Time Out

Istanbul

timeout.com/istanbul

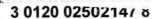

Time Out Guides Ltd
Universal House
251 Tottenham Court Road
London W1T 7AB
United Kingdom
Tel: +44 (0)20 7813 3000
Fax: +44 (0)20 7813 6001
Email: guides@timeout.com
www.timeout.com

Published by Time Out Guides Ltd, a wholly owned subsidiary of Time Out Group Ltd.
Time Out and the Time Out logo are trademarks of Time Out Group Ltd.

Previous editions 2001, 2005, 2007, 2010, 2012.

10 9 8 7 6 5 4 3 2 1

This edition first published in Great Britain in 2012 by Ebury Publishing.
A Random House Group Company
20 Vauxhall Bridge Road, London SW1V 2SA

Random House Australia Pty Ltd 20 Alfred Street, Milsons Point, Sydney, New South Wales 2061, Australia

Random House New Zealand Ltd 18 Poland Road, Glenfield, Auckland 10, New Zealand

Random House South Africa (Pty) Ltd Isle of Houghton, Corner Boundary Road & Carse O'Gowrie, Houghton 2198, South Africa

Random House UK Limited Reg. No. 954009

Distributed in the US and Latin America by Publishers Group West (1-510-809-3700)
Distributed in Canada by Publishers Group Canada (1-800-747-8147)

For further distribution details, see www.timeout.com.

ISBN: 978-1-84670-263-1

A CIP catalogue record for this book is available from the British Library.

Printed and bound in Great Britain by Butler Tanner & Dennis, Frome, Somerset.

The Random House Group Limited supports The Forest Stewardship Council (FSC®), the leading international forest certification organisation. Our books carrying the FSC label are printed on FSC® certified paper. FSC is the only forest certification scheme endorsed by the leading environmental organisations, including Greenpeace. Our paper procurement policy can be found at www.randomhouse.co.uk/environment

Time Out carbon-offsets its flights with Trees for Cities (www.treesforcities.org).

Contents

Introduction

We feel it's best to start this guide with a set of facts that trump the age-old cliché. Istanbul isn't just the bridge between Europe and the Middle East; it's also the largest and – many would argue – most captivating city on both continents. The legacy of its European Capital of Culture 2010 celebrations played out fully in 2011. The year ushered in a volley of new restaurants, a string of new rooftop bars, and a skyline that has been entirely renovated, from the iconic Haghia Sophia to the magnificent Süleymaniye Mosque. If there was ever a city in its prime, it's Istanbul. Right now.

In the same year, Turkey leapt to become the 16th largest economy in the world, sandwiched between the Netherlands and South Korea. (The country boasted the world's fastest growing economy for the first half of 2011.) The trickle-down effect of business patronage on the local cultural scene has been immense. In 2011 Istanbul hosted an art biennial, two international film fairs and several new rock festivals. To put it bluntly, when a city in crisis-hit Europe opens a major art institution, it's headline news. This year Istanbul opened four, including the cultural leviathan SALT Galata, a vast art space overlooking the Bosphorus Straits.

One would be forgiven for thinking that this golden age would make the city crowded, or its citizens complacent. Indeed, it's never been easier – or cheaper – to fly into Atatürk Airport and hop into a taxi for the 20-minute ride downtown. Rest assured, Istanbul is as welcoming and wondrous as it must have been when Emperor Constantine consecrated Constantinople in 330 AD. A case in point is the rambling old Istanbul Archaeology Museum. Its sprawling gardens are home to enough artefacts to make a historian weep, and the museum itself is often empty. The grounds also contain an unexcavated Roman-era hospital in which visitors can play at Indiana Jones in the heart of a vast, head-spinning metropolis. And the thousand-strong list of museums, churches and must-see mosques goes on.

Of course, not everybody visits for cultural immersion. Millions depart the city each year with shopping bags full: of Iranian carpets, Syrian spices and Uzbek ceramics from the Grand Bazaar, or perhaps one-off Turkish designs from the chic stores of Nişantaşı. Others depart with bellies full: of Michelin starred nouveau Ottoman cuisine, or a blowout seafood and *rakı* feast devoured on the banks of the Bosphorus. Whatever your persuasion, you'll love Istanbul's vibrancy. There are two continents' worth of passion here, after all.
Kathryn Tomasetti and Tristan Rutherford, Editors

Istanbul in Brief

IN CONTEXT

The opening section details Istanbul's long and thrilling history: the power and wealth of the empires that shaped it; the bloody events and the bizarre personalities. Elsewhere, there's a look at the 1,500-year story of Istanbul's emotive skyline. Also examined are the challenges facing Istanbul as it develops and grows as a modern city, with a unique position between East and West.

► *For more, see pp17-38.*

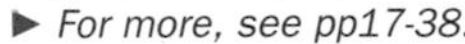

SIGHTS

Sultanahmet is usually the first port of call for visitors. Here, Sultanahmet Mosque, Topkapı Palace and Haghia Sophia are all within walking distance of each other. The world's oldest shopping centre, the Grand Bazaar, is close by too. Across the Golden Horn is modern, secular Istanbul, with hip bars and lively restaurants. Daily life is slower along the Bosphorus, on both European and Asian shores.

► *For more, see pp42-91.*

CONSUME

The quality of food in Istanbul is exceptional. From fish sandwiches alongside the Bosphorus to restaurants with chefs shooting for Turkey's first Michelin stars, Istanbullus eat well. The city is a party town, and we list plenty of stylish clubs and bars. We also give the lowdown on shopping opportunities, from carpets to designer clothes. Completing this section is a rundown of the city's hotels.

► *For more, see pp93-174.*

ARTS & ENTERTAINMENT

Music is an essential part of Istanbul life. Traditional musicians wander the restaurants of Beyoğlu and gypsy singers frequent bars for impromptu gigs. Meanwhile, in the art world, new galleries are opening almost monthly, and Istanbul Modern continues to consolidate its international reputation. We also investigate the Turkish film industry, examine the city's gay culture, and more.

► *For more, see pp175-210.*

ESCAPES & EXCURSIONS

No trip to Istanbul is complete without a cruise along the Bosphorus. This guide covers the highlights as far as the Black Sea, hunting out the best hotels, restaurants and bars. And, for a true escape from the bustle of the city, we take you to the Princes' Islands. With no cars allowed, only the sound of horses' hooves disturbs the peace here.

► *For more, see pp211-218.*

Istanbul in 48 Hours

Day 1 The Historic Heart

7AM Get off to an early start. In fact, it can be very early in Istanbul: the daybreak call to prayer is loud in the old city's mosques. Breakfast in Turkey (*see p127*) is a fortifying affair; it will be needed.

9AM Arrive at the gates of **Tokapı Palace** (*see p44*) as it opens; it gets very busy later on. Be sure to see the Imperial Treasury, to wonder at the opulence of the Ottoman Empire. And don't miss the Harem.

12.30PM From Topkapı Palace's Imperial Gate, walk the short distance to Sultanahmet Square and the entrance to the iconic **Haghia Sophia** (*see p41*). Once a glittering cathedral, it became a mosque after the Ottoman conquest and was declared a museum in the early days of the Republic. Afterwards, divert briefly to examine the **Sultanahmet (Blue) Mosque** (*see p43*). For lunch, follow the locals to **Şar** (*see p129*). Its cafeteria-style decor belies its excellent food.

2.30PM It's a short walk to the Grand Bazaar. Enjoy getting lost in the vaulted passages and haggling with the shopkeepers. Hunt out **Derviş** (*see p171*) for crafty bath products or **Yağlıkçılar Sokak** (*see p55*) for quality textiles.

5PM Take a stroll around Beyazıt Square to the magnificent **Süleymaniye Mosque** (*see p56*). Nearby **Erenler Çay Bahçesi**'s (*see p147*) pretty courtyard is the perfect place to try smoking a narghile, or hubble-bubble pipe.

7PM If you still have energy, head down to the Golden Horn and **Galata Bridge**. As the sun sets, watch the bustle of Istanbul returning home by tram, funicular or ferry.

9.30PM Sultanahment and Eminönü aren't the liveliest areas at night (we've saved the partying for tomorrow), but there are still some good restaurants. **Mozaik** (*see p129*) offers good Anatolian food in an animated atmosphere. Alternatively, head downhill to romantic fish restaurant **Balıkçı Sabahattin** (*see p127*).

NAVIGATING THE CITY

The best way to explore Istanbul is on foot, perhaps crossing from historic Sultanahmet to Beyoğlu by tram. The street layouts can seem daunting, but in Beyoğlu, Istiklal Caddesi is the spine of the area, and the street all others lead to. Likewise, Divan Yolu in Sultanahmet is also a useful marker. The city's main historical sites are within walking distance of each other in Sultanahmet, and most hotels, restaurants, and noteworthy cultural venues are in one of these two areas. For outlying areas, and the Asian Shore, there's a reasonable public transport network. For details, *see pp218-220.*

THE LOCAL CURRENCY

We have listed prices in TL (Turkish Lira) throughout this guide, except in the Hotels chapter. Here we have used euros, as Istanbul hotels usually quote their prices in this currency.

Day 2 Culture & Decadence

9AM Start your day with a caffeine jolt at **Şimdi** (*see p151*) or a traditional Turkish breakfast at **Van Kahvaltı Evi** (*see p127*), before climbing up the 14th-century **Galata Tower** (*see p69*) for incredible panoramic views of Istanbul.

11AM Descend into the streets of **Çukurcuma**, Istanbul's antiques district. Among the meandering streets are shops selling Ottoman furniture and wonderfully kitsch items. Visit **The Works** (*see p172*) for something really quirky or **Eski Fener** (*see p172*) for rural Anatolian treasures.

1PM Climb up to the lively and increasingly trendy **Cihangir** neighbourhood for some lunch. Two tasty options include the open-sided **Smyrna** (*see p149*) and the organic-fantastic **Cuppa** (*see p147*). From here, it's a short stroll down to **Istanbul Modern** (*see p75*).

3PM Edging through earthy **Karaköy**, sit for a while and watch the ferries and boats weave under **Galata Bridge**. If you fancy an afternoon snack, a grilled fish sandwich from the market west of the bridge is hard to beat. You'll need some sustenance for the climb back up to Galata (or take the Tünel funicular) and **Istiklal Caddesi** – Beyoğlu's main pedestrian artery.

6PM On any day of the week, Istiklal will by now be packed with parading Istanbullus. Gone are the days when a necktie was de rigueur for a walk along the street, but people will be looking their best. Art lovers will want to check out the galleries, including **Arter** (*see p186*) and the brand-new **SALT** (*see p187*). Otherwise, dive into the streets around Asmalımescit for a beer. **Badehane** (*see p149*) and **KV Café** (*see p150*) are the busiest. For the best views in Istanbul head to **Leb-i Derya Richmond** (*see p153*) for a cocktail as the sun sets.

9PM There's only one place to go for dinner: **Nevizade Sokak** (*see p139*). This boisterous street is rammed with *meyhanes* (taverns) serving meze and fish dishes. Order a selection of dishes, a bottle of the anise-spirit *rakı* and watch Istanbul at its most exuberant.

PACKAGE DEALS

Given the variety of public transport that you may need, you might find it useful to buy a *mavi* (blue) travel pass, valid for a day, a week, 15 days or a month. The Museum Pass Istanbul Card (*see p46*) offers free or reduced-price entry to museums, without queueing. Otherwise, to avoid queues at the main sights of Topkapı Palace and Haghia Sophia, buy tickets online and in advance, or through your hotel.

GUIDED TOURS

The whole city is one great outdoor museum, with plenty of free sights in the centre. We've included a handful of mapped walks in the sightseeing chapters. For in-depth guided tours, try Istanbul Walks (www.istanbulwalks.net). There's also City Sightseeing Istanbul (0212 458 1800, www.city-sightseeing.com), a company that operates bus tours of the city with commentary from a guide.

Istanbul in Profile

SULTANAHMET

The most unmissable sights are in and around Sultanahmet: Topkapı Palace, Sultanahmet Mosque and Haghia Sophia. If it's your first time in Istanbul, this neighbourhood is where you're going to be spending most time. Its spine is Divan Yolu, the main drag and tram route. With stops beside the main mosques and bazaars, the tram is the best way to get around this side of town.

► *For more, see pp41-50.*

THE BAZAAR QUARTER

Seamlessly blending into Sultanahmet is the Bazaar Quarter. At its heart, the Grand Bazaar was once the economic centre of the Ottoman Empire, where traders from all corners of the empire would come to do business. The area occupies the highest part of a fat thumb of land bordered by the Sea of Marmara and the Golden Horn. It is also home to Istanbul University and the majestic Süleymaniye and Beyazıt mosques.

► *For more, see pp51-56.*

EMINÖNÜ & THE GOLDEN HORN

North of Divan Yolu, the streets slope precipitously down to the waterside transport hub of Eminönü. Here, ferries depart for destinations up the Bosphorus and over to the Asian Shore. Sirkeci Station, once the terminus of the Orient Express, and the Egyptian Bazaar are the main sights around here. Watching the constant waterborne activity around Galata Bridge is mesmerising.

► *For more, see pp57-60.*

THE WESTERN DISTRICTS

Beyond the Bazaar Quarter are the Western Districts, conservative neighbourhoods such as Fatih, Fener, Balat and, further afield, Eyüp. Few visitors make it out here, but there are several interesting churches, mosques and other sights, notably the Byzantine Church of St Saviour in Chora and the city walls. This quiet, traditional area reveals a very different Istanbul from that of secular districts such as Beyoğlu.

► *For more, see pp61-66.*

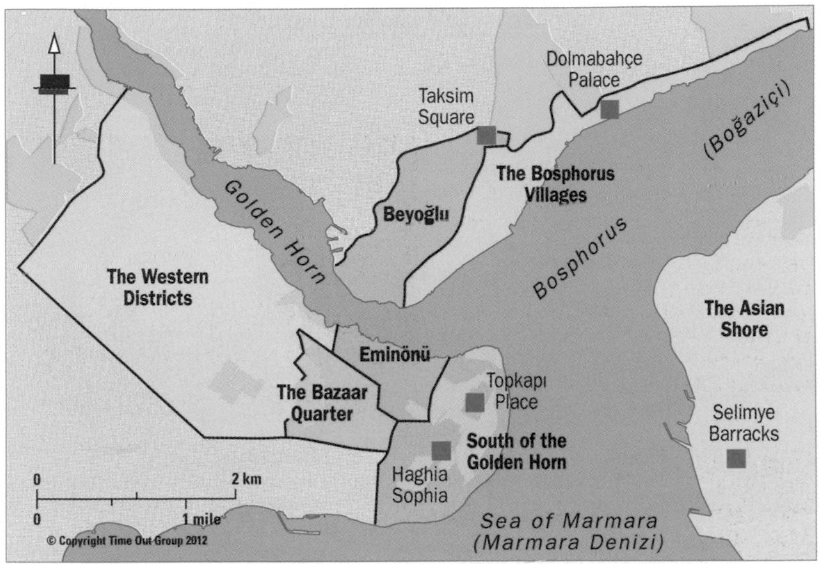

BEYOĞLU & BEYOND

North of the Golden Horn is 'modern' Istanbul, developed largely in the 19th century. Ground zero is Beyoğlu, the place to play after sightseeing. Beyoğlu subdivides into several smaller neighbourhoods, all linked by Istiklal Caddesi, a long, pedestrian boulevard whose narrow off-shoots are filled with shops, cafés, bars, clubs and restaurants. North of Taksim are the newer districts of Harbiye, Şişli, Nişantaşı and Teşvikiye.
► *For more, see pp67-73.*

THE BOSPHORUS VILLAGES

Ortaköy, Arnavutköy and Bebek are picturesque waterside clusters of wooden villas, folksy shops and markets, open-air cafés and restaurants. They make great escapes from the pace of the city. Nearer to the city centre, the more urban former docklands of Karaköy and the bustling neighbourhood of Beşiktaş.
► *For more, see pp74-87.*

THE ASIAN SHORE

The neighbourhood of Kadıköy is home to a lively bar scene, while conservative Üsküdar is better known for its historic mosques – as well as the Maiden's Tower, a popular landmark on a small island just off the coast.
► *For more, see pp88-91.*

Time Out Istanbul

Editorial
Editors Tristan Rutherford, Kathryn Tomasetti
Copy Editor Ros Sales
Proofreader Tamsin Shelton
Indexer William Crow

Editorial Director Ruth Jarvis
Editorial Manager Holly Pick
Management Accountants Margaret Wright, Clare Turner

Design
Art Editor Pinelope Kourmouzoglou
Senior Designer Kei Ishimaru
Group Commercial Designer Jodi Sher

Picture Desk
Picture Editor Jael Marschner
Picture Desk Assistant/Researcher Ben Rowe

Advertising
New Business & Commercial Director Mark Phillips
International Advertising Manager Kasimir Berger
International Sales Executive Charlie Sokol
Advertising Sales Abidin Karabulut

Marketing
Senior Publishing Brand Manager Luthfa Begum
Guides Marketing Manager Colette Whitehouse
Group Commercial Art Director Anthony Huggins

Production
Group Production Manager Brendan McKeown
Production Controller Katie Mulhern-Bhudia

Time Out Group
Chairman & Founder Tony Elliott
Chief Executive Officer David King
Chief Operating Officer Aksel Van der Wal
Editor-in-Chief Tim Arthur
Chief Technical Officer Remo Gettini
Group Financial Director Paul Rakkar
Group General Manager/Director Nichola Coulthard
UK Chief Commercial Officer David Pepper
Time Out International Ltd MD Cathy Runciman

Contributors
This guide was updated, with additional writing throughout, by Tristan Rutherford and Kathryn Tomasetti, except for the Galleries chapter, which was updated by Elif Tirben. **History** Andrew Humphreys, David O'Byrne. **Istanbul Today** Tristan Rutherford, Kathryn Tomasetti. **Sightseeing** Jon Gorvett. Hotels Andrew Humphreys, Daniel Neilson, Cat Scully. **Restaurants** Rene Ames, Vanessa Able, Daniel Neilson. **Bars & Cafés** Vanessa Able, Daniel Neilson. **Shops & Services** Daniel Neilson, Jody Sabral, Lucy Wood. **Calendar** Jon Gorvett. **Children** Yeşim Erdem Holland. **Film** Lucy Wood. **Galleries** Elif Tirben, November Paynter. **Gay & Lesbian** Ken Dakan. **Hamams** Andrew Humphreys. **Music** Andy Footner, Daniel Neilson. **Nightlife** Attila Pelit. **Performing Arts** Attila Pelit. **Sport & Fitness** Jon Gorvett. **Escapes & Excursions** Jon Gorvett, Cat Scully. **Directory** Attila Pelit.

Maps john@jsgraphics.co.uk.

Cover photography Andrew Ward/Life File.
Back cover photography Antony McAulay, Fumie Suzuki, Vladimir Melnik.

Photography Fumie Suzuki except page 3 Martin Froyda; page 7 (middle) Britta Jaschinski; page 7 (bottom left) mahmutceylan.com; page 10 (bottom right), 142 Faraways; page 11 (top) muharremz/Shutterstock.com; page 11 (middle) ollirg; page 11 (bottom) Mikhail Markovskiy; page 18 Corbis; pages 25, 29 Getty Images; page 31 AKG Images; page 32 Antony McAulay; page 33 vvoe/Shutterstock.com; page 37 AFP/Getty Images; page 54 Vladimir Wrangel; page 58 Artur Bogacki; page 73 Ara Güler/Magnum; page 94 Mövenpick Hotels; page 126 Asitane; page 127 Katherine Thamasetti; page 133 Britta Jaschinski; page 145 Berna Namoglu; pages 176, 177 Nathalie Barki; page 183 Daniel Nielson.

The following images were supplied by the featured establishment/artist: pages 107, 115, 119, 123, 137, 139, 141, 193, 196.

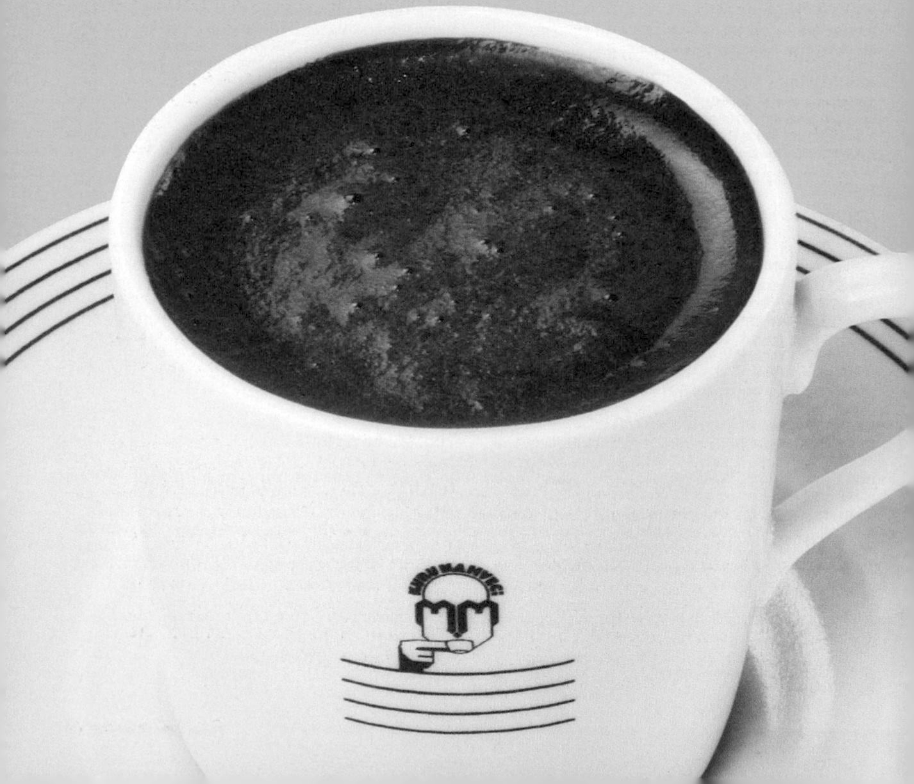

About the Guide

GETTING AROUND

The back of the book contains street maps of Istanbul, as well as overview maps of the city and its surroundings. The maps start on page 239; on them are marked the locations of hotels (❶), restaurants and cafés (❶), and pubs and bars (❶). The majority of businesses listed in this guide are located in the areas we've mapped; the grid-square references in the listings refer to these maps.

THE ESSENTIALS

For practical information, including visas, disabled access, emergency numbers, lost property, useful websites and local transport, please see the Directory. It begins on page 220.

THE LISTINGS

Addresses, phone numbers, websites, transport information, hours and prices are all included in our listings, as are selected other facilities. All were checked and correct at press time. However, business owners can alter their arrangements at any time, and fluctuating economic conditions can cause prices to change rapidly.

The very best venues in the city, the must-sees and must-dos in every category, have been marked with a red star (★). In the Sights chapters, we've also marked venues with free admission with a FREE symbol.

PHONE NUMBERS

The area code for Istanbul is 0212 (European side) or 0216 (Asian side). You don't need from within the city unless you're calling the other side: simply dial the seven-digit number as listed in this guide.

From outside Istanbul, dial your country's international access code (00 from the UK) or a plus symbol, followed by the Turkey country code (90), 212 or 216 for Istanbul (dropping the initial zero) and the seven-digit number as listed in the guide. So, to reach Istanbul Modern, dial +90 212 334 7300. For more on phones, including details of local mobile phone access, *see p228*.

FEEDBACK

We welcome feedback on this guide, both on the venues we've included and on any other locations that you'd like to see featured in future editions. Please email us at guides@timeout.com.

Time Out Guides

Founded in 1968, Time Out has grown from humble beginnings into the leading resource for anyone wanting to know what's happening in the world's greatest cities. Alongside our influential weeklies in London, New York and Chicago, we publish more than 20 magazines in cities as varied as Beijing and Beirut; a range of travel books, with the City Guides now joined by the newer Shortlist series; and an information-packed website. The company remains proudly independent, still owned by Tony Elliott four decades after he launched *Time Out London*.

Written by local experts and illustrated with original photography, our books also retain their independence. No business has been featured because it has advertised, and all restaurants and bars are visited and reviewed anonymously.

ABOUT THE EDITOR

Tristan Rutherford and Kathryn Tomasetti have edited and written for several Time Out titles. Both fell in love with Istanbul after their first *rakı-balık* fish supper on the Bosphorus shores. Tristan and Kathryn regularly write about the city for the *Independent*, the *Guardian* and the *Sunday Times Travel Magazine*.

A full list of the book's contributors can be found opposite.

In Context

Haghia Sophia. *See p41.*

History

Three empires, two thousand years, one city.

As the capital of two world empires – Byzantine and Ottoman – as well as the eastern portion of the Roman Empire, Istanbul has a history that is a fascinating kaleidoscope of faiths, ethnicities, conflict and co-operation. Thanks to a swathe of recent renovations, the city has a newfound pride in its ancient past. From mosques to museums, from synagogues to city walls, this 15-million-strong megacity places 2,000 years of triumph and disaster on display.

Most books will tell you that Istanbul is the only city in the world to straddle two continents, Europe and Asia. The theme of cultural conflict between those continents was already well established by the fifth century BC, when Herodotus devoted much of his *Histories* to the conflict between Greece and Persia, the first of many battles between East and West. His writings came to define the 'them and us' attitude that still dominates relations between Europe and Asia, an attitude still present and relevant in current issues such as Turkey's prospective EU membership.

The role of imagined bridge between East and West has also been thrust on Istanbul as a legacy of its location. The concept is more cliché than reality, but only just. This eclectic city has both 'Western' and 'Eastern' elements forged together by the force of history to create a city that is hard to define as either.

BLIND BEGINNINGS

Despite its geographical advantages, prehistoric finds around Istanbul have been scarce, probably due to the intensity of occupation that followed. Neolithic sites from about 7000 BC have been found near Kadıköy, and Bronze Age remains dated to 3200 BC unearthed in Sultanahmet.

Around 1600 BC, seafaring Greeks began to found colonies around the Aegean and Mediterranean. By 750 BC, they had passed through the Bosphorus and established settlements on the Black Sea coast of Anatolia and in the Caucasus. The 'clashing rocks' episode from the legend of Jason and the Argonauts was probably inspired by the voyage up the Bosphorus Strait. The first Greek settlement in what is now Istanbul was the colony of Chalcedon, founded around 675 BC in today's Kadıköy, on the Asian shore. According to Herodotus (the best source of classical soundbite), Chalcedon was dubbed 'the city of the blind', its founders having foolishly missed the clear geographical advantages of the opposite European shore.

Within fewer than 20 years, more clear-sighted parties had settled across the water on land now enclosed by the walls of Topkapı Palace. Roughly triangular, bounded on two sides by water, it was a natural fortress, with the Golden Horn to the north, a 6.5-kilometre (four-mile) long, deep-water harbour. The site offered access by sea to Africa, the Mediterranean and the Black Sea, and lay at the crossroads of routes between Europe and Asia. It was destined to be a city of world importance. Its founding was attributed to a sailor by the name of Byzas, hence the name Byzantium.

Others were quick to recognise the strategic importance of the new city, and it was repeatedly taken by warring powers: the Persians in 550 BC, then the Spartans, then the Athenians. The Byzantines quickly developed a skill for diplomacy and kept their predatory neighbours at bay through a series of alliances. When that failed, the city dug in, successfully weathering a siege from Philip of Macedon in 340 BC.

Good judgement ran out in AD 196 when, after three centuries of independence as part of the Roman province of Asia, the Byzantines backed the wrong side in an imperial power struggle. After a prolonged siege, the stern emperor Septimius Severus had Byzantium's walls torn down, the city put to the torch and a fair chunk of the population put to death. Such a strategic location couldn't lie wasted for long, though, and within a few years the emperor had rebuilt the city on a far grander scale. For all its pomp, like earlier Greek Byzantium, nothing of Severus's city has survived.

NEW ROME

By the end of the third century, the Roman Empire had become too unwieldy to govern effectively from Rome, and was subdivided, with part of the power shifted to Byzantium. The result was to create internal rivalries that ultimately could only be settled on the battlefield. In 324, Constantine, Emperor of the West, defeated Licinius, Emperor of the East, first in a naval battle on the Sea of Marmara, then on the Asian shore at a place called Chrysopolis, today's Üsküdar. With the empire reunited, Constantine set about changing the course of history, first by promoting Christianity as the official religion of the empire, then by shifting the capital from a jaded and cynical Rome to the upstart city on the Bosphorus. On 11 May 330, Constantine inaugurated his new seat of power as 'Nova Roma'. The name didn't stick, however. Constantinopolis, literally 'Constantine's city', sounded much more catchy.

In Constantinople, the new emperor had a city that he could make over as he saw fit. He embarked on a building programme, plundering the empire to bring in the tallest columns, the finest marble and an abundance of Christian relics, including the True Cross itself. To safeguard his new capital, Constantine had walls erected in an arc from near what is now the Atatürk Bridge over the Golden Horn, then looping south to present-day Mustafa Paşa, enlarging the area of the city fourfold. Other than a burnt and badly aged column, little physical evidence of Constantine's work survives, but he laid the foundations for an empire that was to endure for over 1,000 years.

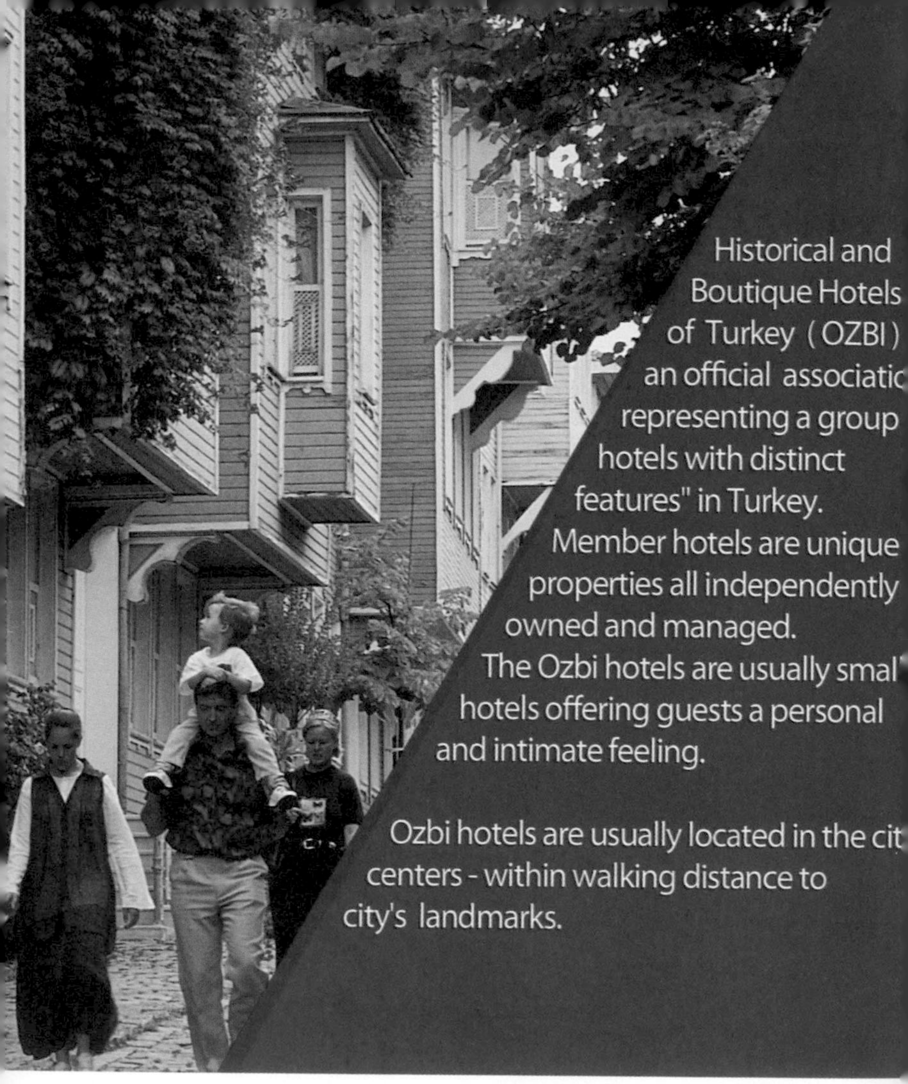

The beginnings were not auspicious, however. On Constantine's death in 337, achievement and stability ended. His three sons quarrelled over the succession and the empire was once again divided between Eastern and Western emperors. Constantinople was largely unaffected by the ensuing two centuries of turbulence, and was even enlarged by the construction of new city walls during the reign of Theodosius II (408-50), completed just in time to halt Attila's advancing hordes. Rome was not so fortunate: it was ripped apart by tribes of Goths and Vandals from the north. With no rival, Constantinople was left to move towards a new era of greatness, reaching its apogee during the era of Justinian (527-65).

CROWD TROUBLE

Justinian's reign was marked by great confidence, which saw the empire extend across most of the Mediterranean coast, including the recapture of the lost dominion of Italy from the 'barbarian hordes'. He was fortunate in having at his service a supremely competent general, Belisarius. Similarly exceptional was Justinian's wife, Theodora, a former street entertainer and prostitute, credited with saving her husband's skin when a revolt broke out among factions at the Hippodrome. Normally rivals, these factions, a cross between political parties and gangs, united to protest at the execution of some of their number. As unrest increased, it was Theodora who dissuaded Justinian from fleeing, and Belisarius who trapped and massacred 30,000 of the rebels in the Hippodrome.

Left presiding over a city of ruins soaked in its citizens' blood, Justinian needed to restore public faith. His answer was to embark on a grand programme of reconstruction, providing for the city spiritually (he endowed over 40 churches) and practically – for example, providing the city with immense water cisterns (among them the **Yerebatan Sarnıcı**, *see p43*). The crowning glory was the new cathedral, Sancta Sophia.

Although the death of Justinian was followed by a prolonged period of decline, largely resulting from internal rivalries, Constantinople remained, as one Byzantine writer put it, 'the city of the world's desire'. There were plenty who acted on those desires. Slavs (581), Avars (617), Persians and Avars (626), Arabs (669-79 and 717-18), Bulgars (813, 913 and 924), Russians (four times between 860 and 1043) and Pechenegs (1087) all marched on the city. Some armies were sufficiently daunted by the walls alone and quit before they'd begun to fight. Others persisted and laid siege. But all failed.

PICTURE PROBLEMS

Trouble was also brewing internally on the theological front when the iconoclast Leo III became emperor in 726. Thus began a 'dark age' of almost 120 years, during which churches were stripped of their decoration and those who stayed faithful to icons (iconodules) were forced to flee to distant monasteries or to worship in secret at risk of denunciation and death. *See p64* **The Great Icon Controversy**.

A restoration in Byzantine fortunes came during the reign of Basil II (976-1025), who succeeded not just in holding the fort but also expanding the empire into Armenia and Georgia. A conscientious ruler, he was also incredibly harsh: in 1014, after taking 15,000 Bulgars prisoner, he had 99 out of every 100 blinded; the remainder were left with one eye to lead their fellow soldiers home. When he saw the ruined army that returned to his capital, Bulgarian tsar Samuel is said to have collapsed and died two days later.

OUT OF THE DARK

The death of Basil marked a turning point in Byzantine fortunes, and the city entered a period of terminal decline. This was signalled to all when, in 1071, a combination of incompetence and treachery led to the annihilation of a Byzantine army at Manzikert in Anatolia. The victors were a new menace: the Selçuk Turks, who flooded across Asia Minor to the shores of the Sea of Marmara. Meanwhile, to the west, Europe had emerged from its Dark Ages to become a patchwork of states owing religious allegiance to the Pope in Rome. But theological differences and the Western Church's envy of its

"At a time when 'heretics' were being burnt alive in Western Europe, the Ottoman regime granted all religions freedom of worship."

older and richer neighbour meant that any common cause was superficial. In 1054, a dispute between papal officials and the Patriarch of Constantinople had resulted in mutual excommunications. The animosity inaugurated the schism between the Roman and Orthodox churches that still exists today.

Threatened by the Selçuk Turks, an increasingly decadent and effete Byzantium was forced to enlist the aid of Latin armies as paid mercenaries. The Latins were crusading to recapture the Holy Lands lost to the Turks and, passing through Constantinople in 1097, they agreed to return to the emperor any formerly imperial territory that they might recapture. This was a promise they failed to keep. Instead, the crusaders set up their own Holy Land states. There followed 50 years of confused bruising between the Byzantine, Latin and Muslim armies, culminating in the Byzantines cutting crusader supply lines and enabling the Selçuks to retake lost territory.

Two or three relatively able emperors, notably John II (1118-43) and Manuel I (1143-80), applied clever diplomacy and judicious use of force to keep the empire intact and even extend its borders; but the good work was undone in 1185 with the accession of the incompetent Isaac II. He was deposed by his brother Alexius III and imprisoned, but Isaac's son escaped and fled west, where he offered enormous sums of money to the armies massing in Venice for the Fourth Crusade, in exchange for helping his father and himself regain the imperial throne. With interest in a long and probably futile struggle in the Middle East never deep, the Latins needed little encouragement to accept.

Threatened with the superior force of the crusaders, the Byzantines agreed to restore Isaac II to the throne. But Alexius III fled with the contents of the treasury and the crown jewels, leaving the reinstated emperor with no money to pay his mercenary allies. On 13 April 1204, the crusaders stormed Constantinople. They sacked the city, stripping it of its treasures and sending them back west; the four gilded bronze horses that now stand over the doorway of St Mark's cathedral in Venice came from Constantinople's Hippodrome. What the crusaders couldn't strip away they destroyed, leaving the city in ruins.

The victorious Latins then appointed one of their own, Baldwin of Flanders, as emperor, and divided up the empire into a patchwork of fiefdoms and city states. Haghia Sophia and many Orthodox churches were converted to the Latin rite. The Latin state lasted until 1261 before the Byzantines mustered enough force to reclaim what remained of Constantinople.

THE OVERWHELMING OTTOMANS

That the Byzantine state was able to survive for another 190 ineffectual years was down to the fact that the rival Selçuk empire had splintered into myriad warring *beyliks*, or fiefdoms. It was only a matter of time, though, before one *beylik* won out. By the first years of the 14th century, a new power had emerged: the Osmanlı Turks, named after their first leader Osman, and better known to Westerners as the Ottomans. During the reign of their first sultan, Orhan Gazi (1326-62), the Ottomans conquered most of western Asia Minor and advanced into Europe as far as Bulgaria, establishing a new capital at Adrianople, now Edirne.

Constantinople had become a Byzantine island in an Ottoman sea. Inevitably, the severely weakened, ruined and depopulated city was confronted with a Turkish army at its walls. This first occurred in 1394, and again in 1400, 1422 and 1442; all were repelled, but this only forestalled the inevitable. Soon after becoming Ottoman sultan

Süleyman the Magnificent. *See p26.*

in 1452, 21-year-old Mehmet II constructed the fortress of Rumeli Hisarı on the European shore of the Bosphorus just north of the city. Fitted with cannons, it gave the Ottomans control of the straits and deprived Constantinople of vital grain supplies.

By April 1453, the Ottoman forces surrounding Constantinople numbered some 80,000; facing them were just 5,000 in a city whose population had fallen to less than 50,000. However, they could not gain access to the Golden Horn because of a great chain that the Byzantines had stretched across its mouth from Galata castle to modern-day Sirkeci. But one night, several weeks into the siege, the Ottomans circumvented the boom by hauling 70 ships on oiled logs up over the ridge above Galata and down to the water on the other side, so that by morning they were in the Golden Horn and up against the city walls.

On 29 May, the final assault was launched. The Ottomans forced an opening near the Golden Horn, and poured into the city in their thousands. By dawn it was all over, with an estimated 4,000 defenders lying dead. A contemporary account describes how 'blood flowed through the streets like rainwater after a sudden storm; corpses floated out to sea like melons on a canal'. With the conquest of Constantinople, Mehmet took the name 'Fatih', or Conqueror. He was apparently shocked at the ruined state of the once-great city.

A MULTINATIONAL CAPITAL

Mehmet was intoxicated by the notion of Constantinople and its heritage as capital of Eastern and Western empires. It fitted perfectly with his own imperial ambitions. Hours after the city walls fell he rode up and prayed in Justinian's great cathedral, Haghia Sophia, which was reconsecrated as a mosque by the following Friday. The Ottomans immediately set about repairing the damage sustained during the siege and the decay of preceding centuries. The sultan's *viziers* (ministers) were encouraged to build and endow the new capital with mosques and the beginnings of what would develop into the Grand Bazaar.

Efforts were made to repopulate the half-deserted city. Greeks, who had fled in the preceding years, were offered land and houses and temporary tax exemption. Craftsmen, merchants and those who would enhance the city's wealth were invited regardless of race or religion. At a time when 'heretics' were being burnt alive in Western Europe, the Ottoman regime granted all religions freedom of worship and the uncontested right to appoint their own religious leaders. Large numbers of Sephardic Jews expelled from Spain and Portugal were ferried by Turkish liberty ships to Istanbul, the only multinational, multi-faith capital in Europe.

On the Conqueror's death in 1481, a scuffle for succession was won by his elder son Beyazıt II, succeeded in turn by his son Selim I, known as 'the Grim' for his habit of having his grand viziers executed. Though Selim's reign lasted only eight years, he presided over significant military victories, adding Syria and Egypt to the imperial portfolio. Further south, he saw off a Portuguese threat to Mecca and was rewarded with the keys to the Holy City, the sacred relics of the Prophet, and the title of Caliph, Champion of Islam. This made Istanbul not only the capital of one of the most powerful empires in the world, but, as it was still the home of the Orthodox Patriarchate, also the centre of two major religions.

But it was during the 46-year reign of Süleyman I (1520-66), known as Süleyman the Magnificent, that the city became a true imperial centre. By the time of his death, he ruled an empire that covered North Africa, stretched east to India, and rolled from the Caucasus through Anatolia and the Balkans to Budapest and most of modern-day Hungary. Süleyman's armies reached the walls of Vienna in 1529, where they were turned back after an unsuccessful siege. Key to Süleyman's military successes were the Janissaries, a crack and fiercely loyal fighting force. Originally of entirely Christian origin, selected boys were forcibly converted to Islam and trained as elite soldiers; they were richly rewarded in return. During the 16th century they were the most disciplined, well-armed and effective of all European armies, universally admired and feared.

Under Süleyman, Istanbul became synonymous with grandeur. Its epicentre was the imperial palace, Topkapı, founded by Mehmet the Conqueror, but gilded by the wealth, tributes and taxes from newly conquered territories. Severe and grave, Süleyman surprised all by falling under the spell of a slave girl, Haseki Hürrem, known universally as Roxelana due to her alleged Russian origins. So besotted was Süleyman that in the early 1530s he married Roxelana and dispensed with the company of all other women. In 1538, as a further expression of devotion, he commissioned a promising young architect, Mimar Sinan, to construct the Haseki Hürrem Mosque complex as a birthday present. This was Sinan's first major commission in Istanbul, launching a glorious career that was to span 50 years, leaving an indelible mark on the city and indeed on most major cities of the Ottoman Empire (*see p32* **Story of a Skyline**).

THE RULE OF WOMEN

Süleyman should have been succeeded by his first son, Mustafa, an able soldier and administrator, but Roxelana schemed against it. Mustafa was not her son. She succeeded in convincing the sultan that he was traitorous and Süleyman had him strangled. Selim, Roxelana's son, became heir apparent.

Such bloodletting to secure the imperial throne was not uncommon. Succession was a matter of life or death, for Mehmet the Conqueror had declared, 'For the welfare of the state, the one of my sons to whom Allah grants the sultanate may lawfully put his brothers to death.' They were strangled with a silken bowstring, preferably by deaf mutes who would not hear their cries.

Far from being 'Grim', like the first Selim, Selim II was known as Selim 'the Sot'. His drunkenness rendered him useless as a ruler. The real power behind the throne was

"One of Selim's wives took control of the harem and the palace, marking the beginning of a period known as 'the rule of women'."

Nurbanu ('Princess of Light'), one of Selim's wives, who took control of the harem and the palace, marking the beginning of an 80-year period referred to as 'the rule of women'. It was an era that saw weak sultans manipulated by their wives and their mothers, between whom there were often power struggles (*see p45* **Hard Times in the Harem**).

Selim drowned in his bath and the ruthless Nurbanu had four of his five sons killed, leaving her own child, Murat III, to succeed as sultan. When Murat died in 1595, Mehmet's successor, Ahmet I, stopped the killing, possibly out of fear of dynastic extinction. From Ahmet's time, male relatives of the sultan were instead confined to the Kafes, literally 'cage', a closed apartment hidden deep inside Topkapı Palace. Here they were kept in complete isolation, apart from a few concubines who had been sterilised by the removal of their ovaries. Guards whose eardrums had been pierced and tongues slit served the prisoners. Although slightly more humane than the earlier fratricidal practices, confinement in the Kafes did little for the captives' mental health. Numerous sultans died prematurely without leaving an heir and their siblings were uniquely unsuited to rule, having spent most of their adult lives incarcerated. In the last years of the empire the problem grew more acute, as successive sultans had little experience of the outside world, or of government. Some simply emerged mad.

THE TURNING POINT

In 1683, the Ottomans failed in a second attempt to take Vienna. This marked the end of Ottoman military successes and expansions and the beginning of a series of reverses. Within three years the imperial armies had lost Buda to the Austrians, and, two years after that, Belgrade. The problem lay not just with addled sultans. In the absence of a strong figurehead, the Janissaries, once the sultan's finest troops, were now completely out of hand, threatening the sultan and killing ministers. Plagues were common. In 1603, a fifth of the population was wiped out, in 1778 a third. Such outbreaks had been eliminated in Europe by the early 1700s by the use of quarantines, but the fatalistic Turks accepted the epidemics as God's will.

Of the advances in science and technology that had begun to revolutionise Western societies and economies in the 18th century, the Ottomans were not only ignorant but arrogantly dismissive. One Turkish dignitary who visited a scientific lab in Vienna in 1748 described it as 'toys' and 'Frankish trickery'.

When Selim III took the throne in 1789, his position was perilous: disobedient guards, recurrent plague, economic decline, military defeats, moribund culture and a restless populace heavily taxed and suffering under poor administration. He looked to the West for inspiration. He established a consultative council and Western architectural influences started to appear at the palaces. More crucially, he attempted to reform the army. For this the sultan earned the enmity of the Janissaries, who felt their privileges were being threatened. They rose up in revolt, deposed Selim and murdered him.

The Janissaries were finally crushed in 1826 by Sultan Mahmut II (1808-39), who had narrowly escaped from the palace with his life the day Selim had been killed. He went on to implement extensive and much-needed reforms, instigating what historian Philip Mansel calls 'revolution from above'. Local government was introduced to Istanbul for the first time, together with the city's first police and fire services.

Mahmut appeared at public functions wearing Western clothes and, most striking of all, banned the wearing of robes and turbans, except by the clergy, introducing the crimson-wool fez from Morocco. This was soon taken to heart by the city, worn by all as a symbol of modernism. More than just a hat, the fez became, in the words of nationalist writer Falih Rifki Atay, 'part of the Turkish soul'.

THE TANZIMAT ERA

Mahmut's successor, Abdül Mecit (1839-61), continued his father's reforming programme, resulting in what was to be a last blossoming of the Ottoman Empire. The sultan further embraced the new era by moving out of Topkapı and into a new Western-style imperial palace at Dolmabahçe. But the real hub of the city was the bridge built across the Golden Horn in 1845. The first bridge to link the two sides of the water, it became very popular; every evening, show-offs would dress up and promenade up and down the bridge. Between palace and bridge, the largely non-Muslim, European districts of Galata and Pera (modern-day Beyoğlu), originally founded as Italian traders' enclaves in Byzantine times, were rapidly developing into a commercial and entertainment district centred on the Grande Rue de Pera, location for an increasing number of theatres, cafés, bars and hotels. Istanbul was shifting its locus from south of the Golden Horn to north.

In the middle of the 19th century, the city began to receive its first proper 'tourists', drawn by the oriental mystique of the capital of the Ottoman sultans. Almost immediately, the sightseeing circuit experienced by visitors today was set. In October 1883, the Orient Express rolled into Sirkeci Station for the first time.

Political reforms culminated in 1876 in the drafting of a constitution and establishment the following year of the first Turkish parliament – albeit with very limited powers. In any case it was short-lived. In 1877, the Russians seized Ottoman lands in the Balkans and the Caucasus. Called to account, Sultan Abdül Hamit responded by dissolving parliament and ruling by decree from his new labyrinthine palace at Yıldız. A paranoid ruler, he hid at Yıldız in constant fear of being bumped off, and had several close members of his family, as well as countless ministers, generals and other court officials, killed. British prime minister William Gladstone called him the 'Great Assassin'. The Turks simply called him 'Abdül the Damned'.

Reform had already progressed too far to allow this reversion to complete imperial rule. Small clandestine groups later known as 'Young Turks' kept up the pressure for change. Most were crushed, but one, the Committee of Union and Progress, succeeded in seizing control of the Ottoman army in Macedonia. By 1908, the CUP was powerful enough to send a telegram to the ageing despotic sultan demanding the restoration of the constitution and parliament. Faced with a rebellious revolutionary army marching on Constantinople, Abdül Hamit acceded to their demands.

Elections to the new parliament saw all but one of the seats won by the CUP, whose elected deputies included Arabs, Greeks, Jews, Armenians and Albanians. It took a pitched battle in Taksim Square to fight off the challenge of Islamic groups, but once that was won reforms were back on the agenda. What should then have been a period of rebirth was instead one of chaos and turmoil, as Europe saw the imminent demise of Ottoman rule as a chance to carve up what remained of its empire.

EMPIRE'S END

In 1912, the Balkan states launched their own offensive, which saw them take all Ottoman possessions in Europe and Bulgarian troops advance to within 40 kilometres (25 miles) of Istanbul. News that Russia, which had long coveted Istanbul and control of the Bosphorus Strait, had joined an alliance with Britain and France left Turkey with little option but to turn to Germany, and the two signed a formal alliance.

Despite a historic victory at Gallipoli, in which they stemmed the Allied invasion and forced a withdrawal, the Ottomans were on the losing side in World War I. In the aftermath, they could do nothing but watch as the former Ottoman Empire was divided up between European powers. The British and French took over the Arab lands, occupied Istanbul in 1919 and enthroned a puppet sultan there.

Turkish leaders in Istanbul seemed incapable of countering the threat from the Greeks, who ran most of the area west of Istanbul. Groups of disillusioned soldiers began slipping out of the city, under the leadership of Mustafa Kemal, the young Turkish general who had masterminded resistance at Gallipoli. In 1919, Kemal led a revolt from the interior, declaring independence and forming a new government in Ankara. 'Henceforth,' he declared, 'Istanbul does not control Anatolia, but Anatolia Istanbul.' In other words: 'Turkey for the Turks.'

After two years of bitter fighting, the Turks forced the Greeks back to Izmir, which was all but destroyed in the final battle. It was a defining moment for the emergent Turkish state, which was now able to negotiate with the Allies on equal terms. In 1922, the sultanate was abolished and the reigning sultan reduced to little more than a ceremonial figurehead.

LET THE GOOD TIMES ROLL

On 29 October 1923, just a few days after reoccupying Istanbul, Turkey adopted a new secular republican constitution, appointed Mustafa Kemal 'Atatürk' ('father of the Turks') as its president, and chose Ankara as its new capital. The latter was a bold break with almost 1,600 years of tradition, which saw the replacement of one of the world's most fabulous cities by a small hillside town that lacked almost every modern amenity, but which was far enough from the new country's borders to make it secure from invasion. Within six months, the 1,300-year-old tradition of the sultanate was completely abolished, and the last members of the Ottoman dynasty were sent into exile, never to return. More sweeping reforms followed, changing the Turkish social, political and cultural world forever (*see p31* **Atatürk's Turkish Transformation**).

Although supplanted by Ankara as the country's political powerhouse, Istanbul continued to prosper as the undisputed cultural and economic capital of the new republic. The Grand Bazaar remained the centre of commerce, while Pera – now renamed Beyoğlu – entered a wild and heady period buoyed by pro-Western reforms that allowed for previously unthinkable levels of freedom.

As a leader, Atatürk was the personification of good-time Turkey. A man of great energy, he enjoyed drinking and could survive on little sleep. He may have moved the capital to Ankara, but his heart was in Istanbul.

Galata Bridge, 1890.

Atatürk died in 1938. His casket was placed in the throne room of Dolmabahçe Palace, where hundreds of thousands came to view the body. Crowds at the palace grew so disorderly that riot police charged and a dozen people were trampled to death. Atatürk's reputation has not been allowed to die: his image is still visible all over Istanbul at every juncture. In 1999, a co-ordinated internet voting campaign almost put him on the front cover of *Time* magazine as the readers' choice of 'Man of the Century', until the ploy was scuppered by Greek and Armenian counter-action.

TURKIFICATION AND TURMOIL

At the renewed outbreak of war in Europe, Turkey, under the wise leadership of Ismet Inönü, opted to remain neutral. Battle of sorts did go on in Istanbul, however, as the city became the espionage capital of World War II. Packed with refugees from all over Europe, Istanbul was also something of a safe haven for Jews escaping the Nazis.

However, Istanbul's indigenous religious minorities, who at the time still accounted for around one-third of the city's total population, were less fortunate. In 1942, on the pretext of combatting war profiteering, the Turkish government introduced an 'asset tax', which was levied primarily on Jews, Armenians and Greeks.

Turkey finally entered the war on the Allied side in February 1945, in order to secure a seat at the United Nations when it was founded later that year. Turkey also sided with the West during the Cold War. Under pressure from its new allies, Turkey introduced parliamentary democracy; in 1950, in the first fully free elections, the Democrat Party (DP) led by Adnan Menderes swept to power with a huge majority.

But the boom proved short-lived. Menderes became increasingly nationalistic and authoritarian. In September 1955, he attempted to exploit tensions over Cyprus by encouraging anti-Greek protests in Istanbul. The protests became a riot and then a pogrom, as mobs attacked the Greek population, killing and looting. The police, apparently under orders not to intervene, stood back and watched. The pogrom sounded the death knell for the Greek community. Today there are only 2,500 Greeks left in Turkey, fewer than the number of expatriate Britons.

In 1960, as Menderes moved to stifle all opposition to his rule, the military staged a coup and, in 1961, hanged Menderes and two of his senior ministers for treason. The 1960s continued to be characterised by political extremism. The streets of Istanbul were the battleground for a low-level civil war between left-wing extremists and far-right groups, who often worked in tandem with elements inside the security forces. In 1971, the military intervened again, toppling the government and appointing an administration of technocrats. Both right and left conducted armed robberies to finance campaigns of assassinations, demonstrations and bombings. On 1 May 1977, unidentified gunmen opened fire on a leftist May Day rally in Taksim Square, killing 39. The violence escalated. By 1980, the daily death toll in Istanbul rarely fell below 20. A succession of weak coalition governments in Ankara seemed unable or unwilling to tackle the problem, with the prime minister Suleyman Demirel dismissing the anarchy as mere hooliganism. On 12 September 1980, to the relief of much of the population, the military seized power again.

For the next three years, Istanbul was under martial law. The ruling military junta banned public meetings, outlawed all existing political parties, closed newspapers and magazines, burned books and arrested tens of thousands of real or suspected political activists, many of whom were subjected to torture. The repression took its toll on public sympathy for the military. When, in 1983, the junta restored civilian rule by allowing free elections, Turks rejected the military's preferred party and voted overwhelmingly for the broad-based Motherland Party and its founder Turgut Özal.

A NEW COSMOPOLITANISM

Faced with an economy that still closely resembled those found throughout Eastern Europe, Ozal implemented a series of market-oriented reforms that helped attract investment, but also brought widespread corruption and sleaze.

Atatürk's Turkish Transformation

How one man forged a nation.

Every 10 November, at 9.05am, Istanbul comes to a halt for a minute's silence to mark the death of Mustafa Kemal 'Atatürk', 'father of the Turkish nation': the man who took a nascent Turkish resistance after World War I and galvanised it into an army able to defeat the might of the Allies and regain Turkish lands, taken from a defeated and ailing Ottoman Empire at the end of the war. And the man who unified disparate strands of that defeated empire to work towards his vision for an emerging – and radically new – Turkish nation.

The new Turkish nation was to be totally 'modern'. Some of Atatürk's innovations would be politically inconceivable today – imposing a dress code that made men exchange fezes for hats, for example, or packing provincials off to performances by the newly founded state opera, would be seen as a demeaning imitation of the West. But there was no such discourse around in 1927, when Atatürk explained, 'It was necessary to abolish the fez, which sat on the heads of our nation as an emblem of ignorance, negligence, fanaticism and hatred of progress and civilisation.' Atatürk's theory was simple: the West was advanced; Turkey would copy and reap the benefits. The European calendar was adopted, then the Swiss civil code and the Italian penal code, abolishing the role of religion in law. Women were granted equal rights. But perhaps the most dramatic piece of social engineering was the adoption of the Roman alphabet. Educated people – normally ones who could read the Holy Koran – became illiterate overnight, while a whole new generation grew up imbibing the new ideology to go with the new script.

Of course, appearing Western was not enough. State intervention in the economy and scientific progress would forge development; social and cultural changes completed the picture. The resulting modernity would become an integral part of a new national identity.

Secularism was another central tenet of the new state, symbolised by the abolition of the caliphate in 1924. Ottomans had not identified themselves as 'Turks'. Their language was Turkish, others called them Turks, but they saw their empire as Islamic, and the caliphate as a divine duty. There was support in some quarters for the idea of a sultan/caliph figure who would act as a sort of Muslim pope. Such an idea was anathema to Atatürk: the Kemalists insisted on the independence of the state from religion. However, this was not quite secularism as understood in the modern West. In Turkey, the state would exercise control over Islam and put it to its service. Here was another crucial marker of the Turkish identity, one that still has repercussions today.

Story of a Skyline

Istanbul's Byzantine and Ottoman architecture explained.

When, in AD 330, Constantine began to build his new capital on the Bosphorus, 'Nova Roma' was literally that, a new Rome constructed in the same style as the old one. But the change in location proved significant, as the proximity to Asia Minor and Syria resulted in an infusion of new ideas and methods. Very quickly the traditional Roman column-and-lintel way of building gave way to a more fluid architecture based on arches, vaults and domes. Supplanting stone, brick became the building material of choice.

Development continued during the reign of the Emperor Justinian (AD 527-565). He was patron to four great churches: SS Sergius and Bacchus, the smaller **Küçük Haghia Sophia Mosque** (*see p50*); the rebuilt **Haghia Irene** (*see p44*); the Church of the Holy Apostles, which was quarried for the Fatih Mosque; and the great cathedral of **Haghia Sophia** (*see p41*). What distinguished these structures from all that had come before was the dome, which had never been built on this scale. With Haghia Sophia, Justinian's goal was to enclose the greatest space possible, creating a physical impression of the kingdom of God. To achieve this he is said to have eschewed traditional builders and craftsmen and instead employed two mathematicians. Such was the impression created that the dome was described by Byzantine historian Procopius as 'appearing to be suspended from heaven by a golden chain'.

Post-Justinian, the Byzantine Empire was to continue for another 800 years, during which time architectural styles evolved further. Later structures tended to be more modest in size and more harmoniously proportioned. Decoration came to play a larger part. For all its spatial grandeur, Haghia Sophia is dull, dull, dull on the outside, whereas surviving later churches such as **St Saviour in Chora** (*see p63*) and the 12th-century Church of the Pantocrator (now the **Zeyrek Mosque**; *see p62*) employ multiple domes, narthexes and apses executed in alternating bands of brick and roughly dressed stone. Glazed pottery set into the external walls forms friezes that echo interior mosaics and tiling, which flourished in the later Byzantine period following the miserable repressions of the Iconoclastic era.

The Ottomans, like the Byzantines, especially those of the early era, shared a predilection for centrally planned structures topped by big domes. In that respect, the Haghia Sophia was inspirational, a benchmark.

Once the Ottomans had captured the city in 1453, the task of constructing a dome larger than Justinian's was to occupy imperial architects for more than a century. It was eventually achieved by a master builder named Sinan during the reign of Sultan Süleyman the Magnificent; the dome in question graced Selimiye Mosque in Edirne.

Islam also defined how Ottoman architecture would develop. An egalitarian religion with no hierarchical orders, no saints in need of side chapels, no use for obfuscating trappings such as naves and apses, its mosques required nothing more than a single, large, open space. A domed central

Haghia Sophia.

IN CONTEXT

Haghia Sophia.

chamber proved to be the best way of achieving this. It's almost incidental that the external effect is so beautiful – a cascade of gracefully descending curves. Slender, pencil-pointed minarets, originally intended as platforms for the five daily calls to prayer, frame the composition, while surrounding courts keep the secular city at bay.

It was Sinan, trained as a military engineer, who gave Istanbul some of its most memorable architectural triumphs. He constructed an incredible 477 buildings, more than 200 still stand, and more than 100 were mosques. He exhibited his style exquisitely in **Süleymaniye Mosque** (*see p56*), which still dominates the city's skyline. Even the much-admired **Blue Mosque** (*see p43*), also known as the Sultanahmet Mosque, built across from the Haghia Sophia in the 17th century, is no more than a reprise of what Sinan had achieved a century earlier.

As the Ottoman Empire declined, so European influence made itself felt. From the mid 18th century, the Ottoman simplicity and clarity of function was wedded to the decorative excesses and indulgences of decadent and redundant imported baroque and rococo stylings. Their bastard offspring goes by the name of 'Turkish Baroque'. One of the earliest and most accessible examples is the **Nuruosmaniye Mosque** (*see p53)*, completed in 1755. Its large dome rests on four huge semicircular arches filled with long vertical windows that brighten the interior, but the absence of semi-domes makes the profile appear stumpy.

By the 19th century, European styles were almost completely dominant, with the 'Turkish' dropping out of 'Turkish Baroque' altogether. Rather than mosques or religious institutions, the defining structures of the time are palaces. **Dolmabahçe** (*see p79*), for example, is a good illustration of the changes taking place, with a showy mix of baroque and neoclassicism, with interiors by Sechan, who worked on Garnier's grand Paris Opera House. Other palaces in a similar ostentatious style include **Çırağan** (now a hotel, *see p119*) and **Beylerbeyi** (*see p91*).

Meanwhile, foreign architects had been making their way to Istanbul. A German named Jachmund designed the wedding cake **Sirkeci Station** (*see p59*), terminus of the Orient Express. And an Italian, Raimondo D'Aronco, introduced Istanbul to art nouveau, especially in the suburbs such as Galata and Pera (now Beyoğlu), which were as wealthy, influential and style-conscious as any in Europe. Europe would continue as the prime inspiration for architecture until the founding of the Turkish Republic in 1923.

Ozal's economic reforms quickened the pace of urbanisation as millions of Anatolian peasants moved to major cities – particularly Istanbul – in search of a better life. These newcomers swelled the population from three million in 1970 to an unofficial estimate of 15 million in 2012, changing the shape of the city. Istanbul has become a collection of villages with names such as 'little Gazientep' and 'little Sivas', named after the Anatolian towns from which most residents originate.

Cheap labour from the *gecekondu* – literally 'overnight homes' – helped fuel the economic boom of the 1980s, although the spread of unplanned suburbs put an unbearable strain on the city's infrastructure, clogging roads and polluting out-of-town reservoirs, leaving some areas without water for weeks at a time. The new arrivals also brought with them the piety of the Anatolian villages, where many paid only lip-service to Atatürk's secularising reforms. In the local elections of March 1994, 40-year-old Tayyip Erdoğan became the city's first Islamist mayor in republican history. Erdoğan used his record as mayor of Istanbul – where even his opponents grudgingly admit he improved services – as a platform to enter national politics. He became prime minister in March 2003, was re-elected in 2007 and returned with an even greater majority in 2011.

THE ROOT OF EXPANSION

The city continues to grow, not just outwards but upwards, with high-rise office blocks and hotels transforming the skyline. Many belong to corporations that have grown rich on the back of Ozal's free-market reforms. Others have been built by newer business-minded migrants from the Black Sea and the Anatolian plains. Illegal immigrants also call Istanbul 'home'. Thousands of Iraqis, Afghans and a rainbow of other nations form communities in the city's backstreets, which have become a stepping stone to Europe 'proper'.

At the same time, the city has regained much of its assertiveness and pride, becoming a regular venue for international conferences, cultural and sports events, including the regular Turkish Grand Prix. Other recent improvements to city life include cleaner streets, pedestrianisation projects, more trees and parks, new tram lines, a speedy Metro, and a clean-up of the Golden Horn. The city's pride swelled during 2010, as Istanbul held the mantle of European Capital of Culture. A volley of renewed civic buildings was inaugurated, alongside new art museums and a yearly calendar of film, art and culture festivals.

There have been setbacks. On 15 November 2003, two truck bombs hit different Istanbul synagogues. Five days later, the British consulate and HSBC bank were hit. More than 60 people were killed. The perpetrators claimed links with Al-Qaeda. Politically, Turkey's EU membership ambitions seem to be no nearer to realisation (*see p35-38* **Istanbul Today**).

NEW FUTURES

In 2006, the Nobel Prize for Literature was awarded to Istanbul novelist Orhan Pamuk, who has written extensively about his native city. Reviled by nationalists, Pamuk's outspoken criticism of taboo issues, such as the treatment of Armenians and Kurds, has got him into trouble with the Turkish state; he has been tried (and acquitted) for 'insulting Turkishness'. But whether or not the Nobel jury's decision was politically motivated, the prize was recognised by Pamuk's friends and foes alike as a coup for contemporary Turkish literature. Brought up in a modern middle-class Istanbul family, Pamuk has, perhaps unwittingly, become a spokesperson for Istanbul's Europe-looking population. He said recently, 'I see Turkey's future as being in Europe, as one of many prosperous, tolerant, democratic countries.'

In the first two quarters of 2011 Turkey became the fastest growing economy in the world – a far cry from its moniker as the 'sick man of Europe' a century before. Prime Minister Erdoğan has been profiled as one of *Time* magazine's '100 most powerful people in the world' – twice. His Islam-friendly pro-business AKP party plans to propel Turkey into the league of the world's top ten economies by 2023, the 100th anniversary of the founding of the modern Turkish state.

Istanbul Today

Culture, commerce and a different kind of politics.

TEXT: KATHRYN TOMASETTI, TRISTAN RUTHERFORD

As European news headlines tell of depression and cuts, Istanbul is booming, awash with new hotels, museums and attractions. Other nations may be jostling for a share of the wealth of the world's new economic powers, but this city's streets are a cacophony of Arabic, Russian, Hindi and Brazilian Portuguese. The 14 million residents of Turkey's largest city walk not with a swagger, but with a quiet, bright confidence: the sick man of Europe is now fighting fit.

BRIDGING THE WORLD

Istanbul's newfound wealth mirrors its newfound cosmopolitanism. And justly so. As protectionism rears its head in the world's traditional economies, Turkey is signing trade agreements with former foes. As right-wing parties in Europe raise anti-immigration banners, Istanbul's economy is empowered by growing legions of expatriate skill. And as border regimes tighten across the globe, 100 nationalities are now welcomed through Atatürk Airport without a prior visa.

The importance of the latter point is hard to overstate. Since 2009, a succession of Arab states has been granted visa-free travel to Turkey. In 2010, Russian tourists got the same treatment. A liberal attitude to budget airlines from Dubai to Düsseldorf has boosted visitor numbers to Istanbul by an average of 20 per cent per year. Mercantile Turks have added new hotels, shops and hamams to cater to these surging crowds, and there's a sense of rediscovery for the foreign visitor too. To Arab tourists, Istanbul is Europe with plenty of mosques. For Russians, the city offers sunshine and shopping, without the costly euro or the long flight. To Europeans, Turkey offers 'Middle East lite' – and it's cheap and cheerful as well as different. The bridge between East and West has never been so neatly trodden.

EUROPEAN TIES

The question of European Union membership is emblematic of Turkey's battle for its own identity. Member countries, led by France and Germany, have made it clear that Turkey's accession to the EU is not going to happen soon. The opinion from current EU chief Herman Van Rompuy that 'Turkey is not a part of Europe and will never be part of Europe' hasn't been lost on locals. But now, the desire to tie up to a single European currency and an intractable political system is fast losing its appeal. Turkish commentators catalogue a sentiment that is pushing away Europe's model, as its political leaders lead trade missions to Russia, China, India and Saudi Arabia. Since Greek, Italian and Spanish debt spiralled out of control at the beginning of 2010, Turkey, with a competitive lira, suddenly became more attractive, both as an investment opportunity and as a tourist destination. It also became a model – for non-EU Europeans and fledgling Arab democracies – for putting national interest above vague political union. As things stand, when it comes to that elusive EU membership, one thing is certain: Turkey can afford to keep her options open until the dust from the euro crisis and the Arab Spring has settled.

CULTURAL CAPITAL

Hosting Europe's Capital of Culture celebrations, as Istanbul did in 2010, is enough to place any city on the cultural map. Securing the backing of the philanthropic city elders during an economic boom cemented this city's status a must-see cultural hub.

The openings of Arter, SALT Beyoğlu and mega-museum SALT Galata in 2011 were the year's biggest cultural draws. Along the Bosphorus from Karaköy to Bebek, art galleries (including Rampa and Borusan Contemporary) have opened at the rate of several per month. Across Istanbul, freshly renovated historic buildings have opened their doors, from hamams (such as the Roxelana in Sultanahmet), to factories (Tophane's cannon foundry turned exhibition hall) and hotels (the Ottoman-chic Georges Hotel). Almost every one of Istanbul's cultural offerings is backed by a public-private partnership. The biggest events of 2013 – the Istanbul Biennial and Film Festival – are sponsored by the municipal council, Turkish Airlines and the art-loving Eczacıbaşı family.

Patronage of the arts has long been a pastime of Istanbul's elite. Emperor Justinian's Hagia Sophia cathedral and Sultan Süleyman's Süleymaniye Mosque were both commissioned in times of plenty, with powerful backers behind them. By coincidence, both emerged afresh from fine renovations in 2011, along with Tophane's Nusretiye Mosque and various sections of Topkapı Palace. In Turkey's 20th-century

Islamism, Turkish-Style

The rise of the AKP.

The Justice and Development Party, or AKP, is a pro-business, mildly Islamist political party far removed from Istanbul's secular nationalist *ancien régime*. Instead, it draws its strength from the Anatolian heartland and brooks little domestic opposition. Indeed, over the last decade the party has smashed Turkey's old elite, breaking the ties that once riddled the country with corruption, and flattening the ability of the military to meddle in the nation's affairs. A force for good, surely?

To many, the party is the saviour of modern Turkey, or a model of democratic Islam in the post-Arab Spring world. But to others it's a force of creeping Islamisation aimed at crippling the country's liberal mores. It is certainly a powerful force. Prime Minister Recep Tayyip Erdoğan reigns as undisputed party leader, while fellow former party member Abdullah Gül is President of the Republic. Both are pious men. Their wives wear headscarves, they've put a lid on alcohol at state functions, and the tax on Turkish wine has gone through the roof. But despite their personal predilections, Istanbul still appears as liberal as ever. After over a decade of AKP power, *rakı* is still drunk as prodigiously, censorship is rare, and swimwear is still worn on the Princes Islands' beaches.

The party is clearly popular. In national elections in 2002, the party won 34 per cent of the vote. In 2004, it picked up 42 per cent, winning in 2007 and 2011 with respective 47 per cent and 49.9 per cent poll victories. To understand why, one only has to compare the bustling streets of Istanbul in 2012 with the city's crumbling infrastructure when the AKP took power. Little wonder that many an Istanbul tearoom has a photograph of Erdoğan under the obligatory portrait of Atatürk. And it's hard to miss the party's slick PR machine. Its English-language website lists election promises for 2023 – the country's centenary year – that appeal to every Turkish voter. Foremost is the aim to put Turkey in the ranks of the top ten global economies, boosting GDP to $25,000 per capita.

Prime Minister Recep Tayyip Erdoğan.

These are not idle promises. In a decade in power, the government has hiked GDP from $3,500 per person to $10,000 today, while increasing foreign trade threefold in the same period. Its much-vaunted 'zero problems' with neighbours policy may have been offset by the implosion of Syria in 2011 and 2012, but other breakthroughs with former foes have been laudable. In 2009, Turkey normalised relations with Armenia. In 2010, it held a joint cabinet meeting with Greece. By staying out of the Iraq War, the AKP drew ire from the country's old military elite, but the strategy proved sound. Instead of participating in the trillion-dollar occupation of its neighbour, it's now Turkey's second biggest commercial partner, with bilateral trade hovering around $12 billion per year. The party really does seem business first, politics second.

rush to modernity, the distant past was looked upon dimly. Ideas are clearly changing, however, leading to charges of Ottomania – a nationalist reboot of previous Turkish glories – from some quarters. Most tourists, however, are over the moon with the wealth of new and refurbished places to visit.

DEMOGRAPHIC CHANGE

While the politicking continues in Ankara, it's Istanbul that remains the country's focus. Turkey's largest city plays an enormous role in the national economy, and is responsible for much of the country's wealth and many of its jobs. It has acted as a magnet for migrants for some 2,700 years now, with little sign of abating. The overriding factor in modern Istanbul's demographics is Anatolian immigration. Over the past 50 years, mass migration has made parts of the city more like a collection of villages, as pockets of people from the same region set up home in the same area. Istanbul's diversity can be seen on the faces of its citizens, as well as in the Black Sea, Aegean and Anatolian restaurants across town.

Recent years have brought vast immigration from abroad too. As Turkey's GDP growth rate rises to world-beating levels, residents from the former Soviet Union (in particular Russia, Dagestan, Moldova and Armenia) and Europe (from English teachers to engineers) have arrived in droves. Suburbs full of workers from Senegal, Ghana, Iraq and Sri Lanka await employment in Istanbul – or a chance to cross the border into the EU.

CONNECTING PEOPLE

Travel on public transport between Taksim and Atatürk Airport, and you'll use three types of vehicle: a 19th-century tramway, a 100-year-old funicular and a modern tram. Istanbul's transport network does hang together – if you are patient. But traffic can be slow, timetables opaque, and the wealthy are addicted to cars. Here, geography becomes a curse, as up to 400,000 motor vehicles make their way across the two Bosphorus bridges every day. At rush hour, a trip from Levent to the Asian shore can take two hours, as opposed to half an hour at other times.

However, after decades of neglect money is now being invested in upgrading the city's creaking transport infrastructure. The metro system is currently clean, efficient and modern. It's expanding, too, with a volley of new stations being opened along the Bosphorus and along the Asian Sea of Marmara in 2012 and 2013. A controversial third Bosphorus bridge near Istanbul's Black Sea coast may provide a speedy through-corridor for vehicles heading from Anatolia to European Turkey. The city's recent Metrobus project, which connects the city suburbs with super-size buses on dedicated roads, now transports up to a million passengers per day. The new Istanbul–Ankara high-speed train line – set to open in 2013 – should trounce both car and plane along the country's busiest land and air corridor.

By far the city's biggest transport undertaking is the Marmaray Tunnel, which is being dug between Sirkeci Station in Eminönü and Üsküdar on the Asian shore. When completed, it will be the world's deepest rail tunnel, set to alleviate the immense strains on the Bosphorus bridges as part of a new and efficient network. The current completion date is 2015, but the project has been plagued with delays, not least because work must stop each time workers come across something of archaeological interest; objects dating back to 6000 BC have been found. Among the items are remnants of the fourth-century port of Theodosius, and the oldest medieval galley ever discovered.

The story of the Marmaray Tunnel can serve as useful shorthand for Istanbul today. The city is meeting the challenges of modernity – with some organisational delay thrown in – while following in the wake of vast historical wealth and heritage. That incredible heritage, and the modern city of today, can perhaps best be understood on a clear day on the Galata Bridge. Istanbul's bewitching beauty tempts from either side, while the busy Bosphorus glimmers below.

Sights

Sultanahmet Mosque. *See p43.*

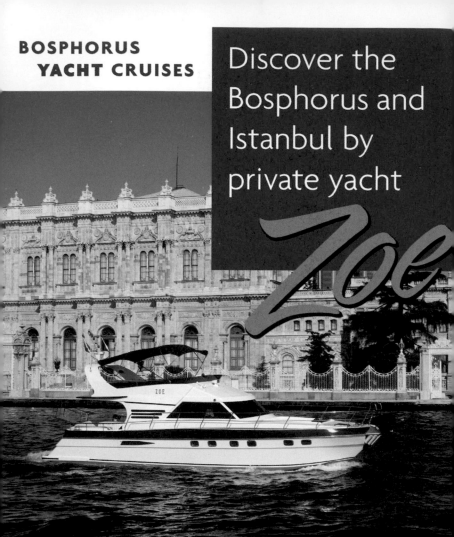

Sultanahmet

Living history.

Sultanahmet is historic Constantinople: thousands of years of history packed into an incredibly picturesque promontory. It's flanked on three sides by the Golden Horn, the Bosphorus and the Sea of Marmara. The heart of the Byzantine and Ottoman Empires, it's layered with world-famous sights, among them the former cathedral (then a mosque and now a museum) of **Haghia Sophia**, the six minareted **Blue Mosque**, the subterranean **Yerebatan Cistern** and the fabulously extravagant **Topkapı Palace** complex. Unsurprisingly, visitors make a beeline here. Yet despite the crowds, Sultanahmet retains its Oriental mystique – both in its atmospheric warren of backstreets and the powerful monuments themselves.

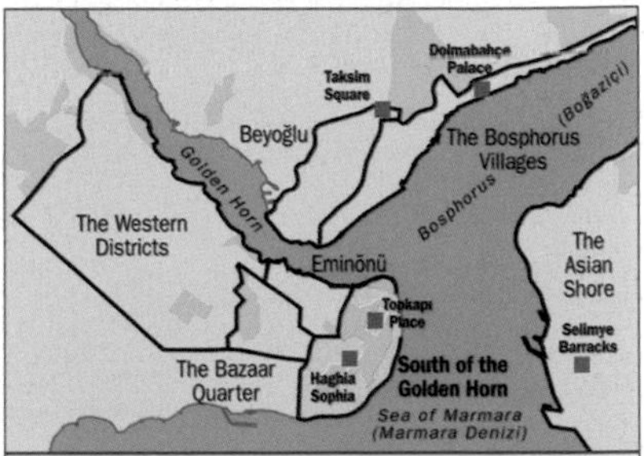

Map pp242-243
Hotels p95
Restaurants p127
Bars & Cafés p145

SULTANAHMET SQUARE

Focal point for disgorging tour buses and a feeding ground for local guides, **Sultanahmet Square** (the fusion of Sultanahmet Meydanı and Ayasofya Meydanı) is the obvious place to begin exploring this historic neighbourhood. Most of the city's major monuments are just a few minutes' walk from here, including the underground cistern **Yerebatan Sarnıcı**, **Sultanahmet Mosque** (commonly referred to as the Blue Mosque) and the **Museum of Turkish & Islamic Art**. **Topkapı Palace** is also a short distance from the square.

Most notably, Sultanahmet Square acts as a forecourt to what was – for close to a thousand years – the greatest church in Eastern Christendom, the **Haghia Sophia** (Ayasofya in Turkish). After the Turkish conquest, it served for five centuries as the chief mosque of the Ottoman Empire, and is now open as a museum.

It's worth remembering that major sights can get very busy, so an early start is a good idea.

★ Haghia Sophia

Ayasofya Müzesi

Sultanahmet Square (0212 522 1750, www.ayasofyamuzesi.gov.tr). Tram Sultanahmet. **Open** *mid Apr-Sept* 9am-7pm Tue-Sun. *Oct-mid Apr* 9am-5pm Tue-Sun. Ticket office closes 1hr earlier. **Admission** TL20. Museum Pass Istanbul Card accepted. **Map** p243 N10.

The third sacred building on the site to bear the name, the existing Haghia Sophia ('Divine Wisdom') was dedicated on 26 December 537 by Emperor Justinian. He had come to power less than a century after the fall of Rome, and was eager to prove his capital a worthy successor to imperial glory. Approached by a grand colonnaded avenue beginning at the city gates, Justinian's cathedral towered over all else and was topped by the largest dome ever constructed – a record it held until the Romans reclaimed their pride just over a thousand years later with Michelangelo's dome for St Peter's (1590). In the meantime, Justinian's dome took on almost fabled status. It was of such thin material, wrote the chroniclers of old, that the hundreds of candles hung high within would cause it to glow at night like a great golden beacon, which was visible to ships far out on the Sea of Marmara.

Adding to the wonder, the church served as a vast reliquary, housing a pilgrim's delight of biblical treasures, including fragments of the True Cross, the Virgin's veils, the lance that pierced Jesus's side, St Thomas's doubting finger, and a large assortment of other saintly limbs, skulls and clippings.

All this was lost in 1204, when adventurers and freebooters on Western Christendom's Fourth

Haghia Sophia. *See p41.*

Crusade, raised to liberate Jerusalem and the Holy Lands, decided they would be equally content with a treasure-grabbing raid on the luxurious capital of their Eastern brethren. At Haghia Sophia they ripped the place apart, carrying off everything they could, and added insult to thievery by infamously placing a prostitute on the imperial throne.

Further destruction was narrowly avoided in 1453, when the Ottoman Turk armies, led by Mehmet II, breached the walls of the city of Constantinople and put its Byzantine defenders to flight. Those who took refuge in the church were slaughtered, but the conquering sultan allegedly rounded on a looting soldier whom he found hacking at the marble floors, telling him, 'The gold is thine, the building mine.'

Haghia Sophia may have been spared, but it was a loss to Christianity. The Friday after the conquest, the church resounded to the chant, 'There is no god but Allah, and Mohammed is his Prophet'. Haghia Sophia had been converted into a mosque. The former basilica soon acquired four minarets, from which to deliver the Muslim call to prayer – although construction was staggered; only two of the minarets are matching. In 1317, a series of buttresses was deemed necessary when the church seemed to be in danger of collapse. These additions aside, what you see today is essentially the church exactly as it was in Justinian's time.

At the death of the Ottoman Empire, with plans afoot to partition Istanbul along national lines, both the Greeks (on behalf of the Eastern Church) and the Italians (on behalf of the Western Church) lobbied for Haghia Sophia to be handed over to them. In Britain, a Saint Sophia Redemption Committee was formed. The Ottoman government posted soldiers with machine guns in the mosque to thwart any attempt at a Christian coup. An expedient solution was effected by the leaders of the new Turkish Republic in 1934, who deconsecrated the building and declared it a museum. This action remains controversial, with Islamists periodically calling for it to be restored as a mosque.

Today, the former cathedral's interior remains impressive, particularly the main chamber with its fabulous dome, 30m (98ft) in diameter. In spring 2011, Haghia Sophia's Byzantine Baptistery Court – later transformed into a mausoleum for 17th-century sultans Mustafa I and Ibrahim – opened to the public, complete with vast fourth-century marble christening font.

The most extraordinary interior feature of Haghia Sophia is its mosaics. Plastered over by the conquering Ottomans, they were rediscovered during renovations in the mid 19th century. But it was only over the course of recent lengthy renovations – which lasted close to two decades and finished at the end of 2010 – that these shimmering creations truly came into their own. Some of the finest mosaics decorate the outer and inner narthexes, which are the long, vaulted chambers inside the present main entrance.

The non-figurative geometrical and floral designs are the earliest and date from the reign of Justinian. Further mosaics adorn the galleries, reached by a stone ramp at the northern end of the inner narthex.

At the eastern end of the south gallery, just to the right of the apse, is a glimmering representation of Christ flanked by the famous 11th-century empress, Zoe, and her third husband, Constantine IX. One of the few women to rule Byzantium, Zoe married late and was a virgin until the age of 50. She must have developed a taste for what she discovered, proceeding to go through a succession of husbands and lovers in the years left to her. On the mosaic in question, the heads and inscriptions show signs of being altered, possibly in an attempt to keep up with her active love life. En route to see Zoe is a slab marking the burial place of Enrico Dandalo, Doge of Venice, a leader of the Fourth Crusade, and the man held responsible for persuading the Latins to attack Constantinople. Following the Ottoman conquest of the city, it is said that his tomb was smashed open and his bones thrown to the dogs.

► *For a drink after touring Haghia Sophia, Yeşil Ev's beer garden is a pleasant stop; see p146.*

★ FREE Sultanahmet (Blue) Mosque

Sultanahmet Camii

At Meydanı Caddesi 21 (0212 518 1319, www.sultanahmetcami.org). Tram Sultanahmet. **Open** 9am-1hr before dusk daily. Closed to non-worshippers during daily prayer times. **Admission** free. **Map** p243 N11.

Seductively curvaceous and enhanced by a lovingly attended park in front, Sultanahmet Mosque (referred to locally as the Blue Mosque) is Islamic architecture at its most alluring. Commissioned by Sultan Ahmet I (1603-17) and built for him by Sedefkar Mehmet Ağa, a student of the great Sinan, this construction was the last of Istanbul's magnificent imperial mosques. It provoked hostility at the time because of its six minarets – such a display was previously reserved only for the Prophet's mosque in Mecca – but they do make for a beautiful silhouette, particularly gorgeous when floodlit at night.

By contrast, the interior is clumsy, marred by four immense pillars, disproportionately large for the fairly modest dome they support (especially when compared to the vast yet seemingly unsupported dome that caps Haghia Sophia across the square). Most surfaces are covered by a mismatch of Iznik tiles: their colour gives the place its popular moniker, the Blue Mosque.

In the north-east corner of the surrounding park is the *türbe* or Tomb of Sultan Ahmet I. It also contains the cenotaphs of his wife and three of his sons, two of whom, Osman II and Murat IV, ruled in their turn, Ahmet being the sultan who abandoned the nasty Ottoman practice of strangling other potential heirs on the succession of the favoured son. *Photo p44.*

INSIDE TRACK MOSQUE ETIQUETTE

At least half of Istanbul's major sights are mosques. Non-Muslims are welcome to visit any of them, but it's best to steer clear of prayer times; noon, especially Friday noon, is the main one (exact times vary throughout the year). Dress modestly: no shorts, short skirts or bare shoulders. Shoes must be removed, and women must cover their hair. Headscarves are frequently – but not always – available to borrow, so you might prefer to bring your own. Photography is often allowed, but it's best to avoid both during prayers and snapping worshippers at any time.

INSIDE TRACK LOSING HEADS

Beside the ticket counters at Topkapı Palace is the Executioner's Fountain. This is where the chief axeman would wash his blade after carrying out his grisly work. The heads of his victims were displayed on top of the truncated columns on either side of the fountain.

The Cisterns

Between the gardens of Sultanahmet Mosque on one side of Sultanahmet Square and Haghia Sophia on the other, **Yerebatan Sarnıcı** (Basilica Cistern) is the grandest of several underground reservoirs that riddle the foundations of this part of the city.

A second cistern, the **Binbirdirek Sarnıcı** (the 'Cistern of 1,001 Columns', although there are only 224), is also open to the public.

★ Yerebatan Sarnıcı

Yerebatan Caddesi 13 (0212 522 1259, www.yerebatan.com). Tram Sultanahmet. **Open** 9am-5.30pm daily. **Admission** TL10. **Map** p243 N10.

Built by the Emperor Justinian at the same time as Haghia Sophia, the Yerebatan Cistern was forgotten for centuries and only rediscovered by a Frenchman, Peter Gyllius, in 1545 when he noticed that people in the neighbourhood got water by lowering buckets through holes in their basements. It's a tremendous engineering feat, with brick vaults supported on 336 columns spaced at 4m (13ft) intervals. Prior to restoration in 1987, the cistern could only be explored by boat (James Bond rowed through in *From Russia with Love*). These days there are concrete walkways. The subdued lighting and cool subterranean air are especially welcome on hot days. Look for the two Medusa heads at the far end from

SIGHTS

the entrance, both recycled from an even more ancient building and casually employed as column bases. There's a café down here and a platform on which occasional concerts of classical Turkish and Western music are performed; check with the ticket office for further details.

Binbirdirek Sarnıcı

Imran Ökten Sokak 4 (0212 518 1001, www. binbirdirek.com). Tram Sultanahmet. **Open** 9am-7.30pm daily. **Admission** TL10. **Map** p243 M10.
Like the more famous Yerebatan, this cistern is a Byzantine forest of pillars and brick-vaulted ceilings, but sadly the restorers have put in a false floor that halves the original height of the chamber (a well at the centre illustrates the original floor level). It's possible to rent out the venue for events, but it's apparent that no one has figured out a use for the place. Currently, it unsuccessfully accommodates a futuristic neon-lit bar and a handful of offices.

TOPKAPI PALACE

Directly behind Haghia Sophia are the walls shielding the Topkapı Palace complex. Part command centre for a massive military empire, part archetypal Eastern pleasure dome, the palace was the hub of Ottoman power for over three centuries, until it was superseded by Dolmabahçe Palace in 1853. For lavish decor and exquisite location, it rivals Granada's Alhambra. At least half a day is needed to explore Topkapı, although you could easily spend a full day exploring the palace's many collections. If you're pushed for time, the must-see features are the Harem (although there's an extra charge), Imperial Treasury and the views from the innermost courtyard. Be warned that any part of the palace may be closed at any time.

The entrance to the palace is via the **Imperial Gate** (Bab-ı Hümayün), erected by Sultan Fatih in 1478 and decorated with niches that during Ottoman times were used to display the severed heads of rebels and criminals. The gate leads into the first of a series of four courts that become more private the deeper into the complex you penetrate. The **First Court** was public and not considered part of the palace proper. It housed a hospital and dormitories for the palace guards, hence the popular name, Court of the Janissaries. To the left is the church of **Haghia Irene** (Aya Irini Kilisesi), built by Emperor Justinian and so a contemporary of Haghia Sophia. It has the distinction of being the only pre-Ottoman-conquest church in the city that was never turned into a mosque. Today, the church serves as an exhibition space and a concert venue, the latter during the **International Istanbul Music Festival** (*see p176*).

Still in the First Court, down the hill to the left, is the superb **Archaeology Museum** (*see p47*), but the palace proper is entered through the Disneyesque gate ahead. Tickets can be bought on the right just before the gate.

A semi-public space, the enormous **Second Court** is where the business of running the empire was carried out. This area is where the viziers of the imperial council sat in session in the divan, overlooking gardens landscaped with cypresses, plane trees and rose bushes. Where once there would have been crowds of petitioners awaiting their turn for an audience, nowadays there are queues lined up waiting to get in to the **Harem**, an introverted complex of around 300 brilliantly tiled chambers on several levels, connected by arcaded courts and fountain gardens. Tickets are sold separately (TL15), from a window located beside the Harem entrance. (*See also right* **Hard Times in the Harem**.)

Around from the Harem ticket window, a low brick building topped by shallow domes is the former **State Treasury**, present home of an exhibition of arms and armour. Across the gardens, a long row of ventilation chimneys punctuates the roof line of the newly renovated kitchens, which catered for up to 5,000 inhabitants of the palace. They contain a collection of ceramics, glass and silverware, much of it imported from China and Japan via Central Asia, along the legendary Silk Route. The earliest pieces are Chinese celadon, particularly valued by the sultans because it was supposed to change colour when brought into contact with poison.

Sultanahmet Mosque. *See p43.*

SIGHTS

All paths in the Second Court converge on the **Gate of Felicity** (Bab-üs Saadet), which gives access to the **Third Court** – the sultan's own private domain. Confronting all who enter is the **Audience Chamber** (Arz Odası), where foreign ambassadors would present their credentials, until the exterior Sublime Porte supplanted this room's role. Although the sultan would be present on such occasions, he would never deign to speak with a non-Turk and all conversation was conducted via the grand vizier.

To the right is the **Hall of the Campaign Pages** (Seferli Koşusu), whose task it was to look after the royal wardrobe. The rotating collection of gorgeous robes on display attests to their excellent job: there's a perfectly preserved 550-year-old, red-and-gold silk kaftan worn by Mehmet II, conqueror of Constantinople.

Things get even more glittery next door in the **Imperial Treasury** (Hazine). Many of the items here were made for the palace by a team of court artisans, which at its height numbered over 600. A lot of what's displayed here has never left the confines of the inner courts. Not that too many people outside the sultan's circle would have had much use for a diamond-encrusted set of chain mail or a Koran bound in jade. Items such as the Topkapı Dagger, its handle set with three eyeball-sized emeralds, are breathtaking in their excessiveness.

More remarkable still are the items in the Privy Chamber. It houses the Chamber of Sacred Relics. To the sound of the Koran being read live, visitors trail around a series of items including Moses's staff, Muhammad's sword, tooth, beard and cloak.

Hard Times in the Harem

The dark world behind those orientalist fantasies.

From its inception in around 1540 until its dissolution in the early 20th century, the Topkapı harem was home, prison and entire world to almost four centuries of palace women. The word means 'forbidden', a ruling that applied to all men except the sultan, the princes and the eunuch guards. Women had no problem getting in, but once admitted they were in for life. Most entered as slave girls presented to the sultan as gifts: it was forbidden to make slaves of Muslims, so they were all Christians or Jews. Circassian girls who came from what is now Georgia and Armenia were favoured because of their fair skin, although even the fairest was still only valued at a fifth of the price of a good horse. The girls were converted to Islam and 'palace-trained', which means they were taught to sing, dance, play instruments and to give pleasure of a more tactile kind.

But notions of the harem as a sensual hothouse are misplaced. It was a highly competitive and cut-throat environment in which each girl sought to catch the eye of the sultan or a prince and so secure a better station. At any one time, a dozen or so girls would be chosen as imperial handmaids and bedmates. Giving birth to the sultan's child ensured exalted status. If it was a boy, there was even the chance he might one day become sultan and his mother *valide sultana*, 'mother of the sultan' – the most powerful woman in the land. At such high stakes, with the sex came violence as the women manoeuvred, plotted, poisoned and knifed their way up the harem hierarchy. A mother with the sultan's child was particularly vulnerable – Murat III (1574-95), for example, fathered 103 children, only one of whom was ever going to make the throne.

All the while, harem girls also had to court the favour of the present valide sultana, responsible for selecting girls for the sultan, while avoiding the displeasure of the *kızlar ağası*, the chief black eunuch. These latter characters were the go-betweens for the sultan and his mother and so privy to all palace secrets. At the same time, physically and psychologically mutilated as they were, the chief black eunuchs tended to be a dangerous combination of corrupt, scheming and vindictive. Some got their kicks by stuffing girls in sacks and dumping them into the Bosphorus, usually on the instructions of the valide sultana (although Sultans Ibrahim and Murat II are both alleged to have ordered their entire harems drowned, one out of boredom, the other through paranoia).

Alev Lytle Croutier sums it up in her fine book *Harem: The World Behind the Veil*, describing it as a world of 'frightened women plotting with men who were not men against absolute rulers who kept their relatives immured for decades'. Far from being a palace of sensual delights, the Topkapı harem must have been more of a nerve-shredding chamber of horrors.

Topkapı Palace.

The final and **Fourth Court** is a garden with terraces stepping down towards Seraglio Point, the protruberance of land that watches over the entrance to the Golden Horn. Buildings are limited to a handful of reasonably restrained pavilions, while the views over the Bosphorus are wonderful, as are the sea breezes on a summer's day. Most notable is the Baghdad Kiosk, built to celebrate Murad IV's Baghdad Campaign in 1638, with remarkable mother-of-pearl furniture. The very last building to be constructed within the palace, the **Mecidiye Pavilion** (Mecidiye Köşkü), built in 1840, now houses an outpost of the historical Konyalı Lokantası, notable for its Ottoman cuisine and much coveted terrace seating.

There are changing exhibitions in buildings around the palace through the year, often celebrating Turkey's diplomatic relationships.

★ Topkapı Palace
Topkapı Sarayı

Entrances off Soğuk Çeşme Sokak or through Gülhane Park (0212 512 0480, www.topkapi sarayi.gov.tr). Tram Gülhane or Sultanahmet. **Open** *May-Sept* 9am-7pm Mon, Wed-Sun. *Oct-Apr* 9am-5pm Mon, Wed-Sun. Ticket office closes 1hr earlier. **Admission** TL20. *Harem* TL15. Museum Pass Istanbul Card accepted for main entrance (not Harem) only. **Map** p243 O9.

Archaeology Museum/Museum of the Ancient Orient
Istanbul Arkeoloji Müzeleri

Alemdar Caddesi, Osman Hamdi Bey Yokuşu Sokak (0212 520 7740, www.istanbularkeoloji. gov.tr). Tram Gülhane. **Open** 9am-5pm Tue-Sun. Ticket office closes 1hr earlier. **Admission** TL10 (incl Museum of the Ancient Orient & Tiled Pavilion). Museum Pass Istanbul Card accepted. **Map** p243 O9.

The collection of classical antiquities displayed here is world class, although a few of the galleries are looking a little tired. Within the grounds of Topkapı Palace, the museum was founded in the late 19th century in an attempt to staunch the flow of antiquities being spirited out of the country by foreigners to fill the museums of Europe. The exhibits were originally housed in the Tiled Pavilion (*see below*) until the commissioning of a new building, since extended on three occasions to keep up with the growing contents. Even so, the bulk of the collection remains in storage due to lack of space and funds.

Greeting visitors is a grinning statue of Bes, a demonic Cypriot demigod of great power and strength, qualities required of anyone hoping to get through even a fraction of the 20 galleries within. Starting with the pre-Classical world, they cover 5,000 years of history, with artefacts gathered from all over Turkey and the Near East and grouped thematically. Highlights include a collection of sixth- to fourth-century BC sarcophagi from a royal necropolis at Sidon, in modern Lebanon, of which the finest is known as the Alexander Sarcophagus because of the scenes of the Macedonian general's victory at Issus (333 BC) adorning its side panels. A great addition is the small children's museum (occasionally closed for temporary shows), complete with ancient toys, 1000-year-old homework samples and a replica Trojan horse.

Up on the first floor, Istanbul Through the Ages is a summary of the city's history presented through a few key pieces, including a serpent's head lopped off the column in the Hippodrome (*see p48*) and a section of the iron chain that stretched across the Bosphorus to bar the way of invaders. The museum also occasionally holds special exhibitions.

Across from the museum stands the **Tiled Pavilion** (Çinili Köşk), which dates back to 1472 and the reign of Sultan Mehmet II, Ottoman conqueror of Constantinople. Built in a Persian style, it was an

INSIDE TRACK MUSEUM PASS ISTANBUL CARD

In late 2011, the Turkish Ministry of Tourism released a multi-entrance museum pass. The aptly named Museum Pass Istanbul Card costs TL72 and is valid for 72 hours, beginning with your first museum entry. It gives free access – and no queuing – at the Haghia Sophia, Topkapı Palace (excluding the Harem), Archaeological Museums, Museum of Turkish and Islamic Arts, Mosaic Museum and Church of St Saviour in Chora, plus discounts on entrance to a handful of additional museums. The pass can be purchased online (www.muze.gov.tr) or at most of the participating venues.

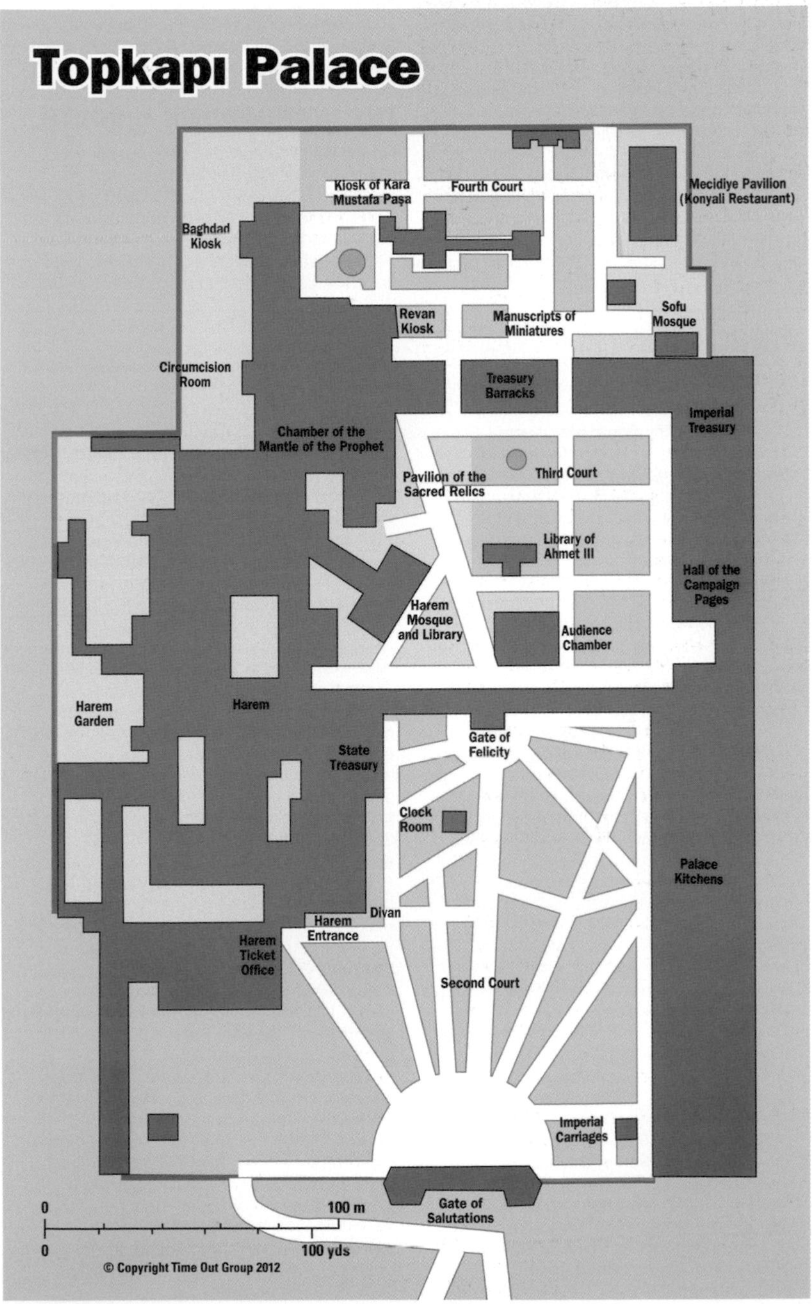
Topkapı Palace
Kiosk of Kara Mustafa Paşa
Fourth Court
Mecidiye Pavilion (Konyali Restaurant)
Baghdad Kiosk
Revan Kiosk
Manuscripts of Miniatures
Sofu Mosque
Circumcision Room
Treasury Barracks
Imperial Treasury
Chamber of the Mantle of the Prophet
Pavilion of the Sacred Relics
Third Court
Library of Ahmet III
Hall of the Campaign Pages
Harem Mosque and Library
Audience Chamber
Harem Garden
Harem
State Treasury
Gate of Felicity
Clock Room
Palace Kitchens
Divan
Harem Entrance
Harem Ticket Office
Second Court
Imperial Carriages
0
100 m
0
100 yds
Gate of Salutations
© Copyright Time Out Group 2012

imperial viewing stand that overlooked a large gaming field, now occupied by the main museum building. The pavilion displays some outstanding samples of Turkish tiles and ceramics from the Seljuk and Ottoman periods, dating from between the end of the 12th century and the beginning of the 20th century.

To the south, beside the main entrance, is the **Museum of the Ancient Orient (Eski Şark Eserleri Müzesi)**, containing antiquities from the Mesopotamian, Egyptian and Hittite cultures, including some monumental glazed-brick friezes from the main Ishtar Gate of sixth-century Babylon. There is also the world's first peace treaty (1283 BC), a clay tablet signed by the Hittite king Hattushilish III and Egyptian pharaoh Rameses II that ended a lengthy conflict between the two ancient rival empires.

THE HIPPODROME & SOUTH

On the north-west side of the Blue Mosque, a strip of over-touristy teahouses and souvenir shops fringes the northern tip of the **Hippodrome** (At Meydanı), formerly the focal point of Byzantine Constantinople.

At one time, this ancient arena was used for races, court ceremonies, coronations and

Istanbul on Foot Sultanahmet

Explore Istanbul's historic centre of faith and empire.

Begin at Karaköy Square for a stroll across the Golden Horn into Sultanahmet. It takes imagination to see Galata Bridge as it was in its golden era, a time when Edmondo de Amicis, an Italian writer who visited the city in the 1870s, gave a literary snapshot of the bridge's human comings and goings in his Constantinople. At that time the bridge was the centre point of the multicultural Ottoman Empire, and flowing across it were Albanians in petticoats with pistols at the ready, Maltese ladies in black faldettas (hooded cloaks), Tartars wearing sheepskin, European ambassadors, necromancers, eunuchs busting skulls making way for the lunchtime social runs of the aristocratic Turkish *hanıms* in their charge, and porters limping along under hundreds of pounds of firewood. These days you're much more likely to see amateur fishermen lining the rails, selling their catch to sandwich vendors; there is also a lively line of touristy restaurants and bars on a lower level between the road and the water. It's still a classic Istanbul walk, though, and an exhilarating one.

Straight ahead on the Sultanahmet side of the bridge lies the **Yeni Camii**, or New Mosque, so called because, as a 17th-century construction, it was a relatively late addition to the skyline.

From here, hit the Mısır Çarşısı, the **Egyptian (or Spice) Bazaar**. As well as shops selling Turkish Delight, 'Turkish Viagra' (variations on dates stuffed with walnuts), and backgammon boards, the market is home to some quality delis, as well as spice and coffee merchants.

Loop back on to Reşadiye Caddesi and, with the Golden Horn on your left, head up Muradiye Hudavendigar, which becomes Alemdar Caddesi. You will pass the entrance of the **Sublime Porte**, once the home of the Ottoman grand vizier, but now relegated to the headquarters of the Istanbul governor. Today, the Porte's wan look says little about what used to happen at this juncture of road. Here the grand vizier held the dangerous job of wielding true power, while the sultans retreated to the harem, went to seed on wine nominally denied to the Muslim masses, or – in the case of 'Mad Ibrahim' (1640-48) – took to **Alay Koksu**, the polygonal kiosk across from the Porte, where the demented sultan would take potshots at pedestrians with a crossbow. Beyond lies the gate to **Gulhane Park**, where picnickers while away the afternoon.

At the top of Alemdar Caddesi, the road leads into Sultanahmet Square. Here, you are at the epicentre of historic Sultanahmet. To the left lies **Haghia Sophia**; **Sultanahmet Mosque** is ahead, visible on the other side of the square past a lovingly attended park with fountains and flowers. **Topkapı Palace** is around the bend off Soğukçeşme Sokak. There are more sights in this area than can be seen on one visit (it's easy to spend a day at Topkapı Palace). Before deciding what to visit, it might be time for a rest in the mosque's gardens. Alternatively, on the other side of Sultanahmet Square, is a place of greenery and park benches, with a road encircling the park that follows the old chariot tracks. A good place in which to find a shady spot, enjoy an ice-cream, and conclude our walk.

parades. Originally laid out by the Roman emperor Septimius Severus during his rebuilding of the city, the arena was enlarged by Constantine to its present dimensions. The modern road exactly follows the tracks of the old racing lanes. Now little more than an elongated park dotted with benches, the Hippodrome does retain an odd assortment of monuments, which stand on what was the *spina*, the raised area around which chariots would have thundered.

Closest to the mosque is an **Egyptian obelisk**, removed from the Temple of Karnak at Thebes (now Luxor). The obelisk was originally carved in around 1500 BC to commemorate the victories of Pharaoh Thutmosis III. In a self-congratulatory mood, the Byzantine emperor Theodosius had the obelisk moved to Constantinople in AD 390, where it was set upon a marble pedestal and sculpted with scenes of himself and his family enjoying a day at the races.

Next to the obelisk is the bronze **Serpentine Column** (also known as the Spiral Column), carried off from the Temple of Apollo at Delphi, where it had been set to commemorate Greek victory over the Persians in 480 BC. When it was brought to the Byzantine capital by

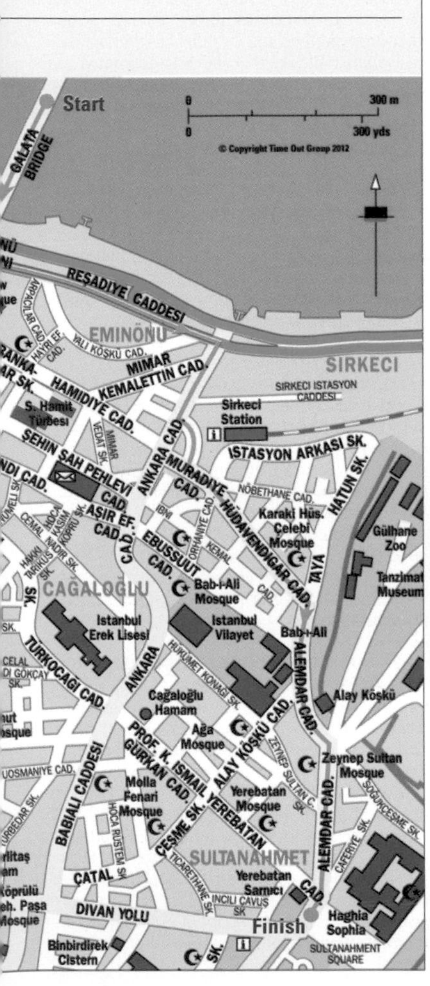

Egyptian obelisk.

Constantine, its three entwined serpents had heads but each one has been decapitated over the years. One detached head survives and is displayed in the Archaeology Museum. A third monument, known as the **Column of Constantine**, was once sheathed in gold-plated bronze, but stripped by the looting Fourth Crusaders. Its pockmarked and crumbling surface is currently swathed in scaffolding, hopefully promising a smooth, fresh renovation.

Overlooking the Hippodrome is the grand **Museum of Turkish and Islamic Art**, while down the hill from its south-west corner is the **Sokollu Mehmet Paşa Mosque**.

The streets around here twist and turn between creaky wooden buildings – a delight to explore. Head south, downhill toward the sea, for the **Küçük Haghia Sophia Mosque**.

Following Küçük Ayasofya Caddesi back uphill leads past the very worthwhile **Mosaic Museum** and the Ottoman-era shopping centre, the **Arasta Bazaar**, beyond which is a sunken terrace café where you can puff an afternoon away with a narghile.

FREE Küçük Haghia Sophia Mosque

Küçük Ayasofya Camii

Küçük Ayasofya Caddesi. Tram Sultanahmet. **Open** prayer times only, daily. **Admission** free. **Map** p243 M12.

Known as 'Little Haghia Sophia' because of its resemblance to Justinian's great cathedral. Like its larger namesake, it was originally a church, in this case dedicated to Sergius and Bacchus, the patron saints of the Christianised Roman army. It possesses both a recently renovated, attractive exterior and a fine interior, including a marble frieze honouring Justinian and his wife, Theodora. There's also a very pleasant garden opposite, which has an adjoining café.

Mosaic Museum

Büyüksaray Mozaik Müzesi

Arasta Çarşısı (0212 518 1205, www.ayasofyamuzesi.gov.tr). Tram Sultanahmet. **Open** *May-Sept* 9am-7pm Tue-Sun. *Oct-Apr* 9am-5pm Tue-Sun. Ticket office closes 1hr earlier. **Admission** TL8. Museum Pass Istanbul Card accepted. **No credit cards. Map** p243 N11.

Behind Sultanahmet Mosque and slightly down the hill towards the Bosphorus is a small, 17th-century shopping street, built to provide rental revenue for the upkeep of the mosque. It has been converted into a cluster of tourist shops, known as the Arasta Bazaar (www.arastabazaar.com). Leading off here is a prefabricated hut that is the unlikely home of a fantastic archaeological find. Uncovered in the mid 1950s, it's an ornamental pavement belonging to the Byzantine Great Palace (Büyüksaray), which stood where the mosque is now, and probably dates from the era of Justinian. The surviving segments depict mythological and hunting scenes, with pastoral idylls disturbingly skewed by bloody depictions of animal combat: elephant versus lion, snake versus gazelle, stags and lizards being eaten by winged unicorns. The museum is also worth a visit for the informative wall panels, particularly the reconstructions of how the Byzantine palace quarter would have looked.

Museum of Turkish & Islamic Art

Türk ve Islam Eserleri Müzesi

At Meydanı 46 (0212 518 1805). Tram Sultanahmet. **Open** *May-Sept* 9am-7pm Tue-Sun. *Oct-Apr* 9am-5pm Tue-Sun. Ticket office closes 1hr earlier. **Admission** TL10. Museum Pass Istanbul Card accepted. **Map** p243 M10.

Overlooking the Hippodrome, the museum occupies the restored 16th-century palace of Ibrahim Paşa. A Greek convert to Islam, Ibrahim was the confidant of Süleyman I and in 1523 he was appointed grand vizier. When his palace was completed the following year, it was the grandest private residence in the Ottoman Empire. When Süleyman fell under the influence of the scheming Roxelana (*see p26*), he was persuaded that Ibrahim had to go, and the vizier was strangled in his sleep.

The palace was seized by the state and was variously used as a school, a dormitory, a court, a barracks and a prison, before being restored as a museum. The collections include carpets, manuscripts, miniatures, woodwork, metalwork and glasswork. Items date from the early Islamic period through to modern times, all presented chronologically and geographically, with full explanations provided.

On the ground floor, a gallery showcases modern Turkish and foreign artists. There's an interesting ethnographic section, which includes a re-creation of a *kara çadır* or 'black tent', the residence of choice for many of the nomadic Anatolian tribes who developed the art of the *kilim*. Upstairs, the Great Hall contains one of the finest collections of carpets in the world.

► *There's an excellent café in the museum's shaded courtyard, as well as seating on a covered terrace overlooking the Hippodrome and the Blue Mosque opposite.*

FREE Sokollu Mehmet Paşa Mosque

Sokollu Mehmet Paşa Camii

Şehit Mehmet Paşa Sokak 20 (0212 518 1633). Tram Eminönü or Sultanahmet. **Open** 7am-dusk daily. Closed to non-worshippers during daily prayer times. **Admission** free. **Map** p243 M11.

One of Sinan's later buildings (constructed between 1571 and 1572), this mosque has been praised by architectural historians for its skilful handling of an uneven, sloping site. If you manage to get inside (hang around long enough, and somebody will usually turn up with a key), notice the lovely tiling and painted calligraphic inscriptions, set among floral motifs. If you don't, the ornate fountain in the courtyard is also beautiful.

The Bazaar Quarter

The hub of Ottoman commerce.

Map p242 **Bars & Cafés** p147
Restaurants p129

Built under Mehmet the Conqueror in the mid 15th century, the covered Grand Bazaar has been the place to sell, exchange and barter – anything and everything – for half a millennium. Camels may no longer drop off silks from Central Asia, but the hundreds of multilingual shop owners still sell woven carpets, antique ceramics, hand-dyed textiles and oodles of gold jewellery, with perhaps a more than healthy dose of knock-off designer jeans and souvenir key rings thrown in.

After loading up on local treasures, be sure to venture out into the streets spiralling around the Grand Bazaar. These crowded alleyways house ancient *hans* (former caravanserais, overnight inns for travelling traders), as well as more practical shopping arcades stocked with scarves, toys, buttons, tulip-shaped tea glasses and much, much more.

DIVAN YOLU

Narrow, sloping, partially cobbled and given over to purring trams, the street known as Divan Yolu is modestly attractive. There's little indication that this was formerly the ancient Mese, or Middle Way – the main thoroughfare of Byzantine Constantinople and, later, Ottoman Stamboul. It ran from the imperial centre (today's Sultanahmet) due west over the city's seven hills to the Topkapı Gate in the city wall. From Byzantium, the Mese continued all the way to Durres (Durazzo) on the Albanian coast. A large marble sliver at the eastern end of Divan Yolu, in the small park behind the Yerebatan Sarnıcı, is all that remains of a Byzantine triumphal arch, known as the **Milion**. It originally marked the point from which all distances were measured.

Modern Divan Yolu is defined by tacky souvenir shops, cheap eateries, money exchange bureaux and bucket-shop travel agencies, with the odd smattering of antiquity. On the corner with Babıali Caddesi is a small, well-tended cemetery with the **Tomb of Mahmut II**. Over the road and down a side street is the **Theodosius Cistern**, sitting under the Eminönü Belediye Başkanlığı building. The **Basın Müzesi** (Press Museum) is rather dull, but has a popular café on the ground floor. Next door, on the corner with Vezirhanı Caddesi, the big, bulbous, yellow-faced dome belongs to the **Çemberlitaş Hamam** (*see p194*). The buildings fall back here to create a crowded combination car park and plaza, marked by the scruffy **Burnt Column**. Otherwise known as the Hooped Column, this easily overlooked pillar is, in fact, one of the city's oldest monuments. Erected by Constantine to celebrate the city's inauguration as new imperial capital in 330, the column was topped by a statue of the emperor until it was destroyed in an 1106 hurricane. Its present blackened state is the result of one of Istanbul's periodic fires. The iron hoops are structural reinforcements that were added in the fifth century and replaced in the 1970s.

By this point Divan Yolu has turned into **Yeniçeriler Caddesi**, which is lined with a string of small mosques, tombs and *medreses* (theological schools), a couple of which have small courtyards that double up as **narghile cafés** (*see p157* **Hubbly Bubbly**). From here, the Grand Bazaar is immediately to the north.

FREE Theodosius Cistern

Şerefiye Sarnıcı

Piyer Loti Caddesi, Sultanahmet. Tram Sultanahmet. Cistern currently closed for renovations. **Map** p243 M10.

This Byzantine reservoir previously offered a glimpse of what the more famous Yerabatan Sarnıcı would have looked like before it was restored. However, it was closed for renovations in mid 2011.

FREE Tomb of Mahmut II

82 Divan Yolu, Sultanahmet. Tram Sultanahmet. **Open** 9.30am-7pm daily. **Admission** free. **Map** p243 M10.

Mahmut II (1808-39) was the sultan who crushed the Janissaries, the Ottomans' elite standing army. He must have been a formidable force in the harem, too, producing 15 sons and 12 daughters, many of whom are now crammed into the domed tomb with him.

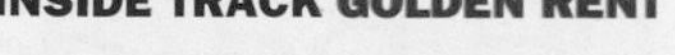

INSIDE TRACK GOLDEN RENT

Many shop owners in the Grand Bazaar still pay their annual rent in gold, particularly jewellery merchants. They can expect to hand over between four and six kilograms of gold a year. On the main avenue, annual rent weighs in at around seven kilograms. However, due to rising gold prices, many shops opt to pay in the more stable euro or Turkish lire.

GRAND BAZAAR

The Grand Bazaar (in Turkish Kapalı Çarşı, or 'Covered Market') is a world apart. A maze of vaulted passages, the bazaar has its own banks, baths, mosques, cafés and restaurants, a police station and post office, not to mention thousands of shops, all glittery and fairy-lit in the absence of natural light. Since the rise of the mall it's no longer the biggest shopping centre in the world, but it can still claim its place as the oldest.

Part of the building dates back to the ninth century, when it was used as something akin to a Byzantine ministry of finance. Trading proper started in 1461, a mere eight years after the Turkish conquest of Constantinople. The Ottomans ushered in a new economic era, with the city at the centre of an empire that stretched from the Arabian deserts almost to the European Alps. Mehmet the Conqueror ordered the construction of a *bedesten*, a great secure building with thick stone walls, massive iron gates and space for several dozen shops. This structure survives in modified form as the Old Bedesten (*Iç Bedesten*), at the heart of the bazaar. It remains a place where the most precious items are sold, including the finest silver and antiques. The Sandal Bedesten was added later; named after a Bursan silk, it was filled with textile traders.

A network of covered streets grew up around the two *bedestens*, sealed at night behind 18 great gates. Whenever the economy was

Grand Bazaar.

SIGHTS

booming, the market would physically expand, only to be cut back by frequent fires. As the Ottoman Empire started to decline after 300 years of wealth, so did the legendary splendour of the bazaar. In 1894, a devastating earthquake hit the traders particularly hard. It wasn't until the 1950s that the bazaar began to revive, as the new republic found its economic footing. These days, it's taking tentative steps into the 21st century with chic boutiques, hip cafés, and even a website (www.kapalicarsi.org.tr).

Much of the current prosperity comes from gold – nearly 100 tonnes of it is sold in the bazaar each year. At the other end of the spectrum, there are the 'black bag' shoppers from Eastern Europe and former countries of the Soviet Union, so called because of their habit of filling numerous bin bags with cheap clothing.

The bazaar definitely has plenty of inessential knick-knacks, tacky souvenirs, nasty leather jackets, hookah pipes and hippie outfits, but there are some unusual and high-quality goods to be had too; you just have to know where to look and be prepared to haggle. For guidance on both, *see p54* **Shopping the Bazaar**.

★ Grand Bazaar
Kapalı Çarşı

Beyazıt (0212 519 1248, www.kapalicarsi.org.tr). Tram Beyazıt or Çemberlitaş. **Open** 8.30am-7pm Mon-Sat. **Map** p288 L9.

► *The smaller Egyptian Bazaar in Eminönü has more souvenirs, food and plenty of spices; see p59.*

AROUND THE GRAND BAZAAR

If you can find your way out of the east side of the bazaar, you emerge into daylight roughly north of the **Nuruosmaniye Mosque**.

From Mahmut Paşa Kapısı (Gate), follow Mahmut Paşa Yokuşu north. This market street is given over to the rag trade: it's lined with wholesalers knocking out fake Lacoste T-shirts and imitation Levi's jeans in insalubrious basement workshops. The street's great stone archways lead into numerous ancient *hans*, medieval merchant hostels with storage rooms and sleeping quarters built around a central courtyard.

To the north of the Grand Bazaar, the market extends much further than the limits of the covered area, spilling over into a crazed warren of narrow streets that zigzag all the way to the districts of Tahtakale and **Eminönü** (*see p59*) beside the Golden Horn. If you're lost, just keep heading downhill. On the way, you'll see the contemporary bazaar at its most frenetic.

Exit the Grand Bazaar on the west side for **Çadırcılar Caddesi**. At No.27 is a large derelict courtyard graced with a mosaic of **Yunus Emre**, a 13th-century Sufi poet ('God is our professor and love is our academy,' quoth he). Ascend the staircase to be greeted by wholesaler Ahmet and his stock of Central Asian kaftans, Pakistani fabrics, shamanistic artefacts and jewellery at prices you won't find anywhere else in the bazaar.

West of Çadırcılar, in Sahaflar Çarşısı Sokak, is the **Booksellers' Bazaar**, a lane and courtyard where the written word has been traded since early Ottoman times. Because printed books were considered a corrupting European influence, only hand-lettered manuscripts were sold until 1729, the year the first book in Turkish was published. Today, much of the trade at this historic bazaar is in textbooks (the university is nearby), along with plentiful coffee-table volumes and framed calligraphy for the tourists. Sadly, the booksellers now have to compete with itinerant merchants peddling everything from Byzantine coins to used mobile phones.

FREE Nuruosmaniye Mosque
Nuruosmaniye Camii

Vezirhanı Caddesi, Beyazıt (0212 528 0906). Tram Beyazıt or Çemberlitaş. **Open** 10am-7pm daily. Closed to non-worshippers during daily prayer times. **Admission** free. **Map** p242 L9.

Constructed on one of the seven hills within the walls of former Constantinople, Nuruosmaniye was the first mosque in the city built in the style known as Turkish Baroque. In summertime, the courtyard shaded by plane trees is lovely; the extensive manuscript library is also worth a peek.

Shopping the Bazaar

Insider tips on finding what you want and paying a fair price.

There are 5,500-odd vendors in the Grand Bazaar. Shopkeepers cajole and entreat passers-by in a dozen languages, determined not to permit visitors to indulge in such a non-commercial activity as sightseeing. Remember, you're not dealing with sales clerks but most likely the owners themselves, or at least a trusted brother or nephew. Many still pay their rent in gold – a hefty seven kilos per year for shops on the main avenue (*see p52* **Inside Track**).

Fortunately, the perception that hardcore hustling is bad for long-term trade has finally started to sink in among the bazaar traders. Visitors will find the Grand Bazaar a kinder, gentler place than it was years ago. But even the sagacious Mehmet the Conqueror, who founded the covered bazaar in the 1460s, would have been surprised by the plasma screens overhead in the bazaar's 65 alleys.

THE PRACTICALITIES

Serious shoppers should come armed with a notepad, a calculator for working out exchange rates and plenty of time – three hours is about the minimum needed for a purchasing expedition here. When you find something you like, the very organised will jot down the price and the location of the seller. Then track down the item elsewhere and get more quotes. Continue for as long as you have the patience.

Don't assume that wildly varying prices for the same item means the higher price is a rip-off. Shopkeepers price their goods according to their needs. You may be lucky: someone may require ready cash to pay overheads or buy new stock and will be happy to settle for a quick, cheap sale. Also, it's not true that large, sleek shops in central locations always charge more. Even though they pay higher rents, higher turnover often allows them to lower prices.

BARGAINING ETIQUETTE

When bargaining, start somewhere well below your ideal price, because the shop owner will start well above his. Hopefully, you can meet in the middle. Remember that it's considered bad form to enter into an elaborate bargaining process if you're not really interested in buying.

WHERE TO BUY WHAT

There are over a dozen main gates into the Grand Bazaar. At least five of them open on to **Kalpakçılar Caddesi**, an opulent east–west thoroughfare lined with gleaming jewellery shops. On this street, you'll also find **Pako** (at No.87), the place for some of the city's best handbags and purses.

South of Kalpakçılar is the **Kürkcüler Çarşısı**, filled with leather jackets and coats. It's also where you'll find **Yörük** (*see p173*), a good carpet shop, located at No.7 at the base of some steps leading up and out of the bazaar.

For more carpets visit the **Rubi Hanı** at the eastern end of Kürkcüler Çarşısı. **Tradition**, tucked away in the courtyard at No.11, is another well-stocked option.

Running north from Kalpakçılar Caddesi, **Kolancılar Sokak** is lined with shops that peddle a typical mix of souvenirs, ceramics, tea sets, silks, water pipes, chess sets and carved wood. It crosses **Keseciler Caddesi** (location of the quality rural crafts shop **Derviş**, *see p171*) before making a beeline for the ancient heart of the bazaar, the **Old Bedesten**. (Check out the Byzantine eagle carved into the stone on the outside face of its eastern entrance.) In here, the atmosphere is hushed, almost scholarly – a suitable setting for dealers in Ottoman-era prayer beads, icons, chess sets,

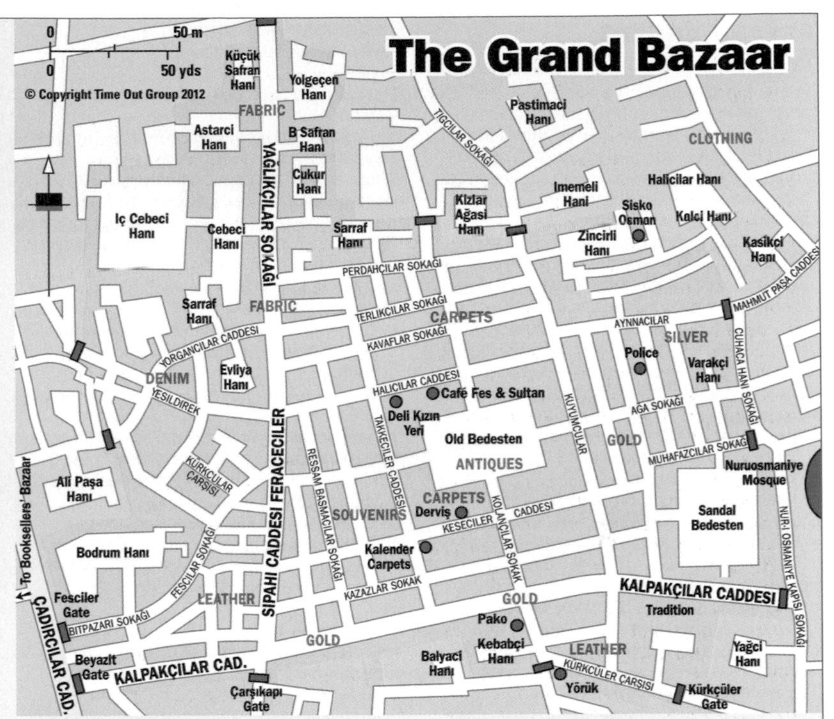

firearms, pocket watches, painted miniatures, snuff boxes, Soviet memorabilia and art nouveau jewellery.

On the north side of the Bedesten is **Halıcılar Caddesi**, no longer 'the Street of the Carpet Sellers', but instead the front line of gentrification, with quaint **Café Fes** and **Café Sultan** selling Illy coffee and fresh flowers, and **Abdulla** (*see p170*) between the two, the latter using chic packaging to shift traditional products.

West along Halıcılar are some more alternatives to carpets, notably at **Galeri Apollo** (Nos.22-6), a shop stocked with silky soft goat-hair rugs and calf-skin hides, hand-stitched into patchwork designs.

Halıcılar connects to **Yağlıkçılar Sokak**, a long street running north–south and the place for bellydancing costumes, incredible fabrics, lamps, knitwear and more unnecessary souvenirs.

Off Yağlıkçılar is the tranquil **Cebeci Hanı** and, beyond, the **Iç Cebeci Hanı**, where a large open courtyard is ringed by a second floor, lined with antiques and metalwork shops, plus a few places selling fabulous Central Asian fabrics and garments.

To visit the most beautiful *han* in the bazaar, head east from Yağlıkçılar along **Perdahçılar Sokak**; at the end follow the signs for **Zincirli Hanı**, the lair of the Grand Bazaar's most famous carpet dealer, **Sisko Osman** (*see p173*).

FOOD & DRINK

Outside the southern entrance to the Old Bedesten are **Julia's Kitchen** (Keseciler Caddesi 92), a great breakfast stop, and Köşk (Keseciler Caddesi 98-100), which serves traditional *sulu yemek* (home-cooked dishes), served up from bains-marie. **Şark Kahvesi**, at the corner of Yağlıkçılar and Fesciler Caddesi, is an old-style coffeehouse decorated with wonderful pictures of old fellows on flying carpets. The courtyard of the **Iç Cebeci Hanı** has an excellent kebab shop and a teahouse where off-duty merchants spend a serious amount of time over games of cards. **Havuzlu Lokantasi** (Gani Çelebi Sokak 3) is a basic, old-fashioned joint that does fine kebabs. Remember that all cafés and restaurants in the bazaar shut by 6.30pm.

BEYAZIT SQUARE

A large, irregularly shaped plaza west of the bazaar, Beyazıt Square was the site of the forum in Roman times. It regained importance when the early Ottomans built a palace here, which served as the pre-Topkapı seat of power until it burned down in 1541. Other significant Ottoman structures still stand, notably the **Beyazıt Mosque**.

Facing the mosque is the monumental gate to **Istanbul University**. In the 1960s and 1970s, the campus was a favourite battleground for both left and right, and is still a centre for political protest. As a result, the university grounds and **Beyazıt Tower**, built in 1828 as a fire lookout (with so many wooden buildings, fire was a constant hazard) and a prominent city landmark, are currently off limits to all but accredited students.

To the left of the monumental gate is a small *medrese*, which was originally part of the Beyazıt Mosque complex but is now occupied by the **Calligraphy Museum**, which is currently being restored.

Follow either of the roads that hug the university walls to reach the architectural perfection of the **Süleymaniye Mosque**. Outside its compound wall, in a walled, triangular garden to the north, is the modest **Tomb of Sinan**, designed by the occupant himself. The mosque's 500-year-old kitchens are now employed by **Darüzziyafe** (*see p129*), where you can have a rather unexceptional lunch in an exceptional setting. Also worth a visit is the neighbouring Lalezar teahouse, which occupies a sunken courtyard with a marble fountain, comfy cushioned seats, and narghile to puff on.

SIGHTS

FREE Beyazıt Mosque
Beyazıt Camii

Beyazıt Square, Yeniçeriler Caddesi. Tram Beyazıt. **Open** 10am-final prayer call daily. Closed to non-worshippers during daily prayer times. **Admission** free. **Map** p242 K9.

Built from 1501 to 1506, Beyazıt was the second great mosque complex to be founded in the city. The first, the Fatih Mosque, was destroyed, which makes Beyazıt the oldest imperial mosque in town. In effect, it's the architectural link between the Byzantine Haghia Sophia – the obvious inspiration – and the great, later Ottoman mosques such as Süleymaniye. The sultan for whom it was built, Beyazit II, is buried at the back of the gardens. Still in use, the mosque is full of market traders at prayer times. Outside is the Sahaflar Çarşısı (book bazaar), where Sufi booksellers tout travelogues and novels in many different languages.

▶ *For a good, cheap Turkish food after visiting the mosque try Şar (see p129), on the opposite side of Divan Yolu.*

Calligraphy Museum
Vakıf Hat Sanatları Müzesi

Beyazıt Square 1, Beyazıt (0212 527 5851). Tram Beyazıt. Museum currently closed for renovations. **Map** p242 K10.

Forbidden to portray living beings by religion (although this rule was not always strictly followed), Islamic artists developed alternative forms of virtuosity. Calligraphy was regarded as a particularly noble art because it was a way of beautifying the text of the Koran. But the sanctity of the text placed restrictions on the flourishes that could be added. Not so with the sultan's tuğra, or monogram, which incorporated his name, titles and patronymics into one highly stylised motif – the precursor of the modern logo. The tile art here is excellent and there are a number of brilliantly illuminated Korans dating from the 13th to 16th centuries. The museum also has a pleasant courtyard that features stone-carved calligraphy. The Dar'ül-Kurra in the courtyard is accessible to visitors during museum opening hours in Ramazan; it contains some holy relics of the Prophet Muhammed.

At the time of going to press this museum was closed for much-needed restoration and it's unclear when it will open again.

▶ *For more calligraphy displays, visit Sakıp Sabancı Museum (see p86) in Rumeli Hisarı, one of the Bosphorus Villages.*

★ FREE Süleymaniye Mosque
Süleymaniye Camii

Tiryakiler Çarşısı, off Prof Sıddık Sami Onar Caddesi, Süleymaniye. Tram Beyazıt or Eminönü. **Open** 9am-7pm daily. Closed to non-worshippers during daily prayer times. **Admission** free. **Map** p242 K8.

Completed in 1557 under Süleyman the Magnificent, this stunning mosque is arguably the crowning achievement of architect Mimar Sinan – all the more stunning since the completion of renovations in 2011. Built on Istanbul's highest hill, it is visible for miles. The approach is along Prof Sıddık Sami Onar Caddesi, once known as 'Addicts Alley' because its cafés sold hashish. This is no longer the case, although the area's teahouses are still popular student hangouts. The low-rise, multi-domed buildings surrounding the mosque are part of its *külliye* (compound), and include a hospital, asylum, hamam and soup kitchen.

Walk through the gardens and arcaded courtyard, whose columns allegedly came from the Byzantine royal box at the Hippodrome, to enter the mosque – remarkable for its soaring central prayer room, illuminated by some 200 windows. The interior decoration is minimal but effective; it includes stained glass added by Ibrahim the Mad and sparing use of Iznik tiles (which Sinan would later use profusely at the Rüstem Pasha Mosque, just down the hill, *see p60*).

Behind the mosque are several *türbes* (tombs), including Süleyman's own beautifully restored grave. Haseki Hürrem, the sultan's wife, a former slave known as Roxelana (*see p26*), is buried beside him.

Eminönü & the Golden Horn

Ferries, spices and the terminal for the Orient Express.

From dawn until dusk, Eminönü's ferry-fringed shoreline is buzzing. Thousands alight here, their daily commute a 20-minute boat ride between Asia and Europe. Spliced among the throngs are clutches of tourists, seeking out spices, coffee and dried fruits at the **Egyptian Bazaar**, or on the hunt for hard-to-find **Rüstem Paşa**, its turquoise tiles making it one of the city's prettiest mosques. Around the corner, ornate **Sirkeci Station** was the final destination of the world's most famous sleeper train, the Orient Express.

Map pp242-243 **Restaurants** p129

Crossing the Golden Horn, an inlet of the Sea of Marmara some 7.5 kilometres (five miles) long, the **Galata Bridge** connects the Sultanahmet peninsula with European Beyoğlu. As the sun drops over the water, there's no better place in the city to kick back with a beer, a narghile or a freshly grilled *balık ekmek* fish sandwich.

GÜLHANE PARK

To get to Eminönü from central Sultanahmet, ride the tram north to the Eminönü stop, or follow the tramlines on foot (a ten-minute walk from Sultanahmet Square). The route curves sharply around the walls enclosing **Gülhane Park**. Formerly part of the grounds of Topkapı Palace, the park is now a verdant enclave. It also contains the compact **Museum of the History of Science & Technology in Islam**, a treasure trove of scientific instruments (all historically accurate re-creations) invented in the Islamic world between the sixth and 16th centuries. Look out for the miniature replica Galata Tower that marks the museum's entrance.

Back on the tram tracks, just west of the Gülhane stop, is an ornate gateway with a rococo roof. At one time, this **Sublime Porte** (Bab-ı Ali) was the entrance to the palace of the grand vizier, the true administrator of the empire during the dotage of the sultans. Foreign ambassadors were accredited to the 'Sublime Porte', and the term became a synonym for the Ottoman government. The current gate dates from 1843 and is now the entrance to the headquarters of the provincial government.

Opposite, jutting out of a corner of the Gülhane Park wall, is the **Alay Köşkü**, aplatform from which the sultans would observe parades or, in the case of Ibrahim the Mad, take pot shots with a crossbow at passing pedestrians.

Museum of the History of Science & Technology in Islam

Islam Bilim ve Teknoloji Tarihi Müzesi

Gülhane Park (0212 528 8065). Tram Gülhane. **Open** 9am-4.30pm Mon, Wed-Sun. **Admission** TL5. **Map** p243 O9.

The exhibits here chronicle scientific instruments – in the fields of astronomy, geography, geometry, medicine and physics, among many others – invented in the Islamic world between the sixth and 16th centuries. All exhibits are models of originals. Highlights include a 13th-century Iranian celestial globe and a 14th-century water clock from Fes.

End of the Line for the Orient Express

The rise and fall of the most elegant train journey in the world.

A byword for glamour and intrigue, the Orient Express existed in several versions on various routes over the years, the most famous being the Paris–Vienna–Budapest–Istanbul route. Its maiden departure was 4 October 1883 from Gare de l'Est, Paris. Between the Western 'city of light' and the Eastern exoticism of its ultimate destination, the train passed through a patchwork of mercurial Balkan kingdoms, always tinged with the promise of war or revolution. A couple of notorious incidents added to the legend: in 1891, bandits held up the train and took its passengers hostage; in 1929, it was stranded in a snowdrift for six days.

Such episodes could be endured in the comfort of carpeted cabins, decked out with damask drapes and silk sheets for the fold-down beds, or the saloon, which evoked the atmosphere of a London gentlemen's club with its leather armchairs and bookcases. Meals were served in the Wagon Restaurant, beneath gas-lit brass chandeliers at tables set with Baccarat crystal, starched napery and monogrammed porcelain. The kind of passengers who could afford all this tended to be minor royals, wealthy nobility, diplomats and financiers, not to mention spies, nightclub performers and high-class prostitutes – the perfect cast list for thriller-writers such as Agatha Christie and Graham Greene, both of whom famously used the Express as a setting for their novels.

The drawing of the Iron Curtain at the end of World War II signalled the beginning of the end for this train, and its final run was in 1961. Sporadic revivals have proved nothing more than sops to moneyed nostalgia buffs. In the age of EasyJet, spending three days, nine hours and 40 minutes – and the price of a second mortgage on the house – just to get from Paris to Istanbul seems a bit extravagant. But then, it always was.

A free museum (9am-12.30pm & 1-5pm Tue-Sat) in Sirkeci Station is dedicated to train travel in Turkey. Among the exhibits are tea services from the Orient Express and a medallion commemorating its final journey into Istanbul. There's only one room, but it's obviously been put together by people who care deeply about the railways.

EMINÖNÜ

After Gülhane, the tramlines descend to **Sirkeci Station** (Sirkeci Istasyonu). On its completion in 1881, this station was the eastern terminus for trains from Europe, including the Orient Express (*see left* **End of the Line for the Orient Express**). Its street-facing façade has been disfigured by modern additions, but the waterfront profile retains an element of grandeur. Despite the station's relegation to the status of suburban shuttle hub (the only international trains are to Thessaloniki, Sofia and Bucharest), the original **Orient Express restaurant** (*see p131*), beside platform one, remains largely intact. Sadly, it's too fancy for the commuters and tends to be empty.

Just past the historic snack spot Konyalı (*see below* **Inside Track**), the tram tracks swing left, terminating at Eminönü, grandly signposted by the **New Mosque**.

FREE New Mosque
Yeni Camii

Eminönü Meydanı (0212 527 8505). Tram Eminönü. **Open** 7am-dusk daily. Closed to non-worshippers during daily prayer times. **Admission** free. **Map** p243 M8.

Construction on the mosque began in 1598, but suffered a setback when the architect was executed for heresy. It was eventually completed in 1663, after the classical period of Ottoman architecture had passed. It is nonetheless a regal structure, particularly uplifting when seen floodlit. The fact that it is so obviously a working mosque tends to keep visitors at bay, but nobody objects to non-Muslims entering.

THE EGYPTIAN BAZAAR

In front of the New Mosque is a pigeon-plagued plaza busy with street sellers and dominated on its south side by the high brick arch leading into the **Egyptian Bazaar**, also known as the Spice Bazaar. The market was constructed as part of the mosque complex, and its revenues helped support philanthropic institutions. The name derives from its past association with the arrival of the annual 'Cairo caravan', a flotilla of ships bearing rice, coffee and incense from Egypt.

While the bazaar's L-shaped vaulted hall is undeniably pretty, at first glance its 90 shops seem to be hustling nothing more than an assortment of oily perfumes, cheap gold and 'Turkish Viagra' (a ubiquitous moniker used for everything from sachets of powders to dried fruit and nuts). It's a tourist magnet, to be sure, but to dismiss it out of hand is to miss one of the world's finest delis: make a beeline for **Erzincanlılar** (shop No.2) for honeycomb and the mature hard Turkish cheese known as *eski kaşar*. Other food shops worth checking out are

Rüstem Paşa Mosque. *See p60.*

Pinar (No.14) for *lokum* (Turkish delight); **Antep Pazarı** (No.50) for nuts, honey-covered mulberries and dried figs stuffed with walnuts; and **Güllüoğlu Baklavacısı** (No.88) for pastries. **Özer** (No.82) has beautiful textiles, as well as pretty, cheap pashmina scarves. Another reason to visit the market is to lunch at **Pandeli** (*see p131*), a Greek-run restaurant up a flight of steps just inside the main entrance.

Running west from the market, **Hasırcılar Caddesi** is one of the city's most vibrant and aromatic streets thanks to a clutch of delis, including **Namlı Pastırmacı** (*see p170*), spice merchants and coffee sellers, among them **Kurukahveci Mehmet Efendi** (*see p169*), where caffeine addicts queue at the serving hatch to purchase the own-brand bags of beans.

INSIDE TRACK
EXPRESS SNACK

Opposite Sirkeci Station, more than holding its own against the neighbouring McDonald's, Konyalı (Ankara Caddesi, Hoca Paşa Hamam Sokak 4, 0212 527 5220) is a Turkish institution. Commuters cram this basic takeaway joint that specialises in pastries: both savoury *börek*, stuffed with minced meat or cheese, and sweet pastries filled with crushed nuts and doused in syrup.

Further along the street, look out for the arched doorways where flights of stairs lead up to the **Rüstem Paşa Mosque**, built in 1561 for a grand vizier of Süleyman the Great.

TAHTAKALE

The view from the Rüstem Paşa's forecourt is dominated by a large dome, which belongs to the nearby **Tahtakale Hamamı Çarşısı**, a 500-year-old bathhouse that has been converted into a shopping arcade. On occasion the space is also used for contemporary arts exhibitions.

This area north of Hasırcılar Caddesi is known as Tahtakale. Its streets heave with locals out to snap up bargain clothing and household accessories. Women shop here to top up their dowries, picking up linens, bedwear, lingerie and towels. This neighbourhood is also the place to buy the traditional circumcision outfits that consist of a crown, a white satin cape and a golden staff. Local traders also do a brisk business in wood and wickerware, handmade wooden spoons and coat hangers, knives and tools. **Tahtakale Caddesi** is renowned for its 'portable stalls' manned by shifty gents peddling pirated DVDs, smuggled electronics and cigars.

Egyptian Bazaar

Mısır Çarşısı

Yeni Camii Meydanı (0212 513 6597). Tram Eminönü. **Open** 8am-7pm daily. **Map** p243 L8.

FREE Rüstem Paşa Mosque

Rüstem Paşa Camii

Hasırcılar Caddesi 90 (0212 526 7350). Tram Eminönü. **Open** 9am-dusk daily. **Admission** free. **Map** p242 L7.

Above the shops (whose rents pay for its upkeep), the mosque is invisible from the street. It's quite a city secret, although it's one of the most beautiful mosques built by Sinan. Smaller than most of his works, it's set apart by its liberal and dazzling use of coloured tiles. The first-floor forecourt, with its colonnaded canopy and potted plants high above the crowded alleys, is one of Istanbul's loveliest hideaways. *Photo p59.*

THE GOLDEN HORN

Eminönü is the departure point for ferries up the Bosphorus and across to Asia. Services from the westernmost ferry terminal Eminönü Haliç Iskelesi also head up the Golden Horn. The maritime traffic here is frantic, as hulking vessels skirmish with tiny motorboats for berthing positions. Pedestrian traffic is intense too – watch your wallet.

Mingling with the smell of diesel is the whiff of chargrilling fish. This pungent aroma comes from the small boats moored at the dockside, cooking up their catch for sale in sandwiches.

The best place to observe the hustle and bustle is from the **Galata Bridge**, the vital link between the two sides of European Istanbul. The current structure, an unsightly concrete ramp with four steel towers at its centre, replaces a much-loved earlier bridge ravaged by fire damage. This one was built in the early 1990s to accommodate growing traffic. The lower deck of restaurants, bars and teahouses right on the waterfront provides ringside seating for cheap beers and boat-watching. It's probably best not to eat along here (or if you do, keep a close eye on the bill); head instead to the fresh fish stalls at the west side of either end of the bridge.

Galata Bridge.

SIGHTS

The Western Districts

Off Istanbul's beaten track.

Fatih, Fener and Balat are religiously conservative neighbourhoods, far from the tourist trail or the bright lights of Beyoğlu. Locals here are some of the city's most welcoming – making a wander through this quarter's low-key lanes a particularly pleasant experience. The Western Districts are also home to a number of synagogues and churches as well as mosques. Spend an afternoon at the **Church of St Saviour in Chora**, home to jaw-dropping frescoes and shimmery gold mosaics. Or stretch your legs with a romp along Istanbul's centuries-old **city walls**. Further afield, the district of **Eyüp** is renowned for its stunning city skyscapes, best taken in from the popular Pierre Loti Café (*see p147*).

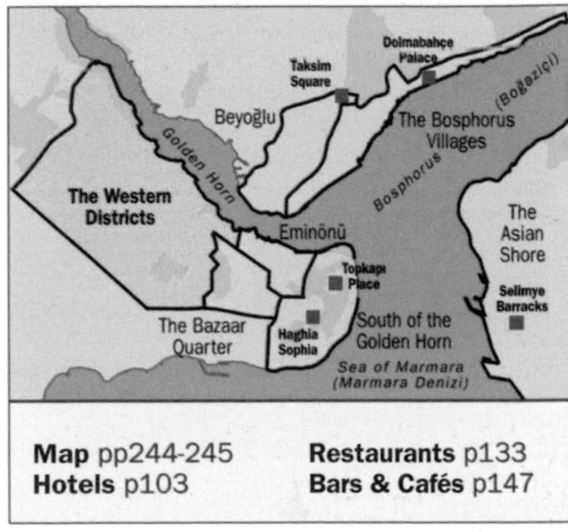

Map pp244-245 **Restaurants** p133
Hotels p103 **Bars & Cafés** p147

FATIH

Immediately west of the Bazaar Quarter, Fatih is easy to reach by tram from Sultanahmet. Hop off at the Üniversite or Laleli stop and walk north to the **Şehzade Mosque**.

Beyond the gardens of the mosque is the Aqueduct of Valens. Constructed by the Roman emperor Valens in the fourth century AD, the aqueduct channelled water from the lakes north of the city to Istanbul's cisterns up until the late 19th century. These days, the aqueduct forms a dramatic entrance to the city as the modern Atatürk Bulvarı thoroughfare passes beneath its two-tiered arches.

Huddled in the shadow of the aqueduct is the attractive little Gazanfer Ağa Medresesi, now the **Cartoon Museum**. A short walk further north is what's now known as the **Zeyrek Mosque**, but was once the Byzantine Church of the Pantocrator. Ten minutes' walk due west is one of the most significant, and underexplored, historical sites in the city: the **Fatih Mosque**. On Wednesdays, streets around the mosque are taken over by Fatih Pazarı, one of the city's largest and best-known street markets.

From the Fatih Mosque follow Darüşşafaka Caddesi north; turn right on to Yavuz Selim Caddesi past the fifth-century Cistern of Aspar (now a sports complex) to find the lovely Selim I Mosque (Yavuz Selim Camii).

FREE Cartoon Museum
Karikatür ve Mizah Müzesi

Kavacılar Sokak 12, off Atatürk Bulvarı (0212 521 1264). Tram Laleli or Üniversite. **Open** 9am-5pm Tue-Sat. **Admission** free. **Map** p242 H8.

Set in a beautiful 17th-century *medrese*, this is one of the city's more unusual museums. Where instructors once lectured students in Islamic philosophy, they now give lessons in illustration, engraving and screen-printing. The permanent collection, with pieces dating back to the 1870s, illustrates the long-standing popularity of caricature and satire in Turkey. Temporary exhibitions are devoted to Turkish and foreign cartoonists. The museum also hosts Turkey's only humour library.

► *For a quirky shop of objects designed by a cartoonist, visit Porof Zihni Sinir (see p164).*

FREE Fatih Mosque
Fatih Camii

Fevzipaşa Caddesi. Metro Emniyet. **Open** 9am-dusk daily. Closed to non-worshippers during daily prayer times. **Admission** free. **Map** p245 G7.

The grounds of Fatih Mosque are a popular place for picnickers. The vast 18th-century baroque structure is built on the site of the Church of the Holy Apostles, burial place of most Byzantine emperors,. The church was already in ruins by the time Mehmet II conquered Constantinople. He used it as a quarry for a mosque built in 1470 to celebrate his victory (*fatih* means 'conqueror'). Most of Mehmet's original structure was

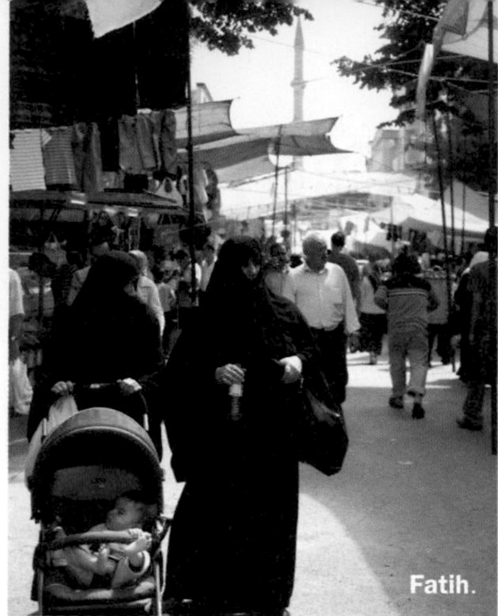
Fatih.

destroyed by an earthquake in 1766; all that remains is the courtyard and parts of the main entrance. The tomb of the Conqueror stands behind the prayer hall.

Panorama 1453 History Museum

Topkapı Culture Park, Merkez Efendi Mahallesi, Topkapı (212 415 1453, www.panoramikmuze.com). Tram Topkapı. **Open** 9am-8pm daily. **Admission** TL10.

In 1453, Sultan Mehmet II conquered the city of Constantinople, marking the end of the Byzantine Empire in the area. This museum, opened by Prime Minister Recep Tayyip Erdoğan in early 2009, depicts the siege of the city and the principal battle that led to its fall in a 2,350sq m panoramic painting that took three years to complete. The multimedia museum also uses the sounds of battle and displays objects from the time. In a neat twist, the Panorama 1453 is located by the very walls that were breached by the Janissaries.

FREE Şehzade Mosque
Şehzade Camii

Şehzadebaşı Caddesi, Saraçhane, Vefa. Tram Üniversite or Laleli. **Open** 9am-dusk daily. Closed to non-worshippers during daily prayer times. **Admission** free. **Map** p242 H8.

Completed in 1548, Sinan dismissed his first royal mosque complex as 'apprentice work'. It is named after Prince Şehzade Mehmet, son of Süleyman, who died suddenly and prematurely. He is buried in the complex. The square courtyard is as big as the interior of the mosque. The combination of the square plan and the central dome surrounded by four half domes is unprecedented in Islamic architecture.

FREE Zeyrek Mosque
Zeyrek Camii

Yeni Akıl Sokak, off Zeyrek Caddesi, Küçükmustafapaşa. Metro Laleli or Aksaray. Currently closed for renovations. **Map** p242 H7.

Built in the 12th century for the wife of Emperor John II Comnenus (1118-43), the Byzantine Church of the Pantocrator became the imperial residence during the struggles with the Latin crusaders. It was turned into a mosque after the Muslim conquest. It has retained some fine internal decoration, including exquisitely carved doorframes and marble mosaic floors – however, the mosque is under partial renovation, so it may be closed. Archaeological oddities are displayed on a terrace overlooking the Golden Horn, which belongs to the swish Zeyrekhane restaurant.

FENER & BALAT

Until the early 20th century, Fener was primarily Greek, while Balat was mainly Jewish. Although lacking major monuments, these neighbourhoods are fascinating areas in which to wander. The most picturesque approach to the two districts is on foot from the attractive Selim I Mosque, just off Yavuz Selim Caddesi.

From the mosque, head downhill past the redbrick Fener Greek School for Boys. A little below and to the left is the only Byzantine church still in Greek hands, the **Church of Panaghia Mouchliotissa**. Immediately north of the church is the stretch of Byzantine sea wall breached by the crusaders in 1204. East along Incebal Sokak is the **Greek Orthodox Patriarchate**, an unprepossessing walled compound that has been the world centre of Greek Orthodoxy for the past 400 years.

Back west along Yıldırım Street are some of the city's finest old Greek residences, including the Fener Mansions, which date from the 17th and 18th centuries.

Equally unique is the **Church of St Stephen of the Bulgars**, one of Turkey's only examples of neo-Gothic architecture.

Inland from St Stephen, the streets take on a grid pattern in what used to be Istanbul's main Jewish district. This area is home to the city's oldest synagogue, the **Ahrida Synagogue**. Around the corner is the fascinating Armenian Orthodox **Church of Surp Hreşdagabet** (Holy Archangels). Heading south-west, towards the city walls, is the **Church of St**

INSIDE TRACK
PILGRIMS PROGRESS

The Church of Surp Hreşdagabet (*see right*) is famous for one thing: every 16 September, a miracle cure is reputedly bestowed on one member of the congregation. Muslims with birth defects or incurable illnesses from all over Turkey crowd into the church, hoping to be the lucky one.

Saviour in Chora, now a museum featuring extraordinarily well-preserved Byzantine frescoes and mosaics.

FREE Ahrida Synagogue
Ahrida Sinagogu

Vodina Caddesi 9, Balat. Bus 35D. **Open** by appointment with the Chief Rabbi (0212 243 5166). **Admission** free. **Map** p245 F3.

Founded by Macedonians from the town of Ohrid (of which 'Ahrida' is a corruption) in the 15th century, the synagogue's congregation later comprised the city's Sephardic Jewish community who had fled Spain during the Inquisition. It is still used by the Sephardic community, many of whom speak the medieval Spanish dialect Ladino. The wooden dome, restored in 17th-century baroque style, is exquisite.

► *For an insight into Jewish life in Istanbul, visit the Jewish Museum (see p78).*

FREE Church of Panaghia Mouchliotissa
Kanlı Kilise

Tevkii Cafer Mektebi Sokak, Fener (0212 521 7139). Bus 55ET. **Open** 9am-4pm daily. **Admission** free. **Map** p245 G4.

Otherwise known as St Mary of the Mongols, this 13th-century church was erected in honour of Princess Maria, daughter of Emperor Michael VIII, who was married off to the Khan of the Mongols. It was reputedly spared conversion into a mosque thanks to a Greek architect employed by Mehmet II; a decree issued by the Conqueror to this effect has pride of place in the church.

Church of St Saviour in Chora
Kariye Müzesi

Kariye Camii Sokak 26, Edirnekapı (0212 631 9241). Metro Ulubatlı or bus 37E, 38E, 91O to Vefa Stadium. **Open** 9am-5pm Mon, Tue, Thur-Sun. **Admission** TL15. Museum Pass Istanbul Card accepted. **Map** p244 D4.

Often overlooked because it's so far off the beaten track, for Byzantine splendour this church (also known as the Kariye Mosque or Museum) is second only to Haghia Sophia. Built in the late 11th century, its celebrated mosaics and frescoes were added when the church was remodelled in the 14th century. Depicting all manner of Christian themes, from the Day of Judgement through to the Resurrection, the works here are arguably the most important surviving examples of Byzantine art in the world, both in terms of their execution and preservation. Ironically, this Christian art owes its excellent state of preservation to the church's conversion into a mosque in the early 16th century, when the frescoes and mosaics were covered over. They remained concealed until they were rediscovered in 1860.

► *The Kariye Hotel at the end of the street is worth visiting for its excellent Ottoman restaurant, Asitane (see p133).*

FREE Church of St Stephen of the Bulgars
Bulgar St. Stephen Kilisesi

Mürsel Paşa Caddesi 85, Fener (0212 521 1121). Bus 55ET. **Open** hours vary. **Admission** free. **Map** p245 G3.

Erected in 1871 for Istanbul's Bulgarian community, this church is still used today by Macedonian Christians. It is constructed entirely from prefabricated iron sections, cast in Vienna and shipped down the Danube to Istanbul.

FREE Church of Surp Hreşdagabet (Holy Angels)
Surp Hreşdagabet Ermeni Kilisesi

Kamış Sokak, Balat. Bus 35D. **Open** Thur am services only. **Admission** free. **Map** p245 F3.

Tentatively dated to the 13th century, this church was taken over by the Armenians in the early 17th century. Although much of the current structure dates from 1835, the side chapel and *ayazma* (sacred spring) are original Byzantine features. Today, the congregation is composed almost exclusively of headscarved Muslim women – many devout Muslims have a devotion to both Christian and Jewish rituals, taking them very seriously as 'precursors' of Islam.

FREE Greek Orthodox Patriarchate
Fener Rum Patrikhanesi

Sadrazam Ali Paşa Caddesi, Fener (0212 531 9670, www.patriarchate.org). Bus 55ET. **Open** 8am-5pm daily. **Admission** free. **Map** p245 G4.

The central section of the seat of Greek Orthodoxy is permanently closed in memory of Patriarch Gregory V, who was hanged from it in 1821 as punishment for

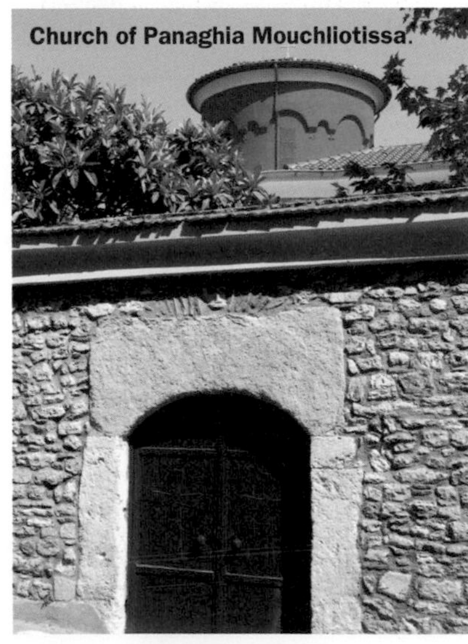
Church of Panaghia Mouchliotissa.

SIGHTS

the outbreak of the Greek War of Independence. The main Church of St George is unremarkable save for three unusual freestanding mosaic icons. During celebrations for Orthodox Easter, the church attracts hundreds of pilgrims and provides a focal point for the Greek community of Istanbul.

CITY WALLS

Constructed during the reign of Theodosius II (408-50), the walls of Constantinople are the largest Byzantine structure that survives in modern Istanbul. These walls withstood invading armies for over 1,000 years, resisting siege on more than 20 occasions until the Ottoman conquest in 1453.

The walls encompass the old city in a great arc, stretching some 6.5 kilometres (four miles) from the Golden Horn to the Sea of Marmara. Together with the sea walls that ringed Constantinople, they constituted Europe's most extensive medieval fortifications.

The Great Icon Controversy

The theological battle that gripped the Byzantine Empire.

In the eighth and ninth centuries, a Byzantine Empire faced with the onslaught of expansionist Islam was also torn apart by an internal controversy: whether or not it was permissible to paint images of Christ and the saints. Should new icons be painted – or should existing ones be destroyed? Strange though it may seem to a modern, secular mindset, this question became the focus of the empire's whole sense of identity.

From the vantage point of the secular 21st century it's easy to say that the Byzantines should have united against the outside threat rather than wasting energy on an internal clash of ideologies. From the vantage point of a Byzantine, it was a matter of crucial importance.

When Emperor Leo III removed an image of Christ from above the doors to the imperial palace in 726, it sparked riots and deaths. However, the emperor was not to be dissuaded. In 730, Leo deposed the Patriarch of Constantinople and ordered the removal or destruction of all icons in the city. All resistance was violently suppressed. So what prompted Leo to plunge his empire into a virtual civil war? The answer lies partly in the Byzantine struggle against Islam. The Byzantines saw success or failure as marks of God's favour or disfavour. Encroachment on Christendom by the aggressively iconoclastic Muslims led some to theorise that God had forsaken them because the veneration of icons was a contravention of the second commandment, forbidding the worship of idols.

The icon-lovers developed an underground resistance movement, hiding icons from the imperial troops in monasteries. They found a powerful spokesman in St John of Damascus, a Christian who was chief councillor to the Ummayad rulers of the city. Safely out of the emperor's reach (or so he thought), John wrote in defence of icons. He pointed out that iconographers were only painting what God himself had done: become flesh and blood in the person of Christ. According to the iconoclasts' logic, he argued, the first and greatest idolater was therefore God himself. Infuriated, the emperor allegedly forged a letter in which John offered to betray Damascus to the Byzantines. An unamused Caliph had John's hand cut off.

The icon controversy raged on for over a century, outlasting four religious councils that provided ecclesiastical backup, several emperors and two empresses. It was these female rulers who eventually decided the case. Empress Irene was the first to reverse the iconoclast policy of her predecessors, and in 843 the Empress Theodore proclaimed the restoration of icons. Since then, the first Sunday of Lent has been celebrated as the triumph of Orthodoxy.

Go into any Orthodox church today and the first things that strike you are the glorious icons, glittering in the candlelight: icons and the faith and art that surround them survived, and it's hard to imagine the Orthodox Church without them. Had the iconoclasts prevailed there would have been none of the later Byzantine religious imagery gloriously preserved in Istanbul – in the **Church of St Saviour in Chora** (*see p63*).

A triumph of engineering, the walls comprise inner and outer ramparts with a terrace in between. The outer wall is two metres (seven feet) thick and around 8.5 metres (30 feet) high, with 96 towers overlooking the 20-metre (70-feet) moat. The five-metre (16-foot) wide inner wall is around 12 metres (40 feet) high and is studded with another 96 towers.

Large sections of the walls have been rebuilt in recent years, drawing criticism from scholars for inappropriate use of modern materials; nevertheless, the restored sections are impressive.

WALKING THE WALLS

There are several ways to get to the walls depending on which part you'd like to visit. It's possible to walk the whole length, along both the inside and outside, although care should be taken as some sections are deserted apart from vagrants. The best place to begin is on the Marmara coast at Yedikule. Take a bus from Eminönü (80) or Taksim (80T) or, for a more scenic ride, a suburban train from Sirkeci to Yedikule. The train passes under the ramparts of Topkapı Palace and winds in and out of what remains of the southern sea walls.

On the Marmara shore, the walls begin with the imposing Marble Tower on a promontory by the sea. It has served as both an imperial summer pavilion and as a prison. You can still see the chute through which executed corpses were dumped into the sea.

On the other side of the coastal road is the near-pristine Gate of Christ, the first of 11 fortified gates. On the northern side of the railway line is **Yedikule Fortress**, whose entrance is in the north-east wall.

From Yedikule to the Belgrade Gate (Belgrad Kapısı) and onwards to the Silivri Gate (Silivri Kapısı) it is possible to walk along the top of the walls or on the terrace below. Near the Silivri Gate is the **Shrine of Zoodochus Pege** ('life-giving spring'). The Mevlevihane Gate bears several inscriptions, including one in Latin boasting how Constantine erected the final phase of the walls in 'less than two months'. Further north beyond Millet Caddesi stands Topkapı Gate, or Cannon Gate.

North of Topkapı, the walls descend into the Lycus river valley, now the six-lane Vatan Caddesi. This low-lying stretch was particularly difficult to defend, and it was here that the besieging Ottomans finally broke through in 1453. Over 500 years later, the battlements here remain in the worst state of repair. A little to the north, Mehmet the Conqueror made his triumphal entry into the city through Edirnekapı (Edirne Gate). A plaque on the south side of the gate commemorates the event.

Approaching the Golden Horn, the city walls end at the Byzantine **Blachernae Palace**.

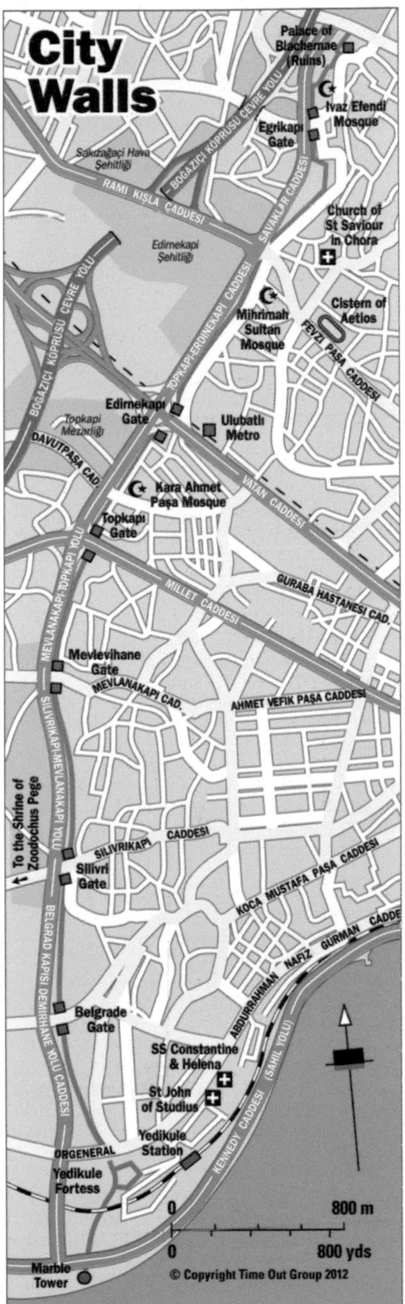

Blachernae Palace
Anemas Zindanları
Ivaz Ağa Caddesi, Ayvansaray. Bus 55ET, 99A.
Open 9am-5pm daily. **Admission** TL2. **Map** p87.
Constructed around AD 500, the palace was extended in the 11th and 12th centuries, by which time it had become the favoured imperial residence. It's now mostly in ruins. The best-preserved sections are the brick-and-marble three-storey façade, the Palace of the Porphyrogenitus, and five floors of tunnels and galleries below the Ahmet tea garden.

Istanbul Aquarium
Istanbul Akvaryum
Şenlikköy Mahallesi, Yeşilköy Halkalı Caddesi 93, Florya (0212 444 9744, www.istanbul akvaryum.com). Florya Station from Sirkeci.
Open 10am-8pm daily. **Admission** TL29.
Despite its location far west of the city walls (and west of Atatürk Airport), as well as its pricey entrance fee, visitors have been pouring into the new Istanbul Aquarium, which opened in June 2011. The aquarium has 16 internationally themed zones – regions that range from the Black Sea to the Pacific – and a dedicated rainforest area. More than 15,000 fish dart through the labyrinth of tanks.

SIGHTS

Shrine of Zoodochus Pege
Balıklı Kilise
Silivrikapı Seyit Nizam 3, Fatih (0212 582 9456). Tram Seyitnizam. **Open** 9am-4pm daily.
Admission free.
Originally an ancient sanctuary of Artemis, the first church on this site was built over the 'life-giving spring' here in the early Byzantine era. Destroyed and rebuilt many times, the present structure dates from 1833. The shrine itself is a pool containing 'sacred' fish, said to have leapt into the spring from a monk's frying pan on hearing him say that a Turkish invasion of Constantinople was as likely as fish coming back to life.

Yedikule Fortress
Yedikule Zindanları Müzesi
Kule Meydanı 4, Yedıkule (0212 585 8933). Yedikule Station from Sirkeci or bus 80, 80T.
Open 9am-5pm Mon, Tue, Thur-Sun. **Admission** TL5. **Map** p87.
Impressively restored, this Byzantine 'castle of the seven towers' was remodelled by the Ottomans. Its western face incorporates the Golden Gate (now bricked up), a triumphal arch erected around AD 390.

EYÜP

Beyond the city walls, a mile west along the shore of the Golden Horn, is the village of Eyüp (pronounced 'eh-oop'). Historian John Freely describes its traditional image as a 'peaceful backwater devoted to religion and death'. These days, the place is on the verge of being absorbed by suburbia, but for now it retains spiritual and rural qualities courtesy of two wooded hills above the village whose slopes are free of development by virtue of being devoted to the dead.

The area's popularity as a burial spot derives from the Eyüp Mosque, the holiest mosque in Istanbul. Its holy status comes from being the reputed burial place of Eyüp Ensari, companion and standard-bearer of the Prophet Muhammad. His tomb is adjacent to the mosque and has a gold-framed footprint of Muhammad and some elaborate Iznik tiling. A constant trail of pilgrims patiently queue to supplicate themselves before the cenotaph. A vast *külliye* (complex) surrounds the mosque, with most buildings dating to 1458 and the reign of Mehmet the Conqueror. Non-Muslims are welcome, but visitors should dress modestly. Headscarves are available for women.

Running north from Eyüp's main plaza is an attractive shopping street full of interesting food shops. From the top end, flag a taxi and ride up the hill to the Pierre Loti Café (*see p147*), named after the 19th-century French romantic novelist who lived in Eyüp for several years. You'll be dropped at a modern tourist development with fantastic views from its terrace, but for something with more charm (and equally good views) follow the path down the hill to a tea shop with tables beneath the trees. Alternatively, hop aboard the panoramic Piyerloti Teleferik (TL2), a two-minute cable car ride that whizzes from behind Eyüp Mosque up to the teahouse.

Also in the area, the Ottoman Empire's first electricity plant, providing electricity for the city from 1911 to 1983, has now been converted into arts and cultural centre **Santralistanbul**.

Santralistanbul
Eski Silahtarağa Elektrik Santrali, Istanbul Bilgi Üniversitesi, Kazım Karabekir Caddesi 1, Silahtar (0212 311 7809, www.santralistanbul.org). Bus 44B. **Open** 10am-6pm Tue-Fri; 10am-8pm Sat, Sun. **Admission** TL15.
The decommissioned Silahtarağa Power Plant has been converted into one of Istanbul's most exciting multidisciplinary arts centres. Old equipment has been retained and restored in two of the former engine rooms, which now form the Museum of Energy, and galleries house eclectic exhibitions. Concerts and festivals are also staged here.

GETTING THERE
Take the 99 bus from Eminönü bus station to Eyüp. It's a 15-minute ride. Alternatively, you can catch a ferry from Eminönü Haliç Iskelesi, stopping off at Kasımpaşa, Fener and Balat en route. The first ferry departs Eminönü at 7.20am, with hourly departures until 8pm. Santralistanbul (*see p66*) also runs free shuttles between Taksim Square to Silahtar from every 20 minutes to every hour.

Beyoğlu & Beyond

Cocktail bars and contemporary arts.

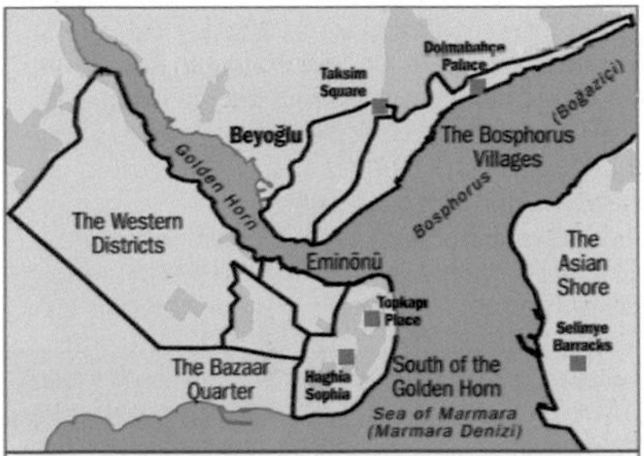

Encompassing the elegant 19th-century neighbourhoods of Pera and Galata, Beyoğlu is Istanbul's vibrant westernised section. **Istiklal Caddesi** sits at its heart, a pedestrianised thoroughfare with **Tünel Square** at one end and bustling **Taksim Square** at the other. Former embassies, sleek boutiques, rooftop cocktail bars and edgy art galleries line Istiklal's popular promenade – and it's here that hip Istanbullus flood come the weekend.

The neighbourhoods of shabby-chic **Çukurcuma** – a treasure trove of antiques and second-hand goods – and cooler-than-thou **Cihangir** lie between Istiklal Caddesi and the Bosphorus. Around the corner, the 14th-century **Galata Tower** offers sublime views over Sultanahmet. Further afield, Beyoğlu also boasts a handful of the city's quirkiest museums, from Atatürk's one-time residence to the planes, trains and automobiles showcased in the Rahmi M Koç Museum.

Maps p246-249 **Restaurants** p134
Hotels p103 **Bars** p147

INTRODUCING BEYOĞLU

Beyoğlu is an area with boundaries that are hard to define, but for the purposes of this guide, this district includes everything up the hill from the Golden Horn, all the way to Taksim Square.

Historically, the sprawling neighbourhood went by two different names: **Galata**, for the hillside just north of the Golden Horn, and **Pera**, denoting what's now the lower Istiklal Caddesi area. Occupied by foreigners since Byzantine times, these trading colonies across the water from the walls of Constantinople proper were founded by merchants from Genoa and Venice. After the Ottoman conquest in the 15th century, it was to Galata that the European powers sent their first ambassadors. By the 17th century, Galata/Pera was a substantial city in its own right, with a multi-ethnic population known collectively as Levantines. Among them were Italians and many other communities, defined thus by a Turkish chronicler of the time: 'The Greeks keep the taverns; most of the Armenians are merchants or money-changers; the Jews are the go-betweens in amorous intrigues and their youths are the worst of all the devotees of debauchery.'

OLD PERA TO NEW

It was during the 19th century that the area acquired its present character. The increased use of iron and brick, instead of the traditional wood, made it feasible to construct buildings that could survive the fires that regularly ravaged the city.

After the foundation of the republic in the 1930s, the area officially became known as Beyoğlu and blossomed with new restaurants, theatres and concert halls. Elderly residents still speak wistfully of never daring to go to Istiklal Caddesi without a collar and tie. However, World War II brought a discriminatory wealth tax that hit the Christians and Jews hard (Muslims were exempt). As a result, many left for Greece, America or Israel. In the 1950s and 1960s, political tensions caused most of the remaining Greeks to depart. In their place came a flood of poor migrants from Anatolia, and Beyoğlu gradually lost its cachet.

By the late 1980s, Istiklal Caddesi and the area around it was run-down, sleazy, even a little dangerous. That began to change in late 1990 after the simple measure was taken of turning it into a pedestrian precinct. The subsequent transformation has been swift and continues apace. Two narrow lanes behind the Galatasaray Lycée got a makeover close to a decade ago, when no fewer than 24 derelict buildings were converted into cafés, bars, galleries, restaurants and a boutique hotel, collectively marketed as the sleek new **Rue Française**. Decrepit apartment blocks have been transformed into cutting-edge galleries, including Arter (*see p186*) and SALT (*see p187*). And most recently, the Art Nouveau Deveaux Apartmani has been heavily restructured, reopening in mid 2011 as the Demirören Istiklal shopping mall. It's now home to international chains such as Virgin Megastore and Sephora.

The boom in trendy cafés, restaurants and bars has turned Beyoğlu, especially expat-heavy **Cihangir**, into the city's hottest destination for many Turks and foreign residents. **Çukurcuma**, the shabby-chic antiques district nestled between Cihangir and Istiklal Caddesi, is also rapidly heating up. Meanwhile, Galata is already a lost cause for anyone looking for a property bargain. Even Tarlabaşı, to the north-west of Taksim Square, one of the city's grimmest, poorest areas, is becoming slowly gentrified.

GETTING AROUND

To get to Beyoğlu from Sultanahmet, simply take the tram across Galata Bridge to Karaköy and take the one-stop, 19th-century Tünel, an underground funicular that clatters up the steep slope to Tünel Square at the southern end of Istiklal Caddesi. Alternatively, ride the tram to Kabataş, the end of the line. From there, another (very modern) underground funicular will speed you up the hill to Taksim Square. Running all the way between Tünel and Taksim, Istiklal Caddesi is the backbone of the whole area. All Beyoğlu destinations are reachable from here, or from Tünel or Taksim – for this reason we don't list transport for individual destinations in this chapter. An old-fashioned, and always busy, tram runs between Tünel and Taksim.

From Sultanahmet, an alternative route is to walk down the hill to Eminönü and across the Galata Bridge, then take the funicular to Tünel, all of which takes around 30-40 minutes.

GALATA

Echoing its mercantile origins, Galata remains almost completely commercial. There's even a row of ships' chandlers still trading along Yüzbası Sabahattin Evren Caddesi.

Central to the area's history, and easily the most distinctive landmark north of the Golden Horn, the conical-capped **Galata Tower** has spectacular views from its pinnacle.

Just downhill from the Galata Tower on **Camekan Sokak**, Beyoğlu Hospital is a large building with a vaguely Gothic tower. It was built in 1904 as the British Seaman's Hospital, designed by Percy Adams, better known as architect of London University's Senate House. The tower afforded clear sightlines to incoming ships, allowing them to signal news of any illness on board, an important consideration in the days before ship-to-shore radio.

Around the corner on **Galata Kulesi Sokak** stands the former British consular prison: the Ottomans allowed favoured nations to imprison their own nationals. This venue – now the Georgian restaurant Galata House – is where the British convicts were banged up.

On the same street is the former parish church of Galata's Maltese community, the **Dominican Church of St Peter and Paul**. It's a superb neoclassical affair built by the Swiss-born Fossati brothers, dating from 1841 but containing a number of much older relics.

From the 18th century onwards, it was the bankers of Galata who kept a declining Ottoman Empire afloat, albeit at ruinous rates of interest. Bankalar (formerly **Voyvoda**) **Caddesi**, at the bottom of Galata Kulesi Sokak, was the city's banking centre. Although the bulk of the financial institutions have since moved out, the street is still lined with imposing 19th-century mansions – many of them transformed into superb new venues, such as the exhibition space **SALT Galata** (*see p187*). Galata's long Jewish legacy is celebrated at the eastern end of Bankalar Caddesi at the **Jewish Museum** (*see p78*), housed in the beautifully restored Zülfaris Synagogue.

South of Bankalar, Perşembe **Pazarı Caddesi** boasts some fine 18th-century merchants' houses, while 100 metres (320 feet) west on Mahkeme Sokak stands the only remaining Genoese church, now the **Arap Mosque**. Just to the north on Yanıkkapı Sokak are more Genoese remains in the shape of the **Burned Gate** (Yanık Kapı), the only remaining gate from the old Galata city walls. It still bears a plaque with St George's cross, symbol of Genoa.

INSIDE TRACK WHIRLING DERVISH SEMA CEREMONY

The newly renovated Galata Mevlevihanesi is due to be unveiled in December 2012. If it's still under wraps during your visit, head instead to the Hodjapasha Art & Culture Center (www.hodjapasha.com), just behind Sirkeci Station. *Sema* ceremonies are performed three to five evenings per week. Tickets cost TL50 a head, and include beverages and Turkish Delight.

FREE Arap Mosque
Arap Camii

Mahkemesi Sokak 16, off Tersane Caddesi (0212 237 6205, www.arapcamii.org). **Open** 9am-dusk daily. Closed to non-worshippers during daily prayer times. **Admission** free. **Map** p246 L6.

Built between 1323 and 1337, and dedicated to St Dominic and St Paul, this former church was the largest of Constantinople's Latin places of worship. In the early 16th century, it was converted into a mosque to serve the Moorish exiles from Spain, which is possibly how it got its current name, the 'Arab mosque'. Despite extensive alterations, the design is clearly that of a typical medieval church, with apses and a belfry.

Galata Tower
Galata Kulesi

Galata Square (0212 293 8180, www.galatatower.net). **Open** 9am-8pm daily. **Admission** TL11. **No credit cards. Map** p246 M5.

Originally named the Tower of Christ, this watchtower was built in 1348 at the apex of fortified walls. After the Ottoman conquest, it was used to house prisoners of war and later became an observatory; during the 19th century, it was a lookout post to watch for the fires that frequently broke out in the city's largely wooden buildings. In the 1960s, the tower was restored and a cheesy restaurant and nightclub were added. The restaurant, which remains, has improved somewhat. However the tower's main attraction is the 360-degree viewing gallery. It's well worth paying the rather hefty entrance fee to ride the lift up and check out the commanding views of the entire sprawling metropolis.

► *For more spectacular views, to be enjoyed with a drink in hand, see p154* **Up on the Roofs**.

Botter House.

TÜNEL

Opened in 1876, the one-stop funicular that runs from Karaköy up to **Tünel Square** at the southern end of Istiklal Caddesi is, after London and New York's systems, the third-oldest passenger underground in the world.

Tünel, the area around the upper station, has long since slipped from shabby-chic to arty affluence. The proliferation of stylish businesses such as **KV Café** (*see p150*), occupying a 19th-century Italianate passage opposite the funicular, extends as far as Sofyalı Sokak, which is lined with fine bars and restaurants, such as **Sofyalı 9** (*see p140*).

Around the corner from Tünel Square, on Galip Dede Caddesi, is **Galata Mevlevihanesi**, a dervish lodge that also goes by the name of the Museum for Classical Literature.

Galata Mevlevihanesi

Galip Dede Caddesi 15 (0212 245 4141). Closed for renovations until late 2012. **Map** p248 M5.

This combination museum and Whirling Dervish centre has long been the best place in the city to take in a *sema*, or dervish ceremony. A peaceful courtyard leads through to the octagonal *tekke* (lodge), a restored version of the 1491 original, which contains various musical instruments and beautifully illuminated Korans. Also within the complex is the tomb of Galip Dede, a 17th-century Sufi poet after whom the street is named.

ISTIKLAL CADDESI

Originally known as Cadde-i Kebir (the high street), and later La Grande Rue de Pera, Istiklal Caddesi gained its present name,'Independence Street', soon after the founding of the republic. In character, it remains resolutely pre-republican, thanks to some wonderful early 20th-century architecture. The **Botter House** at No.235 is an art nouveau masterpiece by Raimondo D'Aronco, built for Jean Botter, Sultan Abdül Hamit's tailor. His daughter offered to leave the building to the city council, but the authorities refused to guarantee its preservation and since her death it has become dilapidated. Opposite, at No.172, the former Markiz Pâtisserie may have been transformed to cheap and cheerful eaterie, but its interior retains French artist JA Arnoux's *Spring* and *Autumn* tiled art nouveau wall panels.

The street's churches are more restrained, often hidden from the street – the result of a restriction forbidding non-Muslim buildings from appearing on the skyline that held sway until the 19th century. The oldest is **St Mary Draperis** at No.215, a fairly humble building from 1789 that once served as the Austro-Hungarian Embassy. This stretch of Istiklal is also lined with former embassies. Some still serve as consulates, while others have been converted to new uses.

West of the main street is the lively neighbourhood of **Asmalımescit**, home of much of the city's buzzing *meyhane* scene. The backstreets are full of laid-back cafés, bars, taverns and cheap eateries. Its western boundary is Meşrutiyet Caddesi, address of the swish **Pera Museum**, as well as the famed **Pera Palas Hotel** (*see p103*), with its Orient Express associations and celebrity-filled guest book.

★ Pera Museum
Pera Müzesi

65 Meşrutiyet Caddesi (0212 334 9900, www.peramuzesi.org.tr). **Open** 10am-7pm Tue-Sat; noon-6pm Sun. **Admission** TL10; TL5 reductions; free under-12s. **Credit** *café & gift shop only* MC, V. **Map** p248 M3.

In an 1893 building that formerly housed Istanbul's famous Bristol Hotel, this well-run museum combines permanent exhibitions, art galleries, an auditorium, shop and café. Exhibits range from the arcane – a collection of Anatolian weights and measures – to the decorative: Kütahya tiles and ceramics. There is a major collection of 17th- to 19th-century European Orientalist art. Also look out for work by Osman Hamdi, including his most famous painting, *The Tortoise Trainer*. The temporary exhibitions of big-name artists, such as Picasso, Botero and Frida Kahlo, are excellent.

▶ *For more on contemporary art in Istanbul, see pp185-187.*

SIGHTS

GALATASARAY

Hardly big enough to constitute a district, Galatasaray refers to the streets surrounding the Galatasaray Lycée (high school), founded in 1868, although the current building dates from 1907. Opposite the school, Galatasaray University's Centre of Culture and Art is home to the Galatasaray Museum, dedicated to Istanbul's top football team, which started life at the school.

The slight widening of Istiklal in front of the Lycée is known as **Galatasaray Square**. Recently, it has become the venue for political demonstrations, notably by the 'Saturday Mothers', relatives of the many political activists who have 'disappeared' in the past 20 years. Such demonstrations are illegal, and the 'mothers' are often met by armoured riot police.

Beyoğlu nightlife once revolved around the *meyhanes* (Turkish tavernas) of **Çiçek Pasajı** (Flower Passage), an arcade in what was originally the Cité de Pera building (1876). Its heavily restored façade faces the school gates. These days, it's almost exclusively frequented by tourists, and it remains a beautiful setting for an overpriced, mediocre meal (*see p137* **Tastes of Turkey Today**). The adjacent Balık Pazarı (Fish Market) is lined with shops fronted by wooden trays of piscine still life on ice. On the east side of the market passage at No.24A, hidden behind big, black doors, is the Armenian Church of the Three Altars (Üç Horan Ermeni Kilisesi) – it's rarely open, but take a look inside if you get the chance.

Istiklal Caddesi.

At the northern end of the fish market is **Nevizade Sokak**, the liveliest and loudest dining spot in Istanbul, crammed full of pavement restaurants. On the west side of the market there are two old arcades, the **Avrupa Pasajı** and **Aslıhan Pasajı**: the former is a mini-Grand Bazaar, the latter is full of second-hand book and record shops. The *pasajı* lead through to Hamalbaşı Caddesi and the **British Consulate** (1845), designed by Charles Barry, architect of the British Houses of Parliament, but completed by WS Smith in neo-Renaissance style. The building was bombed in November 2003, in an attack that killed British Consul-General Roger Short and over a dozen others.

The Çiçek Pasajı is the most famous of a host of covered arcades leading off Istiklal Caddesi. A few steps south is **Haco Pulo Pasajı**, a narrow corridor of fluffy souvenirs that empties out into a lovely courtyard tea garden ringed by one-off boutiques. A few steps north is **Atlas Pasajı**, which has more eccentric stock – anything from furry lampshades to tribal masks. (*See also p168* **Beyoğlu's Fashion Arcades**.)

The side streets sloping south of Istiklal Caddesi at this point filter down into the appealing antiques district of **Çukurcuma**, whose twisting alleys are rife with fascinating finds and junk shops. Among the dealers of carved wedding chests and period furniture are some dim, dusty cubbyholes that offer offbeat treasures such as a temporary London bus stop or cigarette tins painted with scenes of Old Stamboul. Hunt out shops such as the **Works** and **Popcorn** (for both, *see p172*).

FREE Galatasaray Museum

Galatasaray Üniversitesi Kültür ve Sanat Merkezi

Istiklal Caddesi 90 (0212 293 4986, www.galatasaray.org). **Open** 10am-7pm Tue-Sun. **Admission** free. **Map** p248 N3.

Formerly housed in the high school over the road, the Galatasaray Museum, dedicated to the Galatasaray Football Club, was moved into the attractive premises of Beyoğlu's former central post office at the end of 2009. Exhibits include photographs, memorabilia and cases crammed with medals and prizes. The museum also includes displays chronicling the history of Galatasaray Lycée, where the football team began life as the school's sports club.

▶ *Why not see a match too? For details, see p207.*

TAKSIM

If Çicek Pasajı represents old Beyoğlu, the new Beyoğlu is focused on the stretch of Istiklal Caddesi north of Galatasaray, which stretches all the way to Taksim Square. Here, arcades, churches and period architecture give way to malls, megastores and multiplexes, as well as endless bars and cafés.

At its north end, Istiklal Caddesi runs into **Taksim Square**. The name comes from the stone reservoir (*taksim*) on the west side. Built in 1732 on the orders of Mahmut I, the *taksim* was at the end of a series of canals and aqueducts that brought water down from the Belgrade Forest (*see p215*). The centrepiece is the Independence Monument, placed here in 1928 to celebrate the youthful Turkish Republic.

Despite such picturesque associations, the giant square is one of the world's less attractive plazas. Even so, the square is generally regarded as the heart of modern Istanbul and symbol of the secular republic.

The City's Narrator

Orhan Pamuk's books define the city.

Orhan Pamuk has never been shy about giving out his home address, even though the Nobel Prize-winning novelist received death threats and faced imprisonment after speaking out about two Turkish taboos: the Armenian genocide, which the government denies, and the persecution of the Kurdish minority in the south-east.

Some conservative critics argue that it was really his outspoken dissidence that won Pamuk the world's highest literary accolade. In fact, the prolific Pamuk has long been celebrated for his polished prose and Byzantine plot development, as well as his outspokenness. The Turkish authorities might have secretly been infuriated, but the public – or at least the left-leaning intelligentsia – relished this international recognition for one of the nation's best-loved writers.

Pamuk's last name (which means 'cotton' in Turkish) appears above the front door of his childhood home, Pamuk Apartmanı in Nişantaşı, which he called 'the centre of my life' in his 2004 memoir, *Istanbul: Memories and the City*. The family lost the apartment due to dwindling fortunes when Pamuk was a child – a period that inspired his first novel, the three-generation saga *Cevdet Bey and His Sons* – but Pamuk eventually bought it back. Nişantaşı had changed drastically in the interim, with corner shops giving way to designer boutiques. *The Black Book*, Pamuk's complex 1990 novel about a young lawyer searching for his missing wife, features a Nişantaşı apartment playfully called the-Heart-of-the-City, which is probably modelled on Pamuk's own.

Pamuk now has an office in cosmopolitan Cihangir, the neighbourhood where his family relocated after they lost their Nişantaşı home. Journalists often describe how the bay window in his office perfectly frames two minarets rising from the local mosque; they see a symbolism in the contrast between Pamuk's secular space and a religious world beyond. Pamuk rejects the idea: 'I hate both the concept and the reality of a Muslim world clashing with the West.'

Yet contradictions, if not clashes, are very much a part of Istanbul's identity, and identity is a major theme of Pamuk's writing. 'Istanbul's fate is my fate,' he writes in *Memories and the City*. 'I am attached to this city because it has made me who I am.' Pamuk has done for Istanbul what Joyce did for Dublin: the mysteries of human nature lurk around every corner of the city in his brilliant evocations of his birthplace.

Çukurcuma. See p70.

BEYOND BEYOĞLU

Harbiye & Şişli

North of Taksim, there are few sights to capture the visitor's interest in the residential areas of Harbiye and wider Şişli, save for a couple of museums celebrating Turkey's military conquests and republican ideals. Şişli, however, provides a window on to the past, giving a sense of how neighbourhoods such as Cihangir must have felt pre-gentrification. And Şişli could easily be the next area to become trendy, too, with shops, restaurants and hotels opening.

★ FREE Atatürk Museum

Atatürk Müzesi

Halaskargazi Caddesi 250, Şişli (0212 240 6319). Bus 46H. Metro Osmanbey. **Open** 9am-4pm Wed-Sun. **Admission** free.

In northern Şişli, a 15-minute walk north of Taksim Square, is a candy-pink Ottoman house where Mustafa Kemal lived for six months. It now contains three floors of memorabilia of the great Atatürk, from his astrakhan hat to his silk underwear. There's even a wine-stained tablecloth on which he bashed out the new Turkish alphabet over a picnic lunch in 1928. The top floor holds a large collection of propaganda paintings from the War of Independence, with the flag of the perfidious British occasionally fluttering in the background.

★ Military Museum

Askeri Müze ve Kültür Sitesi

Valikonağı Caddesi, Harbiye (0212 233 2720, www.tsk.tr). Bus 46H, 46KY, 69YM/Metro Osmanbey. **Open** 9am-5pm Wed-Sun. **Admission** TL4. **No credit cards**.

The size and wealth of this place says as much about the military's continued clout in Turkey as it does about the country's bloody history. For many years, the Military Museum was one of the few national sights to enjoy substantial funding, so the collection is nothing if not comprehensive. However, all but the most hardened military enthusiasts will suffer serious battle fatigue long before the interminable procession of rooms and corridors comes to an end. Definitely worth seeing are the gloriously colourful campaign pavilions of the Ottoman sultans, created from embroidered silk and cotton. Upstairs, in the 20th-century section, there's a decent display dealing with the 1915 Gallipoli campaign, plus some bizarre furniture constructed out of bayonets and gun parts. For sheer morbidity, nothing beats the car in which the Grand Vizier Mahmut Şevket Paşa was assassinated while travelling along Divan Yolu in 1913.

► *For more military history, visit Topkapı Palace; see p44.*

Hasköy

Heading along the banks of the Golden Horn from Beyoğlu, the coastal road is increasingly residential, populated by a hodgepodge of houses and little parks where locals hang out. School buses regularly make the journey to Hasköy to visit the Rahmi M Koç Museum. If you don't fancy taking a bus, a taxi from Eminönü or Taksim Square takes around 15 minutes. The eccentric Miniaturk (*see p177*) is only a couple of miles further down the coast.

★ Rahmi M Koç Museum

Rahmi M Koç Müzesi

Hasköy Caddesi 5 (0212 369 6600, www.rmk-museum.org.tr). Bus 47, 54HM, 54HT. **Open** *Oct-Mar* 10am-5pm Tue-Fri; 10am-6pm Sat, Sun. *Apr-Sept* 10am-5pm Tue-Fri; 10am-8pm Sat, Sun. **Admission** TL12.5. *Submarine* TL7. **No credit cards**.

Founded by the eponymous industrialist, this converted 18th-century foundry on the waterfront is a showcase for the assorted obsessions of one of the Turkey's wealthiest men. The collection includes hall after hall of antique trains, trams, boats and planes. Many exhibits have moving parts that can be manually activated by buttons or levers; there's a walk-on ship's bridge with a wheel, sonar machines and alarm bells. Try to visit on Saturday or Sunday, when all the working models are in action. Next door to the main complex, a workshop makes a quaint setting for more industrial curios including the forward section of a US air force bomber shot down in 1943 and recovered from the seabed off Turkey's coast some 50 years later. Everything is fully labelled in English.

► *The museum has two top-class eateries in the pricy Café du Levant, modelled after an old-fashioned Parisian bistro, and Halat (see p143), a fish restaurant with tables on the wharf.*

Profile Ara Güler

'The eye of Istanbul'.

Photojournalist Ara Güler, known as 'the Eye of Istanbul', used his lens to chronicle the latter half of Turkey's tumultuous 20th century. Adept at showcasing life at street level, from the grimy to the glamorous, he also carried his trusty Leica from his native Beyoğlu to the world's most colourful corners, including India, Eritrea and the South of France. Güler still resides in his Istiklal Caddesi apartment block, the basement of which houses the Ara Café (*see p151*) and a proud selection of his portraits. It's here that the 83-year-old holds court, reminiscing about a career peppered with memories of Alfred Hitchcock, Pablo Picasso and Sir Winston Churchill.

In his early 20s, Güler started on the staff at the *Yeni Istanbul* (*New Istanbul*) newspaper before transferring his photographic skills to national daily *Hürriyet*. Mastery of the art of speedy shooting – and being in the right place at the right time – became ever more apparent in his work. In 1958, the era-defining photo journal *Life* came to Turkey and employed Güler as its chief correspondent, relaying the minutiae of city life to an audience of millions. As the West's insatiable desire for the Orient continued apace, journals such as *National Geographic*, *Camera* and the *Sunday Times* came knocking. 'The Eye' captured Turkey for all of them.

Two factors place Güler in a different class to his contemporaries. Firstly, he was as quick to catalogue Istanbul's changing landscape as the figures passing through it. In Güler's philosophy, it is better to point and shoot than miss any physical element at all. A figure is always used to illustrate the wider story, be it the steely determination on a fisherman's face as he rides the stormy Bosphorus Straits or the professional grin of a prostitute as her neighbourhood tumbles down around her. Secondly, Güler never shied away from accepting that he was a master of his trade. The photographer has collected global awards including France's Légion d'Honneur and Germany's Master of Leica with tangible self-assurance. As a member of the Magnum photographic agency he had the poise to move into portraiture, shooting global greats such as Maria Callas, Salvador Dalí and Marc Chagall.

Güler's confidence has certainly brought rewards. Look at a black and white print in any Istanbul hotel lobby – or a coffee-table book chronicling Turkey's last half-century – and the vision you see will be his.

The Bosphorus Villages

The chic shoreline of Istanbul-on-sea.

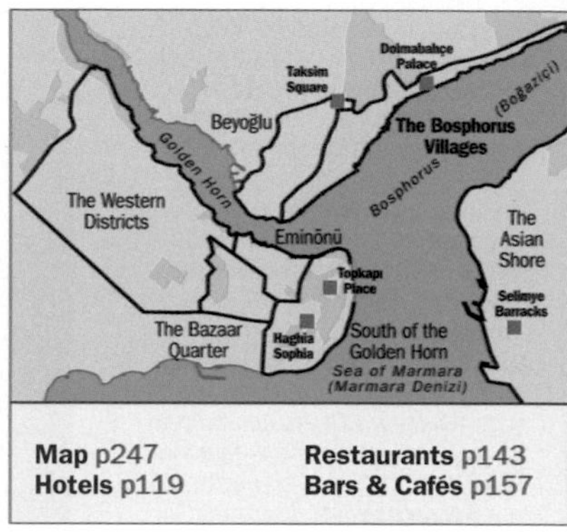

Map p247
Hotels p119
Restaurants p143
Bars & Cafés p157

Ribboning northwards from the Galata Bridge, a wide waterside road traces Istanbul's western Bosphorus banks. At the strait's southernmost tip, the district of **Karaköy** sits along the shores of the Golden Horn. Its crowded streets are home to the **Istanbul Modern**, the city's prime modern art exhibition space, which forms an anchor for Istanbul's contemporary art scene. Heading north, a warren of residential alleyways soon gives way to the utter opulence that is Beşiktaş's **Dolmabahçe Palace**. The Bosphorus villages – now more a volley of chic suburbs – become distinct from here on up, with the wooden *yalı* villas, hip bars and waterfront restaurants of **Ortaköy**, **Arnavutköy** and **Bebek** of particular allure.

In the shadow of Fatih Sultan Mehmet (the Conqueror) Bridge, the second of the bridges to link west and east Istanbul, the 15th-century **Rumeli Hisarı Fortress** was designed by the Conqueror himself. Just north of here, the stellar **Sakıp Sabancı Museum** hosts world-class international art shows.

GETTING AROUND

Several buses run the route, including 22, 22RE and 25E from Kabataş. The metro line (from Taksim) or the tram (from Eminönü) to Kabataş places you at a convenient point on the coastal road. A more relaxed way of travelling is to take one of the half-hourly ferry services from Eminönü, stopping at Beşiktaş, Ortaköy and Bebek. Unfortunately, these commuter services only run in the mornings (around 7-10am) and evenings (around 4-8pm).

KARAKÖY

Karaköy has a refreshingly diverse array of religious monuments. One street inland from the harbour, on Kemankeş Caddesi, is the district's oldest building, the Yeraltı Mosque. Not far from here is the Jewish Museum, housed in a restored synagogue, and further inland are a couple of curious churches. The Russian Orthodox Church of St Andrea on Balyoz Sokak is on the top floor of what appears to be a 19th-century apartment building, but was actually built as a monastery. The monks have long gone, but the church has experienced a revival thanks to the Russian tourists for whom Istanbul is an increasingly popular destination. Around the corner is the Church of St Panagia, belonging to the tiny Turkish Orthodox sect, which broke away from the Greek Church in the 1920s. Mass here is said in the Karamanlı Turkish dialect.

North along **Kemeraltı Caddesi**, the road passes in the shadow of the slightly sinister **Tophane Armoury**. A former Ottoman cannon foundry built during the reign of Mehmet the Conqueror, the current building, with its distinctive row of ventilation towers, only dates to 1803. Recently renovated, it's now used as an occasional arts and exhibition centre.

Opposite are two impressive mosques. **Kılıç Ali Paşa Mosque** is named after a famed admiral who was born in Calabria, captured by pirates, and then, after gaining his freedom, entered Süleyman's navy and rose to become the commander of the entire Ottoman fleet. The mosque was built in 1580 by the celebrated architect Sinan, who was by this time in his 90s. Further north is **Nusretiye Mosque**, built in the late 1820s in baroque style by Kikor Balyan, an Armenian architect whose sons would later design the nearby **Dolmabahçe Palace**. Behind the mosque is a row of cafés specialising in narghiles (*see p157* **Hubbly Bubbly**).

The main road continues past the port. Just up the hill is **Inönü Stadium**, home of Beşiktaş football club (*see p207*). Towering over the stadium is the monstrous, high-rise Ritz-Carlton hotel. High-rollers book suites overlooking the stadium when there's a big match on.

★ Istanbul Modern

Meclis-i Mebusan Caddesi, Liman Işletmeleri Sahası, Antrepo No.4 (0212 334 7300, www.istanbulmodern.org). Tram Tophane. **Open** 10am-6pm Tue, Wed, Fri-Sun; 10am-8pm Thur. **Admission** TL14; TL7 reductions. Free for all Thur. **Map** p248 O5.

Turkey's equivalent of London's Tate Modern, Istanbul Modern has grown comfortably into its role since opening in 2004. Housed in a former customs warehouse on the waterfront in Karaköy, the two-storey museum has 8,000sqm of exhibition space. The permanent collection follows the transformation of Turkish art since the foundation of the Academy of Fine Arts in 1893 and reflects Turkey's shifting economic and political landscape.

Within the chunky cube of a building, you'll immediately encounter the large, site-specific piece from the eighth Biennial – a shattered glass staircase hung from steel chains, created by Monica Bonvicini. Likewise, Richard Wentworth's installation of hundreds of books suspended over the lower level's library, for the Centre of Gravity exhibition, proved so popular that it stayed.

The Lower Floor Galleries house temporary exhibitions. These shows have introduced major international artists, including Anish Kapoor, Juan Munoz and William Kentridge, to a local audience. However, with the surge in Turkish contemporary art's popularity local artists are getting ever more attention, with exhibitions from the likes of photographers Lale Tara and Pınar Yolaç, painter Burhan Uygur and video artist Kutlug Ataman.

One of the museum's galleries is dedicated exclusively to photography; another is devoted to video art. The in-house cinema screens an interesting mix of Turkish and international art-house movies and experimental shorts.

Jewish Museum. *See p76.*

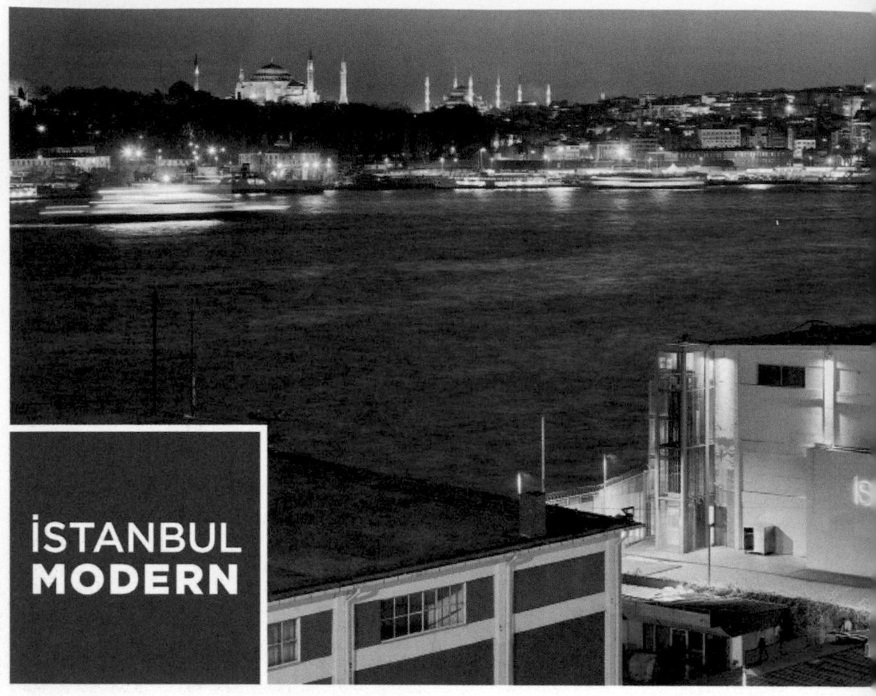

İSTANBUL MUSEUM OF MODERN ART

Set in an 8000 square meter warehouse on the shores of the Bosphorus, İstanbul Modern is Turkey's first private museum of modern and contemporary art. With its exhibition halls, photography gallery, library, cinema, restaurant and store, it constitutes a multi-faceted platform for culture and the arts. Through its collection, exhibitions and educational programs, the museum aims to instill a love of the arts in visitors from all walks of life and provide them opportunities to participate actively in art. The museum also contributes to sharing Turkey's cultural identity with the global art world.

İstanbul Modern offers a broad range of programs that aim to generate greater public interest in museums and contemporary art in particular and create a vibrant connection between the viewer and living art. In parallel with exhibitions, the museum organizes talks, workshops and other special events that explore the ideas and techniques of works displayed and reflect on the role of interdisciplinary thought in art today.

İstanbul Modern's educational programs, cinema program and design products in its store change with each new exhibition.

Exemplary works from İstanbul Modern's permanent collection are exhibited on the museum's main floor. "New Works, New Horizons" as the current selection is called, presents the evolution of modern and contemporary Turkish art from its earliest stage to the present day and features the most prominent artists and works in Turkey as well as exemplary work by contemporary artists from different geographies. Exhibition texts discussing the social, cultural, economic, and political dynamics of the periods in question remind the viewer that art is art is embedded in life and develops in tandem with its context.

The exhibition hall on the museum's lower floor hosts three exhibitions per year, including retrospectives, conceptual and thematic exhibitions, and international exhibitions focused on transformative works or artists in the evolution of modern and contemporary art

PHOTO: MURAT GERMEN

Similarly, photography exhibitions in the museum's Photography Gallery introduce the viewer to the photographic art movements around the world through the works of prominent modern and contemporary photographers, as well as to major works of Turkish photography from its beginnings to the present.

İstanbul Modern Cinema offers an alternative cinema program featuring examples of world cinema, both past and present, new ideas in Turkish cinema, and the latest in film art and unusual films and documentaries.

Through a wide range of educational activities addressing children, young people, adults and families, İstanbul Modern strives to make modern and contemporary art accessible and enjoyable to people of all ages and walks of life. Aside from providing spaces for education and learning, İstanbul Modern is a meeting point for everyone interested in contemporary culture and a communication platform for artists and other members of the art world.

Designs inspired by the museum's collection, items for children, and designer jewelry are prominent in İstanbul Modern Store's original range of products, which combine art and design. These products can serve either as souvenirs of the exhibitions or as unusual gifts. İstanbul Modern Restaurant, with its view of historical İstanbul and the Bosphorus and its varied and tasty menu, welcomes everyone on its spacious terrace or in its stylish interior.

İSTANBUL MUSEUM OF MODERN ART
www.istanbulmodern.org
info@istanbulmodern.org
*twitter.com/istanbulmodern_*
facebook.com/istanbulmodernsanatmuzesi

Meclis-i Mebusan Caddesi
Liman İşletmeleri Sahası
Antrepo 4 Karaköy 34433
İstanbul, Turkey
T +90 212 334 73 00
F +90 212 243 43 19

FOUNDER

EDUCATION SPONSOR

The museum's restaurant is a destination in its own right. Stunning views across the Bosphorus to the minarets of Sultanahmet and out to the Marmara Sea just about justify bumped-up prices for bistro fare.

► *For more contemporary art galleries, see p185-187.*

★ Jewish Museum

Türk Musevileri Müzesi

Karaköy Meydanı, Perçemli Sokak (0212 292 6333, www.muze500.com). Tram Karaköy. **Open** 10am-4pm Mon-Thur; 10am-2pm Fri, Sun. **Admission** TL10. **No credit cards. Map** p246 M6.

Housed in the immaculately restored Zülfaris Synagogue (in existence since 1671, but dating in its present form to the early 19th century), a collection of well-presented objects, documents, photographs and storyboards (in English) tells the history of over 500 years of Jewish presence in Turkey. The Jews first arrived in the Ottoman Empire fleeing the pogroms of Christian Europe. They have made significant contributions to Istanbul life, particularly in the financial sector. An ethnography section presents costumes and accessories related to circumcision ceremonies, dowries and weddings.

FREE Yeraltı Mosque

Yeraltı Camii

Erişteci Sokak, Kemankeş Caddesi. Tram Karaköy. **Open** varies. Closed to non-worshippers during daily prayer times. **Admission** free. **Map** p246 N6.

Often called the Underground Mosque because it's buried beneath a 19th-century wooden mansion, the low, vaulted interior of the Yeraltı Mosque is supported by 54 columns, built on the remains of the Byzantine castle of Galata, which guarded the entrance to the Golden Horn. From here, a great chain was stretched across the waterway, blocking access to enemy ships in times of siege. The upper part of the castle was demolished following the Ottoman conquest, and the remaining lower floor – formerly a prison – was converted to a mosque in 1757.

BEŞIKTAŞ

A celebration of the absolute decadence of 19th-century European design, the excessively opulent **Dolmabahçe Palace** is on most tour group itineraries. A rotating selection of its dubious treasures is now on display in the **Palace Collections Museum** next door. Passing the palace, the road is flanked by colonnades of plane trees leading to **Beşiktaş**, an unsightly concrete shopping and transport hub with a statue of Atatürk for a centrepiece. It wasn't always this way: this used to be a quiet suburb of dignified terraced houses and plush mansions. The last remaining terrace is on **Spor Caddesi**, built to house the staff of Dolmabahçe Palace.

Despite having no real harbour, Beşiktaş has strong nautical connections, revealed

Dolmabahçe Palace.

in the **Naval Museum** beside the ferry terminal. Nearby is the tomb and statue of Hayrettin Paşa, the Ottoman admiral known as Barbarossa. His tomb is only open to visitors on 4 April and 1 July. Nearby, the **Mimar Sinan University Museum of Fine Arts** houses Turkish 19th- and 20th-century painting.

Palace Collections Museum

Saray Koleksiyonları Müzesi

Dolmabahçe Caddesi, Dolmabahçe Palace (0212 236 9000, www.millisaraylar.gov.tr). Bus 25E, 28, 40. **Open** *Apr-Oct* 9am-5pm Tue, Wed, Fri-Sun. *Nov-Mar* 9am-4.30pm Tue, Wed, Fri-Sun. **Admission** TL5 (can vary according to exhibition). **No credit cards. Map** p247 R2.

In the premises of the former Depot Museum, the petite Palace Collections Museum is on the site of the Dolmabahçe kitchens: within the exhibition space, glass floor panels have been arranged to reveal pink and purple neon-lit 19th-century cooking stations. The museum houses a rotating collection of pieces salvaged from the palace's storage rooms – everything from crystal tumblers to copper cauldrons – which alternate with temporary shows. There's also a tiny teahouse in a corner of the museum.

Dolmabahçe Sarayı

Dolmabahçe Sarayı

Dolmabahçe Caddesi (0212 236 9000, www.millisaraylar.gov.tr). **Open** *May-Oct* 9am-4pm Tue, Wed, Fri-Sun. *Nov-Apr* 8.30am-4pm Tue, Wed, Fri-Sun. **Admission** TL30. *Harem* TL20. *Joint ticket* TL40. **Map** p247 R2.

Irrefutable evidence of an empire on its last legs, Dolmabahçe Palace was built for Abdül Mecit by Karabet Balyan and his son Nikoğos. It was completed in 1855, whereupon the sultan and his household moved in, abandoning Topkapı Palace, which had been the imperial residence for four centuries. The outside is overwrought enough – though the façade of white marble is striking when viewed from the water – but it's trumped by the interior, the work of French decorator Sechan, who worked on the Paris Opera. 'Highlights' are the 36m-high (118ft) throne room with its four-tonne crystal chandelier (a gift from Queen Victoria), the alabaster baths and a 'crystal staircase' that wouldn't look out of place in Las Vegas. Atatürk died in Dolmabahçe in 1938, and visitors are treated to a peek at his bedroom. All parts of the palace, which is still used for state functions, are visited by guided tour only. Note that a maximum of 3,000 visitors can tour the palace each day, after which the ticket office will close.

▶ *If you fancy staying in similar opulence, try the Kempinski Çırağan Palace (see p119), a similarly extravagant palace just north along the Bosphorus shore.*

> **INSIDE TRACK**
> **SPORTING COLOURS**
>
> The original colours for Beşiktaş football team were red and white. They were changed to the now-famous black and white in 1913 following the loss of Turkish land on the Balkan peninsula during the Balkan Wars. Beşiktaş, at the time, occasionally stood in for the national team, hence the Turkish flag on the emblem.

FREE Mimar Sinan University Museum of Fine Arts

Mimar Sinan Üniversitesi Istanbul Resim ve Heykel Müzesi

Barbaros Hayrettin Paşa Iskelesi Sokak, off Dolmabahçe Caddesi (0212 261 4298). Bus 25E, 28, 40. Closed for renovations. **Admission** free.

The collection of Turkish art on display in the Museum of Fine Arts' high-ceilinged halls includes some wonderful pieces, all dating from the mid 19th- to mid 20th century, and mostly Orientalist in style. Look out for several notable works by Osman Hamdi Bey, a one-time director of the Archaeology Museum. The hard-to-find museum (it's south of the Naval Museum) is currently undergoing lengthy renovations.

★ Naval Museum

Deniz Müzesi

Barbaros Hayrettin Paşa Iskelesi Sokak, off Beşiktaş Caddesi (0212 327 4345, www.denizmuzeleri.tsk.tr). Bus 25E, 28, 40. **Open** 9am-5pm Wed-Fri; 10am-6pm Sat, Sun. **Admission** TL4. **No credit cards.**

Perched on the shores of the Bosphorus, the city's naval museum is flanked by a garden full of cannons. The museum holds an extensive collection of model ships, mastheads and oil paintings, along with plenty of booty captured from British and French warships sunk during the abortive Dardanelles campaign of World War I. Upstairs are commemorative plaques to Turkish sailors killed on duty from 1319 to the Cyprus war of 1974, as well as the battle flag of Barbarossa, the notorious 16th-century pirate. Downstairs is just about everything that wasn't nailed down on Atatürk's yacht, the *Savarona*, including a set of silver toothpicks. Another area houses an impressive collection of Ottoman caiques. At one time, these elegant vessels were as symbolic of the city as the gondola is to Venice. Back then, boats rivalled the horse and carriage as the common mode of transport. The sultans' caiques were rowed by Bostancı, an imperial naval unit that doubled as palace gardeners. The largest caique on display, a 1648 model, required some 144

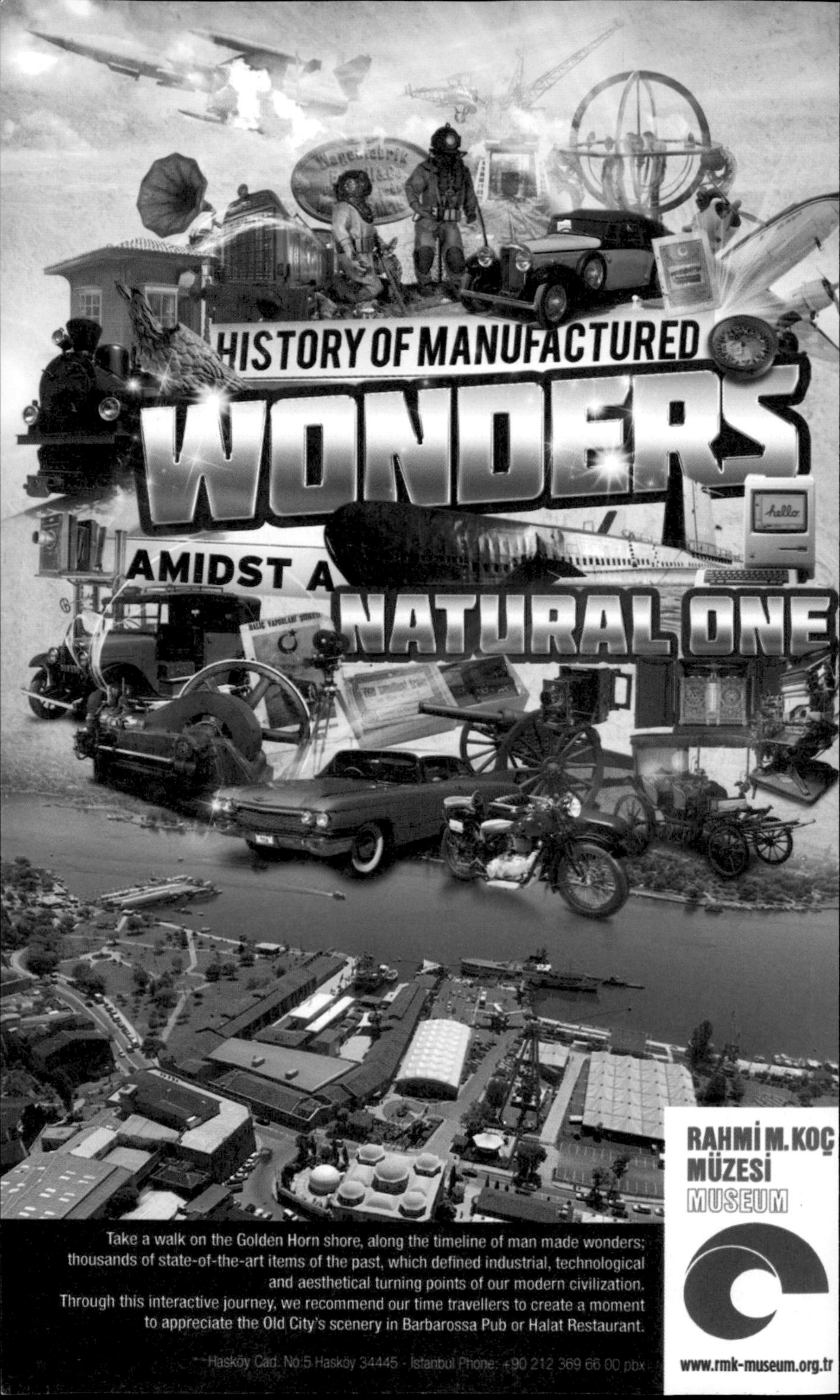

> **INSIDE TRACK**
> **STOP THE CLOCKS**
>
> When Atatürk died on 10 November 1938, all the clocks in Dolmabahçe Palace were stopped at 9.05am, the hour of his death. Most of the clocks have been changed now, but the one in his former bedroom remains at 9.05am.

Bostancı to power it along. The oarsmen were apparently required to bark like dogs as they rowed, so that they wouldn't overhear the sultan's conversations. An enterprising Black Sea firm has made modern replicas that convey tourists to the city's smarter hotels, although, regrettably, the banks of oarsmen have now been replaced by an outboard motor.

▶ *For more on military history, visit the Military Museum in Harbiye; see p72.*

YILDIZ

To the north-west of Beşiktaş are the extensive grounds of **Yıldız Palace**, a sprawling complex of buildings of which only a small part is open to the public. On Yıldız Caddesi is one of the most striking monuments in the city, the **Şeyh Zafir Complex**. Comprising a tomb, library and fountain, it commemorates an Islamic sheikh but is designed in art nouveau style by Italian architect Raimondo D'Aronco.

A little further along, a side road leads off Yıldız Caddesi into **Yıldız Park**, formerly the grounds of **Yıldız Palace** and now a pleasantly overgrown hillside forest. Sadly, the small teahouse built for Abdül Hamit, of which he was the sole patron, is long gone, but there are several former imperial pavilions, including the Şale Pavilion, a D'Aronco-designed building set in private gardens at the top of the park, now open to the public as the **Yıldız Chalet Museum**. While wandering through the park, you might want to stop at the **Imperial Porcelain Factory** and the **Malta Köşkü,** an 1870 pavilion in which Sultan Abdül Hamit had his brother Murad imprisoned. It now makes an attractive café-restaurant, with a terrace overlooking the Bosphorus.

Across from the park entrance, between Yıldız Caddesi and the Bosphorus, is what's left of the **Çırağan Palace**. Last of the Ottoman imperial palaces, it was built for Abdül Aziz who died there (probably murdered) in 1876, two years after it was completed. In 1908, it was restored to house the Ottoman parliament; but it burnt down in 1910 and remained a shell until it was rebuilt as a hotel by the Kempinski chain (*see p119*).

Yıldız Imperial Porcelain Factory

Yıldız Porselen Fabrikası

Yıldız Parkı (0212 260 2370, www.millisaraylar.gov.tr). Bus 25E, 28, 40. **Open** 9am-6pm Mon-Fri. **Admission** TL5. **No credit cards**.

Sultan Abdulhamid II established the Yıldız Porcelain Factory in 1890 at the suggestion of the French ambassador Paul Cambon, to provide a ready supply of fancy china for the Ottoman palace. Today, it mass-produces rather cheesy souvenirs in another splendid building designed by the prolific Italian architect Raimondo D'Aronco.

Yıldız Chalet Museum

Yıldız Şale Müzesi

Palanga Caddesi 23, Yıldız Parkı (0212 259 8977, www.millisaraylar.gov.tr). Bus 25E, 28, 40. **Open** 9.30am-5pm Tue, Wed, Fri-Sun. **Admission** TL10. **No credit cards**.

The obligatory tour takes you down long, dark, musty corridors leading to 60 rooms furnished with ornate furniture. The Grand Salon, a massive court chamber, now stands empty but for a line of chairs that highlight the sense of lost grandeur.

Yıldız Palace

Yıldız Sarayı

Barbaros Bulvarı, Yıldız Caddesi (0212 258 3080). Bus 25E, 28, 40. **Open** 9.30am-4pm Tue, Wed, Fri-Sun. **Admission** TL4. **No credit cards**.

Most of the palace dates from the late 19th century, when the paranoid Sultan Abdül Hamit II ('Abdül

Yıldız Palace.

SIGHTS

the Damned') abandoned waterfront Dolmabahçe for fear of attack by foreign warships. The sultan was so fearful for his safety that no architect was allowed to see the complete plans for the new palace, and the labourers who built it were forbidden to communicate. Only the sultan knew the location of all the secret passages. He never slept in the same suite two nights running and placed large objects in the palatial passageways to obstruct any would-be assassins. The rooms open to visitors contain porcelain, furniture and some of Abdül Hamit's personal possessions, including the carpentry set he used to while away his time after he was deposed in 1908.

ORTAKÖY

Long a thriving social and commercial centre, the coastal area of Ortaköy is a refuge from the crush of the inner city. In the 17th century, Ottoman chronicler Evliya Çelebi noted with a hint of disdain, 'The place is full of infidels and Jews; there are 200 shops, of which a great number are taverns.'

Today, this appealing neighbourhood's narrow, cobbled streets are closed to traffic, its low-rise houses painted in pastel shades. There's a pretty waterfront plaza overlooked by the **Mecidiye Mosque**. Set dramatically on a promontory jutting into the strait, the mosque was built for Sultan Abdül Mecit in 1854 by Nikoğos Balyan, the architect responsible for the Dolmabahçe. Happily, the mosque avoids the ostentation of the palace; instead, it is one of the most attractive baroque buildings in Istanbul.

Beside the ferry landing, waterfront **Ortaköy Square** (Iskele Meydanı) is fringed by open-air cafés and restaurants. The tight nexus of streets inland from the square has been gentrified and filled with gift shops. At weekends, it's the venue for a popular **craft market**.

Nearby are the twin domes of a 16th-century hamam, yet another work by Sinan. Recently restored, it now houses a restaurant.

North of Ortaköy, the road passes under the kilometre-long **Bosphorus Bridge**, finished just in time for the Turkish Republic's 50th birthday celebrations in 1973. Beyond the bridge is a string of exclusive nightspots, where Istanbul's socialites and celebrities strut their stuff (*see p203* **Bosphorus Bling**).

ARNAVUTKÖY

Arnavutköy, the 'Albanian Village', is far more low-key than Ortaköy, and has yet to be spoiled by an influx of venture capital. In Ottoman times, the local population was not Albanian, as the name would imply, but predominantly Greek and Armenian. It's overwhelmingly Turkish today, but a small community of Greeks still lives around here, celebrating mass at the Orthodox **Church of Taxiarchs** in the backstreets. Next to the church is a small chapel containing a sacred spring, or *ayazma*, which is down some marble stairs.

Arnavutköy's picturesque wooden *yalıs* overlook the shore, although the traffic sweeping past detracts from the effect. Many local businesses occupy these 19th-century houses with lace-like trim, pulpit balconies and elaborate ornamentation. As more of them are renovated, Arnavutköy is rapidly taking on a fairytale appearance.

Ortaköy.

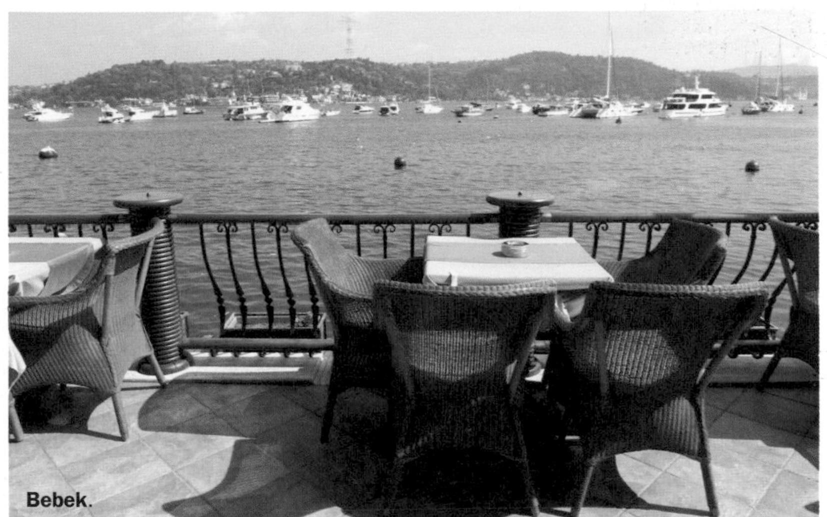
Bebek.

BEBEK

Just north of Arnavutköy, a small white lighthouse marks **Akıntı Burnu**, a promontory jutting out into the straits, named after the strong current that swirls and eddies past the shore. It's a favourite spot for local fishermen who cast out from the shore, but also trawl from rickety wooden boats, battling against a flow so brisk that in days gone by sailing ships often had to be towed around the point by porters.

From Akıntı Burnu it's a ten-minute stroll along a broad, seaside promenade to the next 'village', Bebek. Ranged around a bay backed by wooded hills, this attractive, affluent suburb has some pricey cafés and restaurants.

Beside the small waterfront park is a handsome, white art nouveau mansion. Still in service as the (newly refurbished) **Egyptian Consulate**, it was also designed by prolific architect D'Aronco.

At the top end of the park is Bebek's tiny ferry station and an equally diminutive brown stone mosque dating from 1912. Next door, **Bebek Café** is as basic as they come, but it's a pleasant, unaffected place for a coffee. Round the corner, the high street is a bit of a letdown, lined with modern buildings, including a prominent Starbucks, and choked by traffic. Bill Gates was spotted eating breakfast in these parts. Among the shops selling silk ties and antiques is **Meşhur Bebek Badem Ezmesi**, specialising in exquisite marzipan, which is beautifully displayed in hardwood cabinets.

Follow any of the streets leading uphill off the high street and almost immediately you're surrounded by greenery and wooden terraces. Head north instead and the seafront promenade winds towards the fortress of **Rumeli Hisarı**, a ten- to 15-minute walk. Before the castle, a sign points up a steep road beside the **Kayalar Mezarlığı**, one of Istanbul's oldest Muslim cemeteries, to the **Aşıyan Museum**.

FREE Aşiyan Museum
Aşiyan Müzesi

Aşiyan Yoku u (0212 263 6986). Bus 25E, 40. **Open** 9am-4pm Tue-Sat. **Admission** free.
This attractive wooden mansion was the retreat of celebrated poet Tevfik Fikret (1867-1915), who built it himself. Although the literary exhibits don't amount to much, the views from the upper-storey balconies are wonderful.

RUMELI HISARI

Rounding the headland north of Bebek brings you face to face with the imposing fortress of **Rumeli Hisarı** and, below it, the suburb of the same name. The sleepy village is an unlikely setting for the **Fatih Mehmet Bridge**, which at 1,096 metres (3,634 feet) is one of the longest suspension bridges in the world. Completed in 1988, it spans the straits at the same point where King Darius of Persia crossed with his army via a pontoon bridge in 512 BC.

Two bus stops north of Rumeli Hisarı is **Emirgan**, famous for its tulip gardens (best

Rumeli Hisarı. See p85.

visited in late April or early May), and home to the **Sakıp Sabancı Museum** and the excellent Müzedechanga (see p143) restaurant and café. The museum is about 100 metres beyond the pencil-sharp minaret of the **Hamidiye Mosque**.

★ Rumeli Hisarı Fortress

Rumeli Hisarı Müzesi

Yahya Kemal Caddesi 42, Rumeli Hisarı (0212 263 5305). Bus 25E, 40. **Open** 9am-4.30pm Mon, Tue, Thur-Sun. **Admission** TL3. **No credit cards.**

Consisting of three huge towers joined by crenulated defensive walls, the fortress was raised in a hurry as part of Mehmet II's master plan to capture Constantinople. Facing the 14th-century castle of Anadolu Hisarı (already in Ottoman hands) across the Bosphorus's narrowest stretch, Rumeli Hisarı was designed to cut maritime supply lines and isolate Constantinople from its allies. For this, it earned itself the evocative nickname Boğazkesen, the 'Throat-Cutter'. Designed by the sultan himself, work was completed in August 1452, just four months after it commenced. Garrisoned by Janissaries and bristling with cannon, Rumeli Hisarı proved its effectiveness immediately: a Venetian merchant vessel that attempted to run the blockade was promptly sunk.

Having helped secure the Ottoman conquest of Constantinople, the castle lost its military importance and was downgraded to a prison. The castle was restored by the government in 1953. Today, visitors are free to clamber around the walls, enacting childhood fantasies. An open-air theatre in the courtyard hosts popular musical events throughout the summer.

★ Sakıp Sabancı Museum

Sakıp Sabancı Caddesi 42, Emirgan (0212 277 2200, http://muze.sabanciuniv.edu). Bus 22, 25E. **Open** 10am-6pm Tue, Thur-Sun; 10am-8pm Wed. **Admission** TL10; TL3 reductions.

Owned by one of Turkey's wealthiest families, this museum is housed in a fabulous villa right on the shores of the Bosphorus, built for Egyptian royalty in the 1920s. The steeply sloping lawns are scattered with stone treasures dating from Roman, Byzantine and Ottoman eras. Inside are two floors of exceptionally fine ceramics, with informative English texts. It's particularly strong for Ottoman calligraphy, furnishings and decorative art. A modern extension in glass, steel and marble holds a collection of 19th- and 20th-century Turkish art in sumptuously elegant surroundings: the paintings are back-dropped by panoramic Bosphorus views. The museum also hosts major touring exhibitions by the likes of Picasso, Dali and Rodin.

► *There's an excellent café and restaurant, Müzedechanga (see p143), in the building, with fabulous views over the Bosphorus.*

Istanbul on Foot Karaköy to Dolmabahçe

Churches, mosques and an Ottoman palace.

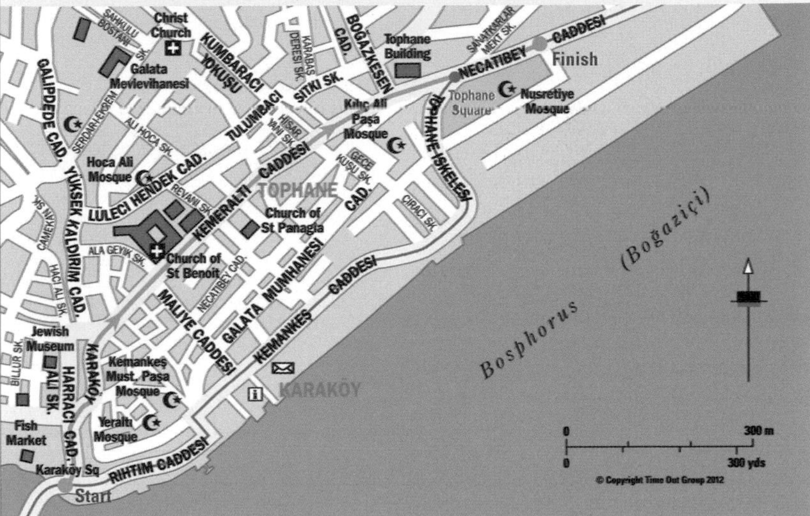

To explore this part of the city, begin at Karaköy Square. Head up busy Haracı Caddesi, then on to Karaköy Caddesi before taking a detour right on to Necatibey Caddesi, and right again to Tulumba Sokak. At the bottom of the street, at the corner of Kemankeş Caddesi, one road back from the shore, is the underground **Yeraltı Mosque** (*see p78*). Buried beneath a 19th-century wooden mansion, the mosque has been described by eminent Istanbul historian John Freeley as a 'strange and sinister place'.

From the ragged shore lined with fish restaurants, private and municipal ferries run back and forth across the Bosphorus from **Karaköy Iskele**. It was around this spot that Byzantine emperors stretched a chain across the Golden Horn to keep enemy ships from accessing the city's waterways.

Bustling Karaköy Caddesi is a warren of kiosks selling all manner of electronics. These shops slip away as the street ascends uphill to Galata. The road forks to the right, becoming Kemeraltı Caddesi, home to several churches. **St Benoit** is on the left, and **St Gregory** is further down on the right.

On the left, past Boğazkesen Caddesi, as it intersects with Necatibey Caddesi, lies the last incarnation of a series of Ottoman munitions foundries that occupied the **Tophane** site. This boxy number, built by Selim III in 1803, with eight domes and scrub growing on the roof, now hosts wedding receptions and art exhibitions.

On the right is the baroque **Nusretiye Mosque**. The Balyans, a family of Armenian architects active in Istanbul during the 18th and 19th centuries, built both the mosque and Dolmabahçe Palace up the road. Past the mosque, cafés set back in the park appeal to those in need of a narghile fix. Slump into a beanbag for a smoke, or keep walking.

You are now in a convenient spot to take the tram from Tophane a couple of stops to Kabataş. From here, it's not far along the coastal road to the neo-baroque fantasy that is **Dolmabahçe Palace** (*see p79*), which stretches the length of nearly three football pitches along the water's edge. In 1453, Mehmet the Conqueror chose this spot – then a small inlet – to haul 70 ships up into Beyoğlu using mules, and down to the Golden Horn, thus avoiding the chain slung across the straits by the Byzantines.

The Asian Shore

On the other side

Opposite Sultanahmet's palaces and Beyoğlu's bars, Istanbul's Asian shore offers another angle from across the Bosphorus. Although its quiet enclaves are certainly less visited, this equally historic section of the city is no less enchanting than its European counterparts.

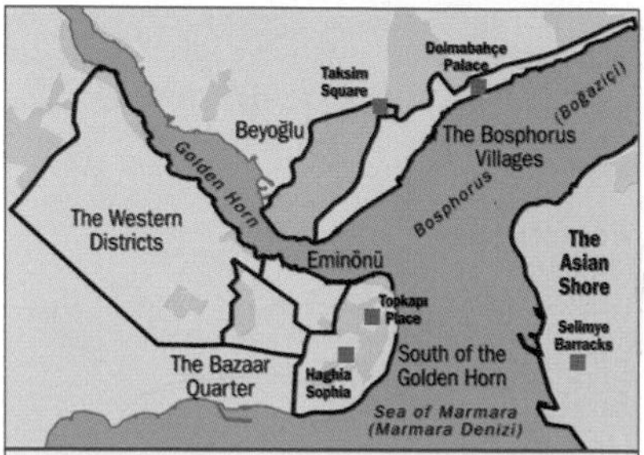

The imposing Haydarpaşa Train Station, gateway to Tehran and all points east, crowns the market-strewn neighbourhood of Kadıköy, while to its south, ritzy Bağdat Caddesi is a shopper's paradise. Affluent Üsküdar is quietly residential, with extravagant wooden *yalı* (villas) dotting its shoreline. To the north, low-key, tasty, terraced fish restaurants pepper the charming waterside villages. And bobbing offshore in the Bosphorus, the Maiden's Tower – made famous by a James Bond movie – makes an idyllic spot to stop and take it all in.

Map pp250-251 **Restaurants** p144
Hotels p125 **Bars & Cafés** p158

INTRODUCING THE ASIAN SHORE

While most sights of interest date from the past 100-odd years, there's a long history of human habitation here. The oldest settlement in the Istanbul metropolitan area, Chalcedon, was discovered near Kadıköy and dates from neolithic times. The first Greek city was also founded at Kadıköy in 675 BC – 17 years before the founding of Byzantium.

Separated by water from their more powerful European neighbour, the Asian settlements suffered over subsequent millennia; the ruthless antics of various invading armies explain the lack of substantial early remains. Before the 19th century, only Üsküdar saw any significant development. That changed in 1852 when a steam ferry company, Şirket-i Hayriye (literally 'the good deeds company'), started plying its trade across the straits. Rich Levantines from Beyoğlu began building elaborate mansions along the shore to the south and east of Kadıköy.

Under the republic, most of the mansions were demolished and replaced by apartment blocks. These homes retained their garden settings, which gives the Asian shore a greener, more suburban feel than the European side.

For information about settlements further along the Bosphorus, *see p212-218.*

GETTING THERE

Although two great suspension bridges now span the straits, the best way to get to the Asian shore is by boat. Between 6am and 9pm, ferries depart every 15 minutes from Eminönü (just west of Sirkeci Station), Kabataş, Karaköy and Beşiktaş for both Üsküdar and Kadıköy. The pleasant crossing takes around 20 minutes.

KADIKÖY

No trace remains of the Greek or Byzantine settlements of Chalcedon, but modern Kadıköy does retain many hints of its 19th-century incarnation as an area largely settled by Greeks and Armenians. To visitors arriving by ferry, this isn't immediately apparent as the two most visible buildings, Kadıköy Municipality and the local theatre, are in an unlovely modernist style.

Bear right for the main Söğütlüçeşme Caddesi and cut into the alleys beside the **Mustafa Iskele Mosque**. This area is the old bazaar, a neighbourhood of narrow streets lined with tiny two- and three-storey buildings, many dating from the 19th century. Some of the best food shopping in Istanbul is on offer here. At the top end of **Yasa Caddesi** are delis stocking a huge range of regional Turkish produce. A few steps south of here, **Mühürdar Caddesi** is almost completely given over to booksellers. Narrow, sloping **Dumlupınar Sokak** has more bookshops, including, at No.17, **Greenhouse Books**, opened by Charlotte McPherson, an American who offers tea and coffee as well as a large English-language stock.

Güneşlibahçe Sokak has more great food shops, including one devoted to honey, another to olive oil, and some fantastic fishmongers. On this street is one of Istanbul's best restaurants, Çiya (*see p144*). One block east, **Dellalzade Sokak** is lined with antiques shops. The area also has a lively café and bar scene centred on **Kadife Sokak**.

Beyond the cinema, Kadıköy gives way to the posher suburb of **Moda**. A few minutes' walk south is the popular waterfront promenade, with a tiny ferry terminal designed in late-Ottoman revival style by Vedat Tek.

Fenerbahçe

East of Kadıköy is **Rüştü Saraçoğlu Stadium**, home of Fenerbahçe football club. Fener is traditionally one of Turkey's top three teams, with a massive fan base across the city. Such is the fanaticism of local supporters that their neighbourhood is often referred to as the 'Republic of Fenerbahçe'. Despite a match-fixing scandal that tarnished the beloved club's reputation in 2011, its supporters remain as loyal as ever.

Behind the stadium is **Bağdat Caddesi**, one of the city's best-known streets. For much of its length it's an unremarkable swathe of asphalt, but passing through the plush suburb of **Suadiye** it is lined with upmarket clothing and design stores, beauty clinics, pavement cafés and restaurants. It's the cruising strip of choice for nouveau-riche Istanbul.

HAYDARPAŞA

Across the bay from Kadıköy stands the imposing edifice of **Haydarpaşa Station**, which would look more at home in the Rhineland – not surprising, given that it was a gift from Kaiser Wilhelm of Germany and was designed by German architects. It's the terminus of the Anatolian railway system, the end of the line for trains from as far east as Tehran (serviced by the weekly TransAsya Express). On the waterfront piazza in front of the station is a small but perfectly formed ferry terminal, designed by Vedat Tek.

The area immediately north of Haydarpaşa is thinly developed, largely because it belongs to the military and Marmara University, which each own one of the two imposing buildings that dominate the area.

The **Selimiye Barracks** were originally constructed in 1799, during the reign of Selim III, as part of his plan to create a 'new army' to challenge the hegemony of the Janissaries. His plan backfired: he was murdered and his barracks were burnt down. Thirty years later, Mahmut II finally succeeded in defeating the Janissaries and he was responsible for putting up the present building, now part of a restricted military zone. During the Crimean War (1853-6) the barracks served as a hospital run by Florence Nightingale; the north-west corner is preserved as the **Florence Nightingale Museum**.

The other grand building is the former **Haydarpaşa High School**, now Marmara University's medical faculty. It's the largest of the many commissions completed by Raimondo D'Aronco. Close by the High School is the **British Crimean War Cemetery**, containing the graves of Crimean War and World War I dead. As far-flung corners of foreign fields go, it's rather pleasant, with manicured lawns tended by the Commonwealth War Graves Commission. Access is through the gate lodge.

Just north-east of here, the largest of the area's cemeteries is the **Karacaahmet Cemetery**, named after a warrior companion of the second Ottoman sultan, Orhan. It was probably founded back in the mid 14th century; estimates put the number of interments at over a million – by far the biggest boneyard in Turkey. In 2009, it became home to the contemporary Şakirin Mosque, the first in the city to be designed by a female architect, Zeynep Fadıllıoğlu.

To get to the barracks and cemeteries, follow Tıbbiye Caddesi fifteen minutes north of Haydarpaşa Station. Alternatively, take any Üsküdar-bound *dolmuş* or bus from the ranks adjacent to Kadıköy's ferry terminal.

FREE Florence Nightingale Museum

Florence Nightingale Müzesi

Birinci Ordu Komutanlığı, Selimiye Kışlası, Üsküdar (0216 343 7310, fax 0216 333 1009). **Open** by appointment 9am-5pm, preferably weekdays. **Admission** free.

INSIDE TRACK
LADY WITH THE LAMP

Florence Nightingale earned the moniker 'Lady with the Lamp' after an article in *The Times* described her at the hospital in Üsküdar. It read, 'When all the medical officers have retired for the night and silence and darkness have settled down upon those miles of prostrate sick, she may be observed alone, with a little lamp in her hand, making her solitary rounds.'

SIGHTS

A visit here requires forward planning: to gain access to the heavily guarded Selimiye army barracks, you must fax your passport details, expected time of arrival and phone number. The army will call back to issue permission. Be sure to take your passport.

Visitors enter through a series of guard posts at which the military rank and level of English improves progressively. During the Crimean War, the vast corridors of the barracks were crowded with wounded British, French and Turkish soldiers, shipped in from the battlefields of Balaclava and Sebastopol. The overcrowded, unsanitary conditions meant that a hospital stay increased the likelihood of death, rather than recovery, and many of the hospital's former patients are buried in nearby Haydarpaşa Cemetery.

It was here that Florence Nightingale and her team of nurses developed modern hospital and nursing practice. The museum in her honour is housed in a corner tower. The lower floor contains life-sized statues of Turkish soldiers from the Crimean War to the War of Independence, as well as a waxwork of Florence Nightingale. On the table is her famous lamp. And up a staircase is the room where she stayed.

Florence Nightingale Museum. *See p89.*

Göztepe

Istanbul Toy Museum
Istanbul Oyuncak Müzesi

Dr Zeki Zeren Sokak, off Ömerpaşa Caddesi 17, (0216 359 4550, www.istanbuloyuncakmuzesi.com). Bus 10B, 10S, 17, 17L, 19F, 19M, 19Y, GZ1, GZ2. **Open** 9.30am-6pm Tue-Fri; 9.30am-7pm Sat, Sun. **Admission** TL8; TL5 reductions.

Founded by poet Sunay Akın in 2005 in an old wooden mansion in Göztepe, the collection at this museum contains some 4,000 toys. Highlights include a French violin made in 1817, an American doll from 1820, 100-year-old porcelain dolls from Germany and a lot of collectable tin toys.

ÜSKÜDAR

Stepping ashore from the ferry, you are pitched into the midst of buses, *dolmuş* and taxis tearing round the central square. All this activity is misleading because, in contrast to Kadıköy, Üsküdar is a conservative area, populated largely by migrants from rural Anatolia. During the Muslim holy month of Ramazan, Üsküdar is the site of one of the city's largest *iftar* (breakfast) tents, with masses of food donated by local businesses for the poor. The main point of interest for shoppers are the antiques shops on **Büyük Hamam Sokak**, which is one block south of the **Mimar Sinan Çarşisi**, a 16th-century hamam converted into a small market.

Otherwise, the district's attractions are its mosques. The **Iskele Mosque** (1548), opposite the ferry terminal, and the **Şemsi Ahmet Paşa Mosque** (1580) are both the work of Sinan. The Şemsi is particularly attractive; you can find it by walking south along the waterfront promenade past a string of floating fish restaurants. Inland on Şemsi Paşa Caddesi stands the earliest of Üsküdar's mosques, the **Rumi Mehmet Paşa Mosque**, built in 1471 for the grand vizier. He was of Greek origin, which may explain the strong Byzantine influence in the design.

The **Yeni Valide Mosque** back on Uncular Caddesi also has a Greek connection. It was constructed for Sultan Ahmet III, whose Greek mother was captured at the age of three and grew up in the harem, where she graduated from concubine to wife to mother of the sultan (*valide sultana*). The building is a late example of classical Ottoman style, with an attractive façade but a disappointing interior.

On a small island off the southern shore of Üsküdar is the stubby white **Maiden's Tower**, which is one of the city's best-loved landmarks.

INSIDE TRACK BRITS ABROAD

For the first 50 years that Bosphorus ferries were in operation, the ships were all products of British shipyards. In fact, overall trade between the Ottoman and British empires was at such a level that by the end of the 19th century the Kadıköy suburb of Moda was more or less an English colony.

Maiden's Tower
Kız Kulesi

0216 342 4747, www.kizkulesi.com.tr. **Open** *Tower* noon-7pm Mon-Sat. *Restaurant* noon-1am Mon-Sat. **Admission** ferry TL5-7. **Map** p296 U3.

Although this little island was occupied by a fortress in Byzantine times, the tower dates from the last century. In Turkish it's known as Kız Kulesi, or Maiden's Tower – after a princess who was supposedly confined here after a prophet predicted she would die from a snake bite. A serpent that eventually arrived in a basket of fruit duly delivered the fatal bite. In English it's even more randomly known as Leander's Tower, after the Greek hero who swam the Hellespont. The tower has been used as a quarantine centre, lighthouse and customs control point. These days, the tower has a café-restaurant decked out like an Ottoman banquet hall, which is very popular with wedding parties. It's a scenic spot for an average lunch, but dinner is an expensive, reservations-only affair. There's also Kuledebar, a panoramic café, and a souvenir shop on site.

To get here, walk along the promenade to Salacak (15 minutes from central Üsküdar), where boats leave every 15 minutes from 9am to 1am. The return trip costs TL5. Alternatively, hourly ferries depart from Kabataş (TL7) on the Bosphorus's western shores.

THE ASIAN BOSPHORUS

Just beyond the first Bosphorus Bridge stands **Beylerbeyi Palace**, the last of the great Ottoman palaces. The eponymous village has a pretty harbour with several teahouses and decent restaurants lining the shore. Nearby **Hamidievvel Mosque** is unusual in having a rose garden. At weekends, the area by the ferry jetty is taken over by craft stalls.

Further north, the landscape gets much greener. In the 1990s, property prices here soared as rich commuters from the European shore moved in. The most exclusive properties are the *yalıs*, vast wooden mansions that hug the strip between the road and the sea. As they're mostly invisible from the road, behind high security walls, you'll need to take a Bosphorus cruise (*see p212*) to catch a glimpse of them.

Çengelköy, the next town up, was a humble village until it featured in a long-running TV soap, *Süper Baba*, precipitating an influx of money and car showrooms. The harbour is still pleasant, and there are a couple of waterside fish restaurants with great views. Çengelköy is home to the excellent Sumahan Hotel (*see p125*), which overlooks the Bosphorus.

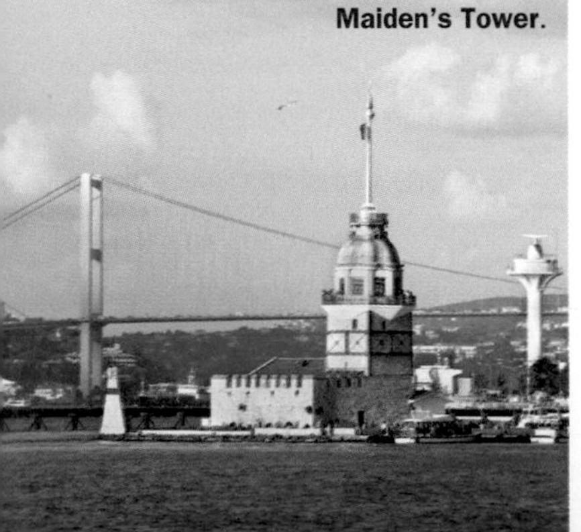

Maiden's Tower.

INSIDE TRACK
THE BOND CONNECTION

The Maiden's Tower (*see left*) was used as a hideout for the villainous Elektra (Sophie Marceau) in the 1999 James Bond movie *The World Is Not Enough*.

The wide valley to the north of **Kandilli** is split by two rivers, Küçüksu and Göksu Deresi, once known as the 'Sweet Waters of Asia'. In Ottoman times, the meadows between them were a popular picnic ground for the rich. Even Sultan Abdül Mecit got in on the act, erecting the modest **Küçüksu Palace** on the shore.

★ Beylerbeyi Palace
Beylerbeyi Sarayı

Abdullah Ağa Caddesi 12 (0216 321 9320, www.millisaraylar.gov.tr). Bus 15 from Üsküdar; occasional ferries direct from Eminönü. **Open** 8.30am-4.30pm Tue, Wed, Fri-Sun. **Admission** TL20. **No credit cards.**

After being deposed in 1908, Sultan Abdül Hamit II spent the last years of his life here. Facing northwest, the palace gets little direct sunlight – it was intended as a summer annexe to the main palace at Dolmabahçe. Beylerbeyi didn't even have its own kitchen: food was brought over from the European shore by boat. Tours only take 15 to 20 minutes, racing through the sumptuous palace and some of its five adjoining pavilions.

Küçüksu Palace
Küçüksu (also called Göksu) Kasrı

Küçüksu Caddesi, Beykoz (0216 332 3303, www.millisaraylar.gov.tr). Bus 15 from Üsküdar/101 from Beşiktaş. **Open** 8.30am-4.30pm Tue, Wed, Fri-Sun. **Admission** TL5. **No credit cards.**

Completed in 1857, this relatively small palace was used by Ottoman sultans for short stays during country excursions and hunting trips. Unlike other imperial buildings, Küçüksu was not surrounded by high walls but by cast-iron railings. The ornate façade and twin staircases sweeping around the ornamental pool and fountain create a grand impression, which is echoed inside. The ceilings are richly decorated with plaster motifs and painted designs, while the many marble hearths make Küçüksu seem like a museum dedicated to 19th-century fireplace design.

The pavilion was extensively restored in 1996 and the surrounding gardens, fountain and quay are being transformed into a park where the public can enjoy picnics as in centuries past.

Consume

Hotels

Hip hotel, loft suite or Ottoman palace by the sea?

A decade ago the Istanbul hotel scene was threadbare. Local flophouses competed with 1970s chains. The city's grande dame hotel, the Pera Palace, lay tired and musty, its ritzy cage lift – the Ottoman Empire's first elevator – a creaky testament to former glories.

But things change fast here. The handful of design hotels that opened in the noughties – including **W**, **Sumahan** and **Tomtom Suites** – inspired a dozen more. Business chic **Edition Hotel** opened in 2011, as did boho Beyoğlu blowout **Le Georges**. A new series of mega hotels pull in big spenders from Europe, the US, Brazil and Asia. The two **Four Seasons** hotels compete with Kempinski's wondrous **Çirağan Palace**, which will both go head-to-head with Istanbul's new **Shangri-La** in 2013. And the **Pera Palace**? After a thorough makeover, it's again adding stars to a gilded guest book that includes Greta Garbo and Jackie O.

WHERE TO STAY

There are basically two choices: in the historic Sultanahmet area south of the Golden Horn, or up the Bosphorus in European Istanbul (the exceptions are the two destination hotels we list on the Asian side, *see p125*). Most tourists who are visiting for a couple of days will head to the former to be near the Grand Bazaar and Topkapı Palace. This area has traditionally been the centre for the city's budget accommodation. Many hotels in Sultanahmet have rooftop terraces and it's hard to beat morning tea and simit bagels nestled between the domes of the Haghia Sophia and Blue Mosque.

To be near the best bars and finest restaurants, find a hotel around Beyoğlu. There are new choices along Meşrutiyet Caddesi such as the newly reopened **Pera Palace** (*see p103*) and **Mia Pera** (*see p105*), as well as the likes of **Tomtom Suites** (*see p107*), **Witt Istanbul** (*see p107*) and **Le Georges** (*see p103*) in the trendy district of Cihangir.

❶ Red numbers given in this chapter correspond to the location of each hotel as marked on the street maps. *See pp242-251.*

Most of the city's high-rise, high-end options for business travellers are clustered around Harbiye, an area of green parkland just north of Taksim Square. There's another cluster of hotels around the business district of Levent, including the **Mövenpick** (*see p119*) and new **Edition Hotel** (*see p115*).

Information & prices

Prices quoted in this chapter refer to the rack rates for standard double rooms. These should at least offer an idea about what you can pay at a given hotel, but note that rates can vary wildly throughout the year and even at the same time within a single property, with some hotels charging more for a view. Prices quoted below are high-season rates, which normally apply from the end of May to the start of September, at Christmas and New Year, and during national holidays. Outside these times you can expect a discount of between 10 and 30 per cent. In all but a few of the high-end hotels, room rates include tax (18 per cent) and breakfast.

Almost every hotel in Istanbul now takes reservations online. Indeed, most establishments rely on international booking websites for custom, including www.booking.com, www.laterooms.com and www.expedia.com. There are also a few useful websites for online reservations, notably www.istanbulhotels.com, which brings together over 200 of the city's hotels and offers discounts for online booking.

Most places quote rates in euros but will also accept Turkish lira. Almost all take credit cards, although hotels in mid-range and budget categories are open to bargaining over rates, especially if you're flexible on paying your bill in either currency and willing to pay cash.

If you arrive without a reservation, there are several booking agents at Atatürk Airport in the international arrivals hall (at the opposite end to the tourist information desk). They have an extensive list of mainly three- and four-star hotels and don't charge any commission.

ABOUT THE CHAPTER

Because hotels in Istanbul commonly list their prices in euros, we have followed suit. Hotels in this guide are divided into the following categories: **deluxe** (more than €400 a night for a double); **expensive** (€200-€400); **moderate** (€100-€200); **budget** (€50-€100); and **hostels** (under €50).

At the end of each review, we've listed a selection of hotel services: restaurants and bars, internet access, spas and the like. If you're bringing a car to the city – not recommended given the ubiquity of cheap taxis and hazardous driving conditions – always check before you arrive. At some hotels parking is limited and may need to be reserved in advance.

South of the Golden Horn

SULTANAHMET

Deluxe

★ Four Seasons

Tevkifhane Sokak 1 (0212 638 8200, www.fourseasons.com/istanbul). Tram Sultanahmet. **Rates** €480-€610 double. **Rooms** 65. **Map** p243 N10 ❶

For 66 years this distinctive building, with its ochre walls and watchtowers, served as the infamous Sultanahmet Prison; inmates included celebrated political prisoners Nazım Hikmet and Orhan Kemal. Sensitively renovated in 1986, the Four Seasons has held on to its position as one of Istanbul's finest hotels. With its manicured gardens and elegant gazebo restaurant (Seasons Restaurant, *see p129*), the former prison yard has been transformed into an oasis of calm in the heart of bustling Sultanahmet. Cells have been replaced by 65 plush, high-ceilinged rooms and suites – a modest number that ensures intimacy and superlative service. The Sunday brunch (*see p139*) is a show-stopping introduction to Turkish hospitality.

Bar. Business services. Concierge. Disabled-adapted rooms. Gym. Internet (wireless). No-smoking rooms. Parking (free). Restaurants (2). Room service. Spa. TV.

► *There's another Four Seasons, the Bosphorus, near Beşiktaş; see p121.*

Expensive

Eresin Crown Hotel

Küçük Ayasofya Caddesi 40 (0212 638 4428, www.eresin.com.tr/eresincrown). Tram Sultanahmet. **Rates** €190-€250 double. **Rooms** 60. **Map** p243 M11 ❷

The Eresin Crown is unusual as a business-friendly high-end hotel amid small boutique competitors in Sultanahmet. It's on the southern side of the peninsula, a stone's throw from the Blue Mosque. Decor in the public spaces is pretty standard, of the marble and plate glass variety, but the hotel's unique selling point are the 50 or so ancient artefacts discovered when the hotel was being built. Some rooms are on the small side, but all are comfortable and well appointed – each comes with a jacuzzi bath. The Terrace Restaurant has amazing views over the city, the Bosphorus and Sea of Marmara. The Eresin is a choice worth considering if you want to be near the sights, but prefer accommodation with international-style features and facilities.

Bars. Business centre. Concierge, Internet (wireless). Room service. Restaurants (2). TV.

Yeşil Ev

Kabasakal Caddesi 5 (0212 517 6785, www.yesilev.com.tr). Tram Sultanahmet. **Rates** €140-€230 double. **Rooms** 19. **Map** p243 N10 ❸

Flagship of the Turkish Touring and Automobile Association's fleet of restored Ottoman properties, the 'Green House' enjoys an unrivalled location on a leafy street midway between the Haghia Sophia and Sultanahmet Mosque. Entering this stately wooden mansion is like stepping on to the set of a 19th-century costume drama. Every room is decked out

INSIDE TRACK TISSUE ISSUES

It's rare to see squat toilets – or *tuvalet alaturca* – in Istanbul hotels, although they still exist in public conveniences across the land. What most toilets do have, however, is a tap to right of the ceramic and a nozzle inside the basin, which provides a sharp splash to the bottom area as the tap is turned. While many still cleanse by hand, a small bin sits beside every WC for those who would rather use tissue. Out of respect for Istanbul's ancient sewage system, make sure all paper is placed in here.

in reproduction furniture, complete with wood-panelled ceilings, creaky parquet flooring and antique rugs. The Pasha Suite has its own hamam. The idyllic garden is one of the highlights, with a pretty pink pond, a fine café and beer garden and the restaurant. With only 19 rooms, booking in advance is essential. Be sure to ask for a room on the first floor, overlooking the cobbled street – with no televisions in the hotel, you'll want the view.
Internet (wireless). Restaurant. Room service.
► *The beer garden is a great spot for a drink, especially after a visit to Hagia Sophia (see p41).*

Moderate

Armada
Ahırkapı Sokak 24, Cankurtaran (0212 455 4455, www.armadahotel.com.tr). Cankurtaran rail. **Rates** €75-€165 double. **Rooms** 108. **Map** p243 O11 ❹

Sandwiched between waterside Kennedy Caddesi and the suburban railway line, the Armada scores low on location, although it is only a ten-minute walk up the hill to the sight-studded heart of Sultanahmet. The real advantage is that most rooms have fantastic, uninterrupted Bosphorus views. Modelled on a row of 19th-century houses that once stood here, the building is now a bit stuck in the 1990s. The fancy lobby has a terrapin pond and café, while the 108 rooms, if not exceptional, are comfortable and slightly bigger than the average Sultanahmet room.
Bars (2). Business centre. Concierge. Disabled-adapted rooms. Internet (wireless). No-smoking rooms. Parking (free). Restaurants (4). Room service. TV.

Ayasofya Pansiyonları
Soğukçeşme Sokak (0212 513 3660, www.ayasofyapensions.com). Tram Gülhane. **Rates** €170-€200 double. **Rooms** 64. **Map** p243 N10 ❺

In the 1980s, the Turkish Touring and Automobile Association reconstructed this row of nine clapboard houses dating from the 19th century. They were painted in pastel colours and furnished in period style. Rooms are all painted different colours and most have big brass beds. The setting is a dream: a sloping cobbled lane hidden between the high walls of Topkapı Palace and the back of Haghia Sophia. Breakfast is served in the pretty garden or the gazebo of the Konut Evi, a four-storey annexe at the end of the alley. At night, the whole place is lamp-lit. Walt Disney couldn't create more magic.
Bars. Internet (wireless). Parking (free). Restaurants (2). Room service.

Citadel
Kennedy Caddesi Sahilyolu 32, Ahır Kapı Sokak (0212 516 2313, www.citadelhotel.com). Cankurtaran rail. **Rates** €90-€120 double. **Rooms** 31. **Map** p243 O11 ❻

Occupying a striking pink three-storey mansion, this Best Western affiliate has 25 rooms and six suites decked out in Barbie colours. The only thing between you and the Sea of Marmara is – alas – six lanes of speeding traffic. It's not far from the fish restaurants of Kumkapı, though, and the conservatory bar and decent restaurant lessen the feeling of isolation.
Bar. Concierge. Internet (wireless). Parking (free). Restaurants (3). Room service. TV.

★ Dersaadet
Kuçuk Ayasofya Caddesi Kapıağası Sokak 5 (0212 458 0760, www.hoteldersaadet.com). Tram Sultanahmet. **Rates** €80-€145 double. **Rooms** 17. **Map** p243 N11 ❼

The Dersaadet (one of the many former names for Istanbul) has become one of the most popular boutique hotels south of the Golden Horn for independent travellers. The hotel's quaint wooden exterior and 19th-century French-influenced Ottoman decor recreate the charms of the Ottoman golden years. The 17 rooms, across four floors, are all comfortable, and some have good views over the Sea of Marmara. The best room is the Sultan's Suite, which has a low wooden ceiling, big windows and jacuzzi baths. Sea view rooms have a €15 surcharge. There is a pleasant rooftop breakfast terrace, with both indoor and outdoor tables, overlooking the Bosphorus. It is a superb spot for enjoying an afternoon coffee to the sound of classical music, only interrupted by the call to prayer at the Blue Mosque and the squeak of canaries.
Bars (2). Internet (wireless). Restaurants (2). Room service. TV.
► *The Hotel Niles (see p99) is run by the same family.*

Empress Zoe
Adliye Sokak 10, off Akbıyık Caddesi (0212 518 2504, www.emzoe.com). Tram Sultanahmet. **Rates** €120-€220 double. 10% discount for cash. **Rooms** 19. **Map** p243 O11 ❽

Named after a racy Byzantine regent, the Zoe is one of the best and quirkiest of the city's small hotels, which means it books up far in advance. Its sunken reception area incorporates parts of a 15th-century hamam; the 'archaeological garden' is ideal for breakfast or a beer. Bear in mind that guests must be agile, as rooms are reached via a wrought-iron spiral staircase. In contrast to the gilt and frills of most other 'period' hotels, the Zoe's 19 small rooms are decorated in dark wood and richly coloured textiles. A new wing of suites has recently been added and the garden expanded. Add a fine rooftop bar for a nightcap with a view and this place is sheer class from top to bottom.
Bar. Internet (wireless). Restaurant. Room service. TV.

Ibrahim Paşa Hotel
Terzihane Sokak 5 (0212 518 0394, www.ibrahimpasha.com). Tram Sultanahmet. **Rates** €115-€225 double. **Rooms** 24. **Map** p243 M11 ❾

CONSUME

Tucked round the corner from the Museum of Turkish and Islamic Art, the Ibrahim Paşa is an eminently likeable small hotel. It doesn't overplay the old Ottoman card and instead is stylishly modern, smart and bright, with just enough judiciously placed artefacts (including some fascinating old photographs in the breakfast area) to remind you that this is Istanbul. Rooms can be small, but careful use is made of space. The buffet breakfast has a good selection of local cheeses, honey, bread, olives and much more. The view from the rooftop terrace is absolutely divine: a seascape taking in two continents plus the Haghia Sophia mosque.
Bar. Internet (wireless). Room service. TV.

Kybele Hotel

Yerebatan Caddesi 33-35 (0212 511 7766, www.kybelehotel.com). Tram Sultanahmet. **Rates** €120 double. 10% discount for cash. **Rooms** 16. **Map** p243 N10 ⑩

The Akbayrak family obviously have a thing about vintage glass lamps – the interior of their hotel is hung with 2,000 of them. The eccentricities continue: every room is crammed with kilims, candlestands, empty bottles and quirky knick-knacks. Garish pink and green paint schemes heighten the sense of fun. It all makes sense when you learn that one of the Akbayrak brothers was formerly an antiques dealer, while another spent three years with an Australian circus. The bedrooms are smallish, but they are comfortable enough and all have marble bathrooms. Breakfast is served in a courtyard as colourful as a gypsy caravan.
Bar. Internet (wireless). Parking (TL10 day). Restaurant. Room service.

★ Hotel Niles

Ordu Caddesi Dibekli, Cami Sokak 19, Beyazıt (0212 517 3239, www.hotelniles.com). Tram Beyazıt. **Rates** €50-€150 double. 10% discount for cash. **Rooms** 29. **Map** p242 K10 ⑪

Significantly refurbished in 2010, Hotel Niles is owned by the same family who are responsible for the highly regarded Dersaadet. They have been involved in every detail of the renovations, from the authentic Iznik tiles to the design on the hand-painted ceiling. Each of the ten new suites is based on French-influenced Ottoman guestrooms, done out in light turquoise, equipped with a microwave and hamam-style bathrooms with Marmara marble. Two duplex rooms were built using the original bricks with inscriptions in old Turkish script. There's a gym, conference room and leafy roof garden where breakfast is served. Service is flawless.
Bar. Internet (wireless). Room service. TV.

► *Dersaadet (see above) is another Sultanahmet hotel run by the same family.*

Sarniç

Kuçuk Ayasofya Caddesi 26 (0212 518 2323, www.sarnichotel.com). Tram Sultanahmet. **Rates** €60-€150 double. **Rooms** 21. **Map** p243 N11 ⑫

Sarniç.

Sarniç, the Turkish word for cistern, takes its name from the fifth-century Byzantine cistern beneath the hotel, which guests can explore from 9am to 6pm. After changing ownership, Sarniç underwent major renovations in 2010. Another five rooms were added on the top floor – recommended for the views of the Blue Mosque. All other rooms have been tastefully decorated, and include flatscreen TVs. The small top-floor terrace makes a lovely setting when the sun sets and there's a bar-breakfast room below ground. There are popular half-day cookery courses in the hotel kitchen.
Bar. Concierge. Internet (wireless). Massage. Restaurant. Room service. TV.

► *For more cookery courses, see p140.*

Hotel Uyan

Utangaç Sokak 25 (0212 516 4892, www.uyanhotel.com). Tram Sultanahmet. **Rates** €60-€130 double; 8% discount for cash. **Rooms** 26. **Map** p243 N11 ⑬

This attractive corner hotel in a 75-year-old building has 16 spacious standard rooms and ten suites spead over four floors. The standard rooms are simply furnished, with small bathrooms. Deluxe suites are a step up and feature a jacuzzi bath and, wait for it, a sound system in the bathroom. Uyan's main selling point is that it has the highest roof terrace in the neighbourhood, with views over the Blue Mosque. If you're not an early riser, avoid

room 309, which lies directly underneath the breakfast room. The hotel offers free airport pick-ups.
Bar. Internet (wireless). Restaurant. Room service. TV.

Budget

Hotel Ararat

Torun Sokak 3 (0212 516 0411, www.ararat hotel.com). Tram Sultanahmet. **Rates** €40-€100 double. **Rooms** 12. **Map** p243 N11 ⓮

Ararat's best feature is its location. Envious of the success of the nearby Empress Zoe (*see p97*), the young Turkish owners of Ararat recruited the same architect, Nicos Papadakis, to revamp their 12-room guesthouse. If the results aren't quite as inspired, the Ararat still breaks the mould, with marbled walls and an orange and ochre colour scheme that works well with the dark, stained-wood floors. Rooms vary widely in terms of size and comfort – some are small with little light, while others have wooden four-posters with wonderful views of the Blue Mosque. Breakfast is served on the roof terrace.
Bar. Internet (wireless). Parking (TL15 day). Restaurant. Room service.

Hanedan

Adliye Sokak 3, Akbıyk Caddesi (0212 516 4869, www.hanedanhotel.com). Tram Sultanahmet. **Rates** €35-€65 double. **Rooms** 10. **Map** p243 O11 ⓯

Hanedan is one of the smartest independent hotels south of the Four Seasons. Clean, bright primrose-yellow rooms, with large beds draped in muslin, all have en suite bathrooms with hairdryers and heated towel rails. The three family rooms have the best Marmara views. There are more unobstructed views from the roof terrace. It can be noisy on summer nights, as neighbouring hotels often host rooftop parties.
Internet (wireless). Room service.

★ Nomade Hotel

Ticarethane Sokak, 15 (0212 513 8172, www.hotelnomade.com). Tram Sultanahmet. **Rates** €100 double. **Rooms** 16. **Map** p243 N10 ⓰

The cosy reception area, with comfortable design-minded furnishings, is perfect for watching the bustling pedestrian traffic outside, while the cushion-strewn, flower-filled roof terrace is one of the prettiest in Istanbul, particularly at night. The hotel's new owners refurbished the 16 rooms and reception area in 2010. The rooms are as cosy and uncluttered as before, with pastel walls, ethnic bedspreads, richly hued wall hangings and modern bathrooms.
Internet (wireless). Restaurant. Room service. TV.

Side Hotel & Pension

Utangaç Sokak 20 (0212 517 2282, www.sidehotel.com). Tram Sultanahmet. **Rates** €35-€70 double. **Rooms** 52. **Map** p243 N11 ⓱

> **INSIDE TRACK PAY PER VIEW**
>
> With great rooftop views two a penny in Istanbul, hotels often stress the vista from the rooms. What they don't usually mention, though, is that the rooms with the best views may come at a premium. It's a good idea to check about the view when you book online or in person.

Rooms are clean and well looked after here, and have en suite bathrooms with shower cubicles (the Istanbul norm for this price bracket is a showerhead that falls straight on to the bathroom floor). Rooms vary widely, so ask to look at a few before you make your choice. Pension accommodation is more basic; the cheapest room has a shared but clean bathroom. There are two self-catering apartments for large groups. Breakfast is served on the rooftop terrace. There's free tea available in the rustic, wood-panelled foyer and a small book exchange. Half the rooms have air-conditioning, the other half fans.
Internet (wireless). TV.

Turkoman

Asmalıçeşme Sokak 2, off the Hippodrome (0212 516 2956, www.turkomanhotel.com). Tram Sultanahmet. **Rates** €69-€99 double. **Rooms** 20. **Map** p243 M11 ⓲

Located just off the Hippodrome and opposite the Egyptian obelisk, the Turkoman has a roof terrace with amazing views of the Blue Mosque, although during the summer months the mosque is hidden from the lower floors by foliage. Bright, unfussy and very yellow rooms may verge on the tacky, but they have brass beds, parquet flooring and big windows. Free one-way airport transfer is available as a perk for guests staying more than three nights.
Bar. Café. Concierge. Internet (wireless). Restaurant. Room service. TV.

Hostels

Orient Hostel

Akbıyık Caddesi 13 (0212 518 0789, www.orient hostel.com). Tram Sultanahmet. **Rates** €9-€15 dorm bed; €35-€55 double. **Map** p243 N11 ⓳

For years the Orient has been the mainstay of the Istanbul backpacker scene, base camp for a constant stream of wanderers tramping across Asia or through the Middle East. Besides the full range of budget traveller services, including cheap internet access, money-changing facilities and discounted airline tickets, the Orient has a lively social scene, with barbecues, belly-dancing and film nights. There is also a women-only dormitory. Both the hostels listed here can fill up with local high school students during holiday time, or school groups from further afield.
Bar. Café. Internet. Restaurant.

CONSUME

WESTERN DISTRICTS

Moderate

Kariye Hotel
Kariye Camii Sokak 6, Edirnekapı (0212 534 8414, www.kariyeotel.com). **Rates** €65-€100 double. **Rooms** 26. **Map** p244 D4 ⑳
Another 19th-century Ottoman residence stripped down and dressed up by the Turkish Touring and Automobile Association and pressed into service as a hotel. There are 26 rooms, all done out in early 1900s fashion. There is also a family annex with one master bedroom and a single room. The restaurant, Asitane (*see p133*), is renowned for its Ottoman cuisine. Next door is the Church of St Saviour in Chora, one of Istanbul's essential sights. But the big snag is the location, out by the old city walls and a TL10 taxi ride from the Blue Mosque. But if you had a reason to be in this part of town, of which a penchant for Byzantine history would be one, this would be the place to stay.
Bar. Concierge. Internet (wireless). Parking (free). Restaurant. Room service. TV.

YEŞILKÖY (AIRPORT)

Expensive

Polat Renaissance Istanbul Hotel
Sahil Yolu 2 Caddesi (0212 414 1800, www.polatrenaissance.com). **Rates** €120-€225 double. **Rooms** 414.
Our airport hotel of choice, the Polat Renaissance is a five-minute taxi ride from the terminal in the coastal suburb of Yeşilköy (it's 18 kilometres, or 12 miles, from the city centre). A 27-storey blue glass skyscraper by the sea, the ultra-modern interior features a soaring central atrium. At least half of the 414 rooms have views over the Sea of Marmara. All the rooms were renovated in 2010 and are now equipped with LCD TVs, broadband internet access and coffee machines. All the facilities you would expect of a Marriott hotel, including a large heated outdoor pool.
Bars (3). Business services. Concierge. Disabled-adapted rooms. Gym. Internet (wireless). No-smoking rooms. Parking (free). Pool (1 indoor, 1 outdoor). Restaurants (5). Room service. Spa. TV.

North of the Golden Horn

BEYOĞLU

Deluxe

Pera Palace
Meşrutiyet Caddesi 98, Pera (0212 377 4000, www.perapalace.com). **Rates** €185-€475 double. **Rooms** 115. **Map** p248 M4 ㉑
Built in 1892 as the last stop on the Orient Express, the Pera Palace is the most aristocratic of hotels. The same company that ran the famed Paris-to-Istanbul trains built it and in the early days its pampered guests were carried on cushioned sedans from Sirkeci Station to waiting hotel transport. After a two-year closure for a €23 million refurbishment, it opened its gilded revolving doors again in September 2010. Care has been taken to restore the hotel meticulously, to an authentic version of its former glory, while incorporating the technology needed for modern comforts including a basement pool and spa. Many of the 115 rooms have brass plaques with the names of famous past guests: Sarah Bernhardt, Greta Garbo, Jackie Onassis, Atatürk (whose room remains as it was when he stayed) and Agatha Christie, who wrote part of *Murder on the Orient Express* during a stay here. *Photos p105.*
Bar. Business centre. Café. Concierge. Gym. Internet (wireless). No-smoking rooms. Parking. Restaurant. Room service. TV.

Expensive

Ceylan InterContinental
Asker Ocağı Caddesi 1, Taksim (0212 368 4444, www.istanbul.intercontinental.com.tr). **Rates** €240-€375 double. **Rooms** 388. **Map** p247 P1 ㉒
The InterContinental is an 18-floor Goliath. Renovated in 2008, the style remains brash, the tone set by a golden staircase spiralling up from the lobby and a glitzy, palm-filled atrium. Decor aside, the hotel is well appointed, and most of the 388 rooms have panoramic views over the Bosphorus. Those on the Club Floor (actually the top four floors) are preferable, but pricey. Mick Jagger and Liz Taylor are some of the celebrities who have stayed in the four lavish Presidential Suites. The hotel is a ten-minute walk from central Taksim Square.
Bar. Business services. Concierge. Disabled-adapted rooms. Gym. Internet (wireless). No-smoking rooms. Parking (free). Pool (outdoor). Restaurants (3). Room service. Spa. TV.

Georges Hotel
Serdar-I Ekrem Sokak 24, Galata (0212 244 2423, www.georgeshotel.com). **Rates** €157-€234 double. **Rooms** 20. **Map** p248 M5 ㉓

INSIDE TRACK BREAKFAST

Breakfast is big news in Istanbul hotels. They are usually extensive and delicious, with cheeses, olives, fresh breads, honeycomb, preserves and cold meats. Some of the best breakfasts can be found at **5 Oda** (*see p111*), Swissôtel (*see p123*), **Mia Pera** (*see p105*) and **Sumahan** (*see p125*).

Contemporary Ottoman best describes this drop-dead gorgeous property, which opened its glass doors in late 2011. Check-in is via the reception desk iPad and luggage – so very cool – is whizzed underground on a subterranean conveyor belt directly to a porter, lest your Samsonite clog up the lobby. The mansion hotel exudes history at every touch. The 20 suite-sized rooms all branch off a vintage marble spiral staircase, and the finely finished wood panelling heralds back to the 1880s. The majority of rooms have capacious terraces and wow-factor views across the Bosphorus. In-room Nespresso machines come with free coffee capsules and staff will hand-deliver the *FT* or the *Herald Tribune* (also for free). The Georges team is currently working on new properties on Istiklal Caddesi and in historic Sultanahmet.
Bar. Business services. Concierge. Internet (wireless). No-smoking rooms. Restaurant. Room service. TV.

Marmara Taksim

Taksim Square, Taksim (0212 334 8300, www.themarmarahotels.com). **Rates** €229-€289 double. **Rooms** 376. **Map** p249 P2 ㉔
One of four Marmara hotels in Istanbul (with sister establishments in Manhattan and across Turkey), this location is a Taksim Square landmark. It is the the place to stay if you want to be at the heart of the action, though bear in mind that Taksim Square is far from picturesque. The rooms have the facilities and feel of a big international hotel. Most have fabulous views, however, but the best lookout spot is from the top-floor Tepe Lounge or the Panorama restaurant, or indeed the top-floor swimming pool.
Bars (3). Business centre. Café. Concierge. Gym. Internet (wireless). No-smoking rooms. Parking (free). Pool (outdoor). Restaurants (2). Room service. Spa. TV.
Other locations Meşrutiyet Caddesi, Tepebasi (0212 334 0300); Muallim Naci Caddesi, Yalıçıkmazı Sokak 20, Ortaköy (0212 334 8300); Ortaklar Caddesi 30, Mecidiyeköy (0212 370 9400).
► *The street-level Kitchenette (see p135) is a stylish location for a long brunch.*

Mia Pera

Meşrutiyet Caddesi 53, Pera (0212 245 0245, www.miaperahotel.com). **Rates** €119-€249 double. **Rooms** 61. **Map** p248 M3 ㉕
One of the latest additions to Beyoğlu's burgeoning hotel scene is also one of the most stylish. Only the façade of this 19th-century French-style Ottoman residence remains intact. Once through the glass doors, Mia Pera is a thoroughly modern experience. Copies of *Wallpaper** magazine are stacked next to coloured glass vases on the shelves in the lobby. Down three steps are the bar, restaurant and breakfast room (the breakfast buffet is excellent). The highlight, however, is the basement spa and

Pera Palace. *See p103.*

CONSUME

heated oval pool – a relaxing and warming hamam-style affair. Massages are available.
Bar. Business centre. Café. Concierge. Gym. Internet (wireless). No-smoking rooms. Parking (free). Pool (indoor). Restaurant. Room service. Spa. TV.

Richmond Hotel

Istiklal Caddesi 227 (0212 252 5460, www.richmondhotels.com.tr). **Rates** €140-€230 double. **Rooms** 103. **Map** p248 M4 26

The Richmond is one of the only hotels on Istiklal Caddesi, Beyoğlu's historic main thoroughfare. The hotel may have retained the building's historic façade, but the interior has been ripped out, and rooms underwent a business class makeover in 2010. What the interior lacks in style, the hotel makes up for with a relaxed atmosphere and friendly staff. Standard rooms are simple and streamlined, while the executive suites cater mainly to commercial travellers.
Bars (2). Business services. Café. Concierge. Disabled-adapted rooms. Gym. Internet (wireless). No-smoking rooms. Restaurants (2). Room service. TV.

► *The sleek Leb-i Derya bar-restaurant (see p135) at the Richmond probably has the best view of any of Istanbul's rooftop bars. The central oval bar is a sublime cocktail spot.*

★ Tomtom Suites

Boğazkesen Caddesi, Tomtom Kaptan Sokak 18 (0212 292 4949, www.tomtomsuites.com). **Rates** €200-€250 double. **Rooms** 20. **Map** p248 N4 27

It's the size of Tomtom Suites that's immediately striking. The standard rooms are 35-45sq m (376-484sq ft), and the senior suites 55-65sq m (582-700sq ft). The high ceilings of this converted Franciscan nunnery only add to the impressive proportions. The beds are enormous, and each marble-clad room boasts a jacuzzi bath. Across the road from the old Italian Embassy, Tomtom was restored and repurposed in 2008 with a modern classic design that paired original features with modern artwork and a glass lift, not to mention iPads at each breakfast table. The terrace restaurant and patio has panoramic views over the Golden Horn.
Bar. Business services. Café. Concierge. Disabled-adapted room. Internet (wireless). No-smoking rooms. Restaurant. Room service. TV.

★ Witt Istanbul

Defterdar Yokusu 26, Cihangir (0212 293 1500, www.wittistanbul.com). **Rates** €169-€499 double. **Rooms** 17. **Map** p249 O4 28

Designed by famed Turkish architects Autoban, Witt is a deeply impressive suite hotel. Every element has been painstakingly considered, from the open-plan arrangement of the suites to the staff uniforms. The lobby, bar and dining/breakfast areas are low lit, with only black tiles reflecting the light. Suites are as envy-inducing as they are spacious,

Tomtom Suites.

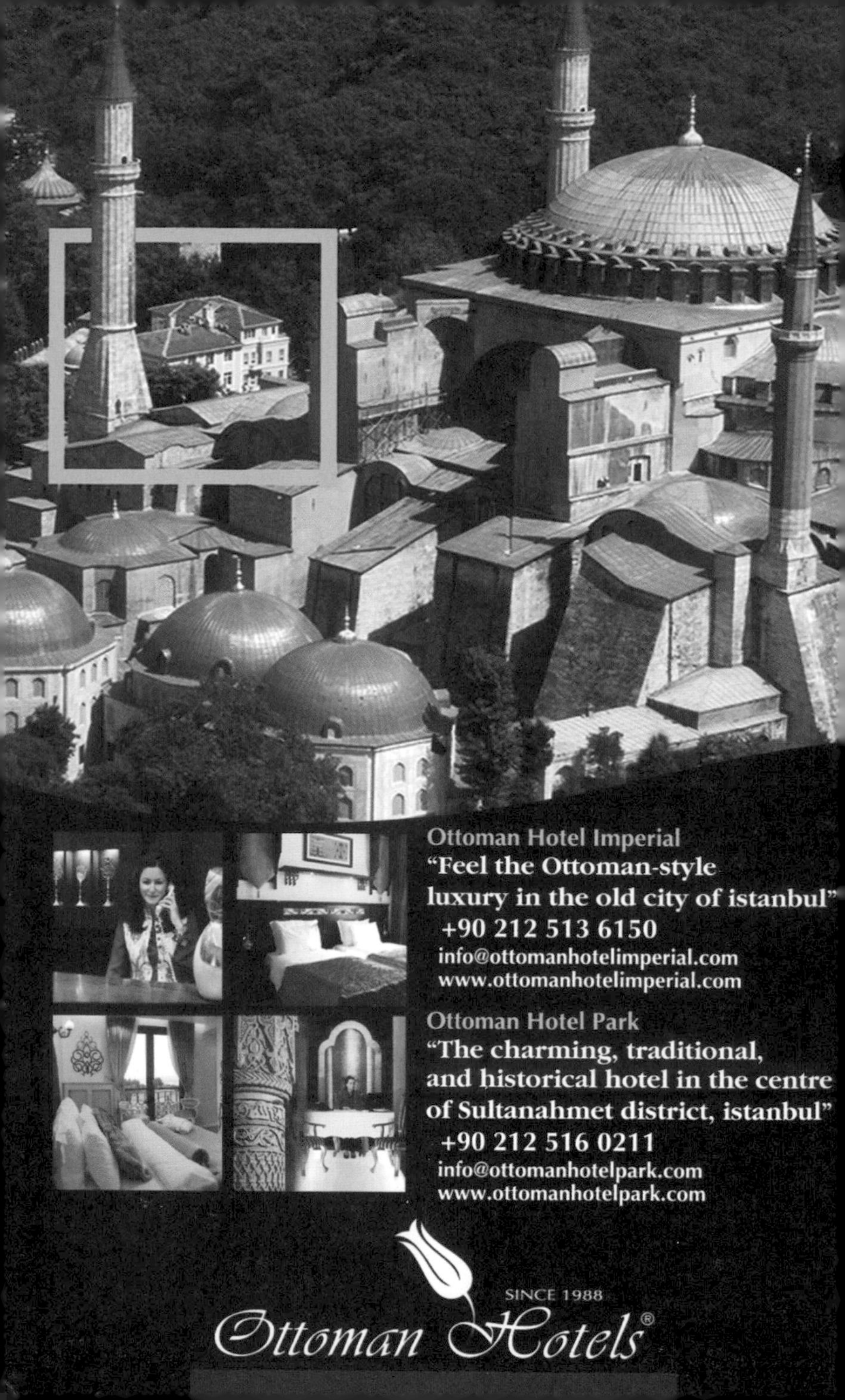

SINCE 1988
Ottoman Hotels®

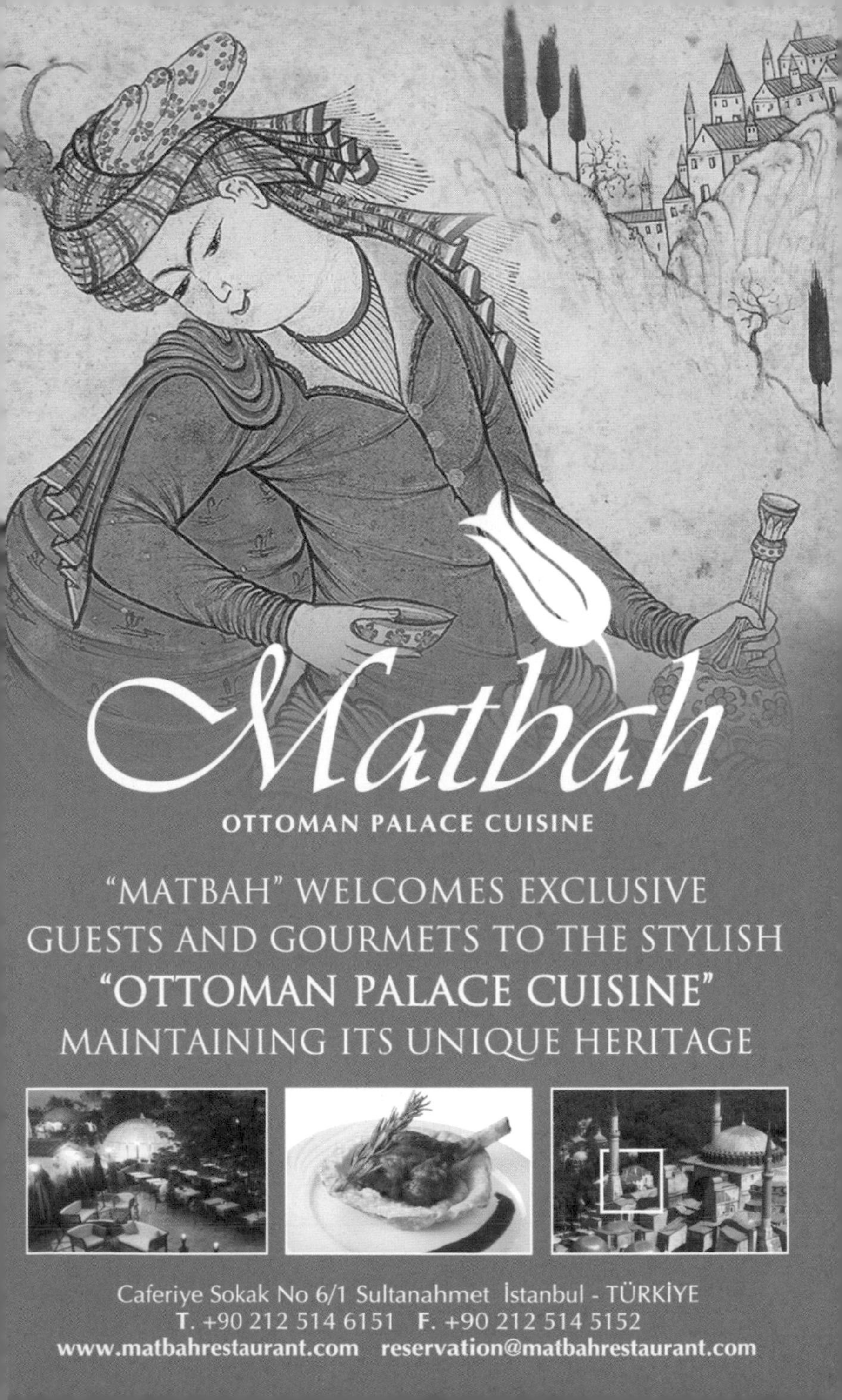
Matbah
OTTOMAN PALACE CUISINE
"MATBAH" WELCOMES EXCLUSIVE
GUESTS AND GOURMETS TO THE STYLISH
"OTTOMAN PALACE CUISINE"
MAINTAINING ITS UNIQUE HERITAGE
Caferiye Sokak No 6/1 Sultanahmet İstanbul - TÜRKİYE
T. +90 212 514 6151 F. +90 212 514 5152
www.matbahrestaurant.com reservation@matbahrestaurant.com

and include a marble kitchenette with sink, kettle, microwave, Nespresso machine and hobs. There is also a seating area, large beds and a desk with an iPod dock. Ross Lovegrove-designed marble bathrooms have five-headed shower units and bespoke towels. Walls are soundproofed. The location is convenient for both the hip cafés along Akarsu Sokak and the antiques shops of Çukurcuma. Simply superb.
Bar. Business services. Café. Concierge. Internet (wireless). No-smoking rooms. Restaurant. Room service. TV.

Moderate

★ 5 oda

Şahkulu Bostan Sokak 164, Galata (0212 252 7501, www.5oda.com). **Rates** €140 double. **Rooms** 5. **Map** p248 M5 ㉙

This new guesthouse, on a quiet street just off Istiklal Caddesi, is perfectly located for the bars and shopping of Beyoğlu. The five rooms are accessed through a reception/kitchen area; a small glass-sided elevator takes you to the upper floors. They are long and airy, with large windows at either side. The architect has used the space well, with an open-plan design that includes a kitchen area with sink, hob, fridge and coffee-making facilities, a couple of chairs and a glass table. With modern design, using wood and white-painted bare brickwork, they are relaxing spaces. Bathrooms are small, with only room for a shower, basin and toilet. Breakfasts, which can be served in guestrooms, are a Turkish spectacular.

★ Eklektik Guest House

Kadribey Cikmazi 4, Galata (0212 243 7446, www.eklektikgalata.com). **Rates** €85-€125 double. **Rooms** 8. **No credit cards**. **Map** p248 M5 ㉚

This thoroughly charming guesthouse, on a quiet cul-de-sac, is popular with gay visitors, but the friendly and knowledgeable staff make everyone feel very welcome. Each of the eight smallish rooms is decorated to a theme: from clean lines, white walls and wood in the Zen Room to drapes and ornate lamps in the Colonial Room, and black linens – and a mirror ball in the bathroom – in the Black Room. The shower in the corner of most rooms is an unconventional touch, but it doesn't seem to bother most patrons, neither does the lack of a lift (and some of the rooms are a hike up several storeys). There is a small terrace with views over the Bosphorus. The breakfast, served around one large table, is superb.
Concierge. Internet (wireless). Parking (TL20 day). Room service. TV.
► *Eklektik is close to several gay venues, such as the Sugar Café (see p191).*

Galateia Residence

Sahkulu Bostan Sokal 9, Tünel (0212 245 3032, www.galateiaresidence.com). **Rates** €130-€250 suite. **Rooms** 13. **Map** p248 M4 ㉛

It's hard to find serviced suites of such size and sumptuousness within striking distance of the Galata Tower. Suites vary inside from capacious 90sqm Junior Deluxe apartments to mammoth 153sqm Bosphorus Duplex flats. All feature walk-in closets, safe, additional beds for guests, fully functioning kitchens and funky bathrooms with Molton Brown products. There's even a concierge on-site, who can arrange restaurant bookings and private shopping trips. Like a hotel, but so much more intimate.
Business services. Concierge. Internet (wireless). Room service. TV.

House Hotel

Firuzağa Mahallesi, Bostanbaşı Caddesi 19, Çukurcuma (0212 252 0422, www.thehouse-hotels.com). **Rates** €150-€220 suites. **Rooms** 20. **Map** p248 N4 ㉜

This stunning hotel is partly owned by the House Café (*see p145*) group, and the same sensitive design aesthetic found in the cafés shines through here. It's located in a converted mansion built in 1850, on a quiet street in the Çukurcuma antiques district. Going through the elegant but unassuming entrance, you'll find the original tiled floors and Italian marble staircase. Decor is a subtly modern take on the traditional, with mixed shades of wood adding pattern to parquet flooring, panelled walls painted white and sleek, updated chandeliers. Furnishings in dove grey add a slightly ethereal touch to the white. All the furniture was designed for the hotel by Autoban (also behind the Witt, *see p107*, and House Café). The bar, on the top floor (bear in mind there are no lifts), has Chesterfield sofas from which to admire views over the Galata Tower. Be aware, however, that both management and reception staff can come across as too cool for school at times. The small lobby makes for chaos at check-out time.
Bar. Café. Concierge. Internet (wireless). Restaurant. Room service. TV.
► *Two larger House Hotels opened in Ortaköy and Nişantaşı in 2010. See the website for details.*

INSIDE TRACK
WHY WIFI CHARGES

Istanbul's museums, cafés, restaurants and public areas bask under various free WiFi clouds. Almost every hotel in town offers free internet connections too. However, a handful of naughty big-name hotels still charge for WiFi, even though it costs only around €100 per month to wire up an entire hotel. Among the worst culprits are Four Seasons and Swissôtel, which both charge around €20 per day per device. At either place, toting two laptops and an iPad on your weekend away would add around €120 to your hotel bill.

★ I'zaz Lofts

Balik Sokak 12 (0212 252 1382, www.izaz.com). **Rates** €78-€106. **Rooms** 4. **Map** 248 N3 ❸❸

There are only four 'lofts' at I'zaz, each replete with considered design touches. They're fabulously well appointed, with large beds, a desk, flatscreen TV, iPod dock and coffee-making facilities. Visitors should bear in mind that the upper rooms can only be accessed by a staircase. The location is excellent for the bars and restaurants of Nevizade, although the hotel entrance is on a nondescript street, nicely out of earshot of the action. There's a lovely seating area with vast views over the minarets of Kasimpaşa and the western side of the city. I'zaz's hands-off philosophy means it can feel more like an apartment outfit than a hotel: if they want to, guests can cook for themselves in the communal kitchen (where there's always a pot of coffee on the go) or do their own laundry. But staff are also on hand and can cater to most whims.

Internet (wireless). TV.

Taksim Suites

Cumhuriyet Caddesi 49, Taksim (0212 254 7777, www.taximsuites.com). **Rates** €169 double suite. **Rooms** 21. **Map** p247 P1 ❸❹

These self-catering suites make an ideal base for business people. The Miyako suites take their inspiration from the East, while the Park and Avenue suites look towards Scandinavia. Fully equipped with everything from microwaves to study desks, the five options range from a 45sq m (480sq ft) studio to a 109sq m (1,150sq ft) penthouse with remote-controlled skylights and Bosphorus views. Additional treats include breakfast in bed (or the Taksim Lounge), jacuzzis, a fitness room and accommodating staff who will buy your groceries if you leave a shopping list at reception. Another plus is the excellent location just minutes from Taksim Square.

Business services. Concierge. Gym. Internet (high-speed). Room service. Spa. TV.

Budget

★ Büyük Londra Hotel

Meşrutiyet Caddesi 53, Tepebaşı (0212 245 0670, www.londrahotel.net). **Rates** €80-€140 double. **Rooms** 54. **Map** p248 M3 ❸❺

The Londra was built in 1892, so it's roughly the same age as the nearby Pera Palace (*see p103*). But while the Pera Palace is grand, the Londra is homely and eccentric. Caged parrots peer dolefully from their cages on the windowsills in the lounge-bar (*see p151*). Portable coal burners, wind-up gramophones, valve radios and plenty of other ancient junk clutter the corridors. Hemingway stayed here in 1922, sent by the *Toronto Daily Star* to cover the Turkish War of Independence, and the place is still favoured by artists, writers and Istanbul's Press Club, who meet every month on the roof terrace bar. Some of the 54 rooms are a little down-at-heel, but they are clean. The upper floors have been renovated to within an inch of their lives with double glazing and plush carpets.

Bar. Internet (wireless). Room service. TV.

Galata Residence

Felek Sokak 27, off Bankalar Caddesi, Karaköy (0212 292 4841, www.galataresidence.com). **Rates** €85-€120 apartment. **Rooms** 15. **Map** p246 M6 ❸❻

An apartment-hotel with history. The house formerly belonged to the Kamondos, an important Levantine banking family, who gave their name to the sculpted steps that lead up to the residence from Voyvoda Caddesi. The solid brick building later served as a Jewish school. It is now split into 15 comfortably furnished apartments, which each sleep four. Smaller two-bedroom apartments are available in the next building. The decor is homely in an old-fashioned way, with four-poster beds, vintage armchairs and sofas. Each apartment has a kitchen, but there's also a restaurant on the roof and a bare-brick café in the vaulted cellar. It is close enough to walk across the bridge to Eminönü and the bazaar, but just downhill from the Galata Tower and Beyoğlu. The entrance and staircases are both tight, however, so may not suit older travellers or those with reduced mobility.

Café. Internet (high-speed). Restaurant. Room service. TV.

La Casa di Maria Pia

Yeni Çarşı Caddesi 37, Galatasaray (0541 624 5462, www.lacasadimariapia.com). **Rooms** 8 apartments, 2 rooms. **Rates** €70-80 double. **Map** p248 N4 ❸❼

Wandering past the flower-clad entryway to La Casa di Maria Pia, the bohemian townhouse appears to be a very cool – and very private – home. Step inside and the intimate feel continues. Apartments and guestrooms, named after animals (Night Owl, Elephants, Octopus) are decorated with a mix of artworks, multilingual books, DVD libraries and personal treasures. A few also boast lovely balconies or a breakfast terrace. Over the years, affable owner Marco has amassed a range of quirky collections, from second-hand glass to magnets; pieces are sprinkled liberally throughout the building.

Internet (wireless). TV.

THE BEST HISTORICAL CONVERSIONS

A whitewashed waterside mansion
A'jia (*see p125*).

Luxury in a former distillery
Sumahan (*see p125*).

Luxury in a palace, a very big palace
Çirağan Palace (*see p119*).

CONSUME

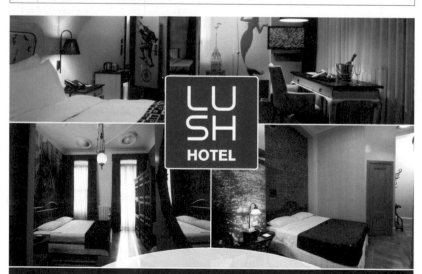

Residence

Sadri Alışık Sokak 19, off Istiklal Caddesi (0212 252 7685, www.hotelresidence.com.tr). **Rates** €59-€96 double. **Rooms** 46. **Map** p249 O3 ㊳

The Residence is a bit difficult to find as it's tucked away on a narrow side street, but it's worth the effort. The rooms, though small and basic, are bright and well equipped and recently refurbished. The location is great, too, right among the bars of Beyoğlu. In short, a simple hotel offering simple Turkish breakfast in a great location.

Bar. Restaurant. Room service. TV.

NIŞANTAŞI, ŞIŞLI & LEVENT

Deluxe

Edition Hotel

Buyukdere Caddesi 136, Levent (0212 317 7700, www.editionhotels.com). Metro Şişli. **Rates** €375-€750 double. **Rooms** 78.

From Ian Schrager, the man who brought the world London's Sanderson and New York's Studio 54, comes this business class boutique hotel. It's so outrageously high-tech and design-led that it gave Istanbul's commercial hotel scene a harsh lesson in

Park Hyatt Maçka Palas. *See p117.*

CONSUME

A glimpse in to the Istanbul of yesteryear

Welcome to Special Class Arena Hotel, located in the old city part of Istanbul called Sultanahmet, which is known as one of the biggest open air museums of the world.

This hotel is an excellent example of a 19th Century Ottoman stone house. The owner was born here. She has restored and decorated it to give guests a glimpse into the Istanbul of yesteryear...

27 rooms, 54 beds, 4 suites. Fully air-conditioned and heated. All rooms come with full bath, direct dial telephone, wireless network system, hair-dryer, safe, cable TV, radio, and minibar. Most rooms have a sea view. **DELIGHT RESTAURANT** offers you the best examples of traditional Turkish cuisine dishes. There is an indoor restaurant that seats 30 and outdoor restaurant with extra 30 seats.

Arena Hotel

Küçükayasofya Mah. Şehit Mehmet Paşa
Yokuşu Üçler Hamam Sk. No: 13 - 15 3440
Sultanahmet İstanbul TÜRKİYE
Tel: +90(212) 458 03 64 - 458 03 65
Fax: +90(212) 458 03 66
İnternet : www.arenahotel.com
E.Mail : arena@arenahotel.com

Suite Istanbul

The city's new breed of apartment-hotels.

Visitor numbers to Istanbul have risen steeply over the last five years, and the local hotel industry has struggled to keep up. As well as a dearth of beds in the busy summer season, the traditional blend of backpacker and businessmen guests – and the constituent hostels and Hiltons that they require – has been snowballed by a surge of culturally aware travellers, who generally demand something more special in the bedroom department. Moreover, these guests routinely seek to stay in the historic Galata and buzzing Beyoğlu areas, two higgledy-piggledy neighbourhoods where the big hotel brands just can't reach. A new breed of suite-only residences and apart-hotels has filled that gap with a great degree of glamour, fun and outright sophistication. In most cases, prices hover between €50 and €100 per night.

Near the Galata Tower, Italian-run **La Casa di Maria Pia** (*see p113*) offers quirkily designed apartments and private rooms with shared kitchen in a pretty townhouse. A more contemporary approach is offered by the four-room apart-hotel **I'Zaz Lofts** (*see p113*), which boasts a high-tech designer suite per floor and a shared terrace and kitchen on the roof.

Another suite-style concept has been pioneered by the **House Apart** (www.thehouseapart.com). Here four smart townhouses (one each in the Tünel, Nişantaşı, Cihangir and Galatasaray neighbourhoods) have been turned into apart-hotels, with vintage fittings and floors, modern kitchens and blanket WiFi. Best of all, all guests receive a breakfast voucher to cash in at any branch of the associated restaurant chain House Café (*see p145*) – and boy are their breakfasts tasty.

New kid on the block **Stories Apart** (www.storiesapart.com) has three larger apart-hotel complexes in even grander fin-de-siècle buildings around Beyoğlu. While the properties aren't quite as hip as the House Apart, each apartment still comes with goosedown pillows, minibar, espresso machine and WiFi.

Highly recommended for weeklong sojourns in the Beyoğlu and Taksim areas are the stunning apartments managed by **Istanbul Sweet Home** (www.istanbulsweethome.com) and the seven properties of **Istanbul! Place** (www.istanbulplace.com).

21st-century service when it opened in 2011. Bedside consoled control curtains and mood lighting. An Espa spa five floors below ground features hot water massage fountains. Treatment rooms have leather floors, lest the staff pass on static electric shocks to guests. The location in Levent is business-friendly, with the HQs of many a Turkish multi-national and one of the city's main highways out front. Tourists can nonetheless hop on the Metro four stops south to Taksim Square.

Bar. Business services. Concierge. Gym. Internet (wireless). No-smoking rooms. Parking (free). Pool. Restaurant. Room service. Spa. TV.

Park Hyatt Maçka Palas

Tesvikiye, Bronz Sokak 4, Şişli (0212 315 1234, www.istanbul.park.hyatt.com). Metro Şişli. **Rates** €255-€455 double. **Rooms** 90.

Leave your preconceptions of international chain hotels in the atrium lobby. This Park Hyatt is one of a new generation of corporate- looking hotels that are responding to the boutique phenomenon. Converted from what used to be the Italian Embassy in Ottoman days, the building is impressive. Each of the 90 rooms has plenty of space, with modern gadgets. Bathrooms have a steam room, which in cheaper rooms is shared with the shower. Some also have a hamam-style area with heated marble floors. Other nice touches include a filtered water sink, alongside a regular one, iPod docks and deep stand-alone baths. Photos from Ara Güler, known as the 'Eye of Istanbul', are hung around the hotel. In the lobby is a wine lounge, but more impressive is the Terrace, with a small pool. The Prime restaurant serves flawless steaks and seafood, grilled in the open kitchen, alongside an impressive, but not cheap, wine list. *Photos p115.*

Bars (3). Business services. Café. Concierge. Disabled-adapted rooms. Gym. Internet (wireless). No-smoking rooms. Parking. Restaurants (2). Room service. Spa. TV.

Sofa Hotel

Teşvikiye Caddesi 123, Nişantaşı (0212 368 1818, www.thesofahotel.com). Metro Nişantaşı. **Rates** €190-€380 double. **Rooms** 82.

The Sofa Hotel offers minimalist chic in the heart of Nişantaşı's upmarket shopping and dining area, and is also within walking distance of the Istanbul Convention and Exhibition Centre. The design-led

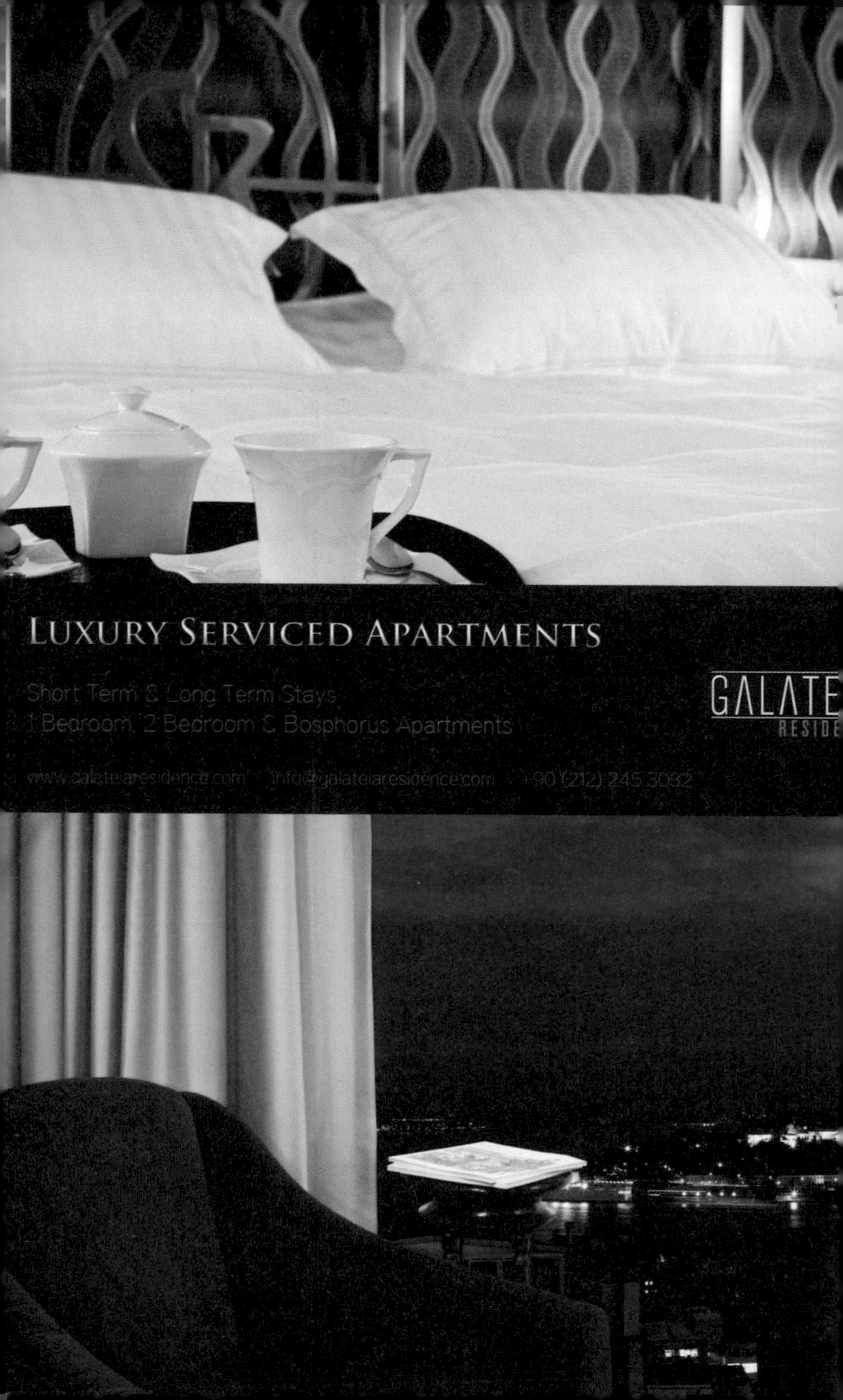
LUXURY SERVICED APARTMENTS
Short Term & Long Term Stays
1 Bedroom, 2 Bedroom & Bosphorus Apartments
www.galatelaresidence.com
info@galatelaresidence.com
+90 (212) 245 3032

Mövenpick.

bedrooms are comfortable, and the well-equipped bathrooms feature rainshowers, natural soaps and fluffy bathrobes. There's a decent spa and fitness room, and the in-house restaurant, Longtable, serves modern New York cuisine in handsome surroundings. Try the signature saffron martini.
Bar. Business services. Café. Concierge. Disabled-adapted rooms. Gym. Internet (wireless). No-smoking rooms. Parking (TL15 day). Restaurant. Room service. Spa. TV.

Expensive

★ Mövenpick

Buyukdere Caddesi, 4. Levent (0212 319 2929, www.movenpick-hotels.com). Metro 4.Levent. **Rates** €90-€290 double. **Rooms** 249.

The pick of the hotels in corporate 4. Levent, the Swiss-owned Mövenpick is a great business option, but its location very near 4. Levent Metro stop means it is handy for the Taksim area too. The 249 rooms are well designed, with plain wood and natural colours, as you would expect from Mövenpick, and rooms on the higher floors have good views. For guests paying the executive rate, there's an airport-style Skyline lounge on the 20th floor. Others have to make do with the chic Baradox lobby bar and lounge. The dimly lit and cavernous wellness centre has a new gym, sauna, jacuzzi and a refreshing swimming pool.
Bars (3). Business services. Concierge. Gym. Internet (wireless). No-smoking rooms. Parking (free). Restaurants (2). Room service. Spa. TV.

BOSPHORUS VILLAGES

Deluxe

★ Çırağan Palace Hotel Kempinski

Çırağan Caddesi 32, Beşiktaş (0212 258 3377, www.kempinski.com). Bus DT1, D2. **Rates** €500-€1,350 double. **Rooms** 313.

The hotel is partly set in a magnificent 19th-century palace on the Bosphorus, built for Sultan Abdülaziz, an ill-fated ruler who killed himself with a pair of scissors. In 1908, the palace became the seat of parliament, but burned down two years later. In 1986, following an ambitious restoration, parts of the original complex were incorporated into this luxurious 313-room extravaganza belonging to the Kempinski chain. Only 11 suites are in the palace itself – including the TL30,000-a-night Sultan's suite (breakfast included) – along with the Tuğra restaurant, which showcases Ottoman cuisine, and other public rooms. All other bedrooms are in the equally luxurious annex. Non-residents can enjoy the hotel's art and culture programme, which includes revolving exhibitions, afternoon tea in the Gazebo Lounge, as well as the belt-tightening 100-dish Sunday brunch, which is a sight to behold. In summer, take advantage of the stunning outdoor infinity pool, which appears to flow into the Bosphorus.
Bars (2). Business centre. Concierge. Disabled-adapted room. Gym. Internet (wireless). No-smoking rooms. Parking (free). Pools (1 indoor, 1 outdoor). Restaurants (2). Room service. Spa. TV.

France
Perfect places to stay, eat & explore
Morocco
Perfect places to stay, eat & explore
France
Britain
Argentina
& Uruguay
Perfect places to stay, eat & explore

PERFECT
PLACES TO
STAY, EAT &
EXPLORE

Hotel Hamams

Get clean, feel beautiful.

Turkey is famous for its hamams, but for those who prefer their treatments more spa-like and less spartan, many Istanbul hotels now have their own, Western-style spas – and most include Turkish baths. Spa facilities aren't restricted to hotel guests, and a few hours' pampering can be a perfect pick-you-up. All the spas recommended below include an indoor pool, sauna, Turkish bath and steam room.

If you can't afford a room at the exclusive **Les Ottomans Hotel** (*see p121*), check into the basement Caudalie Vinothérapie spa instead. Facilities include a tiled hot tub and indoor pool with natural light filtered through the glass bottom of the above-ground pool. For TL130 a day, visitors can use the pools, exercise equipment, sauna (with flatscreen TV), steam room, Turkish bath and 'salt inhalation therapy' room. There's even a meditation room, complete with a cascade of lavender-infused water. Best of all, indulge in one of the treatments using grape-based Caudalie products.

Another luxury hotel that's big on spa treatments is the **Çirağan Palace Kempinski** (*see p119*). In summer, you can take full advantage of your environment by booking a poolside massage in a private cabana with views of the Bosphorus. Otherwise, the treatments are given in the palace section that dates back to 1887. A vast range of treatments using Decléor products is available. The Traditional Çirağan Body Scrub (€120) is pure bliss.

An Asian-inspired ambience and expert staff are the hallmarks of the spa at the **Ritz-Carlton** (Asker Ocaği Caddesi, www.ritz-carlton.com). One of the city's most exclusive spas, its menu features a 'Traditional Turkish Hamam' treatment, including massage (€100).

The treatments at the **Ceylan InterContinental** (*see p103*) begin with a warm steam bath, followed by a full body scrub and a foam massage (TL160).

The **Four Seasons Bosphorus** (*see p121*) boasts Istanbul's largest indoor swimming pool plus mixed and single-sex relaxing and reclining areas. Less expensive massages are on offer, but we love the sound of the Atik Pasha surrender four-handed massage (€250).

For an ultra-modern experience, the **Edition** (*see p115*) has an ESPA den secreted five storeys below the earth. Leather floors and horsehair-clad walls ensure any disturbing static electricity is left at the basement lift doors.

★ Four Seasons Bosphorus

Çırağan Caddesi 28, Beşiktaş (0212 381 4000, www.fourseasons.com/bosphorus). Bus DT1, D2.
Rates €480-€610 double. **Rooms** 170.

The second Four Seasons property in Istanbul is a very different yet equally sumptuous proposition from the Sultanahmet hotel. This one, near Kempinski's Çırağan Palace, is a 19th-century palace on the Bosphorus. Its classic design will reassure those used to the Four Seasons brand, although there are Ottoman touches throughout including Turkish throws and lashings of marble. Rooms and suites all have a TV, DVD and music dock, plus l'Occitane products and a marble bath. The waterside grounds are delightful for taking a stroll before dinner to watch the ships roll past. The spa is truly amazing. Not content with hosting Istanbul's biggest swimming pool, it also boasts a variety of hamams plus luxurious male and female retiring rooms. *Photo p123.*

Bars (2). Business centre. Concierge. Disabled-adapted room. Gym. Internet (wireless). No-smoking rooms. Parking (free). Pools (1 indoor, 1 outdoor). Restaurants (2). Room service. Spa. TV.

Hotel les Ottomans

Muallim Naci Caddesi 168, Kuruçeşme (0212 287 1024, www.lesottomans.com).
Rates €1,200-€5,400 suite. **Rooms** 12.

Opened in spring 2006, this all-suite hotel is designed to lure celebrities, heads of state and millionaires craving something more intimate than the Çirağan Palace. In an impeccably restored white wooden *yalı* (mansion), with spectacular views of the Bosphorus Straits, the style is Oriental opulence – to excess, some might say. Think brocade drapes, Arabic-script inscriptions and giant chandeliers. With just 12 suites, the emphasis is on exclusivity. Butler, yacht and limousine service are all part of the package. There's an intimate Ottoman restaurant, Has Oda, and a waterside restaurant, Su Yani, both of which share the same modern Turkish menu. Les Ottomans also has the fabulously luxurious Caudalie Vinothérapie spa (*see above* **Hotel Hamams**).

Bar. Business services. Concierge. Gym. Internet (wireless). No-smoking rooms. Parking (free). Pool (indoor). Restaurant. Room service. Spa. TV.

Swissôtel the Bosphorus

Bayıldım Caddesi 2, Maçka, Beşiktaş (0212 326 1100, www.swissotel.com/istanbul). **Rates** €150-€280 double; €405-€450 suites. **Rooms** 497. **Map** p247 R1 ㊴

This award-winning hotel is near faultless, right down to its glorious Bosphorus backdrop and legion of kindly staff. Amenities are what mark it out from other luxury options nearby, such as the Çırağan Palace (*see p119*) and Four Seasons Bosphorus (*see p121*). The Swissôtel boasts a mammoth 11 bars and restaurants including sumptuous Gaya and traditional Japanese restaurant Miyako (*see p140*), as well as rooftop tennis courts, the city's biggest boardroom and the Amrita spa – officially one of Turkey's best. Breakfast on the terrace – or the 140-dish brunch (*see p139*) if you have a spare three hours – is sublime. New to Istanbul is Swissôtel's Living concept, a newly renovated block of 63 ultra-luxurious suites. Ranging from studios to three-bedroom apartments designed for long stays and wow-factor weekends, each commands Bosphorus views, has a state-of-the-art kitchen and a design straight out of *Wallpaper** magazine. Guests in the Living block have access to all the hotel's facilities, but share an additional rooftop pool, concierge and high-security reception area.

Bars (4). Business services. Concierge. Gym. Internet (wireless). No-smoking rooms. Parking (free). Pools (1 indoor, 1 outdoor). Restaurants (7). Room service. Spa. TV.

Expensive

Bebek Hotel

Cevdet Paşa Caddesi 34, Bebek (0212 358 2000, www.bebekhotel.com.tr). **Rates** €240-€330 double. **Rooms** 21.

Far from the centre and the sights, this boutique hotel is nonetheless a fine introduction to Istanbul. Its views pan over the Bosphorus and its location in the chic but chilled suburb Bebeb is enviable. From the outside, the four-storey building is nothing special, but inside the 21 suites are all gleaming dark wood, brown leather, pink marble and rattan furniture. The real wow-factor here is the view, and nine of the rooms have balconies over the Bosphorus. Is it worth paying extra for one? We'd have to say yes. Non-guests can enjoy the same view from the waterfront bar downstairs. Beware of Bebek in the summer, when the traffic into town can be agonisingly slow.

Bars (2). Café. Concierge. Internet (wireless). Parking (free). Restaurant. Room service. TV.

W Istanbul

Suleyman Seba Caddesi 22, Akaretler, Beşiktaş (0212 381 2121, www.wistanbul.com.tr). **Rates** €180-€330 double. **Rooms** 136.

Super-stylish W continues its mission to restyle the global hotel industry with this Beşiktaş property. The hotel is in a newly redeveloped area whose terraced buildings once housed officers from the nearby Dolmabahçe Palace. The surrounding Akaretler townhouses have now become clothing stores, art

Four Seasons Bosphorus. *See p121.*

galleries and restaurants so chic it hurts. The W takes boutique to another level with Bose stereos, blanket WiFi, iPod docks, rainforest showers and 350-thread-count linen. The more you pay, the cooler the room. Marvellous rooms come with their own outdoor cabana; Wow suites come with jacuzzis, 3m-high ceilings and kitchens. There is a champagne bar by the lobby, but most of the action happens upstairs in the Minyon restaurants or in the resolutely chilled W Lounge bar. There is also a day spa and café.
Bars (2). Business centre. Concierge. Gym. Internet (wireless). No-smoking rooms. Parking (free). Restaurants (2). Room service. Spa. TV.

THE ASIAN SHORE

Deluxe

★ A'jia

Ahmet Rasim Paşa Yalısı, Çubuklu Caddesi 27, Kanlıca (0216 413 9300, www.ajiahotel.com). **Rates** €260-€460 double. **Rooms** 16.
The first boutique hotel on the Asian shore, A'jia opened in 2004 to great acclaim. The white-washed *yalı* (mansion) was built in 1876 and has at various times been an army barracks, housed Atatürk's advisor Ahmet Rasim Pasha and, later, a primary school. It's now a stunning residence, lapped by the Bosphorus. The 16 sleek rooms contrast successfully with the traditional exterior. Breakfast and dinner can be taken on a large deck overlooking the Bosphorus. A'jia has its own boat, too, which can be used to cross to Emigan opposite, or the fort at Rumeli Hisarı.
Bar. Concierge. Disabled-adapted rooms. Internet (wireless). No-smoking rooms. Parking (free). Restaurant. Room service. TV.
► *The hotel is well placed for the Müzedechanga restaurant (see p143) in the Sakip Sabancı museum directly opposite on the European shore. The free boat will drop guests off and pick them up.*

★ Sumahan

Kuleli Caddesi 51, Çengelköy (0216 422 8000, www.sumahan.com). **Rates** €175-€380 double.
This converted *rakı* distillery, dating from 1875, enjoys a fabulous waterfront setting in Çengelköy, a sleepy fishing village. The architect owners have created polished contemporary interiors featuring grey marble, exposed stonework, and picture windows with extraordinary views of mosques and minarets shimmering beyond the Bosphorus Bridge. Many rooms come with mini-hamams, and beds face the waterfront. Attached restaurant Waterfront Terrace serves fine Turkish fare, although a step up is Kordon Balik next door, one of the city's finest seafood establishments. A private launch zips passengers across the Bosphorus several times daily.
Bar. Business services. Café. Concierge. Disabled-adapted rooms. Gym. Internet (wireless). No-smoking rooms. Parking (free). Restaurant. Room service. Spa. TV.

Hostel

★ Hush

Caferağa Mahallesi Miralay Nazım Sokak 20, Kadıköy (0216 330 9188, www.hushhostel istanbul.com). **Rates** €13 dorm; €35 double. **Map** p251 W8 ⓸⓪
Hush is the first hostel on the Asian shore, and a fine one at that. It's perfectly located for a night out along the lively Kadife Sokak, an area lined with bars and restaurants. As its name suggests, the hostel is on a quiet side street, in a four-storey wooden building dating from the 1920s. Accommodation is in four double rooms, two mixed dorms and one female-only dorm. There's also a cosy lounge and a leafy garden and bar with reasonable prices. It's also handy for the Sabiha Gökçen Airport. The amiable owners will advise you where to go, and may even join you.

W Istanbul. *See p123.*

CONSUME

Restaurants

Turkish delights.

For more than six centuries, Istanbul – or Constantinople – was the capital of the sprawling Ottoman Empire. The city's history is loaded with Middle Eastern, Mediterranean and Balkan influences, and so is its food, ultimately resulting in a cuisine that's both regionally varied and sophisticated. Traditional dishes incorporate signature ingredients from across the former empire, including herbs (dill, parsley, mint), spices (pepper, garlic, cumin, red pepper flakes), cheeses (salty and white), yoghurt, aubergines, tomatoes, lamb, cured meats and fish. As well as kebabs and *köfte* meatballs, Turkish favourites include *mantı* (stuffed pasta similar to ravioli), *pide* (a local version of pizza) and pistachio-laden baklava.

Today, Istanbullus are discovering a new kind of fusion cuisine – one that mixes fresh ingredients from the Bosphorus, spices from the bazaars and techniques learned in the restaurants of France, the US and the UK. Fine-dining establishments such as **Mikla** (*see p135*) and **Mimolett** (*see p138*) may even be in line for Turkey's first Michelin star.

THE LOCAL SCENE

The quintessential Istanbul eating experience remains the *meyhane* (taverna). These places are cheap and frequently boisterous. The meze (shared small dishes) are washed down with plenty of *rakı* (anise-flavoured spirit).

Filling the table with myriad meze to share keeps everyone happy, including vegetarians. *Meyhanes* are found around the city, but there's a heavy concentration around **Nevizade Sokak** (*see p139*) and in the Asmalı Mescit neighbourhood, both in Beyoğlu. Often the meze are wheeled or carried out to your table – a selection is then chosen based on visual appeal, useful when the translated menu includes dishes such as 'sensitive meatballs'. A budget option for Turkish food is canteen-style *lokantas*, where workers eat *hazır yemek* (ready-made dishes) served from bains-marie.

Fish is another local speciality. Visitors are often directed to **Kumkapı** (*see p131*), which has the greatest concentration of seafood restaurants and is close to the hotel district of Sultanahmet. But there are plenty of other enticing options away from the hordes. A city staple is **Doğa Balık** (*see p136*) in Cihangir, or **Balıkçı Sabahattin** (*see right*) in Sultanahmet.

Taste a real kebab at a *kebapçı* or *ocakbaşı*. There are more varieties than you can shake a skewer at (*see p142* **Kebab Cuisine**).

> ❶ Blue numbers given in this chapter correspond to the location of each restaurant as marked on the street maps. *See pp242-251.*

Practicalities

Few restaurants have a dress code, but Istanbullus like to look fabulous when they go out, especially at high-end places. Tipping is expected; ten per cent is sufficient. Service charges are rarely included except at high-end places, where tips are expected anyway. Reservations are a must on Friday and Saturday, and advisable during the week at the most popular restaurants.

Alcohol is expensive in Turkey. *Rakı* is usually served with fish dishes in *meyhanes*, although the ever-improving Turkish wine (*see p150* **Grape Expectations**) is increasingly popular, and can cost between TL25 and TL150 in restaurants.

ABOUT THE LISTINGS

Throughout the chapter, we've listed the price range of starters – these are the meze dishes, which can either serve as an appetiser or a selection can be devoured as the meal itself. The price range of main courses is also provided to offer a rough indication of meal cost. Restaurants often close when the last patron leaves. If paying by credit card, check the machine is working before ordering.

If a restaurant is on a side street (*sokak*), we have also used the name of the adjacent main street where possible.

SULTANAHMET

Big on sights it may be, but Sultanahmet is woefully under-served by decent restaurants. It would be unfair say that all the eateries are tourist traps, but it wouldn't be far off the mark. Below are a few exceptions.

Balıkçı Sabahattin

Seyit Hasan Kuyu Sokak 1, off Cankurtaran Caddesi (0212 458 1824, http://balikci sabahattin.com). Tram Sultanahmet. **Open** 11am-12.30am daily. **Starters** from TL7. **Main courses** TL15-TL45. **Map** p243 N11 ❶ **Seafood**

Many visitors staying around Sultanahmet head to Kumkapı for fish, unaware that there's a far better option on their doorstep. It benefits from a gorgeous setting: a street of picturesque old wooden houses, periodically rattled to their foundations by the commuter trains passing in and out of Sirkeci. There's a basic menu, but far better to await the bow-tied waiters: they'll present you with a tray of various meze and, later, a huge iced platter of seasonal fish and seafood from which to choose. Entertainment comes in the form of skittering cats skilled at doleful looks and pleading meows. Reservations essential.

Dubb Indian Restaurant

Incili Çavuş Sokak 10, off Divanyolu Caddesi (0212 513 7308, www.dubbindian.com). Tram Sultanahmet. **Open** noon-midnight daily. **Starters** TL4.50-TL15. **Main courses** TL13.50-TL33. **Map** p243 N10 ❷ **Indian**

Istanbul is not exactly brimming with Indian restaurants – this little gem in the heart of Sultanahmet may be the closest you'll get to eating authentic dishes from the subcontinent. There are a wide variety of curries, thalis and dishes from the tandoor, plus Indian bevvies such as salty or sweet lassi. All the bread is baked in-house daily. There's a set menu at TL38 (veggie) or TL42. The roof terrace – up seemingly endless flights of stairs – is worth the climb.

The Turkish Breakfast Club

Begin the day with a feast.

Traditional Turkish breakfasts are a table-groaning affair. Locals like to ease into the day with eggs, stuffed puffs of *poğaça* bread, olives, tiny, flavoursome cucumbers and piles of cherry tomatoes. Although Istanbullus usually have more time to enjoy a spread like this at weekends, all of our favourite picks serve breakfast any day of the week. Along with the staples listed above, **Van Kahvaltı Evi** (Defterdar Yokuşu 52/A, Cihangir, 0212 293 6437) dishes up herby village cheeses from Turkey's south-east. At **Kale Cafe** (Yahya Kemal Caddesi 16, Rumelihisarı, 0212 265 0097, www.kalecafe.com), steaming slices of *gözleme* (thin pancakes stuffed with spinach, potatoes or cheese) compete for attention with bowls of honeycomb, *kaymak* (Turkish clotted cream) and Bosphorus views. And just off Istiklal Caddesi, diner-style **Lades** (Sadri Alışık Sokak 14/A, 0212 251 3203) is a shrine to all variations on eggy *menemen* – from the classic version, scrambled with tomatoes and sweet green peppers, to dishes topped with salty white cheese or spiked with *sucuk* sausage.

★ Mozaik

Incili Çavuş Sokak 1, off Divanyolu Caddesi (0212 512 4177, www.mozaikrestaurant.com). Tram Sultanahmet. **Open** 9am-midnight daily. **Starters** TL7-TL18. **Main courses** TL12-TL29. **Map** p243 N10 ❸ **Turkish**

A cut above many of Sultanahmet's more slapdash establishments. When it is too chilly to sit outside, the interior, with wooden floors carpeted with old kilims, copper platters and creaking stairs between the restaurant's three floors, offer romantic potential for dinner à deux. The international menu covers a lot of ground – everything from chicken mandarin to T-bone steak – but the special is *abant kebap*, a spectacular lamb and aubergine West Anatolian dish.

Pudding Shop

Divanyolu Caddesi 6 (0212 522 2970, www.puddingshop.com). Tram Sultanahmet. **Open** 7am-11pm daily. **Starters** TL8. **Main courses** TL8-TL17. **Map** p243 N10 ❹ **Turkish**

A landmark in hippie history. In the pre-*Lonely Planet* days of the late 1960s and early 1970s, the Pudding Shop (founded 1957) was a bottleneck for all the overland traffic passing through on its tie-dyed, spliff-addled way east to Kathmandu. In addition to the food, the place served up travel information, courtesy of the two brothers who owned it, a busy bulletin board, and the like-minded company. It even crops up in the movie *Midnight Express*. Smartened up for the 21st-century tourist – plate-glass windows, gleaming display cabinets and slick staff – the restaurant still doles out basic canteen-style fare, no better or worse than half a dozen similar restaurants along this strip.

Seasons Restaurant

Four Seasons Hotel, Tevfikhane Sokak 1 (0212 402 3000, www.fourseasons.com). Tram Sultahahmet. **Open** noon-2.30pm, 7-11pm daily. **Starters** TL18-TL26. **Main courses** TL29-TL50. **Map** p243 N10 ❺ **Modern European**

A high-end Sultanahmet establishment, the Seasons Restaurant holds its own alongside the flair of newer restaurants such as Ulus 29 and Mimolett. Set in a glass enclosure in the courtyard gardens of the Four Seasons Hotel, the restaurant has an ambience of easy elegance. Its mixed menu changes often, frequently concentrating on Turkish regional specialities. Summertime sees barbeques al fresco; Sunday brunch (*see p139*) is outstanding. Prices and service match the lavish surroundings.

► *The Four Seasons on the Bosphorus (see p121) has a good Mediterranean restaurant, Aqua, in a lovely waterside dining room.*

THE BAZAAR QUARTER

Darüzziyafe

Şifahane Sokak 6, Süleymaniye (0212 511 8414, www.daruzziyafe.com.tr). Tram Beyazıt or Laleli. **Open** noon-11pm daily. **Starters** TL7-TL19. **Main courses** TL27. **Map** p242 J8 ❻ **Turkish**

The former soup kitchens of the Süleymaniye Mosque complex now turn out more varied fare. Although the menu runs to several pages, the food is still canteen cooking – great for lunch (and a favourite with tour buses) but too prosaic for dinner. The setting, a large courtyard filled with rose bushes and trees, is potentially lovely but rendered institutional by cheap furniture and neglect. The restaurant is located to the north of the mosque, separate from the row of small eateries that lines its west side. No alcohol.

★ Şar Lokantası

Yeniceriler Caddesi 47, Beyazıt (0212 458 9219). Tram Beyazıt. **Open** 6am-11.30pm daily. **Starters** TL3-TL5. **Main courses** TL6-TL15. **Map** p242 K10 ❼ **Turkish**

Among tourist restaurants south of the Golden Horn, this canteen stands as an island of Turkish food for Turkish people. The pick-and-point system also serves as a good introduction to the dishes. Pick your starter, main, salad, drink and dessert, pay and head upstairs. Şar has been here since 1957 and is known for its hearty food, such as the moussaka-like *gizli kebap* or the *pide çeşitleri*, a Turkish pizza. It's one of the cheaper options in the area. No alcohol.

EMINÖNÜ & THE GOLDEN HORN

Two blocks south of Sirkeci Station, narrow **Ibni Kemal Caddesi** is a street full of cheap eateries serving the local working population. The presence of neighbouring Hoca Paşa Mosque – plus the steep cost of obtaining an

Seasons Restaurant

okçok thai

Restaurant of The Year

Thai
SELECT
THAI CUISINE
Tepebaşı Meşrutiyet Cad. 51 Beyoğlu, Istanbul
T. +90 212 292 6496 www.cokcok.com.tr

alcohol licence – means no booze is served, but a meal along here tends to cost less than TL15 per person. The underslung section of the **Galata Bridge** is also crammed with budget fish restaurants, with menus in English and beer by the flagon. Much better, however, are the floating fish stalls on the west side of the bridge. Order a *balık ekmek* (mackerel sandwich) and watch the fishermen.

Hamdi Et Lokantası

Kalçın Sokak 17, off Tahmis Caddesi (0212 528 0390, www.hamdi.com.tr). Tram Eminönü. **Open** 11am-midnight daily. **Starters** TL7-TL10. **Main courses** TL12-TL23. **Map** p243 L7 ❽ **Turkish**

Right on Eminönü Square, Hamdi is a favourite among Istanbul natives, particularly business lunchers and carniverous fans of south-eastern Turkish food. Hamdi serves meat *ala turka* at its very best, grilled to succulent perfection on the *mangal*. The restaurant occupies four floors, but the top one is the most memorable. In an enclosed glass terrace, it offers sweeping views of the Golden Horn and Beyoğlu. It's particularly lovely in the summer, when the windows are opened. Otherwise, opt for the curious Oriental Saloon on the first floor, kitted out with cuckoo clocks and startled nymphs.

Orient Express Restaurant

Sirkeci Station, Istasyon Caddesi 2 (0212 522 2280, www.orientexpressrestaurant.net). Tram Sirkeci. **Open** 11.30am-midnight daily. **Starters** TL6-TL12. **Main courses** TL15-TL25. **Map** p243 N8 ❾ **Turkish**

An essential stop for fans of the Orient Express and Agatha Christie, this time warp is bang in the centre of Sirkeci Station, the final stop of the world's most famous train. In warmer weather, tables are set outside on the station platform. The only obvious change in the dining room since the restaurant's launch in 1890 is the incongruous concrete fishpond in the centre, which jars with the Oriental backdrop. The walls are adorned with black and white stills from the 1974 movie *Murder on the Orient Express*. Food is standard Turkish fare, reasonably priced. It's a shame the restaurant is usually empty.

► *For more on the Orient Express, see p58.*

Pandeli

Mısır Çarşısı 1, Eminönü Square (0212 527 3909, www.pandeli.com.tr). Tram Eminönü. **Open** 11.30am-7.30pm daily. **Starters** TL6-TL12. **Main courses** TL15-TL25. **Map** p243 L8 ❿ **Turkish**

Not a bad place for lunch if you're shopping in the Egyptian Bazaar. Occupying a wonderful set of domed rooms above the bazaar entrance, Pandeli is very much the essence of genteel old Stamboul. Decorated throughout in turquoise and white Iznik tiling, it's worth a visit for the lovely interior alone. The food tends to be rich and pricey – and unlike most Turkish eateries, where many menu items are shared, each diner is encouraged to order their own loaded plate. Ask for a table in the front room with views of the Golden Horn. Note the early closing time.

Asitane. *See p133.*

KUMKAPI

Situated inside the city walls on the Sea of Marmara coast, this former fishing port is now an inner-city neighbourhood of cobbled lanes lined with seafood restaurants, where persistent hawkers attempt to waylay passers-by. A shortish taxi ride from Sultanahmet, Kumkapı is not a bad choice for fresh fish, although the popularity of restaurants along **Çapari Sokak** has long been eclipsed by the *meyhanes* at Nevizade and fancy fish places up the Bosphorus.

In total, there are around 50 restaurants in Kumkapı. There are a few that locals rate highly, including **Akvaryum Fish Restaurant**, which has live *fasıl* music,

THE BEST MODERN RESTAURANTS

For inventive Turkish/ Scandinavian fusion
Mikla (*see p135*).

Turkey's best chance for a Michelin star
Mimolett (*see p138*).

Where Mediterranean and Ottoman cuisines meet
Topaz (*see p140*).

as does **Çapari**, one of the district's oldest establishments. **Kartallar Balıkçı** is famous for its *balık çorbası* (fish chowder) and *buğulama* (steamed fish casserole) – and has a large celebrity quotient among its clientele. In business since 1938, **Kör Agop** is known for its top quality fish and *fasıl.*

As at the Grand Bazaar, prices are conspicuously absent from menus, so make sure to agree on the bill in advance. Most places offer fixed meal deals, kicking off with meze followed by fish of the day and dessert. Expect to pay around TL50 per person with alcohol (*rakı*, local wine or beer).

Fasıl musicians roam between the restaurants serenading outdoor diners, while an odd assortment of street vendors flog anything from fresh almonds to Cuban cigars.

Akvaryum Fish Restaurant

Çapariz Sokak 39 (0212 517 3428, www. akvaryumrestaurant.com). Kumkapı Station. **Open** noon-2am daily. **Map** p242 K11 ⓫ **Seafood**

Çapari

Çapari Sokak 22 (0212 517 7530, www. capari.net). Kumkapı Station. **Open** 10am-2am daily. **Map** p242 K11 ⓬ **Seafood**

Menu & Glossary

Your key to the cuisine.

USEFUL PHRASES
Can I see a menu? **Menüye bakabilir miyim?**
Do you have a table for (number) people? **(Number) kişilik masanız var mı?**
I want to book a table for (time) o'clock. **Saat (time) için bir masa ayırmak istiyorum.**
I'll have (name of food). **Ben (name of food) istiyorum.**
I'm a vegetarian. **Et yemiyorum.**
Can I have the bill, please? **Hesap, lütfen.**

BASICS
breakfast **kahvaltı**
lunch **öğle yemeği**
dinner **akşam yemeği**
dessert **tatlı**
menu **menü**
service charge **servis**
cup **fincan**
glass **bardak**
fork **çatal**
knife **biçak**
spoon **kaşık**
napkin **peçete**
plate **tabak**
baked **fırında pişmiş**
boiled **kaynami**
fried **kizarmi**
grilled **ızgara**
roast **kavrulmu**
bread **ekmek**
thin flat bread **pide** or **lava**
brown bread **kepekli ekmek**
pasta **makarna**
rice **pilav**
soup **çorba**
cheese **peynir**
hardboiled/softboiled egg **katı yumurta/ rafadan yumurta**
garlic **sarımsak**
salt **tuz**
red/black/hot pepper **pul/kara/acı biber**

MEAT
beef **dana**
chicken **tavuk**
lamb **kuzu**

FISH
fish **balık**
anchovy **hamsi**
bluefish **lüfer**
crab **yengeç**
lobster **istakoz**
mackerel **uskumra**
monkfish **fener**
sardines **sardalya**
sea bass **levrek**
sea bream **sarıgöz/sinarit**
shrimp **karides**
sole **dil**
swordfish **kılıç**
tuna **torik**

VEGETABLES
aubergine **patlıcan**
carrots **havuç**
cucumber **salatalık**
lentils **mercimek**
lettuce **marul**
onions **soğan**
peas **bezelye**
peppers **biber**
potatoes **patates**
spinach **ıspanak**
tomatoes **domates**
courgette **kabak**

Kartallar Valentino Restaurant
Çapari Sokak 32 (0212 517 2254, www.valentinokartallar.com). Kumkapı Station. **Open** 10am-midnight daily. **Map** p242 K11 ⓭ **Seafood**

Kör Agop
Ördekli Bakkal Sokak 7 (0212 517 2334). Kumkapı Station. **Open** noon-2am daily. **Map** p242 K11 ⓮ **Seafood**

THE WESTERN DISTRICTS

These relatively poor, religiously conservative parts of town draw few visitors, and hence have few restaurants. Asitane is close to the Byzantine church of **St Saviour in Chora** (*see p63*).

★ Asitane
Kariye Hotel, Kariye Camii Sokak 6, Edirnekapı (0212 635 7997, www.asitanerestaurant.com). Bus 28, 77MT, 87. **Open** 11.30am-11pm daily. **Starters** TL12-TL20. **Main courses** TL28-TL40. **Map** p244 D4 ⓯ **Turkish**

It may be a trek to Edirnekapı, but it's worth it for this one-of-a-kind restaurant, which specialises in authentic Ottoman food. Authentic means just that: the menu includes the same dishes that were served at the circumcision feasts of Sultan Süleyman's

FRUIT & NUTS
fruit **meyve**
apples **elma**
banana **muz**
cherries **kiraz**
grapes **üzüm**
hazelnuts **fındık**
honeydew melon **kavun**
lemon **limon**
peanuts **fıstık**
pistachio nuts **şam fıstığı**
oranges **portakal**
walnuts **ceviz**
watermelon **karpuz**

MEZE
börek flaky savoury pastry with parsley and/or white cheese, minced meat, spinach or other vegetables.
çerkez tavuğu shredded chicken served cold in a walnut cream sauce.
çoban salata 'shepherd's salad', composed of tomatoes, cucumbers, hot peppers and onions with lemon and olive oil.
dolma cabbage, grape leaves, pepper or squash, served cold and stuffed with rice, pine nuts, currants and spices. When served hot, *dolma* are usually also stuffed with minced meat.
imambayıldı aubergines cooked with onion, tomato and olive oil, served cold.
karnıyarık baked aubergines stuffed with minced meat, onion, tomato and spices
kısır Turkish-style tabouleh salad with parsley, bulgar, lemon, tomato, onion, olive oil, pomegranate and mint
lahmacun spiced minced meat on a thin crust pizza-like bread called *pide*
mücver deep-fried patties made with grated courgette in a batter of egg and flour
zeytinyağli cold dishes with olive oil

MAINS
güveç casserole cooked in a clay pot
karides güveç shrimps cooked with onions in a peppery tomato sauce
köfte meatballs
pirzola lamb chops

DRINKS
apple juice **elma suyu**
beer **bira**
cherry juice **vişne suyu**
coffee **kahve**
Turkish coffee **Türk kahvesi**; without sugar **sade**; a little sugar **az şekerli**; medium sweet **orta şekerli**; sweet **şekerli**
milk **süt**
orange juice **taze portakal suyu**
peach juice **şeftali suyu**
red wine **kırmızı şarap**
tea **çay**
water **su**
white wine **beyaz şarap**

sons, Beyazıd and Cihangir, in 1539. Expect lots of sweet and sour fruit and meat combos: *kavun dolması* is melon stuffed with mincemeat, rice, almonds, currants and pistachios; *nirbaç* is a stew made with diced lamb, meatballs and carrots, spiced with coriander, ginger, cinnamon, pomegranate and crushed walnuts. The leafy garden is lovely in summer. *Photo p131.*

CONSUME

BEYOĞLU

Beyoğlu has the biggest and best selection of restaurants. Its narrow backstreets are loaded with traditional restaurants and *meyhanes*, with the heaviest concentration around Asmalı Mescit, **Çiçek Pasajı** and **Nevizade Sokak** (*see p139*). The main drag, Istiklal Caddesi, is lined with *lokantas*, serving wholesome fast food, Turkish style. In Beyoğlu, too, you'll find Istanbul's most cutting-edge restaurants, often with superb rooftop views.

360

Mısır Apartmani, 8th Floor, Istiklal Caddesi 311 (0212 251 1042, www.360istanbul.com). **Open** noon-4pm Mon-Thur; 6pm-2.30am Fri; 6pm-4am Sat; 6pm-2.30am Sun. **Starters** TL15-TL26. **Main courses** TL29-TL65. **Map** p248 N3 ⑯ **International**

On the roof of the historic Mısır apartment block, 360 has magnificent 360-degree views of the city. The spacious dining area is a high-tech fusion of steel and glass, with brick walls. The international menu ranges from madras chicken to sushi samba rolls. Reservations are essential on Fridays and Saturdays, with two sittings per night. It turns into a fairly boisterous club and cocktail bar after midnight, when the venue, and the view, is at its best.

▶ *In 2011, 360 opened Fish, an outpost on Suada (see p204), as well as 360 East in the Asian suburb of Moda. For more bars and restaurants with a view, see p154* **Up on the Roofs**.

Canim Ciğerim

Istiklal Caddesi 162 (0212 243 1005, www.asmalicanimcigerim.com). **Open** noon-midnight daily. **Main courses** TL18. **No credit cards. Map** p248 M4 ⑰ **Turkish**

There are only three choices at this popular neighbourhood restaurant: beef, chicken or lamb. Once the meat of choice is ordered, a plate of mint, a plate of parsley, some spicy tomato sauce, a pile of flat bread and grilled veg will be plonked down, followed by around nine skewers of meat. It isn't licensed. The upstairs dining area has ornate Ottoman flourishes.

★ Govinda

Ipek Sokak 15/1, Taksim (0212 252 4015, http://govindaistanbul.com). **Open** 10am-10pm daily. **Starters** TL1-TL3. **Main courses** TL6-TL12. **No credit cards. Map** p249 O3 ⑱ **Indian/Vegetarian**

Tucked away in a backstreet behind Taksim Square, this budget veggie eaterie dishes up tasty Indian delights. Vegan and vegetarian mixed plates both include falafel, rice and spicy vegetables, and the veggie burger (TL6) is a popular bargain. No alcohol is served, although top-notch sweet and savoury lassis are available.

Hacı Abdullah

Atfi Yılmaz Caddesi 9/A, off Istiklal Caddesi (0212 293 8561, www.haciabdullah.com.tr). **Open** 11am-10.30pm daily. **Starters** TL9. **Main courses** TL16-TL33. **Map** p248 N3 ⑲ **Turkish**

One of the oldest restaurants in Istanbul, Hacı Abdullah is deservedly famous for traditional Ottoman fare. Three old-school dining rooms are brightened by a few contemporary flourishes. Opt for the pale pink room at the rear, complete with skylight and chandelier. The restaurant is renowned for its pickles, stored in colourful jars, and bizarrely described in the English menu as 'the symbols of pooped politicians'. An array of pre-cooked dishes is on display in the front room. No alcohol is served.

Kitchenette

Marmara Hotel, Tak-ı Zafer Caddesi 3, Taksim Square (0212 292 6862, www.kitchenette.com.tr). **Open** 8am-1pm daily. **Starters** TL8-TL25. **Main courses** TL16-TL33. **Map** p249 P2 ⑳ **French/Modern European**

From the can-do-no-wrong Istanbul Doors Group, which also owns Anjelique (*see p157*) and Vogue (*see p144*), this venture is brasserie, bakery, bar and breakfast joint. The space is stunning, with chrome booths and long wooden tables making for a large, but atmospheric, interior. The in-house bakery provides the bread for the large breakfasts. There is also a wide selection of pastas, meat dishes and salads. It's not cheap, but for a long brunch in stylish surroundings it's worth it.

Other locations throughout the city.

Leb-i Derya Richmond

6th Floor, Richmond Hotel, Istiklal Caddesi 227 (0212 243 4375). **Open** 11am-2am Mon-Thur; 11am-3am Fri; 10am-3am Sat; 10am-2am Sun. **Starters** TL14-TL28. **Main courses** TL28-TL40. **Map** p248 M4 ㉑ **Modern European**

Located on the sixth floor of the Richmond Hotel on Istiklal Caddesi, Leb-i Derya has probably the best views of any restaurant in the city, even by Istanbul standards. The tables are placed by vast windows: very romantic, especially if the meal is timed with the setting sun. Using the best ingredients, the dishes are simple but perfectly rendered. Highlights include sea bass in a parmesan crust, beef cheek ragu and scallop ravioli. And while the menu changes with the seasons, one constant is the extraordinary Forty-Spice Steak. The restaurant stops serving lunch in July and August due to the greenhouse effect of its glass panelling. Reservation recommended.

► *Leb-i Derya's sister restaurant in Kumbaracı (Kumbaracı Iş Hanı 57/6, Tünel) is equally enchanting.*

★ Mikla

The Marmara Pera, Meşrutiyet Caddesi 15 (0212 293 5656, www.miklarestaurant.com). **Open** 6pm-11.30am Mon-Sat. **Starters** TL24-TL36. **Main courses** TL44.50-TL59.50. **Map** p248 M4 ㉒ **Modern European**

On the roof garden of the 18-storey Marmara Pera Hotel, Mikla is one of Istanbul's most exclusive eateries. The project of Turco-Finnish chef Mehmet Gürs, the menu reflects both sides of his heritage and is brief but inventive. Starters are big enough to share (just as well, as prices are steep). Mains might include grilled grouper with tomatoes, aubergines, anchovies, capers, olive oil and poached artichoke, or pistachio-crusted lamb chops with potato, pistachio purée and pomegranate molasses. The place doesn't fill up until 10.30pm; you'll miss the buzz if you book too early.

► *Other fine-dining restaurants include Topaz (see p140) and Mimolett (see p138).*

INSIDE TRACK FINE FISH

For the day's catch in refined surroundings, head up the Bosphorus to the village of **Arnavutköy**, which is packed with fish restaurants – including the excellent **Adem Baba** (*see p143*) – and has a scenic walkway by the water. A little further along the Bosphorus is upmarket **Poseidon** (*see p144*) in **Bebek**, and **Rumeli Iskele** (*see p144*) up at **Rumeli Hisarı**.

Nature & Peace

Büyükparmakkapı Sokak 15, off Istiklal Caddesi (0212 252 8609, www.natureandpeace.com). **Open** 11am-11.30pm Mon-Thur, Sun; 1-11.30pm Fri, Sat. **Set lunch** TL10-TL18. **Starters** TL5-TL12. **Main courses** TL11-TL25. **Map** p249 O3 ㉓ **Vegetarian**

Vegetarian restaurants are rare in Istanbul, and even this pretender to the title serves several chicken and meat dishes. The set lunch is great value and the dinner menu includes a soup and salad with any main course; pasta and falafel are reliable choices. One of the most popular dishes is a lentil 'meatball', with cabbage and nettle soup. The small, unpretentious space is cosy.

► *The restaurant transforms into a club after 11pm, open until 5am.*

Rejans

Olivya Geçidi 7/A, Galatasaray (0212 243 3882, www.rejansrestaurant.com). **Open** noon-3pm, 7pm-midnight Mon-Sat. **Starters** TL9-TL24. **Main courses** TL16-TL66. **Map** p248 N3 ㉔ **Russian**

Founded by White Russians who relocated to Istanbul in the wake of the Russian Revolution, Rejans was reputedly one of Atatürk's favourite restaurants. Left-wing Turkish intellectuals would come here to gripe over borscht and vodka. Since the red star was spurned in favour of the gold card, Rejans is now frequented by visiting Russians with deep pockets, who knock back flavoured vodkas as they gorge on 'tsar's zakuski'. If the Slavic food is so-so, Rejans still oozes charm, with its polished wood, high ceilings, musicians' gallery and a drunken doorman to hang customers' coats on hooks personalised with the names of long-dead regulars.

Tokyo Restaurant

Meselik Sokak 24, off Istiklal Caddesi (0212 293 5858, www.tokyo-restaurant.com). **Open** noon-10.30pm daily. **Starters** TL9-TL15. **Main courses** TL29-TL64. **Map** p249 O2 ㉕ **Japanese**

With its modern-traditional scarlet decor and tatami rooms, Tokyo is a hit with the local Japanese. The menu includes dozens of noodle, rice and teriyaki dishes, plus good sushi and sashimi. The sushi chefs show off their skills behind an open counter.

Zarifi

Çukurlu Çeşme Sokak 13 (0212 293 5480, www.zarifi.com.tr). **Open** 8pm-4am daily. Closed June-Aug. **Starters** TL5-TL10. **Main courses** TL22-TL35. **Map** (winter venue) p249 O3 ㉖ **Turkish**

An update on the *meyhane* that's very popular with fashionable young Turks. Zarifi's extensive menu covers all the classic meze and grilled meats, as well as Ottoman dishes and recipes inherited from the former Greek residents of the Pera neighbourhood, such as shrimp *saganaki* and octopus stew. The soundtrack is equally eclectic – a mix of Turkish folk, chill-out tunes and mainstream pop. Once the *rakı* is flowing freely, the spirit of the *meyhane* usually takes over and spontaneous table-top dancing breaks out.

Zencefil

Kurabiye Sokak 8, Taksim (0212 243 8234). **Open** 11am-midnight Mon-Sat; noon-10pm Sun. **Starters** TL4-TL8. **Main courses** TL11.50-TL20. **Map** p249 O2 ㉗ **Vegetarian**

Beşinci Kat (5.Kat).

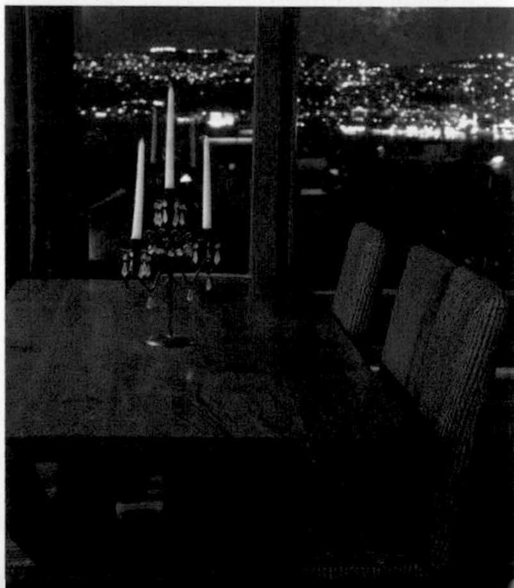

Probably the best vegetarian restaurant in Istanbul (though purists may be infuriated by the fact that chicken makes an occasional appearance on the menu). The setting is urban café meets country kitchen, with shelves lined with jars of produce and giant blackboards listing the daily specials, from soups to spicy stews and freshly baked breads. The home-style food is unfalteringly delicious, likewise the home-made lemonade. In summer tables cluster in the restaurant's beautiful gated garden as well.

Cihangir

Rehabilitated from its dirty days as a shady part of town, Cihangir is now one of Istanbul's most coveted neighbourhoods. This transformation has been accompanied by the arrival of a quirky selection of restaurants, cafés and bars catering to the area's predominantly arty and foreign residents. In warm weather, restaurants and cafés remove their doors and windows entirely, and are buzzing well into the small hours.

★ Beşinci Kat (5.Kat)

5th Floor, Soğancı Sokak 7, off Sıraselviler Caddesi (0212 293 3774, www.5kat.com). **Open** 10.30am-2am Mon-Thur, Sun; 10.30am-3am Fri, Sat. **Starters** TL12.90-TL35.90. **Main courses** TL22.50-TL46.90. **Map** p249 O3 ㉘ **International**

With its bright colours, velvet furnishings and an eye-catching floor piece of a nude young Norma Jean Baker, 5.Kat has one of the city's most striking interiors. As its name implies (*kat* means floor), it occupies the fifth floor of a backstreet building. A giant neon angel shines at street level. A rooftop terrace, lit with red lanterns, opens during the summer and has fabulous views over the Asian shore. The menu is a culinary mishmash (Turkish, French, Italian, Oriental) but everything is good. There are two fixed price menus, each one including three 'local' drinks, for TL70 and TL80. 5.Kat's actress proprietor, Yasemin Alkaya, keeps a close eye on proceedings, even after hours, when dance music takes over from chilled jazz, and the atmosphere gets clubby.

▶ *For more bars and restaurants with a view, see p154* **Up on the Roofs**.

Doğa Balık

7th Floor, Hotel Villla Zurich, Akarsu Yokuşu 46 (0212 243 3656, www.dogabalik.com.tr). **Open** noon-11pm daily. **Starters** TL5-TL15. **Main courses** TL15-TL50. **Map** p249 O4 ㉙ **Turkish**

Don't let the entrance, via the lobby of the Villa Zurich Hotel, put you off: Doğa Balık is a splendid neighbourhood fish restaurant. The dining room is on the seventh floor and is best known for its roof terrace, which has stunning views across to Sultanahmet and Beyoğlu. The cooking is equally

Tastes of Turkey Today

From raucous meyhanes to Ottoman fine dining.

It's stating the obvious but we'll say it anyway: there's so much more to Turkish cuisine than kebabs. And along with the variety in the cuisine, there's a range of places that serve it. Here, we take you on a culinary tour of the various breeds of places to eat you'll find in Istanbul.

Esnaf lokantas Turkey's equivalent to a basic canteen, *esnaf lokantas* are cheap eateries that serve neighbourhood workers who don't have the time to head home for lunch. Food is cooked in a simple, home-style way – which also means dishes tend to be as seasonal as they are sensational. *Esnaf lokantas* generally don't have menus – just check out what's cooking in the steaming trays and point out what you want. And they hardly ever serve alcohol.

The city's top *esnaf lokanta* is **Ciya** (*see p144*). **Şar** (*see p129*) and **Kanaat** (*see p144*) are also superb.

Meyhanes Everyone needs a place to let loose. The British down pints in pubs, the French guzzle wine in brasseries, and the Greeks smash plates in tavernas. The Turks? They make merry in the *meyhane*, the age-old Istanbul version of a tapas bar. It's here that locals most frequently meet, eat meze, drink *rakı* and are cajoled by house musicians into belting out folk songs.

Order plenty of meze, since sharing is what it's all about. Cold dishes cost about TL6, hot ones around TL10, and seafood appetisers TL12-TL20. For two people, six dishes are usually enough; you can order main courses later if you have room. Most meze will be paraded before you on a tray. Some *meyhanes* offer a set menu of meze, fish and dessert, with unlimited *rakı*, beer or wine (around TL50-TL80 a head).

Meyhanes differ drastically in terms of food and prices, but everyone has their favourites. We like **Boncuk** (*see p139*), which specialises in Armenian dishes and features live *fasıl* music. Owned by a friendly Greek family from Imroz (the Aegean island of Gökçeada), **Krependeki Imroz** (*see p139*) was founded in 1941 and is one of the city's oldest *meyhanes*. **Cumhuriyet Meyhanesi** (*see p139*), once frequented by Atatürk, is notable for its *fasıl* musicians. For quality fish (rather than a thrilling atmosphere), **Mer Balık's** (*see p140*) lantern fish kebab is outstanding. The Asmalı Mescit neighbourhood's **Refik**, **Sofyalı 9** and **Yakup 2** are also lively, very tasty *meyhanes*, although a bit more upscale (for all, *see p140*).

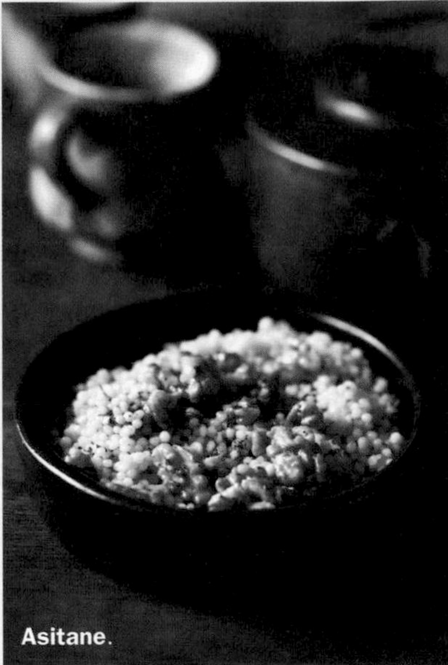
Asitane.

Ottoman cuisine Istanbul sits at the heart of the former Ottoman Empire. At its powerful peak, the frontiers of these lands stretched from Egypt to Eastern Europe, and swept across Asia Minor. For centuries, Topkapı Palace's finest chefs – inspired by produce and recipes from the edges of the empire – competed to craft the most exotic dishes for the sultan, his royal court and esteemed visitors. The result? Mouth-watering, slow-cooked meals, flavoured with nutty spices such as sumac and spicy red pepper, and seasonal fruits, including quince, figs and pomegranates.

To sample the best of this creative cooking, head to **Asitane** (*see p133*), where hundreds of elaborate Ottoman recipes have been sourced from the kitchens of Topkapı and Dolmabahçe palaces. For simple, old-school Ottoman cuisine, low-key **Hacı Abdullah** (*see p134*) makes a delectable spot for a midday stop. Nişantaşı's upscale **Hünkar** (*see p141*) is also excellent.

INSIDE TRACK
EAT LIKE A SULTAN

The kind of food that pleasured the palates of sultans – wildly elaborate dishes mixing rice, fruit and vegetables with meat and fish – was coined with equally flamboyant names. Look out for *dilberdudağı* ('lady's lips'; pastry soaked in syrup), *karnıyarık* ('slit stomach'; aubergine stuffed with minced meat), *imambayıldı* ('the imam fainted'; slow-roast aubergines with onions and tomatoes) and *kadınbudu köfte* ('ladies' thighs'; battered, fried meatballs).

impressive. The kitchen specialises in lightly cooked greens (up to 18 varieties, including unusual sea grasses) and perfectly grilled seasonal fish drizzled with garlicky olive oil. This cuisine is the quintessential Aegean comfort food – and it's good for you too. On Wednesday, Friday and Saturday evenings, there's live traditional music.

★ Mimolett

Sıraselviler Caddesi 55/A (0212 245 9858, www.mimolett.com.tr). **Open** 7-11.30pm Mon-Sat. **Bar** 3pm-2am Mon-Sat. **Starters** TL18-TL29. **Main courses** TL49-TL72. **Degustation menu** TL125-TL145. **Map** p249 O3 ㉚ **Modern European**

Head chef Murat Bozok worked at Michelin-starred restaurants in France and the UK (including a stint as head chef at Gordon Ramsay's Devonshire), before returning to his native city to open Mimolett, one of Istanbul's new breed of fine-dining restaurants. The menu is a Michelin-friendly selection of modern European dishes; Turkish twists, seen in dishes such as a lamb chop and sweetbread *dolma*, bring originality and a sense of place. Quality is incredibly high, and the service flawless. The opulent, yet modern, interior befits a restaurant of this stature, but the terrace is the best place to take dinner, just as the sun sets and the moon rises over the Bosphorus. Mimolett also has a bar and wine shop.

★ Miss Pizza

Hayvar Sokak 5/A, off Akarsu Yokuşu (0212 251 3278). **Open** noon-midnight daily (last orders 10.30pm). **Pizzas** TL12-TL33. **Side orders** TL15-TL20. **Map** p249 O4 ㉛ **Pizza**

Arguably the best pizzeria in town, this stylish but cosy eaterie in the heart of Cihangir is a big hit with resident foreigners. Selen and Elif, who both have backgrounds in textiles, were inspired to create Miss Pizza by their trips to Italy. An Italian chef created the menu and taught them to make pizza dough. Pizza *funghi*, made with gorgonzola and porcini mushrooms marinated in truffle oil, is our recommendation here. Besides pizza, there are good cheese and charcuterie platters and salads. There are only a few tables, but you can also order home delivery. Reservations are essential on Fridays and Saturdays. **Other location** Meşrutiyet Caddesi 86/A (0212 251 3234).

★ Savoy Balık

Bakraç Sokak 32, off Sıraselviler Caddesi (0212 249 3382, www.savoybalik.com). **Open** noon-midnight daily. **Starters** TL6-TL17. **Main courses** TL15-TL25. **Map** p249 O3 ㉜ **Seafood/Turkish**

Tucked at the back of a petite car park in the heart of Cihangir, this lively seafood restaurant is a delight. Work through marinated *lakerda bonito*, fish-stuffed *börek*, and giant seasonal salads before moving on to deep-fried calamari, grilled sea bass or plump fillets of red mullet. Patrons are laid-back and almost entirely local. During warm weather, reservations are essential for tables on the small outdoor terrace.

Galatasaray, Tünel & Karaköy

Filled with an interesting mix of restaurants, cafés and bars frequented by locals, the narrow, atmospheric streets stretching from **Tünel Square** down past the **Galata Tower** to the former docks area of Karaköy are a trendy but low-key area. **Nevizade Sokak** and **Çiçek Pasajı**, as well as the streets criss-crossing the nearby Asmalı Mescit neighbourhood, form the city's most famous *meyhane* district.

Akın Balık

Perşembe Pazarı, near Karaköy Square (no phone). **Open** 11am-midnight daily. **Main courses** TL5-TL15. **No credit cards. Map** p246 M6 ㉝ **Seafood**

There are a handful of budget eateries tucked around the fish market by Galata Bridge. This one, on the west side of the market, is consistently the most popular with locals. The setting – outdoors and overlooking the Golden Horn – is sublime, as is the fresh fish. Try the simply grilled sea bass, fried calamari with walnut dipping sauce, or hearty fish soup.

★ Antiochia

Minare Sokak 21, Asmalı Mescit (0212 292 1100, www.antiochiaconcept.com). **Open** noon-1am Mon-Sat. **Starters** TL8-TL14. **Main courses** TL16-TL30. **Map** p248 M4 ㉞ Turkish

A tiny, semi-subterranean spot tucked into a backstreet off Istiklal Caddesi, Antiochia serves delicious specialities from Turkey's south-eastern Hatay region, on the Syrian border. Sample houmous, smoky aubergine *abagannuç*, walnut and pepper *muammara* or crushed olive salad, followed by tender marinated lamb. Note that the restaurant's ambience is simple – some may find it a shade too basic; the food is the main star here.

Boncuk

Nevizade Sokak 7, Balık Pazarı (0212 243 1219). **Open** 11.30am-2am daily. **Map** p248 N3 ㉟ **Turkish**
See p137 **Tastes of Turkey Today**.

Cumhuriyet Meyhanesi

Sahne Sokak 47, Balık Pazarı (0212 293 1977, www.tarihicumhuriyetmeyhanesi.com.tr). **Open** noon-2am daily. **Map** p248 N3 ㊱ **Turkish**
See p137 **Tastes of Turkey Today**.

★ Karaköy Lokantası

Kemankeş Caddesi 37A, Karaköy (0212 292 4455, www.karakoylokantasi.com). **Open** noon-4pm, 6pm-midnight Mon-Sat. **Starters** TL8-TL16. **Main courses** TL15-TL33. **Map** p246 N6 ㊲ **Turkish**

Set within Istanbul's former docklands of Karaköy, this buzzing restaurant is classified as a *meyhane* – but it's definitely a top-end example of these often-rowdy eateries. The meze selection is particularly sublime, ranging from smoky aubergine purée to wilted sea greens and an unbeatable *ahtapot ızgara* (grilled octopus). The interior – with a mosaic of gorgeous turquoise tiles – is as attractive as the cuisine. Visit at lunchtime if you're on a budget; evening reservations essential.

★ Krependeki Imroz

Nevizade Sokak 16, Balık Pazarı (0212 249 9073, www.krependekiimroz.com). **Open** 11.30am-2am daily. **Map** p248 N3 ㊳ **Turkish**
See p137 **Tastes of Turkey Today**.

Lokal

Müeyyet Sokak 5/A, Asmalı Mescit (0212 245 5744). **Open** 10am-midnight daily. **Starters** TL7-TL15. **Main courses** TL15-TL25. **Map** p248 M4 ㊴ **Modern European/International**

Once one of the hippest eateries in town, Lokal has graduated to classic status. On a tiny side street off Asmalımescit, this buzzing venue is easy to locate thanks to the films projected on the wall opposite, ranging from footage of skateboarders to spaghetti westerns. Menus bound by kitsch LP covers read like an encyclopaedia of global fusion: pesto linguine, chicken tikka, pad Thai, salmon teriyaki and chicken wings. All are surprisingly good.

► *There are two Lokal outposts in the side streets around the original: Flavio (Gönül Sokak 1/A-3/A, 0212 243 2843, http://flavio.com.tr) focuses on Italian food, while Lokal-Tünel (Tünel Meydanı 186/A, 0212 245 4028, www.lokal-tunel.com) offers modern Turkish dishes, as well as coffee, smoothies and snacks.*

★ Lokanta Maya

Kemankeş Caddesi 35/A, Karaköy (0212 252 6884, www.lokantamaya.com). **Open** noon-5pm Sun; noon-5pm, 7-11pm Tue-Sat. **Starters** TL9-TL22. **Main courses** TL12-TL34. **Map** p246 N6 ㊵ **Modern Turkish**

Opened in mid 2010, Lokanta Maya has rapidly become one of Istanbul's most sought-after spots for intimate fine dining. Owner-chef Didem Şenol spent years working in New York and a decade researching on Turkey's Aegean Datça peninsula. Today,

Sunday Brunch Istanbul-style

The most relaxing meal of the week.

Given Istanbullus' adoration of long, lingering breakfasts (*see p127* **The Turkish Breakfast Club**), it's little surprise that Western-style brunch has taken off here in a big way. Most of the city's top hotels and restaurants have jumped on the brunch bandwagon, serving up to 100-plate buffets every Sunday from around 11am until 3pm. Expect a range of Turkish favourites, from sizzling skillets of *menemen* (scrambled eggs with tomatoes and peppers) to scoops of rich *kaymak* cream, as well as pancakes, tropical fruit salads, cured meats, jams and pâtisserie-worthy desserts. **Vogue** (*see p144*) serves a brunch (TL50) that includes towers of salmon sandwiches and tahini-slathered *börek*, on a stunning rooftop terrace with views from the Blue Mosque to the Bosphorus Bridge. Brunch (TL110) at the **Four Seasons Sultanahmet** (*see p129*) is elegance itself, with elaborate cloche-topped salads, an open-air barbecue and a clutch of staff on hand to proffer the gourmet delights. And for total decadence? Head to the 140-plate brunch at **Swissôtel** (*see p123*, TL135), which has a fresh fish bar, an edible garden and a dedicated sushi chef.

Four Seasons Sultanahmet.

she brings her diverse experiences together with heirloom ingredients, traditional cooking techniques and cosy, contemporary decor. Menu offerings are all top drawer, but favourites include caramelised sea bass with apricots, and crispy *mücver* courgette fritters, served with cucumber yoghurt dipping sauce.

Mer Balık Restaurant

Sahne Sokak 23, Balık Pazarı (0212 244 9797, www.merbalik.com). **Open** 11.30am-2am daily. **Map** p248 N3 ❹❶ **Turkish**
See p137 **Tastes of Turkey Today**.

Refik

Sofyalı Sokak 10-12, Asmalı Mescit (0212 243 2834, www.refikrestaurant.com). **Open** noon-2am daily. **Starters** TL8-TL12. **Main courses** TL20-TL25. **Map** p248 M4 ❹❷ **Turkish**
Established in 1954, this upmarket *meyhane* is a great starting point to immerse yourself in meze culture and acquire a taste for *rakı*. Patrons have always included a devoted clientele of leftie hacks and intellectuals. Most regulars drink more than they eat, but the place is renowned for seafood dishes. There's no music, as it would interfere with the animated conversation.

Sofyalı 9

Sofyalı Sokak 9, Asmalı Mescit (0212 245 0362, www.sofyali.com.tr). **Open** noon-1am Mon-Sat. **Starters** TL4-TL10. **Main courses** TL13-TL25. **Map** p248 M4 ❹❸ **Turkish**

A *meyhane* maybe, but *très* genteel. This cosy local haunt feels like someone's front room – someone with money, taste and a fine old house. The ground-floor space is small, with mustard walls, exposed brickwork, wooden floors and hanging lanterns, but tables fill the two floors upstairs. Even so, reservations are a must, as the city's literati, fashionistas and theatre crowd love this place. The food is a cut above – superior meze, followed by meat and fish dishes prepared with the freshest ingredients and a lightness of touch.

★ Yakup 2

Asmalı Mescit Sokak 35-37, Asmalı Mescit (0212 249 2925, http://yakup2restaurant.com). **Open** noon-2am daily. **Starters** TL8-TL24. **Main courses** TL12-TL30. **Map** p248 M4 ❹❹ **Turkish**
Thriving since Yakup Arslan (nephew of Refik Arslan of Refik, *see left*) opened these doors in 1982, Yakup 2 is particularly popular with actors, writers and artists. The *meyhane*'s walls are still covered with photos, drawings and notes from favourite former patrons, although today the place draws a varied crowd. Top meze, rolled out on an old-style wheely cart, include octopus salad, *arnavut ciğeri* (Albanian-style liver), pickled mackerel, grilled red peppers and shrimp *güvec*, baked in a casserole. Mains concentrate on seasonal fresh fish, from tiny fried anchovies to plump turbot steaks. Reservations recommended.

Şişli

★ Miyako

Swissôtel The Bosphorus, Bayıldım Caddesi 2, Maçka (0212 326 1100, www.swissotel.com). **Open** 7-11pm Tue-Sun. **Starters** TL18-TL40. **Main courses** TL28-TL57. **Map** p247 R1 ❹❺ **Japanese**
Widely recognised as the best Japanese restaurant in Istanbul, Miyako emanates understated Asian elegance. Blonde wood booths are packed with hushed patrons, many of them visiting Japanese. The restaurant is renowned for its teppanyaki, and one of Miyako's rooms is dedicated to these large iron griddles. Set menus offer a choice of teppanyaki fish, beef or chicken (TL80-TL140), and are served with rice, veggies, miso soup and seasonal nibbles. Maki, sashimi and hand rolls are also exceptional – although best value are Miyako's raw dinner sets (TL75-TL95).

Topaz

İnönü Caddesi 50, Gümüşsuyu (0212 249 1001, www.topazistanbul.com). **Open** noon-midnight daily. **Starters** TL20-TL36. **Main courses** TL24-TL36. **Degustation menu** TL105-TL115 (matched with wines additional TL75-TL95). **Map** p247 Q2 ❹❻ **Modern European**
Views from Topaz are superlative: picture windows run the length of the restaurant, which looks over

INSIDE TRACK
COOK LIKE A TURK

Saying goodbye to Turkish cuisine can be heartbreaking. However, Istanbul is home to a handful of English-language cooking schools that can teach you how to recreate your favourite Turkish treats back home. At **Cooking Alaturka** (Akbiyik Caddesi 72A, Sultanahmet, 0212 458 5919, www.cookingalaturka.com), Dutch chef Eveline Zoutendijk and Turkish sous-chef Feyzi Yıldırım offer half-day classes followed by a five-course meal (€60 per person including meal and wine). **Istanbul Culinary Institute** (Meşrutiyet Caddesi 59, Tepebaşı, 0212 251 2214, www.istanbulculinary.com) has three-hour workshops dedicated to both Turkish and international cuisine (TL120-TL150). And at **Turkish Flavours** (Vali Konağı Caddesi Uğur, Apt 14/3, Nişantaşı, 0532 218 06 53, www.turkishflavours.com), Istanbul native Selin Rozanes teaches traditional Turkish cooking to children and adults (€75 per adult; one child under 12 free; two children under 12 €37.50).

Topaz.

the first Bosphorus bridge. The interior is comfortably modern, sleek and luxurious, and the food and service match the look. Alongside the carte, there are two six-course *degustation* menus: the first is a modern interpretation of traditional Ottoman cuisine, with dishes such as artichoke with wild rice and grilled lamb loin with smoked aubergine purée. The second is a more modish Mediterranean selection, albeit with Turkish touches: saffron-infused seafood soup with coconut foam, and oven-braised beef cheek with goose liver crème brûlée, perhaps. All ingredients are rigorously sourced. The service is flawless, and the French sommelier can recommend Turkish or international wines. Cocktails are great too. Book ahead for a table by the window.

NIŞANTAŞI

Few visitors make it up the hill to this upmarket neighbourhood, with its impressive selection of designer boutiques and equally swanky eateries.

Hünkar

Mim Kemal Öke Caddesi 21 (0212 225 4665, www.hunkar1950.com). Metro Osmanbey. **Open** noon-midnight daily. **Starters** TL7-TL15. **Main courses** TL12-TL20. **Turkish**

The original Hünkar opened in 1950 in the working-class Fatih neighbourhood. This offshoot in Nişantaşı has taken the old-school Ottoman brand upmarket. Diners include Chanel-suited ladies who lunch and deal-clinching businessmen who schmooze over homely dishes such as sheep's trotter soup, stuffed cabbage, anchovy pilaf, or the signature dish *hünkar beğendi* – 'sultan's delight' – a rich lamb stew with aubergine purée. Decorative touches (jars of preserves, copper artefacts) maintain one foot in the past; street sideseating allows clients to keep an eye on the present.

Salomanje

Belkıs Apartmanı 4/1-2, Atiye Sokak (0212 327 3577, www.salomanje.com.tr). Metro Osmanbey. **Open** 1pm-2am Mon-Sat; 1-7pm Sun. **Starters** TL8-TL18. **Main courses** TL21-TL34. **Modern European**

This place is a hit with Nişantaşı's most stylish residents, although entering the undersized venue you might wonder why. With a bar, a handful of tables and a small terrace out the back, the decor is unremarkable but cosy. The menu combines Turkish and international standards. In summer, Salomanje moves to Sortie nightclub in Kuruçeşme, *see p204*.

LEVENT & ETILER

A couple of Istanbul's wealthier business districts – comprising glass skyscrapers, monolithic malls and bumper-to-bumper SUVs – Levent and Etiler are home to a handful of fine restaurants.

Sunset Grill & Bar

Yol Sokak 2, off Adnan Saygun Caddesi, Ulus Parkı, Ulus (0212 287 0357, www.sunsetgrillbar.com). Metro Levent. **Open** noon-2am Mon-Sat; 6pm-2am Sun. **Starters** TL15-TL40. **Main courses** TL35-TL80. **International**

A gorgeous setting for a romantic tryst – a tree-lined terrace set on a hilltop high above the Bosphorus. The menu is an unlikely but well-executed mix of Californian fusion, meat-heavy modern Turkish dishes and superior sushi. The restaurant is a five- or ten-minute walk from Levent metro station. Predictably, it's hugely popular at sunset, when you are advised to book ahead.

Ulus 29

Kireçhane Sokak 1, Adnan Saygun Caddesi, Ulus Parkı, Ulus (0212 265 6181, www.group-29.com). Metro Levent. **Open** noon-3pm, 7pm-2am daily. **Starters** TL18-TL30. **Main courses** TL30-TL60. **Mediterranean**

Someone to impress? Something to celebrate? Ulus 29 fits the bill. Thanks to yet another spectacular hillside setting (just above the Sunset Grill & Bar, *see above*), the views from the veranda are unbeatable. Models

Kebab Cuisine

No longer just filling fodder for boozers, kebabs are going gourmet.

Not too long ago, sophisticated Istanbullus would turn their noses up at the kebab (the word *kebap* means simply 'roast meat'), dismissing it as uncouth provincial grub. Kebabs are synonymous with south-eastern Turkey. The stereotypical kebab restaurateur is a moustachioed sort from rural Droolsville. But over the years the foodie snobs have gradually come around. So much so that these days it's a case of *kebap c'est chic*.

For all its south-eastern associations, the initial spotting of the gourmet potential of grilled meat took place in western Turkey. Back in 1867, a chef in the city of Bursa, 250 kilometres (155 miles) south of Istanbul, by the name of Iskender Usta hit upon the idea of layering slabs of boneless lamb on to a spit, then revolving the resulting meaty mass in front of glowing coals. He then shaved off thin layers with a long knife, and there you have the birth of the döner kebab and Turkey's contribution to worldwide post-booze bingeing. Not content to stop there, Iskender Usta went on to jazz up the döner with *pide* bread, tomato and yoghurt to create his namesake, the Iskender kebab. His contribution to kebab cuisine was enshrined in law in 2002, when Usta's descendants were awarded a patent to protect their family delicacy from imitators. Thousands of restaurants throughout Turkey were obliged to relabel their 'Iskender kebabs' as 'Bursa kebabs' in order to forestall potential lawsuits.

His name may be protected but Iskender's crown has been lost for good. The current king of kebabs is Beyti Güler. His family opened **Beyti's** (Orman Sokak 8, Florya, 0212 663 2990, www.beyti.com) restaurant, in the outskirts of Istanbul, back in 1945. By the 1960s, Turkophile diplomat and author Lord Kinross was declaring that it served 'the best meat in Europe'. The plaudits continued and the celebrity guests kept coming – Richard Nixon, Jimmy Carter and Arthur Miller have all eaten here. And, of course, there's a trademark 'Beyti kebab'.

With these varieties and many more, the kebab has come a long way since Mr Usta sliced his first döner. Here's our quick guide to help you choose:

Adana kebap minced lamb seasoned with red peppers and grilled on a spit.

begendi kebap chunks of beef cooked with onions and tomatoes and served on a bed of puréed aubergine.

beyti kebap chopped lamb flavoured with a hint of garlic and red pepper. Served either wrapped in filo pastry or on cubes of toasted *pide* bread.

Çöp şiş tiny bits of slightly fatty lamb grilled on a skewer, then rolled up in paper-thin *pide* with onions and parsley.

döner kebab compressed meat sliced in strips off a vertically rotating spit. Lamb, beef or chicken.

fıstıklı kebab minced low-fat suckling lamb studded with pistachios.

Iskender kebab slices of döner drizzled with tomato sauce and melted butter served with a side of yoghurt on cubes of toasted *pide* bread.

patlican kebab minced lamb grilled with chunks of aubergine.

şiş kebap chunks of marinated lamb, chicken or fish grilled on skewers.

testi kebab diced meat, tomatoes, shallots, garlic and green peppers simmered in a clay pot for several hours.

CONSUME

make eyes at moguls against an opulent oriental backdrop, decked with muslin drapes and lit by oil lamps. The restaurant is immaculately designed by local nightlife impresario Metin Fadıllıoğlu and his interior designer wife, Zeynep. Food is impressive, focusing on the eastern Mediterranean.

HASKÖY

Halat

Kumbarhane Caddesi 2, Hasköy (0212 369 6616, www.halatrestaurant.com). Bus 54HM, 54HT. **Open** 10am-10pm Tue-Sun. **Starters** TL7-TL15. **Main courses** TL18-TL29. **Mediterranean**

In addition to being a world-class museum, the Rahmi Koç has a couple of excellent restaurants including Café du Levant, a fancy French bistro, and Halat, with quayside dining under canvas awnings. The menu ranges from a 'tea-time' selection of sandwiches and tarts to breaded crab claws and heavenly desserts. Black-waistcoated staff and classical music suggest formality, but the vibe is laid-back. The views – across the Golden Horn to the tumbling orange roofs of Balat – are stunning.

► *For the Rahmi Koç Museum, see p72.*

THE BOSPHORUS VILLAGES

This string of waterfront settlements starts at **Beşiktaş** and runs north through **Ortaköy**, **Arnavutköy** and **Bebek**, as far as **Rumeli Hisarı**. Restaurants in this district tend to be pricey, cashing in on their seaside setting, but remain popular.

★ Adem Baba

Beyazgül Caddesi 2, Arnavutköy (0212 287 2648, www.adembaba.com). Bus 25E, 40. **Open** noon-10.30pm daily. **Starters** TL5-TL12. **Main courses** TL10-TL45. **No credit cards. Seafood**

Beginning life as a tiny boat famed for frying up the freshest of Bosphorus fish, today Adem Baba may have more permanent premises in the postcard-perfect fishing village of Arnavutköy, but it's still renowned for its seasonal fish and seafood. The simple wooden decor takes a back seat to the expertly prepared cuisine. Picks of the menu include savoury fish *köfte* and a special Sunday-only fish soup.

Banyan Ortaköy

Salhane Sokak 3, off Muallim Naci Caddesi, Ortaköy (0212 259 9060, www.banyan restaurant.com). Bus 25E, 40. **Open** 7pm-midnight daily. **Starters** TL12-TL32. **Main courses** TL29-TL58. **Asian**

With spectacular views of the original Bosphorus Bridge and floodlit Ortaköy mosque, Banyan comes into its own on summer nights. Bonsai trees scattered around the tables lend an exotic twist to the refined interior. Living up to the slogan 'Food for the Soul', all ingredients are organic and ethically sourced. The menu is a melange of Asian influences. Chinese, Japanese, Vietnamese and Indian delicacies are all beautifully presented and prepared: fusion food at its best – good for the soul, but hard on the wallet.

House Café

Salhane Sokak 1, off Muallim Naci Caddesi, Ortaköy (0212 227 2699, www.thehousecafe.com). Bus 25E, 40. **Open** 9am-1am Mon-Thur; 9am-2am Fri, Sat; 9am-midnight Sun. **Starters** TL8-TL22. **Main courses** TL15-TL35. **Modern European**

The expansion of the House Café group is something of a phenomenon. Since opening the original branch in Teşvikiye (the Ortaköy branch was the second), another ten venues have been added to the list. With industrial-chic interiors from Istanbul super-designers Autoban, all the locations offer lovely surroundings in which to enjoy global comfort food made with gourmet ingredients. This Ortaköy café has a blissful terrace right on the Bosphorus. Weekend brunch is a fixture for the young and well-heeled. Try the superlative House burger, thin-crust pizzas, imaginative bruschette and salads. Pint-sized fresh fruit cocktails are a joy to behold and delicious to boot.

Other locations throughout the city.

► *The House Hotel, p111, and the House Apart, p117 are owned by the same group.*

Mangerie

Cevdetpaşa Caddesi 69, Küçük Bebek, Bebek (0212 263 5199, www.mangeriebebek.com). Bus 25E, 40. **Open** 8am-midnight daily. **Starters** TL11-TL25. **Main courses** TL25-TL35. **Modern Turkish**

Tucked away behind the fancy waterside eateries in Bebek, this delightful restaurant is worth seeking out. (Head for the Küçük Bebek end of the high street and follow the steps leading up past a hairdresser.) The airy interior is all white wood, with a balcony that looks over the rooftops to the Bosphorus. The relaxed atmosphere makes this an ideal lunch spot, with simple salads and sandwiches served on great breads, baked on the premises. Mangerie's menu was revamped and expanded in 2011; courgette flowers stuffed with goat's cheese and toasted pine nuts come highly recommended.

★ Müzedechanga

Sakıp Sabancı Museum, Sakıp Sabancı Caddesi 22, Emirgan (0212 323 0901, www.changa-istanbul.com). Bus 25E, 40. **Open** 10.30am-midnight Tue-Sun. **Starters** TL16-TL27. **Main courses** TL23-TL39. **Turkish-Mediterranean**

In the Sakıp Sabancı Museum, Müzedechanga is much more than a museum café. A spin-off from the acclaimed Changa restaurant in Taksim, it's housed in a space remodelled with a modern mixture of glass, wood and steel, with custom-made furniture by renowned local designers Autoban. The terrace has amazing views across the manicured museum gardens to the Bosphorus. The Turkish-Med menu, supervised by consultant chef Peter Gordon of Sugar Club fame, is faultless and well priced for this quality. Highly recommended.

▶ *The original – and outstanding – Changa is at Sıraselviler Caddesi 47, Taksim (0212 249 1348, closed June-Aug).*

Poseidon

Cevdet Paşa Caddesi 58, Küçük Bebek, Bebek (0212 287 9531, www.poseidonbebek.com). Bus 25E, 40. **Open** noon-midnight daily. **Starters** TL7-TL25. **Main courses** TL20-TL40. **Seafood**

A supremely stylish affair with a beautiful location on the Bosphorus in Bebek, Poseidon serves superior seafood at vertiginous prices. Sampling the meze menu will hike up the bill, but specialities such as stuffed calamari, marinated sea bass and fish croquettes are worth it for the high quality. The catch of the day is priced by the kilo. Your dining companions will be well-bred and well-manicured big spenders. The large deck is virtually suspended above the Bosphorus and has gorgeous views of Bebek bay; the view from inside is almost as magical.

Rumeli Iskele

Yahya Kemal Caddesi 1, Rumeli Hisarı (0212 263 2997, www.rumelihisariiskele.com). Bus 25E, 40. **Open** noon-midnight daily. **Starters** TL8-TL16. **Main courses** TL18-TL44. **Seafood**

Despite competition from newer seafood restaurants, this place is always packed. The best tables are on the waterfront deck, with a view of the hilltop castle of Anadolu Hisarı across the strait. The menu holds few surprises – meze and Mediterranean fish – but the food is excellent. Service is unobtrusive and efficient.

Vogue

Spor Caddesi 92, BJK Plaza A Blok 13, Akaretler, Beşiktaş (0212 227 4404, www.voguerestaurant.com). Bus 25E, 40. **Open** noon-2am daily; from 10.30am Sun. **Starters** TL20-TL35. **Main courses** TL30-TL55. **Modern European**

Despite being eclipsed by newer, trendier joints, Vogue has managed to retain its stylish clientele and high standards. Curiously situated on the top floor of an office block, the restaurant serves sophisticated Californian-fusion dishes and freshly prepared sushi. Reservations are still essential at weekends.

▶ *Vogue is owned by the Doors group. Its other restaurants include Kitchenette (see p135) and Angelique (see p157).*

THE ASIAN SHORE

Çiya and **Kanaat** offer a fantastic array of classic, and more unusual, Turkish dishes at bargain prices, while exclusive **A'jia** is worth crossing continents to visit.

A'jia

A'jia Hotel, Ahmet Rasim Paşa Yalısı, Çubuklu Caddesi 27, Kanlıca (0216 413 9300, www.ajiahotel.com). Ferry from Beşiktaş or Eminönü to Üsküdar then taxi. **Open** 7am-midnight daily. **Starters** TL20-TL30. **Main courses** TL20-TL50. **Modern European**

A'jia's remote location – a boutique hotel in a converted *yalı* on the shores of the Bosphorus – makes for a peaceful setting. Far from the hustle of the city centre, the waterfront terrace has sweeping views of European Istanbul, while the sleek interior marries Ottoman elegance with contemporary designer pieces. Highlights of the international menu include fresh pasta and octopus carpaccio.

▶ *For A'jia hotel, see p125.*

★ Çiya

Güneşlibahçe Sokak 43, Kadıköy (0216 330 3190, www.ciya.com.tr). Ferry from Eminönü or Karaköy to Kadiköy. **Open** 11am-10pm daily. **Starters** TL4-TL8. **Main courses** TL8-TL14. **Map** p251 W7 ㊼ **Turkish**

Most of the little local eateries on Güneşlibahçe are indistinguishable, but Çiya is so good – and so successful – that it is taking over most of them. Çiya Sofrası specialises in traditional dishes from around Turkey. The interesting starters are on a buffet. Choose what you like and then your plate will be weighed. Mains are also of the pick and point variety: stuffed artichoke, meatballs, a fabulous stuffed intestine stew or a bit of everything. Or just let the affable waiters choose for you. Opposite is Çiya Kebapçı, heaven for kebab aficionados, where chefs in white hats conjure up a mind-boggling selection of skewered meats and freshly made flat breads in the open kitchen. The venues are smart and clean, with tiled white floors, pine furniture and sepia photos of pastoral scenes. Friendly staff are the picture of brisk efficiency. Very highly recommended: do not miss a meal here. No alcohol.

★ Kanaat

Selmanipak Caddesi 9, Üsküdar (0216 341 5444, www.kanaatlokantasi.com.tr). Ferry from Eminönü or Beşiktaş to Üsküdar. **Open** 6am-11pm daily. **Starters** TL4-TL8. **Main courses** TL8-TL14. **No credit cards. Map** p250 W2 ㊽ **Turkish**

Kanaat is a perfect example of a historical *lokanta* that has changed little since it was founded in 1933. The vast menu of traditional but increasingly hard-to-find Turkish dishes is excellent value. Choose from dozens of stuffed, stewed and spiced vegetables and a mouth-watering array of grilled, baked and roast meat dishes, from rich lamb stew to spicy meatballs. There's a separate section dedicated to desserts. Baked quince with clotted cream and delicate milk puddings with various combinations of dried fruit and nuts are especially memorable.

Bars & Cafés

Roof-terrace sundowners, or tea with the locals.

It may come as a surprise to some, but Turkey has a historical and emphatically enthusiastic relationship with alcohol. Over the past few years, Turkish wine, cultivated in the western part of the country for close to three millennia, has received the international recognition it deserves. Designer bars, often on roof terraces at the top of Beyoğlu's most beautiful art nouveau townhouses, are the hippest spots to imbibe with abandon. And for visitors keen on simply sipping a tulip-shaped glass of strong Turkish tea at sunset, Istanbul delivers – in sleepy city courtyards, tea gardens along the Bosphorus or overlooking the Golden Horn.

WHERE TO DRINK

The Ottoman *kıraathane* – traditional coffee- or teahouses that catered to men only – has morphed and come back into fashion thanks to the current popularity of the narghile (hookah pipe): *see p157* **Hubbly Bubbly**. These joints still don't serve alcohol, but are now popular with young people of both sexes. Otherwise, most places blur the boundaries between bar and café, serving coffee and food throughout the day, and becoming increasingly boozy after dark.

Heaven for bar-hoppers, Beyoğlu has a density of drinking venues that would do any German city proud. There's not much worthwhile on the main drag, Istiklal Caddesi, but the surrounding side streets are packed with watering holes, ranging from the good, the bad to the ugly. An evening in Ortaköy or Arnavutköy is pleasant, but quality options are limited. The same is true in swanky Nişantaşı and Teşvikiye. A night on Kadife Sokak in Kadıköy, on the Asian shore, has the potential to turn into something enjoyably regrettable, but if you're staying in Sultanahmet or Beyoğlu, getting home could prove to be a problem.

Café culture, as it's known in Western Europe and the US, has come to Istanbul with zeal. It was kick-started by the wonderful House Café chain, which was the first to encourage a lazy coffee with free Wi-Fi access, good food and award-winning design from Autoban. Starbucks has a firm foothold in the city, with apparently more than 80 outlets. Gloria Jean's is an Australian competitor with branches across the city. A relatively recent addition, along the same lines as House Café, is Big Chefs (Meşrutiyet Caddesi 176, www.bigchefs.com.tr).

WHAT TO DRINK

There are now countless places where you can order a cocktail with confidence (try **Leb-i Derya** for a well-mixed cocktail with a view). Local vintners are also producing and marketing a greater variety of wine (*şarap*) of steadily improving quality (*see p150* **Grape Expectations**), although ordering an unspecified glass of house red or white will still generally result in remorse. There are some reliable labels, though: you won't go wrong with Kavaklıdere's Angora (red and white), Çankaya (white) and Yakut (red), or Doluca's Villa Doluca (red and white). Wine isn't cheap, and there's a very high tax on imported booze. Turks consume twice as much *rakı* – the anise-flavoured spirit similar to the Greek *ouzo* or French *pastis* – as all other alcohol combined; it's generally drunk with *meze*; it's especially good with fish.

SULTANAHMET

With the exception of **Mozaik** restaurant's basement bar (*see p129*) and the Şah Bar (*see p146*), there's a shortage of decent bars in

❶ Green numbers given in this chapter correspond to the location of each bar as marked on the street maps. *See pp242-251.*

Sultanahmet. Options are limited to a row of nondescript tourist cafés east of the Hippodrome, the odd rowdy backpacker joint on **Akbıyık Caddesi** and one or two somnolent hotel bars. Or forgo the booze and give your lungs a workout at one of the local narghile cafés.

Enjoyer Café

Incili Çavuş Sokak 7 (0212 512 8759). Tram Sultanahmet. **Open** 9am-2am daily. **Licensed. Map** p243 N10 ❶

Tucked off Sultanahmet's main Divan Yolu drag, Enjoyer Café is indeed an enjoyable spot for a snack or a drink. Open all day, the friendly venue boasts tasty – and budget-friendly – Turkish and Ottoman dishes, such as chicken marinated in honey or garlicky salmon. There's a solid selection of wines and fine Turkish coffee.

Fes Café.

Fes Café

Ali Baba Türbe Sokak 25-27 (0212 526 3070, www.fescafe.com). Tram Çemberlitaş. **Not licensed. Open** 9am-9pm daily. **Map** p243 M9 ❷

On a quiet backstreet near Nuruosmaniye Mosque, just off Nuruosmaniye Caddesi, this café's modern design blends surprisingly well with its antiquated surroundings. With a sister establishment smack in the centre of the Grand Bazaar, Fes Café is something of a local institution. The fresh-pressed lemonade and mint tea are refreshing after a heavy shopping session. Be sure to check out Abdullah, a little shop in the café that sells gorgeous natural textiles, plus an assortment of olive oil-based soaps.

★ Meşale

Arasta Bazaar 45 (0212 518 9562). **Open** 24-hrs daily. *Tram Sultanahmet.* **Not licensed. Map** p243 N11 ❸

For review, *see p157* **Hubbly Bubbly**.

North Shield

Ebusuud Caddesi 2 (0212 527 0931, www.thenorthshield.com). Tram Gülhane. **Open** 11am-1am Mon-Thur, Sun; 11am-2am Fri, Sat. **Licensed. Map** p243 N9 ❹

The North Shield transports its regulars to suburban middle England. Think tartan carpets, Famous Grouse mirrors, etched glass screens, wooden benches and a dark, polished bar. There's even Abba, Elton John and Santana on the sound system. Homesick Brits gather here and at seven other North Shields around town. It's big on sports.

Other locations Thoughout the city.

Şah Bar

İncili Çavuş Çıkmazı 9 (0212 519 5807, www.sahbar.com). Tram Sultanahmet. **Open** noon-2am daily. **Licensed. Map** p243 N10 ❺

This is a true drinking bar, with loud Western music, Efes flowing and a rowdy backpacker crowd enjoying the vibe. It's something rare in Sultanahmet, and welcome for that. There are some snacks, but it's best to visit after dinner elsewhere for drinking into the night and singing along to soul classics.

Yeşil Ev Beer Garden

Kabasakal Caddesi 5 (0212 517 6785, www.yesilev.com.tr). Tram Sultanahmet. **Open** 7am-11pm daily. **Licensed. Map** p243 N11 ❻

This idyllic garden of towering laurel, tulips and horse chestnut trees belongs to the quaint Yeşil Ev guesthouse. It's the finest place for an aperitif this side of the Golden Horn. In winter, guests are sheltered in a large conservatory amid hanging plants. Pricey, but worth it.

► *For the Yeşil Ev hotel, see p95.*

THE BAZAAR QUARTER

Divan

Kapalıçarşı (Grand Bazaar) Cevahir Bedesten 143-151 (0212 520 2250). Tram Beyazıt. **Not licensed. Open** 9am-7pm Mon-Sat. **Map** p242 L9 ❼

This place in the Old Bazaar, or Cevahir Bedesten, stands out. It's a simulated slice of the suave old days of the republic, with burgundy walls, red leather couches, a huge Turkish flag draped from the ceiling, and a crystal chandelier beside a giant portrait of Atatürk. The extensive coffee menu features the likes of frappuccinos, plus decent sandwiches and sweets.

Beyazıt

Erenler Çay Bahçesi

Çorlulu Ali Paşa Medresesi, Yeniçeriler Caddesi 36/28 (0212 511 8853). Tram Beyazıt. **Open** *Summer* 7am-3am daily. *Winter* 7am-midnight daily. **Not licensed. No credit cards. Map** p242 L10 ❽

For review, *see p157* **Hubbly Bubbly**.

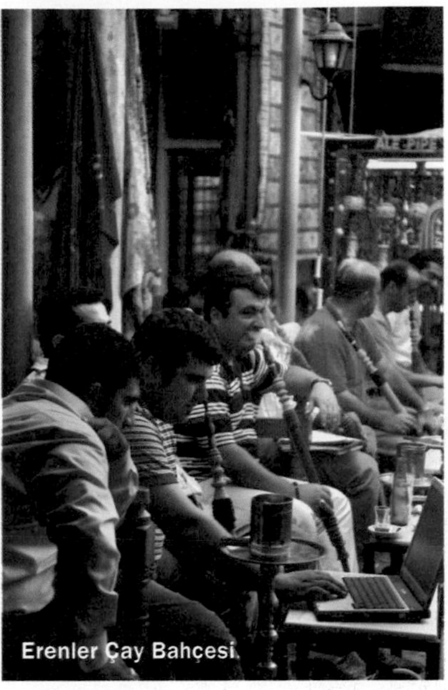

Erenler Çay Bahçesi.

WESTERN DISTRICTS

Eyüp

Pierre Loti

Balmumcu Sokak 5, off Gümüşsuyu Caddesi (0212 581 2696). Bus 55ET or ferry from Eminönü Haliç Iskelesi. **Open** 8am-midnight daily. **Not licensed. No credit cards.**

On a hilltop with a stunning vantage point over the Golden Horn, this café is dedicated to French naval officer Pierre Loti, who was so obsessed with Istanbul that he took to masquerading as a Turk and remodelled his house as a 'Sultan's palace'. Legend has it Loti would sit at this spot for hours, gazing over the city and gathering inspiration for his literary masterpiece, *Aziyade*. To get to this modest teahouse, climb up through the scenic cemetery near Eyüp Mosque or take the cable car, which is signposted from the mosque.

INSIDE TRACK COFFEE TIME

Boiled in a miniature copper or brass beaker known as a *cezve*, Turkish coffee is served in miniature porcelain cups (*fincan*). Types include *çifte kavrulmu* (double-roasted), *mirra* (bitter with cardamom), *közde* (coal-cooked) and *melengiçi* (with nettle tree). After draining your cup, turn the remaining sludge upside down to have your fortune read from the dregs. Turkish coffee is still a much-cherished ritual: as the local saying goes, *Bir fincan kahvenin kırk yıllık hatrı vardır* (one cup of coffee brings 40 years of gratitude).

BEYOĞLU

Cihangir

This bohemian enclave boasts countless style-conscious cafés and bars. Most are concentrated along and around Akarsu Sokak. Things really liven up after dark and at weekends, when a leisurely brunch can easily last all day.

★ Cuppa

Yeni Yuva Sokak 26 (0212 249 5723, www.cuppajuice.com). **Open** 9am-10pm daily. **Not licensed. Map** p249 O4 ❾

On one of the smaller streets behind Cihangir's main drag, this juice bar is the perfect antidote to Beyoğlu's boozy bars. Choose from around 40 fruit and veggie cocktails, plus nutritious extras such as wheatgrass, guarana or Echinacea. The healthy menu extends to salads, wraps and sandwiches. The decor, like many places in the neighbourhood, is retro, with classic furniture, shelving holding up *National Geographic* magazines and *Peanuts* cartoon books, and a record player providing the tunes. Free Wi-Fi.

► *You'll find lots of fruit juice stalls along Galipdede Caddesi, off Tünel Square.*

CONSUME

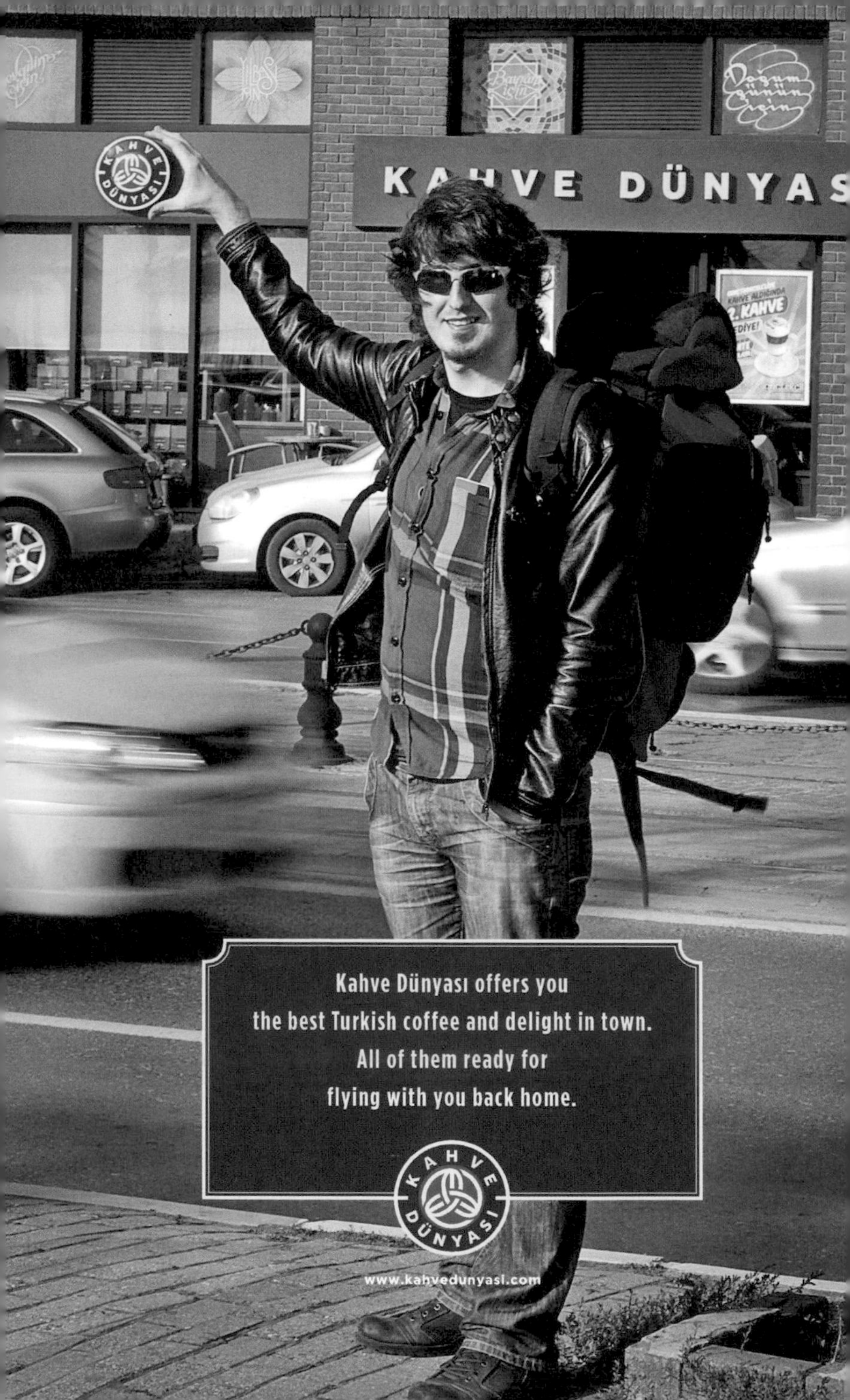
KAHVE DÜNYASI
KAHVE DÜNYAS
Kahve Dünyası offers you
the best Turkish coffee and delight in town.
All of them ready for
flying with you back home.
KAHVE DÜNYASI
www.kahvedunyasi.com

Meyra

Akarsu Caddesi 36A (0212 244 5350, www.hotelvillazurich.com). **Open** 8.30am-2am Mon-Fri; 8.30am-4am Sat, Sun. **Licensed.** **Map** p249 O4 ⑩

Meyra (formerly Leyla) is a popular café that is unpretentiously cool. The retro designer furniture, chalkboard specials and airy interior with large windows opening on to street tables make it the perfect location for whiling away an afternoon. Menu highlights include all-day breakfasts (available until 6pm), with geographical themes running from Istanbul to Oslo, Madrid and London. The English breakfast is a generous plate of bacon and eggs, with orange juice, tea and a selection of rolls. Decent salads, burgers and meat dishes are also available. There's wine by the glass and Efes beer is on tap.

★ Smyrna

Akarsu Caddesi 29 (0212 244 2466). **Open** 9am-2am daily. **Licensed.** **Map** p249 O4 ⑪

Traditionally, Cihangir's favourite hangout has been the cluster of teahouses by the mosque, where local loafers can spend a whole day or evening ensconced beneath the plane trees, nursing a dirt-cheap glass of tea. Nearby Smyrna is where the teahouse regulars come when they're feeling flush, to rub shoulders with the actors and artists who live in the area. The fabulous decor has been put together using items from second-hand shops in the area and is a mix of the antique, modern and downright whimsical. The old typewriters reflect the bohemian vibe. Food includes a variety of salads, pastas and grilled meats. Laid-back enough for daytime lounging and lunching, Smyrna shifts up a few gears after dark.

Susam Café

Susam Sokak 11 (0212 251 5995). **Open** 10am-2am daily. **Licensed.** **Map** p249 O4 ⑫

A low-key corner bar on one of Cihangir's backstreets, hip little Susam has a menu with hot and cold coffees, teas, freshly squeezed juices, lemonade, cookies, cakes and other sweets. There are waffles and pancakes, plus mains of toasted sandwiches, salads and sandwiches. Decor is delightfully retro.

Galata & Tünel

The cobbled streets found around **Galata**, **Asmalımescit** and **Tünel** are home to some of the city's most exciting and distinctive venues. At the time of writing, bars and cafés in Asmalımescit were suffering due to a 2011 restriction on outdoor seating. It wasn't clear if this is permanent or if rules will be softened in the near future; for the moment, be prepared to find the traditional terrace sprawl severely curtailed.

Badehane.

★ Badehane

General Yazgan Sokak 1/D, Tünel (0212 249 0550). **Open** 9am-3am daily. **Licensed.** **Map** p248 M4 ⑬

A modest, single-room venue just off Tünel Square, Badehane began as an eaterie, but quickly evolved into one of the most popular bars in town. On Wednesdays, live gypsy music (including local legend Selim Sesler) gets the crowd dancing around the tiny, packed tables. There is also live music on Tuesdays and at weekends – see in-house posters for details. During summer, windows are removed and the action edges outdoors, with crowds sharing backgammon tournaments and large beers.

► *For more information on Istanbul's live music venues, see p195-201.*

CONSUME

Grape Expectations

Turkey has 3,000 years of winemaking heritage. It's taken that long to succeed.

Wine may not be the first thing that comes to mind when discussing Turkish products. Turkish Delight, pashmina scarves, evil eye ornaments... But wine? Yet this attitude is undergoing big changes. Wine writers Oz Clarke and Charles Metcalfe, and Masters of Wine Susan Hulme and Tim Atkin, toured Turkey's wine-producing areas in 2010 and returned pleasantly surprised. An impressed Tim Atkin reported, 'This historic but little-known wine-producing country has an exciting range of indigenous varieties that deserve to reach a wider audience. I am very impressed by the quality.' Flash in the pan? Judges at the 2011 London International Wine Fair lauded the local production yet again, with Turkish wines scooping numerous medals and awards, including a whopping 67 medals from the Decanter World Wine Awards. Turkish producer Kavaklidere was even awarded the Decanter Regional Trophy for its sweet Tatlı Sert Narince, pressed from the indigenous Narince grape.

It's been a challenge to get Turkish wine up to competitive standards when the favoured local tipple, anise-based *rakı*, fills bar glasses and accompanies meals as a matter of course. In addition to convincing local taste, the fact that the country's three principal producers – Doluca, Kavaklidere and Kayra – have dominated winemaking has pushed small-scale vineyards to the sidelines up until now. However, with international acknowledgement and increased exposure, there are signs that Turkey is on its way to becoming a significant exporter. 'There's a long wine history in Turkey, but at the moment there's not much competition,' explained Murat Bozok, head chef of Mimolett (*see p138*), one of Istanbul's leading restaurants. 'When there is, the quality of wine will go up. We have a lot of boutique vineyards and the baby boom generation are beginning to learn about wines.'

Educating the average consumer about Turkish wines is half the battle. Not only have most wine-lovers probably never considered them, but – unless you're Turkish – the names of local grapes are tongue twisters themselves. Below is a short rundown.

RED

Öküzgözü (okoo-zgoo-zu). Translates as 'bull's eye', referring to its large, dark grape. Medium body, not too fruity. It doesn't taste as heavy as it looks. Öküzgözü is to Turkey what Malbec is to Argentina.

Boğazkere (bo-aahz-kere). Dark and rich but typically used to make light-bodied blends. However, the single variety, premium quality, makes for a full-bodied, tannic, fully loaded glass.

CONSUME

★ Enginar

Şah Kapısı Sokak 4A, Kuledibi, Galata (0212 251 7321). **Open** noon-2am daily. **Licensed. Map** p246 M5 ⓮

The neighbourhood around the Galata Tower has had a major facelift in the last few years: streets have been repaved and sleek new cafés populate the spruced-up square surrounding the tower. Enginar, one of the area's most popular bars, has a claim to fame as a set for a local soap opera, and with its stained-glass windows and rustic interior, it's a perfect pit-stop after a tour of the tower or midway on the steep climb from Karaköy to Tünel. There's occasional music during the winter months.

KV Café

Tünel Geçidi 10, Tünel (0212 251 4338, www.kv.com.tr). **Open** 8am-2am daily. **Licensed. Map** p248 M4 ⓯

Opposite Tünel station, an elaborate iron gate leads to an enchanting 19th-century arcade overgrown with potted plants. Of the handful of cafés lucky enough to share this secret passageway, KV is the largest and most atmospheric. Couples cosy up on wrought-iron furniture, snacking on cakes or lingering over cheese and wine. Inside, the café occupies three beautiful bare-brick rooms with tiled floors, arched windows and unusual antiques. At dusk, the setting is even more romantic, lit by candles and Victorian lamps, with live piano music wafting through the arcade. The music programme is usually from September to March.

Otto Sofyalı

Sofyalı Sokak 22/A, Tünel (0212 252 6588, www.ottoistanbul.com). **Open** 11am-2am Mon-Sat. **Licensed. Map** p248 M4 ⓰

With authentic pizzas, light bites and good cocktails, Otto has been an important part of Istanbul food and drink, as well as nightlife, since the first branch opened back in 2005 (Küçük Otto, around the corner; the second branch is located just outside the

Kalecik Karası (kal-ee-jik kar-a-si). Not so deep in colour, but lively on the palate. Soft tannins, with aromas of dried fruits, cocoa and spices. It is a classy number. If you like pinot noir, you'll like this one.

WHITE

Emir (eh-meer). Refreshing and dry with lingering floral and faintly fruity notes. Low acidity. It's also used to make excellent bubbly. The type of wine that slips down oh-so-easily on its own.
Narince (nah-reen-jeh). An aromatic white with a smooth texture. The flavour of this grape varies greatly because it can be aged for quite a while, though younger bottles have a nice, fresh flavour.
Sultaniye (sul-ta-na). The Ottoman sultans drank this by the gallon. Light and citrus with a low level of acidity. The perfect wine to sip sitting by the Bosphorus with a freshly grilled fish sandwich.

WHERE TO TRY TURKISH WINE

If you'd like to learn more and sample some of Turkey's top tipples, visit **La Cave** (Sıraselviler Caddesi 109, Cihangir, Beyoğlu, 0212 243 2405, www.lacave sarap.com) or **Sensus** (Büyükhendek Caddesi 5, Galata, Beyoğlu, 0212 245 5657, www.sensuswine.com). Both offer 'flights' by wine regions for around TL20 for five samples.

Santralistanbul arts centre; *see p66*). This branch has a similar industrial chic look as the others. Its most attractive detail is the bar, which spans from the entrance down to the back of the narrow venue.
Other locations Otto Santral: Kazım Karabekir Caddesi 2/7 (0212 427 1889); Küçük Otto: Şehbender Sokak 5/1 (0212 292 7015).

Şimdi

Atlas Apt, Asmalımescit Sokak 5, Tünel (0212 252 5443). **Open** 8am-2am daily. **Licensed**. **Map** p248 M4 ⑰

This relaxed refuge off Istiklal is one of the most stylish all-day café-bars in Istanbul. Hipsters hang out in the retro front room, where low seating and low lighting encourage lounging. Free wireless internet also makes it a good place to work on a quiet afternoon. There's an above-average selection of wine by the glass, accompanied by addictive balls of spiced cheese. Simple but delicious Mediterranean dishes are served in the dining area at the rear.

Galatasaray

Discerning drinkers head to the stylish cafés and bars around the **Galatasaray Lycée**, where Istanbul's intellectuals, designers and media types congregate. Photographers favour **Kafe Ara**, named after Magnum snapper Ara Güler, who lives upstairs.

Büyük Londra

Meşrutiyet Caddesi 53 (0212 293 1619, www.londrahotel.net). **Open** 4pm-2am daily. **Licensed**. **Map** p248 M3 ⑱

Fans of colonial watering holes tend to head for the bar at the Pera Palas Hotel. that's because they don't know about the Büyük Londra. A late 19th-century time warp, it may be a less grand than the newly renovated Pera Palas, but it's definitely more eccentric. Hemingway stayed here in 1922, sent by the *Toronto Daily Star* to cover the Turkish war of independence, and the bar remains a monthly meeting place for Istanbul's Foreign Press Club. The bar's two gilded salons are plushly carpeted and decked with giant chandeliers. An immaculate barman occasionally sallies forth from the tiny bar at the back to change the 78 on the wind-up gramophone; otherwise, caged songbirds on the windowsills provide the soundtrack. In summertime, action moves upstairs to the hotel's panoramic Teras Bar. *Photo p153.*
► *The Büyük Londra is also a good, moderately priced hotel (see p113).*

Cezayir

Hayriye Caddesi 12 (0212 245 9981, www.cezayir-istanbul.com). **Open** 9am-2am daily. **Licensed**. **Map** p248 N3 ⑲

Behind the Galatasaray Lycée, this fabulous 19th-century building was originally a school for the Italian Workers' Association. Now beautifully converted into a glamorous bar and modern Turkish restaurant, Cezayir throngs with the city's literati and glitterati late into the night. The baroque silvery dining room is stunning. The golden back room, with original floor tiles, soaring ceilings and a long wooden bar, is a stylish place for sharing some of the kitchen's inventive meze. There's a louche lounge with large mirrors and sofas, and a courtyard garden downstairs that opens on to the twee restaurants of French Street. *Photos p155.*

Kafe Ara

Istiklal Caddesi, Tosbağa Sokak 2, off Yeniçarşı Caddesi (0212 245 4105). **Open** 8am-midnight Mon-Thur, Sun; 8am-midnight Fri, Sat; 10am-midnight Sun. **Not licensed**. **Map** p248 N3 ⑳

A continental-style café owned by local Magnum photographer Ara Güler, whose evocative black and white shots of Istanbul adorn the walls and place-mats. Year-round, the smart, split-level interior buzzes with cultured patrons armed with portfolios, notebooks or laptops. No alcohol is served, but the

fresh-pressed lemonade with mint and milkshakes are great. Snack on a mix of Mediterranean salads and Turkish meze, plus sandwiches, pasta and desserts. *Photo p156.*

► *To view photos by Ara Güler, see www.araguler.com.tr.*

★ Leb-i Derya Richmond

Richmond Hotel, Istiklal Caddesi 227 (0212 243 4375, www.lebiderya.com). **Open** 11am-2am Mon-Thur; 11am-3am Fri; 10am-3am Sat; 10am-2am Sun. **Licensed. Map** p248 M4 ㉑

On the sixth and top floor of the Richmond Hotel, right on Istiklal Caddesi, this bright and airy bar and restaurant has one very attractive proposition: jaw-dropping views over Istanbul. The food is excellent, but avoid lunch in summer as the glassed-in terrace creates a greenhouse effect. Instead, go in time for a sundowner – try the Derya cocktail (green apple vodka, cointreau, lime and fresh mint) – accompanied by breathtaking views over the Bosphorus.

► *Don't miss the equally spectacular Leb-i Derya nearby at Kumbaracı Han 57/6, Kumbaracı Yokuşu, Tünel (0212 293 4989).*

Limonlu Bahçe

Yeniçarşı Caddesi 74 (0212 252 1094). **Open** *Nov-Mar* noon-11pm daily. *Apr-Oct* 9.30am-2am daily. **Licensed. Map** 248 N3 ㉒

Part-way down the precipitous slope of Yeniçarşı, Limonlu Bahçe is hidden away in a bucolic courtyard garden. This pretty setting draws a self-conscious young crowd who loll on cushions, flop in hammocks or gather around chunky wooden tables. There are plenty of tight T-shirts and cute tattoos on display. And if there aren't enough staff, nobody seems to mind.

Nu Teras

Meşrutiyet Caddesi 67 (0212 245 6070, www.nupera.com.tr). **Open** noon-1am Mon-Thur, Sun; noon-4am Fri, Sat. **Licensed. Map** p248 M4 ㉓

On the rooftop of the Nu Pera building, Nu Teras is the epitome of hip Istanbul – with the backdrop of a stunning view of the Golden Horn. The area behind the bar is given over to long tables for diners, who tuck into chef Esra Muslu's contemporary meze, such as red pepper dolma stuffed with seasonal fish, and tasty organic breads. Dancing is tolerated, but swaying is considered cooler. Unlike other new venues that were crowded out then swiftly abandoned, Nu Teras is a survivor that can be considered a classic.

► *For more bars with views, see p154* **Up on the Roofs.**

Pano

Hamalbaşı Caddesi 12/B (0212 292 6664, www.panosarapevi.com). **Open** 11am-2am daily. **Licensed. Map** p248 N3 ㉔

INSIDE TRACK TEA TIME

Turkish tea, made from black tea leaves grown in the Black Sea region, brewed in a teapot and sipped from elegant little tulip-shaped glasses, is as ubiquitous as ever.

Over a century old, Pano is an Istanbul institution. This atmospheric wine bar is like an updated take on a typical Greek taverna, with wood-panelled interior and rows of giant barrels above the bar. The later it gets, the more people pile in, and there's often standing room only. Then customers squeeze around the narrow counters, sampling Turkish and imported wines by the glass or bottle. Beer is also plentiful and cheap. Tasty finger food includes a generous cheese platter. Only the lucky few will find a table for a proper meze dinner.

► *For more on Turkish wines, see p150* **Grape Expectations.**

Public

Meşrutiyet Caddesi 84 (0212 251 5131). **Open** noon-midnight Mon-Thur; noon-4am Sat, Sun. **Licensed. Map** p248 N3 ㉕

Public is a relatively new Beyoğlu addition among the hotels and design bars along Meşrutiyet. By day, it serves an impressive range of snacks and light

Büyük Londra. *See p151.*

lunches. The evening menu is more substantial, with Mediterranean dishes and a few Turkish standards. The music gets going at night too; some of Istanbul's more cutting-edge DJs and a few international names have put in an appearance. After dark, Public is all about the partying.

SALT Bistro

Istiklal Caddesi 136 (0212 251 6628, www.bistro.com.tr). **Open** noon-midnight Tue-Sun. **Licensed**. **Map** p246 N3 26

Opened by stellar chef Murat Bozok in 2011, SALT Bistro occupies the first floor of brand-new art gallery SALT Beyoğlu. The tiny café and eaterie is slighter softer on the wallet than Bozok's upscale restaurant Mimolett (*see p138*) but still pricey, so bargain-hunters should aim to drop in 6-8pm for discounted drinks. In summertime, tables spill out on to a tiny streetside terrace.

Zoe

Yeniçarşı Caddesi 38 (0212 251 7491, www.zoeteras.com). **Open** noon-2am daily. **Licensed**. **Map** p248 N3 27

Despite the gruff bouncers manning the red velvet entrance, Zoe is actually a relatively laid-back

A Bar with a View

Head up high for stunning panoramas.

Yesterday I watched you from a noble hill,
Noble Istanbul
I know every street, every alleyway,
I love you Istanbul
Yahya Kemal Batah (1884-1958)

Now, as then, the best way to see Istanbul is from above, as Istanbul's nightlife impresarios have discovered – a revelation that has revolutionised dining and drinking in recent years. Rooftop bars and restaurants have sprung up everywhere, desperately trying to outdo each other with the most sweeping skyline and exotic cocktail list.

The frontrunner of this trend is **5.Kat** (*see p136*), owned by actress Yasemin Alkaya: it's a heady mix of art deco and kitsch, starlit romance and late-night shenanigans. Another pioneer of the roof-terrace scene is **Leb-i Derya Richmond** (*see p153*), owner Cem Sancer's second bar (visit the first at Kumbaracı Han 57/6) boasting breathtaking views over the Bosphorus.

Nu Teras (*see p153*) is another stunner: up on the seventh floor, and with amazing views over the Golden Horn, this spot is a place to be seen – it's summer central for hip Istanbullus.

In recent years, ever more bars, restaurants, cafés and cake shops have launched open-air outposts offering fabulous cityscapes. The glass-walled pleasure palace that is **360** (*see p134*), a restaurant, bar and club rolled into one, sits atop one of Beyoğlu's most famous apartment blocks, smack in the middle of Istiklal Caddesi. As its name suggests, it boasts 360-degree views – with sky-high prices to match.

Rooftop revelry is not confined to the rich. Many of Beyoğlu's *meyhanes* and humble coffee shops have also opened up their top floors to the elements – though they can't all boast the same views.

Nu Teras.

CONSUME

bar-restaurant that puts equal emphasis on food and drink. On a budget? During Happy Hour (5-7.30pm) all drinks are discounted. Zoe is also one of many venues that makes the most of its rooftop; in the summer, lively groups of revellers party under the stars until dawn.

Nevizade

Nevizade Sokak is a safe bet for a lively night out. At the time of writing, it is one of the few streets off Istiklal Caddesi that has been allowed to retain its outdoor terraced seating, giving it an all-hours, lively buzz. Young Turks down *raki* in packed *meyhanes* or huddle around tankards of beer in the nearby pubs.

Gizli Bahçe

Nevizade Sokak 25 (0212 249 2192). **Open** 2pm-2am daily. **Licensed. Map** p248 N3 ㉘
To pick this 'Secret Garden' out from the dozens of other establishments on Nevizade Sokak, keep an eye out for the old '27' crudely painted alongside the entrance. There's a mellow terraced bar on the ground floor and a livelier space up two flights of stairs, littered with low tables and armchairs. The music, pumped on to the outdoor patios upstairs, is an odd medley of modern electro and obscure 1980s tracks.

James Joyce

Balo Sokak 26, off Istiklal Caddesi (0212 244 7973, www.theirishcentre.com). **Open** noon-2am Mon-Thur, Sun; noon-4am Fri, Sat. **Licensed. Map** p248 N3 ㉙
The first and only Irish pub in Istanbul. The decor is predictably clichéd, although recently renovated, but the punters are a mixed bag of worldly Turks, expats and tourists who come for the decent range of fairly pricey beers (Guinness included). Irish breakfast is served all day and there's often live music. The place gets packed for international football matches, when the atmosphere can be electric. There's also regular live music on the new stage.

Şahika

Nevizade Sokak 5 (0212 249 6196). **Open** noon-4am daily. **Licensed. Map** p248 N3 ㉚
Another lively but laid-back venue with dozens of stools and tiny tables packed into the small space outside, from where a predominantly younger crowd watches the world go by. Inside, wooden stairs lead to five levels of dining rooms and a summer roof terrace where the good times roll to a mix of 1980s, electronica and alternative rock. The simple menu is good value for money.

Taksim

Almost every side street off two-and-a-half kilometre-long Istiklal Caddesi is riddled with

Cezayir. *See p151.*

CONSUME

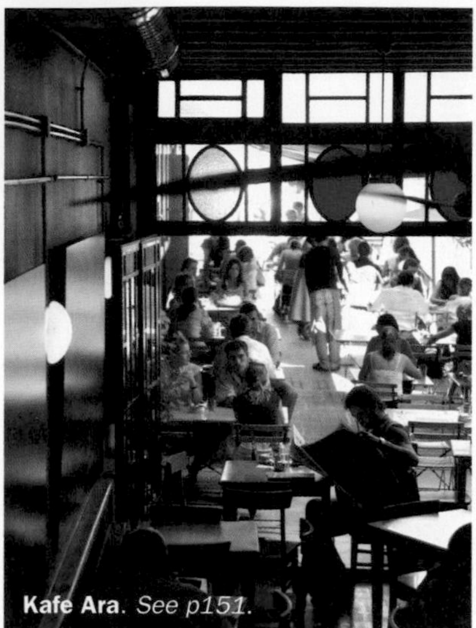
Kafe Ara. See p151.

bars and cafés. The greatest concentration is near **Taksim Square**, with venues for every tribe: Africans, Anatolians, goths, bikers, students, intellectuals, gays and transvestites. Patrons in search of a cheap beer or a puff on a narghile loiter around **Mis Sokak** and **Büyük Parmakkapı Sokak**.

Kaktüs

Imam Adnan Sokak 4/A, off Istiklal Caddesi (0212 249 5979). **Open** 9am-2am daily. **Licensed**. **Map** p249 O2 ㉛

Kaktüs's elegant dark-wood interior owes a great deal to the classic French café. Its patrons do their best to recreate the ambience of a Godard movie by chain-smoking (outside) and sipping blonde beers or black coffee. Standoffish staff process the short-order menu that changes daily. Since opening in the early 1990s, Kaktüs has spawned countless imitators, but it still manages to remain the coolest.

Other locations Cihangir Caddesi 16, Cihangir (0212 243 5731).

Klub Karaoke

Zambak Sokak 7 (0212 293 7639, www.klub-karaoke.com). **Open** 8pm-3am Mon-Thur, Sun; 8pm-5am Fri, Sat. **Licensed**. **Map** p249 O2 ㉜

This karaoke club near Taksim Square consists of a small bar and three private rooms that are available for hire – the intimate, red-leather Tokyo Room, the darker Fetish Room and the vast, jungle-inspired Zoo Room. Look out for the theme nights dedicated to ladies, men, Turkish tunes or disco hits. Things don't really get going until around 11pm, then everyone wants a turn on the mic.

Pia

Bekar Sokak 4/A, off Istiklal Caddesi (0212 252 7100). **Open** 10am-2am daily. **Licensed**. **Map** p249 O2 ㉝

The uncluttered decor and gallery-style mezzanine create a sense of space where there isn't much at all. Ornate mirrors and a single George Grosz print set the tone. This is a hangout for writers, filmmakers and other creative types. It's also the kind of place where single women will feel comfortable – in fact, some of the city's most beautiful women have been seen to drop into Pia – or so the local rumours go. Dishes inspired by the owners' travels are served all day. The daily specials are usually worth a gamble.

NIŞANTAŞI

For a different take on Istanbul's bar life, head up to **Nişantaşı**, an upper-class neighbourhood north of Taksim with a lively bar scene. Much of the action centres around Teşvikiye Caddesi.

Corridor

Milli Reasürans Çarşısı 47/48, Abdi Ipekci Caddesi (0212 343 0241). Metro Osmanbey. **Open** 6pm-2am Mon-Sat. **Licensed**.

A shopping mall may seem like a rather strange place for a bar, but Nişantaşı's Milli Reasürans Çarşısı is full of them. Corridor has a lively but laid-back atmosphere, without the snob factor and dismissive doormen of many Nişantaşı locations. And the hipsters don't seem to mind taking their drinks out to the closed shopping centre.

Hubbly Bubbly

Put this in your pipe and smoke it.

Waterpipe, hookah, or 'hubbly bubbly'. Call it what you will, Turks have been smoking the narghile since the early 17th century, despite religious authorities periodically denouncing the practice and calling for it to be banned. The tyrannical Murat IV (1623-40) decreed that anyone caught having so much as a quick puff should be sentenced to death.

In the late 19th and early 20th century, narghile smoking was all the rage in high society, particularly among women. That fad passed and in republican Istanbul the narghile was relegated to a pastime of the peasantry. Why it should suddenly be making a comeback in the 21st century is anybody's guess. But in the last few years a slew of cafés devoted to the waterpipe has opened. A few are aimed at tourists, but most custom comes from students.

Narghile tobacco is typically soaked in molasses or apple juice, giving it a slightly sweet flavour; but you can get it straight and strong by asking for *tömbeki*.

Narghile cafés serve tea and coffee, but traditionally they do not serve alcohol. Prices are around TL10-TL15 a pipe, which lasts a good hour or more. Contrary to popular misconception, hashish is not an option, nor, sadly, is the traditional Ottoman blend of opium, perfume and crushed pearls.

The best place to sample a narghile is on the nameless pedestrian strip between the old cannon foundry at Tophane and the Istanbul Modern. Until recent years there was just a row of small shops; now it's lined with nothing but narghile cafés. At any time of day or night, there might be 300 to 400 people here, an extraordinary mix of students, couples and families, all puffing great clouds of pale smoke. Certain cafés along the strip have drawn fire in the press for providing beanbags and cushion-strewn banquettes, which apparently encourage al fresco canoodling. But with or without the bodily contact, this is a fine place to wind down after a night out in Beyoğlu.

Over in Beyazit, in the idyllic courtyard of an Ottoman seminary, **Erenler Çay Bahçesi** (*see p147)* has low tables and benches, shaded with ivy-hung trellises. Despite signs advertising 'Magic Waterpipe Garden', few tourists visit; it's filled with students from nearby Istanbul University and a good sprinkling of elderly locals.

Perhaps the most popular place in Sultanahmet is **Meşale** (*see p146*). This sunken café beside Arasta Bazaar, an arcade of tourist shops, is very pleasant when the shops close and locals descend. There are usually nightly performances of Turkish classical music and dervish dancing shows on Friday, Saturday and Sunday between 8pm and 10pm.

Touchdown

Milli Reasürans Çarşısı 61/D11, Abdi Ipekci Caddesi (0212 231 3671, www.touchdown.com.tr). Metro Osmanbey. **Open** 11am-midnight Mon-Thur; 11am-2am Fri, Sat. **Licensed.**

Touchdown manages to successfully recreate the atmosphere of an American corner bar, despite the fact that it's located in a shopping mall. It's a popular spot for locals to gather for drinks after work; on busy nights, customers trickle down the stairway of the Reasürans Centre. Although a particular favourite with media and advertising executives, it's not at all flashy. In fact, it feels more like a student union bar.

THE BOSPHORUS VILLAGES

On the shores of the Bosphorus, picturesque, well-to-do **Ortaköy**, **Arnavutköy** and **Bebek** are made for indolent afternoons measured out in coffee cups and moonlit evenings fuelled by martinis. The most successful venues owe as much to their waterfront settings as their designer decor and fancy drinks.

Anjelique

Salhane Sokak 5, Muallim Naci Caddesi, Ortaköy (0212 327 2844, www.istanbuldoors.com). Bus 25E, 40T. **Open** 6pm-4am daily. **Licensed.**

INSIDE TRACK ON THE RAKI

When it comes to alcohol, Turkey is best known for *rakı* – the anise spirit that turns milky when mixed with water, hence its nickname 'lion's milk' (*aslan sütü*). Careful drinkers fill a third of their glass with *rakı* and top up with water and ice. Unlike beer, *rakı* contains no malt, which allegedly saves drinkers from killer hangovers. Even so, you can have a very bad *rakı* experience unless you wash it down with plenty of water and soak it up with copious meze. *Rakı* should never be drunk without an edible accompaniment. White Turkish cheese and melon is a classic combination.

Anjelique, which is run by the prolific Doors Group, is an upmarket restaurant serving Asian and Mediterranean dishes – which after hours turns into a club and cocktail bar. In a restored three-storey mansion, it has superb views over the Bosphorus. The music policy is key, and it even issues its own *Sounds of Anjelique* volumes. Big-name DJs regularly attend, including Argentinian DJ Hernan Cattaneo.

Aşşk Kahve

Muallim Naci Caddesi 64/B, Kuruçeşme (0212 265 4734, www.asskkahve.com). Bus 25E, 40T. **Open** 9am-2am Tue-Sun; noon-2am Mon. **Licensed**.

Once you get past that name – the Turkish word for 'love' drawn out into a lisping 'ashk' – this place has a lot to offer. To find it, follow the unmarked staircase down to the Bosphorus from the Macrocenter in Kuruçeşme. The setting is gorgeous: a clubhouse beside the Bosphorus with a lovely garden. The lavish breakfasts and organic salads are deservedly renowned, but rather expensive.

Corvus Wine and Bite

Şair Nedim Caddesi 5, Akaretler (0212 260 5470, www.wineandbite.com). Bus 25E, 40T. **Open** 10am-10pm Mon-Sat. **Licensed**.

This brand-new wine bar is tucked into the trim townhouses that formerly sheltered Dolmabahçe Palace's stables. Stocked entirely with wines produced by Bozcaada Island vintners Corvus, the contemporary bar boasts sleek wooden furnishings and exposed brick. Plenty of wines are available by the glass, and each one can be paired perfectly with Aegean nibbles.

▶ *For more the best Istanbul wine bars, see p150* **Grape Expectations**.

★ Lucca

Cevdetpaşa Caddesi 51/B, Bebek (0212 257 1255, www.luccastyle.com). Bus 25E, 40T. **Open** 10am-2am Tue-Sun; noon-2am Mon. **Licensed**.

If you're caught in a traffic jam in Bebek, the likely cause is the string of SUVs double-parked outside this neighbourhood hotspot. By night, sleek society girls pick at plates of sashimi and check each other out from the pavement seating or through the floor-to-ceiling windows. At weekends, the party people like to kick off the night with exotic cocktails, and big-name DJs hit the decks (Gilles Peterson has been here recently). By day, it's a pleasant café with Mediterranean mains (TL20-TL40) and tapas. The modern decor works well, and different artists show their work every month.

ASIAN SHORE

Savvy residents of the Asian side turn their noses up at the prospect of crossing the Bosphorus for a night out. And why should they? Kadıkoy's **Kadife Sokak** is packed with bars and cafés offering cheap beer and excellent live music. It's also worth checking out the lively nightlife scene in the chic residential area of Moda, south of Kadıköy, including bars such as **Moda Teras** (Moda Mektebi Sokak 1).

Dunia

Kadife Sokak 19, Kadıköy (0216 336 7505, www.kadyagrup.com/dunia). Ferry from Karaköy or Beşiktaş to Kadıköy. Bus 112. **Open** noon-2am daily. **Licensed**. **Map** p251 W8 34

A heady mix of café, art gallery, concert venue and dive bar, newly opened Dunia is spread over multiple floors of an enchanting old Ottoman townhouse. Sink into one of the plush velvet sofas, or order a cocktail at the long wooden bar. Both hip and delightfully unpretentious.

Isis

Kadife Sokak 26, Kadıköy (0216 349 7381, www.isis.com.tr.tc). Ferry from Karaköy or Beşiktaş to Kadıköy. Bus 112. **Open** 11am-2am daily. **Licensed**. **Map** p251 W8 35

This Egyptian-themed bar, with wall paintings and statues, is incongruously located in a converted three-storey townhouse. The top-floor wine bar holds regular tastings accompanied by live music. The large garden gets crammed on summer nights.

Karga

Kadife Sokak 16, Kadıköy (0216 449 1725, www.kargabar.org). Ferry from Karaköy or Beşiktaş to Kadıköy. Bus 112. **Open** 11am-2am daily. **Licensed**. **Map** p251 W8 36

This much-loved haunt in the heart of Kadıköy's bar strip is known for three things: alternative music, cheap beer and fine art. The music policy can only be described as eclectic, with themed nights ranging from Belgian pop to Bill Laswell. These usually take place in the ground-floor bar, which is like a pub, with lower lighting and louder music. Changing art exhibitions are held in the quieter space upstairs.

Shops & Services

Boutique buys and carpet conundrums.

That unique blend of ancient and modern that is integral to Istanbul's identity is present in shops too. Europe's largest city is home to the world's oldest mall, the **Grand Bazaar** (*see p52*), a labyrinth of intricate carpets, kilims and ancient kaftans, as well as coloured glass lamps, hand-painted ceramics and high-quality textiles. Back in Eminönü, the piles of spicy dried pepper, sumac and Turkish Delight that line the stalls of the **Egyptian Bazaar** (*see p59*) are aromatic proof of Istanbul's historic position as nexus of the international spice trade. Tastes tend instead towards the 21st century? Then the boutiques of Beyoğlu, Akaretler and Nişantaşı are the place to pick up custom-made leather slippers, contemporary knitwear and Made in Turkey designs. And if antiques or mid 20th century is your thing, head to Çukurcuma, a neighbourhood dense with antique finds and second-hand shops.

General

DEPARTMENT STORES

Armaggan
Nuruosmaniye Caddesi, Sultanahmet (0212 522 4433, www.armaggan.com). Tram Çemberlitaş. **Open** 8.30am-10pm Mon-Sat. **Map** p243 M10.
Opened in summer 2011 just east of the Grand Bazaar, high-end Armaggan has seven floors of unique artworks, jewellery, textiles and leather, plus an art gallery and the top-floor Nar Gourmet restaurant. Note that many of the items for sale here are produced in limited editions; prices can be equally exclusive.
Other locations Bostan Sokak 8, Nişantaşı (0212 291 6292).

Beymen
Akmerkez Mall D101, Nispetiye Caddesi, Etiler (0212 316 6900, www.beymen.com). Metro Levent. **Open** 10am-10pm daily.
Beymen started life as a men's clothing store, but is now synonymous with designer clothing and accessories for men and women, combining own-label products with select international brands. You'll also find cosmetics and home accessories.
Other locations Abdi Ipekçi Caddesi 23/1, Nişantaşı (0212 373 4800); Bağdat Caddesi 330/1, Erenköy, Asian Shore (0216 468 1500).

Boyner
Metrocity Mall, Büyükdere Caddesi 171, Levent (0212 344 0566, www.boyner.com.tr). Metro Levent. **Open** 10am-10pm daily.
Part of the eponymous Boyner Group, which also owns Beymen, Boyner is a less label-conscious version of its sister store. It stocks a comprehensive selection of clothes, shoes, sportswear, cosmetics, fabrics, china, glass and home accessories.

Vakko
Kanyon Mall, Büyükdere Caddesi 138-140, Levent (0212 353 1080, www.vakko.com.tr). Metro Levent. **Open** 10am-10pm daily.
Vakko was once Turkey's authority on fashion and it still has huge cachet locally. Aside from some eye-

INSIDE TRACK
FIT FOR A SULTAN

Akaretler is a newly redeveloped area in Beşiktaş. Its terraced buildings were once the homes of officers who worked at nearby Dolmabahçe Palace, residence of Ottoman sultans, as well as the palace stables. The pretty townhouses now house top labels, Corvus Wine & Bite (*see p158*), hip restaurants and a W hotel. For details, see www.akaretler.com.tr.

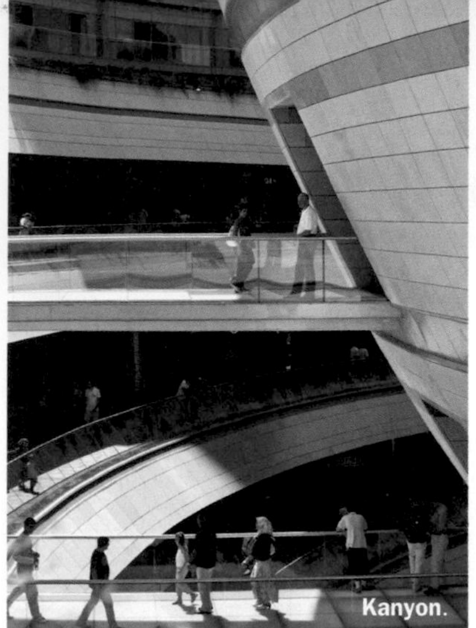
Kanyon.

catching window displays, the store has lost much of its originality today. The exceptions are own-label scarves and ties (also worth checking out in the duty free store at Atatürk Airport) and the lavish Ottoman-design furnishings and fabrics.
Other locations Akmerkez Mall 122, Nispetiye Caddesi, Etiler (0212 282 0695); Bağdat Caddesi 422, Suadiye, Asian Shore (0216 463 2606).

YKM
Halaskargazi Caddesi 368, Şişli (0212 248 4120, www.ykm.com.tr). Metro Şişli. **Open** 10am-10pm Mon-Sat; noon-7pm Sun.
Turkey's oldest department store started life as a humble shop behind the Spice Bazaar in 1950. Today, it's the closest thing Istanbul has to a Western department store. Unlike its more exclusive rivals, it caters to a broad market, selling everything from clothing to sports gear, toys, homeware and electronics.
Other locations Cevahir Mall, Büyükdere Caddesi, Şişli (0212 382 0342).

MALLS

Shopping mall (*alışveriş merkezi*) mania has seized the city since the arrival of the first one in 1988. **Kanyon** and the paparazzi-friendly **Istinye Park** are relatively recent additions to Istanbul's mall roster. **Akaretler** isn't a mall, but this redeveloped area, once stables and an estate of houses for workers at Dolmabahçe Palace, is now a row of shops, including Marc Jacobs and other luxury brands. The centrepiece is the W Hotel (*see p123*).

Akmerkez
Nispetiye Caddesi, Etiler (0212 282 0170, www.akmerkez.com.tr). Metro Levent. **Open** 10am-10pm daily.
An upmarket mall with 250 shops, a food court, cinema and a branch of Milan's excellent restaurant Paper Moon (www.papermoon.com.tr). However, its crowds and complex design do mean it's hard to find your way out. Akmerkez also suffers from an inconvenient location around ten minutes' walk from the metro.

Cevahir
Büyükdere Caddesi 22, Şişli (0212 368 6900, www.istanbulcevahir.com). Metro Şişli. **Open** 10am-10pm daily.
A vast shopping mall, the sixth largest in the world and formerly the biggest in Europe; its six storeys are permanently packed. Besides direct access from the metro, one of the mall's greatest assets is Koçtaş, one of the city's only DIY stores reachable by public transport.

Istinye Park
Istinye Bayırı Caddesi 73, Sarıyer (0212 345 5555, www.istinyepark.com). Bus 22RE, 29, 29B, 29P, 29S, 40B, 42, 59A. **Open** 10am-10pm daily.
The exclusive Istinye Park is home to Gucci, Louis Vuitton, Prada and the usual roll call of designer stores. It's mostly covered, but there's a more pleasant outdoor precinct area. Among the mall's various restaurants and cafés, it is Masa where shoppers go to be seen; paparazzi often hang about the place.
► *Istinye Park is also fairly close to Müzedechanga (see p143), the summertime-only restaurant located in the Sakıp Sabancı Museum in Emirgan.*

★ Kanyon
Büyükdere Caddesi 185, Levent (0212 317 5300, www.kanyon.com.tr). Metro Levent. **Open** 10am-10pm daily.
Kanyon is a mall with a difference. Open to, and yet sheltered from, the elements, its canyon-inspired design houses 170 boutique-style shops, a plethora of restaurants, including branches of fashionable Kitchenette (*see p135*) and the House Café (*see p143*), not to mention the plushest cinema in town. When it comes to shopping, the accent is on prestige fashion and lifestyle labels, both local and foreign: the likes of Harvey Nichols, Georg Jensen-Moser, Vakko and Swarovski. There's also an Apple store.

Metrocity
Büyükdere Caddesi 1, Levent (0212 344 0660, www.metrocity.com.tr). Metro Levent. **Open** 10am-10pm daily.
Like nearby Kanyon, this four-storey mall is served by a direct link to the metro. What's different is that it pitches to a far more middle-of-the-road clientele. Among the 140 stores, you'll find Marks & Spencer vying for business with Benetton, Zara, Mavi Jeans and the like. There's also a very good food court offering a range of traditional Turkish fare.

Where to Shop

Istanbul's best shopping neighbourhoods in brief.

SULTANAHMET
Sultanahmet is prime tourist territory, and is well supplied with tacky souvenir stores and pushy carpet sellers. Prices are marked up accordingly. That said, some of the handicraft places and rug stores, particularly off the main drag, can turn up some interesting finds – just don't expect bargains. Things get spicier as you head west towards the Grand Bazaar area, which may have lost its lustre to locals now attuned to the mall, but remains the oriental shopping experience par excellence (*see p54* **Shopping the Bazaar**).

BEYOĞLU
By comparison, Beyoğlu offers an altogether more Western shopping experience. The street that is the backbone of the area, Istiklal Caddesi, is fast becoming bland anywhere-in-the-world high-street territory. The current line-up includes Top Shop, the Body Shop, Mango, Nike and multiple Starbucks, and now boasts the massive Demirören Istiklal shopping mall, which opened mid 2011. But duck into the side streets, or be enticed by the Parisian-style passages, and things start to get more interesting. The same holds true as you head away from the mainstream Taksim end of Istiklal towards the more off-beat Tünel end.

ÇUKURCUMA
This neighbourhood is the principal art, antiques and collectibles district. There are dozens of dealers in the labyrinth of steep, narrow streets. Antiques, mid-century modern furniture and quirky knick-knacks from the last century can all be found, along with paintings in various artists' ateliers. Bostanbaşı Caddesi and Turnacıbaşı Sokaks are the best streets to start, but nothing beats wandering.

NIŞANTAŞI
For committed shoppers in search of sophistication, head to Nişantaşı and neighbouring Teşvikiye, two districts about a kilometre and a half north of Taksim Square: these neighbourhoods are serious label territory. On Abdi Ipekçi Caddesi, the likes of Armani, Louis Vuitton and Tiffany sit alongside Turkish jewellers.

THE ASIAN SHORE
The Asian shore is great for food. In Kadıköy, at the top end of Yasa Caddesi, are delis stocking a huge range of regional Turkish produce. Güneşlibahçe Sokak has more excellent food shops, including one devoted exclusively to honey, another to olive oil, and some fantastic fishmongers. Tellalzade Sokak is lined with antiques shops.

Çukurcuma.

Market Day

A bit of everything.

Once a week, in most Istanbul neighbourhoods, a few streets are taken over by the *mahalle pazarı*, or local market. The awnings go up, wooden stalls jam the streets, and stallholders compete for custom at high volume.

Stalls are heaped with everything from jumbo olives and village cheese (*köy peyniri*) to cheap clothing, cooking pots and tools. Apples, melons and all manner of seasonal fruit and vegetables are stacked in colourful pyramids.

Bargain-hunters can sometimes find well-known European and American clothing brands at knockdown prices. Turkey's factories produce garments for the likes of Gap and Calvin Klein, and manufacturers sometimes sell surplus stock to market traders. But be sure to check items for faults. (For more on picking up surplus fashion stock, *see p168* **Beyoğlu's Fashion Arcades**.)

As a general rule, trading kicks off around 9am and winds down around 5pm (later during summer), when prices are slashed for the remaining small pickings.

For some of the city's best-known markets, *see right*.

Salı Pazarı.

MARKETS

For food markets, *see p169*.

Fatih Pazarı

Around Darüşşafaka Caddesi, Fatih. **Open** Wed. **Map** p291 G7.

This vast open-air market surrounds the Fatih Mosque and fills its rambling courtyard. Join the neighbourhood residents every Wednesday to tussle over leopard-print lingerie, clothing and household items. It also has an excellent reputation for food: expect to find top village produce, including cheeses, baskets of rosehips and, in season, cornelian cherries.

Ortaköy Market

Ortaköy Quayside. **Open** Sun.

Istanbul's answer to London's Camden Market. Go for mounds of mass-produced jewellery and plentiful kitsch imported from India and Africa. You might also happen to find the odd interesting antique, reproduction print or choice piece of trinketry.

► *For a post-shopping snack visit the House Cafe (see p143).*

Salı Pazarı

At Uzunçayır Caddesi & Mandıra Caddesi, Kadıköy. **Open** Tue, Sun.

This sprawling 'Tuesday' bazaar is the best-known, biggest and most popular of the city's street markets, so be prepared to mix it up with middle-class matrons and Anatolian mamas in search of bargain bras and the freshest of figs. Note that the new location means the market is further out of town; hop aboard bus 8A from Kadıköy bus station. Sunday sees fewer vendors.

Specialist

BOOKS & MAGAZINES

English-language

Galeri Kayseri

Divan Yolu 58, Sultanahmet (0212 512 0456, www.galerikayseri.com). Tram Sultanahmet. **Open** 9am-8.30pm daily. **Map** p243 M10.

This shop is devoted exclusively to books about Istanbul and Turkey. Whatever genre you're after, you'll find it here.

Other locations Divan Yolu 11 (0212 516 3366).

★ Homer Kitabevi

Yeniçarşı Caddesi 12A, Galatasaray (0212 249 5902, www.homerbooks.com). **Open** 10am-7.30pm Mon-Sat. **Map** p248 N3.

This smart, air-conditioned bookshop has what is widely considered to be the best collection of foreign non-fiction in Istanbul. It's particularly strong on art and academic subjects.

Pandora Kitabevi

Büyük Parmaklık Sokak 8, Beyoğlu (0212 243 3503, www.pandora.com.tr). **Open** 10am-8pm Mon-Wed; 10am-9pm Thur-Sat; 1-8pm Sun. **Map** p249 O3.

A fine little bookshop packed with English-language titles, including fiction, poetry, art, local interest and a very good history section. Flyers and posters advertise events around town. Note that there are two Pandora bookshops opposite each other – the English one is on your right if arriving from Istiklal Caddesi.

★ Robinson Crusoe

Istiklal Caddesi 195/A, Beyoğlu (0212 293 6968, www.rob389.com). **Open** 9am-9.30pm Mon-Sat; 10am-9.30pm Sun. **Map** p248 M4.

A beautiful, cluttered space graced by tall ceilings, this store has an especially well-chosen selection of English-language fiction, international music and art mags, plus an array of titles on Istanbul and Turkey. **Other locations** SALT Beyoğlu, 1st Floor, Istiklal Caddesi 136.

Robinson Crusoe.

Specialist

Denizler Kitabevi

Istiklal Caddesi 199/A, Beyoğlu (0212 249 8893, www.denizlerkitabevi.com). **Open** 10am-8pm daily. **Map** p248 M4.

Next door to the Dutch Consulate, this shop specialises in books on a maritime theme (*deniz* means 'sea'), but is also strong on travel guides, especially on Turkey.

Used & antiquarian

There are about half a dozen shops packed with second-hand books, many in English, in the **Aslıhan Pasajı**, an inconspicuous passage just off the Balık Pazarı (fish market) halfway down Istiklal Caddesi. Some shops also deal in vinyl, magazines and old film posters.

> **INSIDE TRACK**
> **TAXES AND REFUNDS**
>
> VAT (KDV) on goods and services is a standard 18 per cent, with the exception of textiles and leather, which are charged at 8 per cent. Non-residents are eligible for refunds on purchases of goods (not services) over TL100 from stores displaying the tax-free sticker, and reclaiming the money is not the tedious process it used to be. The retailer fills out a special receipt in quadruplicate and gives you three copies, which you then present to customs – along with your purchases – upon departure; this must be within three months of the purchase. You can then get a cash refund in the currency of your choice on the other side of passport control.

★ Booksellers' Bazaar

Kapalı Çarşı, Beyazıt (0212 522 3173, www.kapalicarsi.org.tr). Tram Beyazıt or Çemberlitaş. **Open** 8.30am-7pm Mon-Sat. **Map** p288 L9.

West of Çadırcılar is Sahaflar Çarşısı, the Booksellers' Bazaar, a lane and courtyard where the written word has been traded since early Ottoman times. Because printed books were considered a corrupting European influence, only hand-lettered manuscripts were sold until 1729, the year the first book in Turkish was published. Today, much of the trade at this historic bazaar is in textbooks (the university is nearby), along with plentiful coffee-table volumes and framed calligraphy. Booksellers now have to compete with itinerant merchants peddling everything from Byzantine coins to used mobile phones.

Librairie de Pera

Galipdede Caddesi 8, Tünel (0212 243 7447, www.librairiedepera.com). **Open** 9am-7pm daily. **Map** p248 M5.

Situated just downhill from Tünel Square, this shop carries old and rare books in numerous languages, many covering history and travel throughout Turkey.

CHILDREN

Toys

★ Porof Zihni Sinir

Hacı Bekir Apt 13, Ağahamamı Caddesi, Cihangir (0212 252 9320, www.zihnisinir.com). **Open** 10am-7.30pm Mon-Sat. **Map** p249 O3.

This remarkable store is at its core a toyshop, but the inventiveness of Irfan Sayar's creations could have found it a place in this guide's Galleries chapter.

Irfan is a cartoonist, whose character, a teacher called Porof Zihni Sinir, features in many Turkish children's books. His sculptures, at once tactile, fantastical and imaginative, have one thing in common: fun. Alongside the large-scale pieces, there are plenty of unique souvenirs and knick-knacks that would fit perfectly in a suitcase.

► *To learn more about the Turkish cartoon culture, visit the Cartoon Museum (see p61).*

ELECTRONICS & PHOTOGRAPHY

General

The best place to buy electronics – both big-name and discount brands – is in the underground arcade in **Karaköy Square**, directly under the tram stop.

Photographic shops can be found on almost every high street. Many will do portrait and passport-size (*vesikalık*) photos, as well as selling and developing film. There are dozens of photographic shops around **Ankara Caddesi** and **Hüdavendigar Caddesi** in Eminönü. Lenses, filters and parts for all the major brands can be bought here.

Giycek Nostaljik Fotograf Studyosu

Serdar-ı Ekrem Caddesi, Doğan Apt 30-C, Galata (0212 251 8181, www.giycek.com). **Open** 10am-7pm Tue-Sun. **Map** p248 M5.

Fancy yourself as a bit of a sultan? This quirky photography studio sets up faux historical shoots, providing the necessary costumes, backdrops, props and printed photos for all aspiring Ottomans. From TL50 per person.

Stüdyo Mor Ipek

Selvi Han, Sıraselviler Caddesi 27, Taksim (0212 249 5877, www.moripek.com). **Open** 8.30am-8pm Mon-Sat. **Map** p249 O3.

This basement shop caters to both professionals and amateurs. Staff are also able to take colour passport photographs.

Teknosa

Kanyon Mall, Büyükdere Caddesi 185, Levent (0212 353 0480, www.teknosa.com). Metro Levent. **Open** 10am-10pm daily.

In Kanyon Mall, this branch of the popular electronics chain Teknosa sells laptops, telephones, white goods, TVs and cameras.

Yalçınlar

Ankara Caddesi 179, Sirkeci (0212 512 3134, www.yalcinlar.com.tr). Tram Sirkeci. **Open** 8.30am-8pm Mon-Sat. **Map** p243 M10.

One of around a dozen branches offering developing and printing services for both professional photographers and amateurs.

Specialist

Bilgisayar Hastanesi

Inönü Caddesi 38, Gümüşsuyu, Taksim (0212 252 1575, www.bilgisayarhastanesi.com). **Open** 9am-6pm Mon-Fri. **Map** p247 P2.

An authorised service provider for Compaq, Hewlett Packard and Epson. Staff will clean, maintain and repair computers and order spare parts. Bilgisayar Hastanesi ('Computer Hospital') also operates an emergency service, but you pay a 50% premium for any work done outside office hours. Otherwise, expect a long wait. You can also buy second-hand laptops and rent iPads here.

Troy Apple Centre

Kanyon Mall, floor B2, Büyükdere Caddesi 185, Levent (0212 353 0460, www.troyapr.com). Metro Levent. **Open** 10am-10pm daily.

All the usual Apple goods you'd expect from a certified reseller. Repairs and spare parts are also available here.

FASHION

Designer

★ Berrin Akyüz

Akarsu Yokuşu 20, Cihangir (0212 251 4125, www.berrinakyuz.com). **Open** 10am-8pm Mon-Fri; 10am-5pm Sat, Sun. **Map** p249 O4.

Designer Berrin Akyüz works half the time in her atelier in Üsküdar, and the other half in this Cihangir shop that sells her skirts, tops, scarves, bags, children's wear and jewellery. She works with Polish designer Lucasz Budzisz, who specialises in corsets, and between them they offer four collections every year.

Damat Tween

Akmerkez Mall 214, Nispetiye Caddesi, Etiler (0212 282 0112, www.damat.com.tr). Metro Levent. **Open** 10am-10pm daily.

A local boy made good, Damat has branches in a dozen countries in addition to his mini-empire in Turkey. His stock-in-trade is classic menswear, ranging from suits to knitwear. The Tween label features casual collections in bold styles that are distinctive both for design and quality.

Fashion Tunnel

Serdar-ı Ekrem Sokak 33/B, Galata (0212 292 4206, www.fashiontunnel.com.tr). **Open** 9am-7pm Mon-Sat. **Map** p248 M5.

Set up by fashion guru Tuba Benian in collaboration with five up-and-coming designers, Fashion Tunnel opened in late 2011. Look out for cutting-edge design mixed with vintage favourites, including exotic handbags, sleek cocktail dresses and quirky hats. Monthly events and rotating themes keep collections fresh.

★ Gönül Paksoy

Atiye Sokak 1/3, Teşvikiye (0212 236 0209). Metro Osmanbey. **Open** 1-7pm Mon; 10am-7pm Tue-Sat.
Ms Paksoy claims her designs are unique, not just in Turkey but worldwide. She's probably right. Her collections reinterpret Ottoman designs, using original fabrics and the finest natural weaves hand-dyed in subtle shades. She also does a great line in Ottoman-style slippers, handbags and shoes.

Koton

Istiklal Caddesi 54, Beyoğlu (212 251 2958, www.koton.com.tr). **Open** 10am-10pm daily. **Map** p248 N3.
This trendy Turkish chain sells sporty and stylish men's and women's wear at very reasonable prices. Keep an eye out for hip Istanbul- and Turkey-printed T-shirts, which are a cut above the usual tourist fare and make for top souvenirs.
Other locations Metrocity Mall 171, Büyükdere Caddesi, Levent (0212 344 0464).

Mavi Jeans

Istiklal Caddesi 123/A, Beyoğlu (0212 244 6255, www.mavi.com). **Open** 10am-10pm Mon-Sat; 11am-10pm Sun. **Map** p249 O3.
Since making it big in the US, Mavi's prices have rocketed, but compared with imported brands, prices are still reasonable. Designs are fun, contemporary and very wearable. T-shirts, sweatshirts and casual co-ordinates complete the look.
Other locations Akmerkez Mall, Nispetiye Caddesi, Etiler (0212 282 0423); Metrocity Mall, Büyükdere Caddesi 171, Levent (0212 344 0070).

Nr. 39

Süleyman Nazif Sokak 33, off Valikonaşı Caddesi, Nişantaşı (0212 241 4059, www.nr39.com). **Open** 10.30am-7pm Mon-Sat.
Gorgeous handcrafted shoes – many of them one-of-a-kind – by designer Ipek Yılmaz. Look out for sky-high patent leather heels and flower-fringed Mary Janes. Or customise your own dream booties.

★ Simay Bülbül

Derya Apt 5, Camekan Sokak, Galata (0212 292 7899, www.sim-ay.com). **Open** 10am-7pm Mon-Fri; 11am-8pm Sat, Sun. **Map** p248 N5.
At the bottom of a quiet cobbled street off Istiklal Caddesi, designer Simal Bülbül's eponymous store sells her delicate clothes: she manages to integrate leather into dresses and blouses elegantly, using the lightest of touches. The newly expanded space also offers Bülbül's shoes and leather accessories.

Ümit Ünal

Ensiz Sokak 1/B, Tünel (0212 245 7886, www.umitunal.com). **Open** 10am-7pm daily. **Map** p248 M5.
Ümit Ünal is an Istanbul-based designer who is plugged into the international fashion scene. His avant-garde fashion shows are more like performances, and his multi-layered, complex creations are art installations as much as garments. Ünal's influences are diverse – Celtic banshees, Himalayan mountain tribes, gypsies. He travels the globe in search of unusual fabrics and accessories.

Yargıcı

Valikonaşı Caddesi 34/A, Nişantaşı (0212 225 2952, www.yargici.com.tr). Metro Osmanbey. **Open** 9.30am-7.30pm Mon-Sat; 1-6pm Sun.
Middle-of-the-road fashion for both sexes. You're talking dependable quality rather than cutting-edge design. Beware the sizing, which can be baffling. (You thought you were a 36? Well, here you're a 32.)
Other locations Akmerkez Mall, Nispetiye Caddesi, Etiler (0212 282 0501).

Discount

See p168 **Beyoğlu's Fashion Arcades**.

Leather

For the best selection of leather (*deri*) head to the **Grand Bazaar** (*see p53*). Be careful, though, because quality can vary: 'antelope

Yargıcı.

skin', for example, is unlikely to be genuine. As always, you'll have be comfortable bartering in order to get a fair price. If it all seems like too much hassle, there are stores that specialise in quality leather at fixed prices, but they aren't that much cheaper than stores at home.

Derimod

Akmerkez Mall 362, Nispetiye Caddesi, Etiler (0212 282 0668, www.derimod.com.tr). Metro Levent. **Open** 10am-10pm daily.

Classic and contemporary designs in top quality leather for both men and women, as well as an extensive range of leather accessories.

Matra

Akmerkez Mall, Nispetiye Caddesi, Etiler (0212 282 0215, www.matras.com). Metro Levent. **Open** 10am-10pm daily.

Classic, high-quality designs from Turkey's leading leather accessories label. As well as handbags, wallets and belts, pieces also include briefcases, luggage and smaller items such as leather purses and cardholders.

Used & vintage

Binbavul

Galipdede Caddesi 66, Galata (0212 243 7218). **Open** 11am-9pm Sun-Thur; 11am-11pm Fri, Sat. **Map** p248 M5.

Binbavul is located in the basement of an old building, along an alley off the touristy Galipdede Caddesi at the southern end of Istiklal Caddesi. The small street stall only hints at the cavernous space behind, rammed with vintage clothes, military regalia, theatre props, luggage, ball dresses, vinyl, designer goods and any whimsical item the owner picks up.

★ Mozk

Aşa Hamam Caddesi 13, Cihangir (0212 252 3499, www.mozk.co.uk). **Open** 9am-9pm Mon-Sat; 3-9pm Sun. **Map** p249 O3.

Run by two fashion designers, this vintage store exudes cool. Retro sunglasses, leatherwear, floral dresses, shirts, hats: just about anything you could want can be found in this little shop. Only items in excellent condition are sold. Some other vintage items, such as telephones, clocks and chandeliers, are also available.

Roll

Turnacıbaşı Sokak 13, Galatasaray (0212 244 9656). **Open** 10am-10pm Mon-Sat; noon-10pm Sun. **Map** p248 N3.

Most vintage stock here is from Europe and dates from the 1960s and '70s – loud nylon shirts, suede and velvet jackets, retro shades and vintage Adidas tracksuit tops.

FASHION ACCESSORIES & SERVICES

Accessories

See also p171 **Seyitağaoğulları Kilim**.

Antique Objet

Zenneciler Caddesi 48-50, Grand Bazaar (0212 526 7451, www.antiqueobjet.com). Tram Beyazıt. **Open** 9am-7pm Mon-Sat. **Map** p79.

Crammed into an awkward space by the entrance to the market's Iç Bedesten, this den of delights stocks own-label boots, Cinderella slippers and jackets in velvet Suzani cloth, sleek short coats of rich Ottoman fabric and a line of bags in Suzani and *ikat*. Workmanship is top notch.

Ipek

Istiklal Caddesi 120, Beyoğlu (0212 249 8207). **Open** 9am-8pm Mon-Sat. **Map** p248 M4.

If it's neckwear you're after, this shop is the place to head. Along with charmingly persuasive service, you'll find an exhaustive range of scarves, shawls and ties.

Cleaning & repairs

The bespoke tailoring business may be foundering, but there's still a living to be made from mending and alterations. Tailors (*terzi*) are found throughout the city.

Laundries can be found throughout the city, though they're much harder to track down now that most people have washing machines at home. Dry-cleaners are plentiful and reasonably priced.

Acar Terzihane

Yeni Yuva Sokak 30, Cihangir (0212 251 3745). **Open** 8am-8pm Mon-Sat. **No credit cards**. **Map** p249 O4.

A long-running outfit, competent at all kinds of stitching and mending, as well as more ambitious custom-made outfits for ladies and gents.

Can Laundry

Bakraç Sokak 32/A, off Sıraselviler Caddesi, Cihangir (0212 252 9360). **Open** 8.30am-7.30pm Mon-Fri; 8.30am-4pm Sat. **No credit cards**. **Map** p249 O4.

Neighbourhood laundry services come with a smile at this Cihangir laundry. You can either pay per load or by individual item. Ironing is optional and is charged per item.

Celal Akagün Tuhafiye

Marputçular Alacahamam Caddesi 53, Eminönü (0212 526 3857). Tram Eminönü. **Open** 8.30am-6pm Mon-Fri; 8.30am-4pm Sat. **Map** p243 M8.

Mor.

After 60 years in the business, Mr Akagün is the oldest haberdasher in town, and still works from his original store. His stock, which is 90% Turkish-made, includes a bewildering array of buttons, lace, embroidered trimmings and ribbons.

Çınar
Sıraselviler Caddesi 152/A, Cihangir (0212 251 4204/252 1938). **Open** 8am-7.30pm Mon-Sat. **Map** p249 O3.
A dry-cleaner and laundry running a pick-up and delivery service in the Taksim area (hotels included). A same-day service is available. Mending/alteration jobs are outsourced to a local tailor.

Hats

For felt hats visit **Cocoon** (*see p170*).

Hat Quarters
Kanyon Shopping Mall, Büyükdere Caddesi 185, Levent (0212 353 0926). Metro Levent. **Open** 10am-10pm daily.
All manner of designer hats, berets and various other accessories.

Jewellery

The **Grand Bazaar** (*see p53*) houses the largest selection of jewellery and gold under one roof. And where designs once stopped at the classic, a new tide of creativity has been creeping in over the last few years. For definitively modern pieces, try the Teşvikiye area of **Nişantaşı**, home to several small showrooms.

Gasia
Nil Apt 21, Abdi Ipekçi Caddesi, Teşvikiye, Nişantaşı (0212 219 2715, www.gasia.com.tr). **Open** 9am-7pm Mon-Sat. **Map** p248 N3.
Specialising in contemporary handmade creations in 24-carat gold, Gasia offers a unique range of pendants, rings and bracelets, taking inspiration from Ottoman imagery. The studio designed pieces for Sarah Jessica Parker's character in *Sex in the City 2*.

Mor
Turnacıbaşı Sokak 16, Galatasaray (0212 292 8817). **Open** 10am 7.30pm Mon-Sat. **Map** p248 N3.
A stylish, glass-fronted studio just down from the Galatasaray Hamam, selling inspired originals designed by an in-house team. Most pieces are fashioned from silver and bronze, often combining scraps of ethnic jewellery from eastern Turkey, Turkmenistan and Afghanistan.

Nelia
Halil Bey Pasajı 49, Valikonaşı Caddesi, Nişantaşı (0212 291 1123, www.nelia.com.tr). Metro Osmanbey. **Open** 10am-7.30pm Mon-Sat.
Nelia produces funky, chunky jewellery with a tribal twist. In-house designer Banu Kosifoğlu works with a multitude of materials – from semi-precious stones and sterling silver to ribbon, silk tassels and snippets of ethnic cloth – crafting weird and wonderful combinations that work as unique pieces.

★ Urart
Abdi Ipekçi Caddesi 18/1, Teşvikiye, Nişantaşı (0212 246 7194, www.urart.com.tr). Metro Osmanbey. **Open** 9am-7pm Mon-Sat.
Sophisticated jewellery with an Anatolian slant. Designs are drawn from the countless civilisations that have peopled Anatolia from Palaeolithic to Ottoman times, using a combination of silver, gold and semi-precious stones. Pricey, but beautiful.
Other locations Swissôtel, Bayıldım Caddesi, Beşitkaş (0212 259 0221).

Lingerie & underwear

Zeki Triko
Akkavak Sokak 63/E, off Valikonaşı Caddesi, Nişantaşı (0212 233 8279, www.zekitriko.com.tr). Metro Osmanbey. **Open** 9.30am-7.30pm Mon-Sat.
Not only is Zeki the premier swimwear label at home, it's also one of Turkey's most successful exports. Prices are high, but so is the quality. The own-label lingerie is also well worth checking out.
Other locations Akmerkez Mall 366, Nispetiye Caddesi, Etiler (0212 282 0591); Cevahir Mall 22, Büyükdere Caddesi, Şişli (0212 380 0807).

Luggage

Paşalar Çanta
Istiklal Caddesi 56, Beyoğlu (0212 293 9080). **Open** 10am-10pm Mon-Sat; 10am-8pm Sun. **Map** p248 N3.
Budget luggage, handbags and accessories for the traveller can be found at this shop along Istikal. Be

Beyoğlu's Fashion Arcades

Hunt out budget clothes in a hidden pasaj.

In the last few decades, Turkey has become one of the world's most prolific producers of clothing, with over 40,000 factories nationwide. Many leading American and European brands now manufacture their clothing in Turkey.

Savvy local shoppers can reap the benefits by visiting factory outlets, where seconds and overruns can be bought for a fraction of the retail price. In Istanbul, you don't even have to trek to the suburbs to find a factory outlet: you can find seconds at unofficial outlets right in the city centre, if you know where to look.

Off Beyoğlu's Istiklal Caddesi are a number of *pasajs* (covered arcades) tucked away in backstreets, bursting with cheap clothing, stacked in bins or hung on rails, at knock-down prices. A pair of jeans, say, might be TL35 or TL40. Be prepared to rummage, as clothes are often crammed indiscriminately on to racks and it's up to you to find the right size.

As part of the trade agreement between the fashion companies and factories, extras usually have their labels removed. Part of the fun is trying to figure out whether you've got your hands on the latest style from H&M or Miss Sixty. Some companies don't allow their factory cast-offs to be resold, although you may well find faithful rip-offs of well-known brands anyway.

Popular with the alternative crowd, the **Atlas Pasajı**, behind the Atlas cinema, is more structured than most, and its stock is of a higher quality, with a better claim to street cred than the Beyoğlu *pasaj* norm. Atlas is also home to an interesting selection of jewellery, second-hand clothes, kitsch collectibles, records, posters and comics. Its vaguely gothic vibe is reminiscent of London's Camden Market.

Beyoğlu Merkezi, opposite the Odakule building (Istiklal Caddesi 142), is a vast *pasaj* that has three underground floors packed with real bargains. Most of the clothes are casual and sporty, with the emphasis on denim.

With a rather hard-to-find entrance across from the Dutch Consulate at Istiklal Caddesi 197, **Terkoz Çıkmazı Karaaslan Merkezi Pasaj** has piles of clothing at rock-bottom prices, as well as small boutiques with more discriminating selections.

sure to pop down to the basement for its range of cheap backpacks.

FOOD & DRINK

Bakeries

Galata Konak Café

Hacı Ali Sokak, Galata, Beyoğlu (0212 252 5346, www.galatakonakcafe.com). **Open** 7am-7pm daily; *terrace* 7am-midnight. **Map** p246 M6.

This French-influenced pâtisserie has been serving its colourful cakes and sweet Turkish bite-sized pastries since 1975. The view from the terrace, taking in the Golden Horn and the historic Sultanahmet peninsula, is sublime.

★ Güllüoğlu

Rıhtım Caddesi 3-4, Karaköy (0212 293 0910, www.karakoygulluoglu.com). Tram Karaköy. **Open** 7am-10pm Mon-Sat.

The Güllüoğlu family – originally hailing from Gaziantep, and having opened its shop here in Karaköy in 1949 – is the city's undisputed king of baklava. Sample sweet pistachio, walnut, chocolate or cheese. Its *su böreği* (baked layers of cheese and filo pastry) is also top notch.

Kitchenette

Marmara Hotel, Tak-ı Zafer Caddesi 3, Taksim (0212 292 6862, www.kitchenette.com.tr). **Open** 8am-1am daily. **Map** p249 P2.

The in-house bakery at this successful brasserie sells its superior bread to outside customers as well.

► *For a review of the restaurant, see p135.*

★ Savoy Pastaevi

Sıraselviler Caddesi 181/183A, Cihangir (0212 249 1818, www.savoypastanesi.com). **Open** 7am-10pm daily. **Map** p249 O3.

One of Istanbul's best cake shops, thriving since 1950 and now something of an institution. There's a reasonably sized café up on the first floor, which gets especially busy at breakfast.

Drinks

La Cave

Sıraselviler Caddesi 109, Cihangir (0212 243 2405, www.lacavesarap.com). **Open** 9am-9pm Mon-Sat; 9am-8pm Sun. **Map** p249 O4.

One of the city's first speciality wine shops and certainly the most serious. Owner Esat Ayhan keeps a comprehensive cellar filled with wines from all over Turkey, Europe and the New World. He also stocks imported spirits, bar accessories and a limited range of Havana cigars.

Mimolett

Sıraselviler Caddesi 55/A, Taksim (0212 245 9858, www.mimolett.com.tr). **Open** 10am-11.30pm Mon-Sat. **Map** p249 O3.

There's a selection of around 350 wines at the wine boutique attached to the Mimolett restaurant and bar. Aimed at a discerning, upmarket clientele, it excels in stocking wines from Turkey's boutique vineyards. There are plenty of wines that you can try by the glass too.

▶ *For a review of the restaurant, see p138.*

★ SenSus

Büyükhendek Caddesi 5, Galata, Beyoğlu (0212 245 5657, www.sensuswine.com). **Open** 10am-10pm daily. **Map** p246 M5.

There are more than 300 different types of exclusively Turkish wine in this underground cellar by the Galata Tower. A tasting bar allows customers to try 50 wines by the glass (a five-glass flight is around TL20; for an additional fee this tasting can be accompanied by regional cheeses).

▶ *For more on Turkish wines, see p150* **Grape Expectations**.

General

Carrefour Expres

Sıraselviler Caddesi 74/A, Cihangir (0212 293 5158, www.carrefourexpress.com). **Open** 10am-10pm daily. **Map** p249 O3.

This central and well-stocked supermarket also offers a home delivery and online ordering service.

Other locations Büyükdere Caddesi 5, Şişli (0212 219 6439).

Macro Center

Abdi İpekçi Caddesi 24-28, Nişantaşı (0212 233 0570, www.macrocenter.com.tr). Metro Osmanbey. **Open** 8.30am-9.30pm daily.

Macro caters for the upper end of the market, with a wide selection of imported foods and prices to match. The deli, fresh fish and meat counters are especially good and there's a wide, fairly priced selection of local wines.

Other locations Muallim Naci Caddesi 170, Kuruçeşme (0212 257 1381).

Markets

For the freshest, best-quality fish, visit the upmarket **Balık Pazarı** (fish market) next to the historic Çiçek Pasajı, off Istiklal Caddesi. As well as fish, you'll find delicacies from quail's eggs to fresh clotted cream. Alternatively, Karaköy's Perşembe Pazarı is stocked with piles of cheaper seasonal – but equally fresh – fish. For regional specialities such as like pepper paste, dried aubergines and herby cheeses, head for the stalls lining the west side of the **Egyptian Bazaar** or the many delicatessens in the backstreets of **Kadıköy** on the Asian shore. For general markets, *see p162.*

Specialist

★ Ali Muhiddin Hacı Bekir

Hamidiye Caddesi 83, Sirkeci (0212 522 0666, www.hacibekir.com.tr). **Open** 8am-10pm Mon-Sat; 9am-10pm Sun. **Map** p243 M8.

You can't come to Turkey without trying Turkish Delight. Hacı Bekir, official confectioner to the Imperial Palace, is credited with creating this delectable sweet in 1777 – there's no better place to try it and buy it. Be sure to sample *akide* as well: these colourful boiled sweets come in every conceivable flavour. Other tasty gifts include halva, baklava and marzipan (*badem ezmesi*), which all come in beautiful gift-wrapped boxes.

Other locations Istiklal Caddesi 83/6, Beyoğlu (0212 245 1375).

Ambar

Kallavi Sokak 12, off Istiklal Caddesi, Beyoğlu (0212 292 9272, www.nuhunambari.com). **Open** 8am-8pm Mon-Fri; 9.30am-8pm Sat. **Map** p248 M3.

One of the few places in Istanbul that sells fresh tofu. Other worthwhile buys include wholegrain bread, organic grains and pulses, hulled pumpkin and sunflower seeds and a range of organic fruit and veg.

★ Antre Gourmet Shop

Akarsu Caddesi 40/A, Cihangir (0212 292 8972, www.antregourmet.com). **Open** 9am-9pm Mon-Sat; 9am-8pm Sun. **Map** p249 O4.

Antre stocks around 40 regional cheeses, all bought from local producers and free from additives. There's also a fair selection of cold meats, Austrian wholegrain breads, teas, home-made meze and jams, olive oil, honeycomb (in season), Turkish wines and natural yoghurt.

Kurukahveci Mehmet Efendi

Tahmis Sokak 66, Eminönü (0212 511 4262, www.mehmetefendi.com). Tram Eminönü. **Open**

8.30am-7pm Mon-Sat; 9am-6pm Sun.
No credit cards. **Map** p242 L8.
Reputedly the first shop to sell roasted, ground Turkish coffee, Mehmet Efendi has been doing a roaring trade since it opened in 1871. It's opposite the west entrance to the Egyptian Market – just follow your nose. Besides the traditional Turkish variety, there's filter and espresso coffee, whole roasted beans, cocoa and *sahlep*, a winter drink made from ground orchid root.

Namlı Pastırmacı
Hasırcılar Caddesi 14-16, Eminönü (0212 511 6393, www.namlipastirma.com.tr). Tram Eminönü. **Open** 8.30am-8pm Mon-Sat. **Map** p242 L8.
A hugely popular deli just along from the west end of the Egyptian Market. It specialises in *pastırma* (Turkish spicy cured beef) but also has a tantalising selection of cold cuts, cheeses, halva, honeycomb, *pekmez* (grape molasses), olives and pickles.

Saray Muhallebicisi
Istiklal Caddesi 173, Beyoğlu (0212 292 3434, www.saraymuhallebicisi.com). **Open** 6am-2am daily. **Map** p248 N3.
Delectable Turkish desserts, from milk puddings to *aşure*, popularly known as Noah's pudding. Since 1949, this branch has served as a sugar-fuelled, very popular pit stop during or after a night out in the bars and cafés of Beyoğlu. There's also a takeaway service.
Other locations Teşvikiye Caddesi 105, Teşvikiye (0212 236 1617).

Şütte
Dudu Odaları Sokak 21, Balık Pazarı, Galatasaray (0212 293 9292, www.suttebeyoglu.com). **Open** 9am-8pm Mon-Sat. **Map** p248 N3.
This long-established deli, owned by Macedonians, is one of the few places in Istanbul that stocks pork products other than bacon. It also carries pricey but wonderful imported cheeses, plus cheaper local cheeses, ready-made meze and condiments.

GIFTS AND SOUVENIRS
Handicrafts

Besides carpets, Turkey offers a wealth of lesser-known – and equally traditional – handicrafts. The ceramics trade dates back to the Selçuk Empire of the 11th century. Tiles, vases and plates with the traditional Ottoman tulip motif are now displayed in museums worldwide. The tradition lives on in Kütahya and Iznik, both in western Anatolia, where artists handcraft reproductions and more contemporary designs. Then there's *ebru*, a Central Asian variation of paper marbling, which took off during calligraphy's heyday. Today, the technique is also applied to fabrics. Other craftwork includes carved meerschaum pipes, prayer beads, backgammon sets and silks. Most of these crafts can be found at the **Grand Bazaar** (*see p54* **Shopping the Bazaar**).

For carpets and rugs, *see p172* and *p173* **The Rug Trade**.

Abdulla
Halıcılar Caddesi 53, Grand Bazaar (0212 522 3070, www.abdulla.com). Tram Beyazıt. **Open** 9am-7pm Mon-Sat. **Map** p54.
Abdulla is all about a contemporary take on traditional crafts. The bywords are 'natural' and 'handmade'; the main product line is hamam accessories, so you will find *peştemal* towels, scrubs and olive oil soaps in scents from cinnamon and tea to sesame. Other good buys include sheepskin throws and hand-spun silk and wool.

★ Cocoon
Küçükayasofya Caddesi 13 & 17, Eminönü (0212 638 6450, www.cocoontr.com). Tram Sultanahmet. **Open** 9am-7pm Mon-Sat. **Map** p243 N11.
Cocoon is housed in two fabulous shops by the Blue Mosque, on Küçükayasofya. The first (no.13) has an incredible array of felt hats. Coupled with four floors of accessories, hamam wear, shirts, scarves and all manner of knick-knacks, it is the only souvenir shop you'll need. A couple of doors down is a more serious affair. Owner Şeref Özen has collected antique rugs, clothing and textiles from across Turkey and Central Asia for collectors and enthusiasts.
Other locations Halıcılar Caddesi 38, Grand Bazaar (0212 528 3515); Arasta Bazaar 93, Sultanahmet (0212 638 6450).

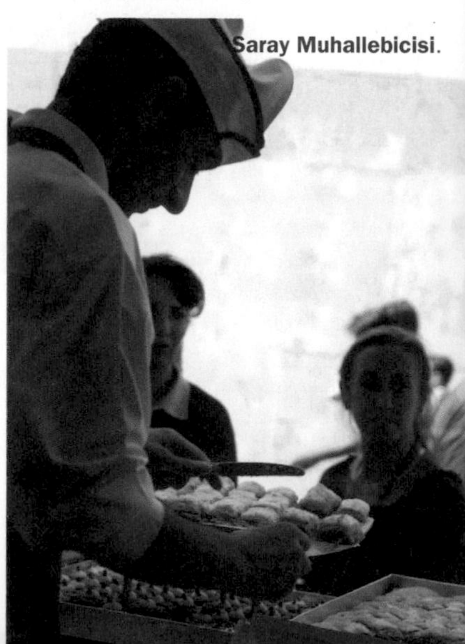
Saray Muhallebicisi.

Derviş

Keseciler Caddesi 33-35, Grand Bazaar (0212 514 4525, www.dervis.com). Tram Beyazıt. **Open** 9am-7pm Mon-Sat. **Map** p54.

Derviş nestles behind the narrowest of shop fronts. Here, Anatolian traditions are reinvented. Bathroom accessories are big, including handmade soaps in a host of natural flavours, super-soft unbleached cotton towels, and *peştemal* towels in linen, cotton and silk. But there are also shimmering scarves of hand-spun silk, felt slippers, rugs and throws, and mohair and patchwork fur blankets; plus brimming shelves of original dowry items, trawled from the depths of Anatolia by owner Tayfun Utkan. Look out for the hand-stitched bolero jackets, ethnic coats and dresses in fabulous colours and fabrics, and exquisitely embroidered linens.

Istanbul Handicrafts Centre

Kabasakal Caddesi 5, Sultanahmet (0212 517 6784/8). Tram Sultanahmet. **Open** 9am-6.30pm daily. **Map** p243 N10.

The Istanbul Handicrafts Centre is located in a restored *medrese* (religious school), opposite the Baths of Roxelana. It now houses a warren of workshops, each with its own specialisation. The most accomplished handicrafts are the illuminated manuscripts, miniatures and calligraphy. Other highlights include cloth-painting, dolls, ceramics, glassware and hand-bound books. The artists work on site, so you can watch them at their trade.

Seyitağaoğulları Kilim

Tavukhane Sokak 30, Sultanahmet (0212 518 1295). **Open** 9.30am-8.30pm daily. **Map** p243 M11.

Kilim accessories are everywhere these days, but what you'll find here – from belts and footwear to bags, purses and stationery – is a cut above the rest. The products are all handmade, the kilims are kosher and the leather trim really is leather. Tucked behind the Blue Mosque.

HEALTH & BEAUTY

Hairdressers & barbers

Grooming is next to godliness for Turkish girls, which means that the beauty salon (*güzellik salonu*) is a second home and the city is brimming with them. For the face, it's tweezers and expertly teased thread; for the body it's waxing (*ağda* – Turkey is the home of the all-over wax), plus manicures (*manikür*), pedicures (*pedikür*), and all manner of hair treatments. Dyeing (*boya*) is a favourite, and the blow-dry (*fön*) – involving at least two attendants and an army of brushes – essential.

Hüseyin Günday

Sıraselviler Caddesi 80, Cihangir (0212 251 0005). **Open** 8am-8pm Mon-Sat. **Map** p249 O3.

A typical neighbourhood *kuaför* offering the full range of beauty services. Bright young things attend to your every whim. Prices are very reasonable.

MOS

Bronz Sokak 65, off Abdi Ipekçi Caddesi, Maçka (0212 240 1970, www.moskuafor.com.tr). Metro Osmanbey. **Open** 9am-7pm Mon-Sat.

MOS equates with class on the Istanbul hairdressing scene. Despite being production-line stuff, it's a great favourite with the well-heeled of both sexes, who book in for all manner of treatments. But beauty doesn't come cheap: prices are high by Turkish standards.

Other locations Akmerkez Mall 122, Nispetiye Caddesi, Etiler (0212 282 0554).

Herbal remedies

Bünsa

Dudu Odaları Sokak 12, Balık Pazarı, Galatasaray (0212 243 6265). **Open** 9am-8pm Mon-Sat. **Map** p248 N3.

Herbal remedies and healing tonics, from medicinal teas to ginseng, karakovan honey and rare varieties of *pekmez* (fruit molasses). Tell staff your ailment, and they'll prescribe a potion. The most popular panacea is a concoction of honey, royal jelly, nettle and ginseng, guaranteed to beat fatigue.

Kalmaz Baharat

Mısır Çarşısı 41, Eminönü (0212 522 6604). Tram Eminönü. **Open** 8am-7pm Mon-Sat. **No credit cards. Map** p243 L8.

One of the oldest stores in the Egyptian Bazaar, this atmospheric place – just east of the main intersection – still has its original drawers and tea caddies. Specialities include spices, medicinal herbs, healing teas and aromatic oils.

Toiletries & cosmetics

Toiletries and a limited range of cosmetics are available in most supermarkets. Some pharmacies also stock imported brands such as Vichy and RoC. For upmarket labels, go to a specialist *parfümeri*, but note that prices are pushed up by stiff import taxes.

Erkul Kozmetik

Istiklal Caddesi 163, Beyoğlu (0212 251 7662). **Open** 10.30am-10pm Mon-Sat; noon-10pm Sun. **Map** p248 N3.

A one-stop cosmetics store where you can find every grooming product imaginable.

Opticians

Emgen Optik

Istiklal Caddesi 47, Beyoğlu (0212 292 3577, www.emgenoptik.com). **Open** 9am-7.30pm Mon-Sat. **Map** p249 O2.

Emgen Optik does a roaring trade in fashion-conscious frames and shades. Around since 1925, this local institution carries a huge selection of big brands such as Ray-Ban, Police, Gucci and Armani. It also deals in prescription lenses and repairs.

Pharmacies

Pharmacies (*eczane*) are plentiful. Pharmacists are licensed to measure blood pressure, give injections, clean and bandage minor injuries and suggest medication for minor ailments – many prescription medicines are available over the counter in Turkey. However, few pharmacists speak English. Opening hours are typically 9am-7pm Mon-Sat. Every neighbourhood also has a duty pharmacy (*nöbetçi*) that is open all night and on Sundays.

Filibeli Eczanesi

Istiklal Caddesi 27A, Beyoğlu (0212 245 6440). **Open** 9am-7.30pm Mon-Sat. **Map** p248 L2.
There are dozens of pharmacies on Istiklal Caddesi, as there are throughout the city. Some of the staff at this branch near Taksim Square speak some English and they're very helpful.

Spas & salons

For the best spas and salons, *see p121* **Hotel Hamams**.

HOUSE & HOME

Antiques

One of the best places for browsing is **Çukurcuma**, a quiet Beyoğlu neighbourhood behind the Galatasaray Lycée. Its rollercoaster streets harbour a plethora of small shops with a wealth of antiquaria from rural Anatolia – anything from oil lamps and painted trunks to carved doors. There's also a fair amount of sophisticated glass and porcelain ware, Ottoman screens and chandeliers, as well as shops specialising in single items such as tin toys. Items over a century old must be cleared by the Museums Directorate before being taken overseas. Dealers should know the procedure.

★ Artrium

Tünel Geçidi Iş Hanı 7, Tünel (0212 251 4302, www.artrium.com.tr). **Open** 9am-7pm Mon-Sat. **Map** p248 M4.
A shop attracting a sophisticated breed of collector, with three spacious display rooms and a prime location in the passage just across from KV Café. It has a fine selection of miniatures, maps, prints and calligraphy, along with Kütahya ceramics and the odd film and advertising poster.

Can Shop

Avrupa Pasajı 16, off Meşrutiyet Caddesi, Galatasaray (0212 249 3280). **Open** 10am-7pm Mon-Sat. **No credit cards. Map** p248 N3.
Tins, pins, coins and toys, from clanky cars to planes and tanks. There's a lot of Turkish stuff, dating mostly from Ottoman and early republic times.
Other locations Hak Pasajı 5, off Teşvikiye Caddesi, Teşvikiye (0212 225 2903).

Eski Fener

Ağa Hamam Sokak 7/B, Çukurcuma (0212 251 6278). **Open** 11am-7pm Mon-Sat. **No credit cards. Map** p249 O3.
A select assortment of furniture, doors, oil lamps and copperware, mostly picked up in rural Anatolia. Look out for practical items such as low-legged dough-rolling tables, wooden butter churns and storm lamps. All items have been painstakingly restored.

Leyla Eski Eşya Pazarlama

Altıpatlar Sokak 6, Çukurcuma (0212 293 7410). **Open** 10am-7pm Mon-Sat. **Map** p249 O3.
A massive selection of antique clothes, hats, embroidered linens, wall hangings and tapestries. Prices are quite high, but it's all top quality stuff.

Popcorn

Faik Paşa Sokak 2, off Turnacıbaşı Caddesi, Çukurcuma (0212 249 5859, www.popcornistanbul.com). **Open** 10am-7pm Mon-Sat. **No credit cards.**
This eclectic shop specialises in rare books, furniture and knick-knacks from the 1950s.

★ The Works: Objects of Desire

Faik Paşa Sokak 6/1, off Turnacıbaşı Caddesi, Çukurcuma (0212 252 2527, www.fleaworks.com). **Open** 11am-6.30pm Mon-Sat. **No credit cards.**
A remarkable shop that goes the extra mile in collecting the kitsch, the old and the downright bizarre. Owner Karaca Borar follows his own whims, and those of the collectors and film crews that buy and rent the goods. The shop, dubbed 'for the slightly deranged collector seeking identifiable memories', is stuffed with coats, hats, mannequins, old porn, unworn designer clothes, snow globes, and pretty much anything else. Prices are good, and as the sign says, 'no bargaining under TL10, it's embarrassing'.

Carpets

For tips on buying carpets, *see right* **The Rug Trade**.

Ahmet Hazım

Takkeciler Caddesi 61-63, Grand Bazaar (0212 527 9886, www.ahmethazim.com). Tram Beyazit. **Open** 9am-7pm Mon-Sat. **Map** p54.
One of the oldest rug merchants in the bazaar, specialising in kilims and carpets from Turkey, Iran and

CONSUME

The Rug Trade

Follow our guide to getting the best deal, and having fun while you do it.

Buying a carpet in Istanbul has unfortunate associations with hassle, hustle and hoodwinking. It doesn't have to be that way. With a bit of homework and common sense, you can enjoy the buying process and go home with a beautiful carpet at the right price.

To be a confident and successful bargainer and buyer, first you need to determine how much you are prepared to spend. If you're interested in handmade carpets or kilims made of natural fibres, expect to spend TL450 and above. Unless you're an expert, don't bother paying a premium for vintage; modern carpets are just as high quality and are usually made with natural dyes (*kök boya*). Under no circumstances should you tell the dealer your budget. Instead, ask the prices, get a feel for what's on offer, and be prepared to shop around. Look at carpets that are double your price range, then offer what you have.

Carpet dealers have all the time in the world. It is their job to answer your questions, explain details of origin and design, and unroll hundreds of kilims, all the while keeping you fortified with miniature glasses of strong tea.

Ultimately, the final price depends a great deal on your rapport with the dealer and your determination to buy a carpet. It all comes down to one thing: how much do you want it? If you have the slightest hesitation concerning patterns or colours, keep looking.

Nearly all shops have English-speaking staff, can be trusted to handle overseas shipping, and allow exchanges if you are unhappy with your purchase. And if you find the Grand Bazaar too bewildering, try browsing at the more peaceful **Arasta Bazaar** (www.arastabazaar.com) on Küçük Ayasofya Caddesi in Sultanahmet (map p243 N11) – also home to a branch of Cocoon (*see p170*).

CONSUME

the Caucasus and Suzani embroidery from Uzbekistan. What you get is quality service and none of the hard sell.
Other locations Istinye Bayırı Caddesi 27, Istinye (0212 345 5620).

EthniCon

Kapalıçarşı Takkeciler Sokak 58-60, Grand Bazaar (0212 527 6841, www.ethnicon.com). Tram Beyazit. **Open** 9am-7pm Mon-Sat. **Map** p54.

EthniCon (short for 'ethnic contemporary') creates kilims with a contemporary twist. Products are made without the use of child labour; it also ensures environmentally friendly processes, so colours tend to be muted. Browsing in EthniCon is a very different – and more peaceful – experience compared to the rest of the bazaar. Prices are fixed.

Kalender Carpets

Takkacılar Caddesi 24-26, Grand Bazaar (0212 527 5518, www.kalendercarpet.com). Tram Beyazıt. **Open** 9am-7pm Mon-Sat. **Map** p54.

Kalender stocks a great collection of full-size, deep pile Anatolian carpets, which start from as little as TL1,500. A good place to start your mission in 'carpet row', in the heart of the bazaar.

Sisko Osman

Zincirli Han 15, Grand Bazaar (0212 528 3548, www.siskoosman.com). Tram Beyazıt. **Open** 9am-6.30pm Mon-Sat. **Map** p54.

Sisko 'Fat Man' Osman is acknowledged around the Grand Bazaar as the leading authority on carpets and kilims. His well-stocked shop fills most of the historic Zincirli Han, and his international clientele has included many well-known people over the years. So while you can be sure of quality, don't expect a bargain.

Yörük

Kürkçüler Çarşısı 7, Grand Bazaar (0212 527 3211). Tram Beyazıt. **Open** 9am-7pm Mon-Sat. **Map** p54.

The shop may be tiny, but it has some of the finest treasures to be found in the bazaar. There are lots of kilims here, although the emphasis is on old ethnic rugs, mostly from the Caucasus. The dashing young sales staff promise entertainment, little pressure to buy and, quite probably, the rug of your dreams.

General

Turkey has a strong textile industry, so towels, linens, curtains and fabrics are excellent buys. Quality towels and linens are found in Sultanhamam, around the back of the **Egyptian Bazaar** (*see p59*) – look out for the Taç label.

Özgül Çeyiz

Mısır Çarşısı 83, Eminönü (0212 522 7068, www.begonville.net). Tram Eminönü. **Open** 8am-7.30pm Mon-Sat. **Map** p243 L8.

The east end of the Egyptian Bazaar was once crammed with stores in the trousseau (*çeyiz*) business. In days of yore, young ladies were wheeled along by their female relatives to make wholesale purchases that would improve their prospects. Özgül is one of the few survivors from those days. It's a minimal store packed with fancy embroidered sheets, quilts, towels and robes. Trousseau-hunting or not, there's some great stuff at very reasonable prices – such as the fluffy Begonville towels.

Paşabahçe

Istiklal Caddesi 150, Beyoğlu (0212 244 0544, www.pasabahce.com.tr). **Open** 10am-8pm Mon-Thur; 10am-8.30pm Fri, Sat; 11am-7pm Sun. **Map** p248 M4.

Spread over three floors, this stylish shop is a favourite with Istanbul's upwardly mobile, and Turkey's answer to Habitat. Head to the basement for kitchenware, basic china and glass, the ground floor for vases and ornaments, and the first floor for special collections. The latter includes some impressive hand-blown glass, using traditional motifs – a conscious revival of time-honoured techniques.

Other locations Teşvikiye Caddesi 47/A, Teşvikiye (0212 233 5005).

MUSIC & ENTERTAINMENT

CDs, records & DVDs

Ada Kafe

Istiklal Caddesi 158/A, Tünel (0212 251 5544, www.adakitapcafe.com). **Open** 9am-10pm Mon-Thur, Sun; 9am-11pm Fri, Sat. **Map** p248 M4.

Owned by local record company Ada, this was Istanbul's first shop to specialise in Turkish rock and protest music. There's a small café attached, and a decent range of foreign CDs, books, newspapers and magazines.

★ De Form Müzik

Turnacıbaşı Caddesi 45, Çukurcuma (0212 245 3337). **Open** noon-8pm Mon-Sat; 1-7pm Sun. **Map** p248 N5.

Vinyl fans look no further. De Form, run by two friends, is an old-school music shop, with a turntable to test your potential purchases. Most of the records are Turkish editions of international artists, but there is a small selection of Turkish folk too. There is also dance music and, shhh, some CDs.

★ Lale Plak

Galipdede Caddesi 1, Tünel (0212 293 7739, www.laleplak.com). **Open** 9am-7.30pm Mon-Sat; 11.30am-7pm Sun. **Map** p248 M5.

The city's top jazz, ethnic and classical music retailer is a favourite hangout of visiting jazz musicians. There is also a comprehensive selection of traditional Turkish music. Staff are knowledgeable and helpful.

Musical instruments

Look no further than **Galipdede Caddesi**, which extends towards Galata Tower from Tünel, at the southern end of Istikal Caddesi. There are dozens of music shops along this street and many more in the close vicinity. Each has a speciality, whether it be stringed instruments, wind instruments, percussion or electronic goods. It is also the place to pick up traditional Turkish instruments, such as the *saz* long neck lute, *bağlama* or *tar*.

SPORTS & FITNESS

There are sports shops all around the city. Along Beyoğlu's main thoroughfare are Nike, Adidas and other general sports stores. All the shopping malls will also have stores where you can pick up a pair of running shoes and sporting equipment. Kanyon (*see p160*), for example, has Adidas and Intersport (www.intersport.com.tr).

TICKETS

Sporting events and musical events are listed in the local press, including the monthly *Time Out Istanbul* magazine (www.timeoutistanbul.com). Tickets for many events are available from online ticketing agencies **Biletix**, which is an arm of Ticketmaster, and **Ticket Turk** (www.ticketturk.com). Both have good websites in English.

Biletix

0216 556 9800, www.biletix.com. **Open** *Call centre* 8.30am-10pm Mon-Fri; 10am-10pm Sat, Sun.

Tickets can be booked on the phone or the website (in English and Turkish), or at one of the many desks in selected outlets of Vakkorama, supermarket Migros and at music retailer D&R (Istiklal Caddesi 55, Beyoğlu).

TRAVELLERS' NEEDS

For luggage, *see p167*. For shipping, *see p223*. For mobile phone rental, *see p228*. For a computer repair shop, *see p164*.

CONSUME

Arts & Entertainment

Crystal. *See p202*.

Calendar

Culture ala turka.

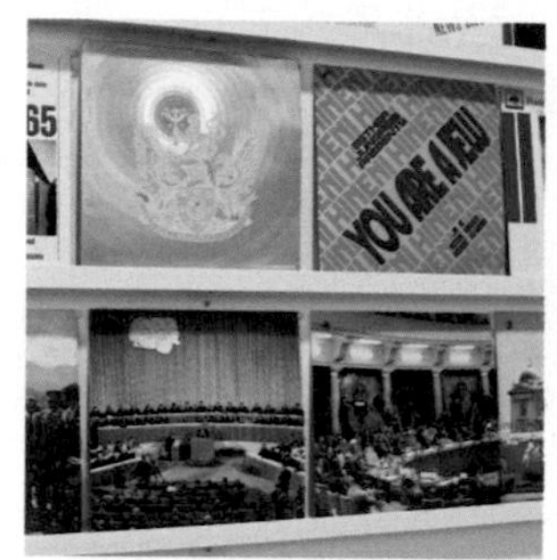

Turks will use pretty much any excuse for a party. Historically, the Ottoman sultans were renowned for their revelry, organising indulgent celebrations in honour of the empire's victories as well as personal rites of passage. Today, with a population of 13 million – and some estimates placing more than half of Istanbul's demonstrative, music-crazy residents under the age of 25 – there's plenty of reason to let loose.

Istanbul's buzzing calendar of events includes festivals ranging from the critically renowned Istanbul Art Biennial to open-air rock concerts and orchestral performances in millennia-old Byzantine churches. Many of these events are superbly managed by the Istanbul Foundation for Culture and Arts (Istanbul Kültür ve Sanat Vakfı; www.iksv.org). Tickets can usually be purchased in advance online (*see p174*).

SPRING

★ International Istanbul Film Festival

Various venues (0212 334 0700, www.iksv.org). **Date** Mar-Apr. **Tickets** venues, Biletix. **Admission** TL2.50-TL15.

An annual highlight, eagerly anticipated for the glamour factor of visiting movie stars. Be warned: this is the city's most popular cultural jamboree, and tickets sell out in advance. For more information on this and other film festivals, *see p184.*

★ Istanbul Tulip Festival

Various venues. **Date** Apr. **Admission** free.

Every April, the Istanbul municipality celebrates the tulip – a favourite Ottoman symbol – by planting millions of bulbs in just about every green space in the city. Gülhane and Ermigan parks are both fantastic spots to wander among the carpets of colour. The flowerbeds throughout Sultanahmet are also brilliant.

Orthodox Easter

Fener Rum Patrikhanesi (Orthodox Patriarchate Building), Sadrazam Ali Paşa Caddesi, Fener (0212 531 9670, www.patriarchate.org). **Date** Apr/May. **Admission** free. **Map** p245 G4.

The city's Greek residents – as well as hundreds of pilgrims from Greece – flock to Easter Sunday mass in the Patriarchate (*see p63*) in Fener on the Golden Horn. In a church illuminated by hundreds of candles, the aura of ancient ritual is extremely powerful.

★ International Istanbul Theatre Festival

Various venues (0212 334 0700, www.iksv.org). **Date** May (even years). **Tickets** venues, AKM, Biletix. **Admission** varies.

One of the few opportunities to see international theatre in Istanbul. In the past, big draws have included Robert Wilson, Pina Bausch, the Berliner Ensemble, the Piccolo Teatro di Milano and the Royal Shakespeare Company. Most performances are held at city theatres including the Atatürk Cultural Centre, the Kenter Theatre and the Aksanat Cultural Centre (for venues, *see p205*). A few events take place at more unusual venues, such as Rumeli Hisarı (*see p85*) on the Bosphorus.

International Istanbul Puppet Festival

Akkarga Sokak 22, Elmadağ (0212 243 4704, www.kuklaistanbul.org). **Date** May. **Tickets** venues, Biletix. **Admission** free-TL20.

Puppet, marionette and shadow theatre was big in Ottoman times, but is rarely performed today. This festival is an opportunity to witness this almost forgotten art, with around a dozen shows by Turkish and international companies at the Kenter Theatre (*see p206*) and various other venues. Most plays are silent and suitable for children and adults.

Conquest Week Celebrations

Various venues (0212 449 4000, www.ibb.gov.tr). **Date** late May. **Admission** free.

A lively celebration of the Turkish conquest of Constantinople (29 May 1453) featuring exhibitions of traditional Turkish arts and parades by the 'Ottoman' Mehter band, plus concerts, conferences, lectures, screenings, fireworks and some rabble-rousing by nationalist and Islamist parties.

► *The Panorama 1453 History Museum (see p62) details the siege of Istanbul.*

SUMMER

International Istanbul Music Festival

Various venues (0212 334 0700, www.iksv.org). **Date** June-July. **Tickets** AKM, Biletix. **Admission** TL20-TL450.

Inaugurated in 1973 on the occasion of the 50th anniversary of the republic, the IMF is the most prestigious event on the city's cultural calendar. It comprises about 30 performances of orchestra and chamber music, dance and ballet. Big hitters at past festivals have included Kiri Te Kanawa, Philip Glass, the Michael Nyman Ensemble, Cecilia Bartoli and the Kronos Quartet. Performances often take place in the lovely Haghia Irene church (*see p44*), open to the public for this festival and temporary exhibitions only.

★ Efes Pilsen One Love Festival

Various venues (0212 334 0700, www.efespilsen onelove.com). **Date** July. **Tickets** venues, Biletix. **Admission** TL55 (1 day), TL80 (2 days).

This massive two-day rock and alternative music festival is held annually on the grassy fields surrounding Santralistanbul. Expect big international acts, including the likes of 2011's lineup of Suede, Manic Street Preachers and Happy Mondays.

INSIDE TRACK TICKETS & INFORMATION

For information about festivals and events, try the English-language *Time Out Istanbul*, or www.istanbul.com, which lists events on a day-by-day basis. Tickets for festivals are often available through Biletix (www.biletix.com), MyBilet (www.mybilet.com) or Ticket Turk (www.ticketturk.com).

★ International Istanbul Jazz Festival

Various venues (0212 334 0700, www.iksv.org). **Date** July. **Tickets** venues, Biletix. **Admission** TL20-TL350.

This two-week festival pushes the boundaries of what defines modern jazz. Keith Jarrett, Wynton Marsalis and Dizzy Gillespie have all performed in the 4,000-seat Harbiye open-air theatre, as have less likely musicians such as Grace Jones, Nick Cave, Paul Simon, Lou Reed and Martha Wainwright. Consistently the best programme of any Turkish music festival.

Traditional Istanbul Açıkhava (Open-Air) Concerts

Harbiye Cemil Topuzlu Açıkhava Tiyatrosu (0212 257 6200, www.mostproduction.com). **Date** mid July/early Aug. **Tickets** Açıkhava Tiyatrosu (box office 0212 232 1652), Biletix. **Admission** varies.

This season of open-air concerts in Harbiye is worth checking out. The line up mixes mainstream names from Turkish pop, rock and folk with a variety of

International Istanbul Biennial. *See p178.*

alternative genres. Past performers have included the Mercan Dede Fusion Project, alongside Balkan stars such as Goran Bregovic.

Rock 'n' Coke

Hezarfen Airfield (0212 334 0100, www.rockncoke.com). **Date** July. **Tickets** Biletix. **Admission** TL60 (1 day), TL220 (camping, 2 days).
Since it began in 2003, Rock 'n' Coke has become Istanbul's largest open-air summer festival – making it the perfect opportunity to stand in a beer queue with 50,000 of your closest friends. In 2011, groups appearing included Limp Bizkit, Motörhead and 2 Many DJs. Smashing Pumpkins, the Prodigy and Muse have also appeared.

AUTUMN

Efes Pilsen Blues Festival

Lütfü Kırdar Convention Centre, Harbiye (0212 334 0100, www.pozitif-ist.com). **Date** Sept-Oct. **Tickets** Biletix. **Admission** varies.
This hugely popular festival, running since 1990, is a showcase for new talent, with three bands performing every night. Although it certainly doesn't stop the occasional star (Lucky Peterson, Bobby Rush, Long John Hunter) from showing up.

★ International Istanbul Biennial

Various venues (0212 334 0700, www.iksv.org). **Date** Sept-Nov, odd years only. **Tickets** venues. **Admission** TL8-TL20; Festival Pass TL50.
Every other year since 1987, more than 50 artists from some 50 countries exhibit around a theme set by a guest curator. Expect to find paintings, installations, screenings, walkabouts, films, panel discussions, lectures and guided tours (in English). With the sharp increase in worldwide popularity of Turkish contemporary art, it was little surprise that 2011's Biennial drew thousands of international visitors. *Photo p177.*

> **INSIDE TRACK**
> **PARTY LIKE A SULTAN**
>
> The Ottomans certainly knew how to celebrate. For the circumcision of three of Emperor Süleyman's sons in 1530, tents sewn with tulips were raised on gold-plated poles at the Hippodrome, where crowds were entertained by tightrope walkers on a cord stretched from the Egyptian obelisk. The public was fed on roast oxen, from which fled live foxes when the feast was served. During the annual Tulip Festival, small armies of tortoises were released to roam the imperial gardens with candles fixed to their shells.

Akbank Jazz Festival

Various venues (0212 334 0100, www.akbanksanat.com). **Date** Oct. **Tickets** venues, Biletix. **Admission** TL10-TL115.
Unlike July's international jamboree (*see p177*), this festival is less about big names and more about jazz. Some ten bands perform every day over a two-week period, with jam sessions at venues including Babylon (*see p195*), Ghetto (*see p195*) and Nardis (*see p197*). Joe Lavano, Marilyn Mazur and Cecil Taylor have all participated in recent years. In addition to great music, there are film screenings and workshops.

Istanbul Arts Fair

Istanbul Convention & Exhibition Centre, Gümü Caddesi 4, Harbiye; Istanbul Congress Centre, Taşkışla Caddesi, Harbiye (0212 244 7171, www.contemporaryistanbul.com). **Date** Nov. **Admission** TL20.
Relocated from its less accessible airport venue to two exhibition centres just behind Taksim Square, this vast, week-long sales fair is increasingly popular. Close to 100 Istanbul galleries, a handful of local institutions (including Santralistanbul, *see p66*, and Istanbul Modern, *see p75*) and hundreds of artists come to exhibit (and sell) paintings, sculpture and ceramics to an increasingly receptive local market.

Anniversary of Atatürk's Death

Date 10 Nov.
Every 10 November at 9.05am, the death of Mustafa Kemal Atatürk is commemorated with a minute's silence. Sirens howl and the Bosphorus ferries sound their foghorns, while buses, cars and people come to a sudden standstill. The experience is both moving and eerie – a testament to the great leader's lasting grip on the Turkish public's imagination.

Istanbul Book Fair

Tüyap Centre, E – 5 Karayolu Üzeri, Gürpınar Kavşağı, Büyükçekmece (0212 867 1100, www.istanbulbookfair.com). **Date** Nov. **Tickets** at the door. **Admission** TL5; students free.
Over 600 Turkish and international publishing houses, as well as dozens of authors from abroad, gather for one week to trade their wares. Leading writers, academics and intellectuals participate in non-stop conferences and round-table discussions. Attendees get discounts on new publications. Free shuttle services run from AKM on Taksim Square, Atatürk Airport, the Bakırköy ferry stop and Esenler bus terminal.

WINTER

!f Istanbul Independent Film Fest

Various venues (0212 254 1060, www.ifistanbul.com). **Date** Feb. **Tickets** venues, MyBilet. **Admission** TL7-TL13.
One of the few events on Istanbul's wintertime calendar, the !f Film Fest screens an excellent range of themed international films at cinemas around town.

Children

Explore the city with your own Young Turks.

Travel with young children in Turkey and you'll find your little ones the centre of attention. Here, kids are adored, indulged, spoiled and squeezed. Waiters slip them specially prepared nibbles. Grannies coo and reach out for cuddles. Children are a cherished part of daily life and are welcomed pretty much everywhere.

And when kids tire of grown-up sights and activities – delightful as boat rides on the Bosphorus can be – it's time to head for Istanbul's child-friendly museums: the magic shows at the **Toy Museum**, or the real submarine at the **Rahmi M Koç Museum**. Or spend an afternoon slipping around an ice-skating rink, spying on fish in the city's new **aquarium** or learning kitchen skills at a traditional Turkish cooking lesson.

MUSEUMS

The museum with the most immediate appeal to kids is probably the **Toy Museum** (*see p90*). As well as old Anatolian toys and *karagoz* puppets, there is a Wild West section highlighting the lives of native Americans, and puppets of American presidents from George Washington to Nixon. At weekends there are puppet shows, magic shows and plenty of other activities. Check the website for a detailed schedule.

The **Archaeology Museum** (*see p47*) has a small area set aside for children, with displays at youngsters' eye level. The **Military Museum** (*see p72*) is crowded with tanks and soldiers' uniforms. The **Ural Ataman Classical Car museum** (Nuripaşa Caddesi 41, Tarabya, 0212 299 4539, www.atamanmuseum.com) displays cars, trucks, motorbikes and war vehicles dating back more than 100 years.

Best of the lot is the **Rahmi M Koç Museum** (*see p72*), which has heaps of interactive displays, working models of trains, an aeroplane and a submarine to clamber around.

Sakıp Sabancı Museum (*see p86*) and **Istanbul Modern** (*see p75*) both arrange free programmes and workshops to make visual arts fun for children. At the time of writing they take place in summer only; check the websites for more information.

PARKS & PLAYGROUNDS

There are good outdoor playgrounds in Cihangir (Güneşli Caddesi) and Bebek (Cevdetpaşa Caddesi). Both tend to get overcrowded on sunny weekends.

There are also some lovely parks further from the centre. Just north of the city centre, in Beşiktaş, **Yıldız Park** is beautiful and leafy. The small fairground **Maçka Luna Park** is in a park north of Taksim. A little further north of Bebek is the large **Emirgan Park**, located just beside the Bosphorus, with an ornamental lake, playground and some of the prettiest landscaping in Istanbul. The coast road is heavy with traffic at the weekends; go early and leave early to beat it.

Parkorman is a lovely woodland area in Maslak, north of the city, with sports facilities including a swimming pool, picnic areas, a playground and fast-food outlets. It also hosts organised parties and activities for children.

OUTSIDE THE CENTRE

Kilyos and **Demirciköy** (*see p218*), villages on the Black Sea coast north of Sarıyer on the European side, have beaches that are popular in summer, with cafés, umbrellas and loungers available. The Black Sea has some strong currents, so be sure that children do not swim outside the designated areas. But wave-surfing and the beach itself will provide plenty of fun for the kids. Just make sure you leave home early so you can have a decent time at the beach and leave before the early evening rush; the journey can stretch as long as two hours each way, instead of the usual 30 minutes, at peak times.

Polonezköy, the old Polish village on the way to Şile on the Asian side, is also a 30-minute drive (traffic permitting). For many Istanbullus, a visit here is a rare opportunity to see large patches of grass you're actually allowed to walk on. It's a great place for children to run around, kick a ball and ride horses. There are several restaurants. **Leonardo's** (Cumhuriyet Caddesi 1, 0216 432 3082, www.leonardo.com.tr) in the centre is among the best. Brunch, served 11am-5pm daily, costs TL45 per person (with a 50 per cent discount for children between three and seven). A swimming pool (and a small pool for kids) and a large playground are major assets.

ACTIVITIES

For babies under two, the British International School (www.bis.k12.tr) organises free mother-and-baby groups; the International Women of Istanbul (www.iwi-tr.org) organises similar groups.

BaB Bowling Café

Yeşilçam Sokak 24, Beyoğlu (0212 251 1595, www.babbowling.com.tr). **Open** 10am-midnight daily. **Games** TL5 daytime, TL7.50-TL10 evening Mon-Fri; TL8-TL10 Sat, Sun. **Map** p246 N3.

This six-lane bowling alley is enduringly popular among teenagers in Istanbul. There are also pool tables, and a café serving fast food and snacks.

Bosphorus Zoo

Tuzla Caddesi 15, Bayramoğlu, Darıca, Gebze (0262 653 6666, www.farukyalcinzoo.com). **Open** *May-Oct* 8.30am-8pm daily. *Nov-Apr* 9am-4.30pm daily. **Admission** TL15; TL10 5-17 years; free under-4s.

Located way out in Darıca, 45km (30 miles) from the city centre, but worth the trip for its wide range of exotic birds and animals, gardens and playground. An hourly feeding schedule gives children the opportunity to check out penguins, lions, jaguars and crocodiles.

> **INSIDE TRACK**
> **COOING OVER KIDS**
>
> Turks are physically affectionate towards kids – sometimes in ways that can seem unusual to the uninitiated. Gestures can vary from a gentle kiss or cuddle to vigorous pinches and even bites on the cheeks or thighs.

Enka Sports Centre

Enka Spor Kulübü, Sadi Gülçelik Spor Sitesi, Istinye (0212 276 2297, www.enkaspor.com). Bus 40, 40T or Metro 4. Levent then dolmuş. **Open** 7am-10pm daily.

Facilities for swimming, tennis, basketball, football, volleyball and athletics, with nine-week courses for children in swimming and tennis (TL295).

★ Istanbul Aquarium

Istanbul Akvaryum

Şenlikköy Mahallesi, Yeşilköy Halkalı Caddesi 93, Florya (0212 444 9744, www.istanbulakvaryum.com). Florya Station from Sirkeci. **Open** 10am-8pm daily. **Admission** TL29; TL22 3-17s; free under 2s.

West of Atatürk Airport, this brand-new aquarium, home to more than 15,000 fish, is a hit with children, who are particularly keen on the replica of an ancient shipwreck recently discovered in the Sea of Marmara.

► *For more on the aquarium, see p66.*

Learning Center

Keramibey Sokak 11, Yeniköy (0212 223 9700, www.thelearningcenteristanbul.com). **Open** hours vary.

A wonderful little centre that offers English-language after-school tutoring sessions, homework clubs and 'Little Genius' programmes for under-threes. Saturdays there are also dance, cooking, drama and literacy courses (from TL60 each).

★ Miniaturk

Imrahor Caddesi, Sütlüce (0212 222 2882, www.miniaturk.com.tr). Bus 47, 47E, 54HS. **Open** *Nov-Apr* 9am-5pm daily. *May-Oct* 9am-7pm Mon-Fri; 9am-9pm Sat, Sun. **Admission** TL10; free under-9s.

An absolutely magical attraction, which recreates 105 of Turkey's most famous sights in miniature. The models range from a palm-sized Leander's Tower to a Sultanahmet Mosque the size of a small car and an Atatürk Airport complete with taxiing jumbos; the level of detail is incredible. Card-operated speakers deliver commentary in English and Turkish. There is also a train going around the sights, a playground and a maze for the kids.

Optimum Ice Skating

Buzluk Buz Pisti, Optimum Mall 10, 1st Floor, Istiklal Sokak, Yeni Sahra, Ataşehir (0216 664 1164, www.optimumoutlet.com). **Open** 10am-10pm daily.

This brand-new ice-skating rink is located within the popular Optimum Shopping Mall, just inland from Kadıköy on Istanbul's Asian shore. Private lessons are available for TL40 a session.

Play 'n' Learn

Havyar Sokak 46, Cihangir, Beyoğlu (0212 244 9151, www.playnlearn-tr.com). **Open** 8.30am-6pm Mon-Sat. **Admission** TL22.5/hr. **Map** p247 O4.

Activities for children up to six. There are workshops on arts and crafts, drama, experiments and games. Arrangements are flexible: you can join in with your child, or drop him off for a few hours.

★ Turkish Flavours

Vali Konağı Caddesi, Uğur Apt 14/3, Nişantaşı (0532 218 0653, www.turkishflavours.com). Metro Osmanbey. **No credit cards.**

Istanbul native Selin Rozanes teaches traditional Turkish cooking to both children and adults within the 1930s kitchen of her Nişantaşı home. One child under 12 years may accompany an adult for free (adult price €75); two children under 12 are charged €37.50.

RESTAURANTS

Although almost all Istanbul restaurants welcome children, and it's usual to bring children to restaurants, few offer special amenities such as children's menus. If asked, though, most will serve children's portions and cook special requests. The restaurants we list in this section go out of their way to cater for children.

Metropolis

Terbiyik Sokak 19, off Akbiyik Caddesi, Sultanahmet (0212 517 6826, www.metropolisrestaurant.net). **Open** 8am-11.30pm daily. **Main courses** TL15-TL20. **Map** p243 N11.

This lively restaurant has been a favourite with locals and visitors alike since it opened in 2003. Excellent Ottoman-style dishes, as well as child-friendly pizzas, pastas and bakes.

> **INSIDE TRACK GETTING ABOUT**
>
> Children can be taken almost everywhere in Istanbul, though it's not always physically easy to do so: pushing a pram is a battle involving encounters with steep hills, high kerbs and narrow passes – which is why most Turks carry their children in their arms.

Secret Garden

Kalender Üstü, Atadan Sokak, Yeniköy (0212 299 0077, www.secretgardenistanbul.com). **Open** 10am-1am daily. **Main courses** TL10-TL15.

In summer, tables are laid out in this big hilly garden overlooking the Bosphorus, which also has a play area with swings, slides and a large lawn. The restaurant serves simple, tasty food: pancakes and sausages, barbecued meatballs and lamb chops.

TGI Fridays

Nispetiye Caddesi 79, Etiler (0212 257 7078, www.fridays.com.tr). Metro Levent. **Open** 11.30am-midnight daily. **Kids' courses** TL10-TL15.

Burgers, hot dogs and fancy ice-cream desserts. There is a dedicated kids' menu.

SHOPPING

Kids' clothing and toy stores can be found at all the large malls (*see p160*). There are pharmacies (*eczane*) in most neighbourhoods. Almost all supermarkets sell a good selection of Milupa baby food and Turkish brands such as Ülker. Nappies and wipes can be found at most grocery stores. For supermarkets, *see p169*.

Gelar

Nispetiye Caddesi, Petrol Sitesi 1, Blok 4, Levent (0212 351 9515). Metro Levent. **Open** 9am-6pm Mon-Fri.

Imported educational tools, wooden toys and playground equipment of excellent quality. Prices are high but the range is unique in Turkey.

Toys 'R' Us

Beyazıt Han 86, Büyükdere Caddesi, Gayrettepe, Beşiktaş (0212 217 9616). Metro Gayrettepe. **Open** 10am-10pm daily.

The largest selection of toys in the city. It also has kids' clothing, shoes, baby food and nappies.

BABYSITTING

Deluxe hotels provide babysitting services. Smaller hotels will usually make every effort to find someone. Beyond that, TLC Nannies (0212 223 9700, www.tlcnanniesandaupairs.com) provides nannies and babysitters in Istanbul.

Film

Popcorn and popularism.

Istanbul has long been enthralled by moving pictures: the first films were shown here al fresco in the dying days of the Ottoman Empire. Local cinema came into its own half a century later, when hundreds of mostly action films were produced annually around Beyoğlu's Yeşilçam Sokak – Turkey's answer to Hollywood. Between the 1950s and 1970s, scores of open-air cinemas sprung up throughout the city, and dreams of becoming a movie star swept the nation.

Today, Turkish film production is once again taking the country – and now the world – by storm. Directors such as Semih Kaplanoğlu, who won Berlin's Golden Bear award for his film *Bal* (*Honey*) in 2010, are earning international acclaim. Istanbul has many cinemas, most of which screen films in their original language with Turkish subtitles. The city also hosts four top-notch annual film festivals.

CINEMAS

All films, except animation and big blockbusters, are shown in the original language with Turkish subtitles, but don't expect English subtitles for Turkish films. Contrary to expectations, the once over-zealous censors have retreated into virtual oblivion under the current Islamist government.

Tickets cost an average of TL10-TL15. Most cinemas have a 'People's Day' (*halk günü*) once or twice a week, when all seats are reduced. The first screening of the day is often cheaper, and students and OAPs generally qualify for a discount at all times with proof of identity.

Phone and online reservations are accepted at some cinemas, and a growing number take credit cards. Seating is assigned. In the older cinemas, ushers often expect a tip; the going rate is around TL1. Be prepared for an intermission during all screenings. To find out what's, check the *Hürriyet Daily News* (www.hurriyetdailynews.com).

Sultanahmet

Çemberlitaş Şafak Movieplex

Darüşşafaka Pasajı, Yeniçeriler Caddesi, Çemberlitaş (0212 516 2660, www.ozenfilm.com.tr). Tram Çemberlitaş. **Tickets** TL12; TL8 Mon. **Map** p242 L10.

Sultanahmet's only cinema couldn't be better positioned, right by a tram stop. All screens have Dolby Digital sound and offer a range of current US, European and local releases.

Beyoğlu

AFM Fitaş

Fitaş Pasajı, Istiklal Caddesi 24 (0212 251 2020, www.afm.com.tr). **Tickets** TL10-TL14. **Map** p249 O2.

Just below Taksim Square, this US-style multiplex has 11 screens, showing a mix of Hollywood hits, indie and Turkish films.

Atlas

Atlas Pasajı, Istiklal Caddesi 209 (0212 252 8576). **Tickets** TL10; TL8 Mon, Thur. **No credit cards. Map** p248 N3.

This once-imposing cinema has been carved into three smaller screens. The largest still boasts the city's most steeply raked auditorium. *Photo p180.*

Sinepop

Yeşilçam Sokak 22, off Istiklal Caddesi (0212 251 1176, www.ozenfilm.com.tr). **Tickets** TL10-TL14; TL8 Mon, Thur. **Map** p248 N3.

During the golden age of Turkish cinema, Yeşilçam Sokak was Turkey's answer to Hollywood. No more: historical cinemas such as the Emek have closed indefinitely over recent years. Sinepop, although modern, was used as a club by the Germans during World War I. Two screens show local and international fare.

And... Action

Turkish cinema comes of age.

The Turkish film industry didn't really get going until the 1950s – yet from the '50s to the '70s, around 250 films were made a year. By the 1990s, the average number had dipped down to ten. But these days filmmaking is on the rise again, with around 60 Turkish films being released annually over the last couple of years.

Commercial success usually calls for a star-studded cast borrowed from TV soaps, pop bands and the catwalk, with a celebrity director to boot. Slapstick comedy is perennially popular, but there are plenty of highbrow films too. Ömer Faruk Sorak's *G.O.R.A.*, a sci-fi parody written by comedian Cem Yılmaz, in which a carpet seller is abducted by aliens, is crammed with cultural references, with subtle swipes at Turkey's deference to the US and Europe. Another hit was actor-director Yılmaz Erdoğan's 2005 comedy *Organize Işler* (*Magic Carpet Ride*), a spoof on Istanbul's organised crime racket.

But box office bounty is not confined to comedy. A case in point is Çağan Irmak's drama *Babam ve Oğlum* (*My Father and My Son*), a rural tale set against the backdrop of Turkey's troubled political past. And action thrillers are entering the fray, among them the crudely nationalistic *Kurtlar Vadisi – Irak* (*Valley of the Wolves: Iraq*), a spin-off of a TV series that raised hackles across the Atlantic early in 2006 and earned record box office takings at home. Built around a real-life event in 2003, when US troops arrested and hooded a group of Turkish officers in northern Iraq, the film sets the scene for hero Polat Alemdar to avenge the incident. It was followed by the equally controversial *Valley of the Wolves: Gladio* in 2008 and *Valley of the Wolves: Palestine* in 2010.

Turkish cinema is not simply successful at home: over recent years, Turkish films have begun winning prizes and recognition abroad too. One of Turkey's best-known directors is Nuri Bilge Ceylan, creator of the acclaimed *Uzak* (*Distant*), whose feature *Bir Zamanlar Anadolu'da* (*Once Upon a Time in Anatolia*) was a co-winner of Cannes Film Festival's Grand Prix in 2011. Ceylan's cinema is a simple but subtle reflection on the human condition. By contrast, director Zeki Demirkubuz has made waves with his ruthless realism, including *Kader* (*Destiny*), the compelling story of a grim love triangle.

Özer Kızıltan's debut feature *Takva* (*Takva – A Man's Fear of God*), an ironic look at the inner workings of an Islamic sect, won the Swarovski Cultural Innovation Award at the Toronto Film Festival in 2006. Yüksel Aksu's debut *Dondurmam Gaymak* (*Ice Cream, I Scream*) took the comic tale of a small trader struggling against globalisation to the Oscars in 2007 as Turkey's official entry for Best Foreign Language Film.

But it's director Semih Kaplanoğlu who has attracted most international attention recently. His 2010 film *Bal* (*Honey*) won the Berlin International Film Festival's Golden Bear award. The story of a young boy searching for his father, *Bal* is the third film in a trilogy: it was preceded by *Yumurta* (*Egg*) in 2007 and *Süt* (*Milk*) in 2008.

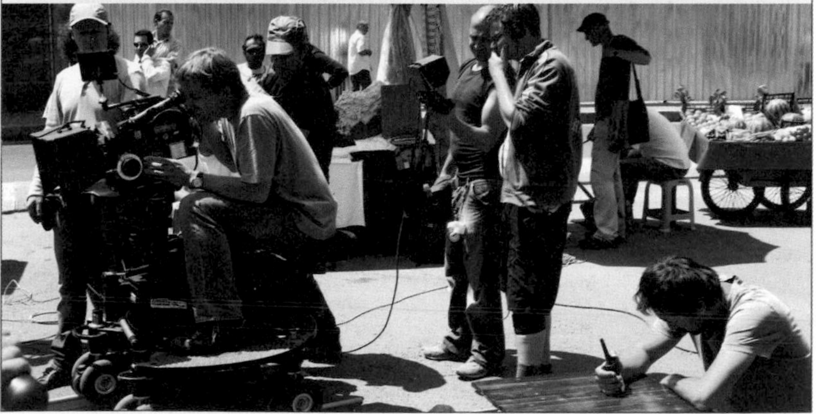

Taksim-Beyoğlu

Halep Pasajı, Istiklal Caddesi 62 (0212 251 3240, www.beyoglusinemasi.com.tr). **Tickets** TL12; TL8 Wed. **No credit cards. Map** p248 N3.

The Beyoğlu has an authentic art-house feel with a programme to match. From July to September, there's a daily programme of critics' picks from the past year, but this soon slides into anything from the past decade. Across from the foyer/café is the small-screen Pera, with the same management.

★ Yeşilçam

Imam Adnan Sokak 8, off Istiklal Caddesi (0212 293 6800, www.yesilcamsinemasi.com). **Tickets** TL7. **No credit cards. Map** p249 O2.

At this small, basement art-house cinema, the programming leans towards local and European independent film. The charming foyer is full of old projection machines and fading film posters.

Levent

★ Cinebonus Kanyon

Kanyon Mall, Büyükdere Caddesi 185 (0212 353 0853, www.cinebonus.com.tr). Metro Levent. **Tickets** TL16.50-TL17.50; TL11 Wed.

The ultimate cinema experience. Step into the cutting-edge complex and you're in a world of plush design and smooth service, from the ticket booths to the conveniences. Worth every (pricey) penny.

Levent Kültür Merkezi Sinema

Çalıkuşu Sokak 2 (0212 325 7371). Metro Levent. **Tickets** TL5. **No credit cards.**

Run by TÜRSAK (the Turkish Foundation of Cinema and Audiovisual Culture), this art-house venue shows indie fare plus popular recent films. It also hosts various festivals. There's a pleasant café with seats outside in summer.

Karaköy

★ Istanbul Modern

Liman Işletmeleri Sahası, Antrepo 4, off Meclis-i Mebusan Caddesi (0212 334 7300, www.istanbulmodern.org). Tram Karaköy. **Tickets** free with museum admission (TL14). **No credit cards.**

A state-of-the-art theatre within the museum (*see p75*), which runs a monthly programme dedicated to home-grown and international art-house movies, including retrospectives, documentaries, animation and shorts. The annual four-day Pera Fest (Nov) is also held here, over which ten international and Turkish films are screened.

FESTIVALS

★ !F Istanbul Independent Film Festival

Various venues (0212 254 1060, www.ifistanbul.com). **Date** Feb. **Tickets** venues, MyBilet.

The programming of this hugely popular event is distinctly right-on, with strands dedicated to digital, political and gay/lesbian cinema, plus horror, shorts, international award-winning and cult films. Try to book tickets in advance.

★ International Istanbul Film Festival

Various venues (0212 334 0700, www.iksv.org). **Date** Mar-Apr. **Tickets** venues, Biletix,.

A highlight of the Turkish cultural calendar, this glamorous festival brings a real buzz to Beyoğlu. Hundreds of films from around the world, plus all the latest Turkish productions, are crammed into a two-week programme. Alongside national and inter-national competitions, themes include tributes, documentaries, animation, adaptation and world cinema. Festival season is also a chance to stargaze, with an impressive contingent of heavyweight directors and actors in attendance most years. Buy tickets in advance to guarantee seats and qualify for a discount.

International 1001 Documentary Film Festival

Various venues (0212 245 8958, www.1001belgesel.net). **Date** late Sept.

This one-week festival run by the Association of Documentary Filmmakers (BSB) includes unusual factual films, as well as panel discussions, master classes and Q&A sessions. Admission is free.

Istanbul International Short Film Festival

Various venues (0212 252 5700, www.istanbulfilmfestival.com). **Date** late Nov.

A long-running event masterminded by short film aficionado Hilmi Etikan, this week-long festival screens shorts at the Dutch Consulate's Chapel, the Goethe Institute and the Institut Français. The programme includes short fiction, experimental fare and animation from all over the world. All films have English subtitles and all screenings are free.

INSIDE TRACK MOVIE MANIA

As of 2011, Beyoğlu is the new home of the Türkvak Cinema-Theatre Museum (Türkvak Sinema-Tiyatro Müzesi, Yeniçarşı Caddesi 24, Galatasaray, 0212 245 8091, www.turvak.com.tr, closed Mon, TL10). The museum, which houses all sorts of movie paraphernalia, including thousands of Turkish films, equipment, photos, posters, scripts and a hall of wax statues, was founded by Turkish director Türker Inanoğlu.

Galleries

Painting the town.

Istanbul's art scene has grown exponentially in the last few years. Scores of new galleries opened in 2011 and 2012, many in time for the Istanbul Biennial, the city's biggest ever art show, on the banks of the Bosphorus. This in a city that only welcomed its first museum of contemporary art (Istanbul Modern, *see p75*) in 2004.

Some of Istanbul's most cutting-edge galleries – **Arter**, **Edisyon**, **Non** and the two new **SALT** spaces – are along Beyoğlu's main thoroughfare of Istiklal Caddesi or in the waterside district of Tophane. All are easily accessible by tram or on foot.

GALLERIES

For many years, the **International Istanbul Biennial** (*see p178*) was the only specialist art event that invited international artists to exhibit in Istanbul, and also gave local artists the opportunity to present their work in large-scale, professionally curated exhibitions. With the Biennial taking place only every other year, the city lacked a more permanent support structure for ongoing artistic production and presentation.

Over the last few years, the situation has shifted to the opposite extreme. Although there is almost no state funding for contemporary culture in Turkey, wealthy patrons and banks, which have a history of providing charitable financial support to the arts, have now created their own 'branded', non-commercial galleries, cultural centres and museums. It is currently so fashionable to own an art institution that Istanbul – or rather the relatively small area around Beyoğlu, Karaköy and the Golden Horn – is bursting with new developments and prospective projects.

In 2004, the **Istanbul Modern** (*see p75*) kickstarted this trend. Located in an old customs warehouse on the Bosphorus, it showcases a comprehensive collection of modern Turkish art alongside interesting photography and art-house films, and stages several outstanding temporary exhibitions each year.

Hot on the heels of Istanbul Modern came a crop of equally captivating museums, including the **Pera Museum** (*see p70*), the **Sakip Sabanci Museum** (*see p86*) and **Santralistanbul** (*see p66*). But in recent years, it's not the art museums, but the sudden swathe of independent galleries that has taken the city by storm. Among the dozens that seem to open their doors on an almost daily basis, **Arter**, **SALT Beyoğlu** and **SALT Galata** are stunning spaces to take in Turkish and international contemporary art.

Note that in many of the smaller galleries, artworks are for sale to the general public. Unless otherwise indicated, admission to all of these spaces is free.

Akbank Culture & Arts Centre
Akbank Kültür Sanat Merkezi

Istiklal Caddesi 8, Beyoğlu (0212 252 3500, www.akbanksanat.com). **Open** 10.30am-7.30pm Tue-Sat. **Map** p249 O2.

INSIDE TRACK GALLERIES GALORE

Thanks to a thriving economy and several art shows a year, it's almost impossible to keep up with wave after wave of local gallery openings. In addition to this list, **C.A.M. Galeri** (www.camgaleri.com), **Dirimart** (www.dirimart.org), **Elipsis Gallery** (www.elipsisgallery.com) and **Pi Artworks** (www.piartworks.com) are also well worth checking out. For more galleries and up-to-date listings, check the monthly *Time Out Istanbul* magazine.

Galerist.

Open since 1993, this newly renovated space is home to a gallery, café and art library. The programme fluctuates between externally curated shows of international artists and exhibitions by Turkish art students. There are also theatre and dance workshops.

★ Arter

Istiklal Caddesi 211, Beyoğlu (0212 243 3767, www.arter.org.tr). **Open** 11am-7pm Tue-Thur; noon-8pm Fri-Sun. **Map** p249 M4.

An initiative of the Vehbi Koç Foundation opened in 2010, this 'Space for Art' showcases temporary exhibitions of some of Turkey's most interesting artists from the last 50 years. Videos, paintings, photography and installation pieces are displayed over five floors.

BAS

Necati Bey Caddesi 32/2, Karaköy (0555 503 3847, www.b-a-s.info). **Open** noon-6pm Tue-Sat. **Map** p246 N6.

Launched by artist Banu Cennetoğlu to display and produce art books and publications, BAS has already published several books by Turkish artists, which can be purchased here. The rest of the collection is a useful reference resource. The gallery also hosts temporary exhibitions, focusing on Turkish contemporary art.

★ Edisyon

Bostanbaşı Caddesi 20A, Beyoğlu (0212 245 4310, www.edisyonlar.com). **Open** noon-7pm Tue-Sat. **Map** p248 N4.

A small gallery selling editioned works by independent artists, including prints, photos, illustrations, drawings and design objects. Both up-and-coming and established artists are showcased, making it a good place to discover unknown local talent.

Galeri Apel

Hayriye Caddesi 5A, Galatasaray, Beyoğlu (0212 292 7236, www.galleryapel.com). **Open** 11.30am-6.30pm Tue-Sat. **Map** p248 N3.

Apel hosts exhibitions in a variety of media that verge on craft and design. Expect weird and wonderful creations from Turkey's avant-garde, as well as works by international artists. As you might expect for an underground space, it's a little hard to find: up a few steps at the corner of the street right behind the Galatasaray Lycée.

Galeri Nev

Istiklal Caddesi Mısır Apt 163, Beyoğlu (0212 252 1525, www.galerinevistanbul.com). **Open** 11am-6.30pm Tue-Sat.

Founded in 1984 by architects Ali Artun and Haldun Dostoğlu, Galeri Nev has a sister gallery in Ankara. Essentially a commercial space, it mostly represents internationally recognised Turkish artists such as Inci Eviner, Canan Tolon and Erdag Aksel as well as exhibiting work by artists from abroad. The gallery is also one of the oldest initiatives publishing artist books.

Galerist

Meşrutiyet Caddesi 67/1, Beyoğlu (0212 252 1896, www.galerist.com.tr). **Open** 10am-6pm Mon-Fri; noon-6pm Sat. **Map** p248 M4.

Galerist has the strongest international reputation of any contemporary art gallery in Istanbul, with a roster of illustrious local artists. The gallery stages about eight temporary exhibitions a year; Julian Opie showed here in 2010.

Galeri X-Ist

Artı Sanat Üretim, Kaşıkçıoğlu Apt 42, off Abdi Ipekci Caddesi, Nişantaşı (0212 291 7784, www.artxist.com). Metro Osmanbey. **Open** noon-7.30pm Mon; 11am-7.30pm Tue-Sat.

Galeri X-Ist is committed to working with young Turkish artists, giving them the opportunity to show and develop their work from an early stage in their career. Photography and painting are high on the agenda. Cutting-edge pieces by artists such as Nuri Kuzucan, who focuses on urban landscapes, and contemporary photographer Sinem Dişli are well worth checking out.

SALT Beyoğlu

Istiklal Caddesi 136, Beyoğlu (0212 377 4200, www.saltonline.org). **Open** 12am-8pm Tue-Sat; 10.30am-6pm Sun. **Map** p248 N3.

Sponsored by Garanti Bank along with SALT Galata (*see below*), SALT Beyoğlu is a wow-factor new addition to Istanbul's arts scene displaying art over four vast floors. Temporary exhibitions, including Turkish retrospectives, vie for attention alongside SALT's walk-in cinema, first-floor Bistro and outpost of quality bookshop Robinson Crusoe (*see p163*).

★ SALT Galata

Bankalar Caddesi 11, Karaköy (0212 334 2200, www.saltonline.org). **Open** 12am-8pm Tue-Sat; 10.30am-6pm Sun. **Map** p246 M6.

Opened in November 2011, SALT Galata is a multi-functional cultural centre, dedicated to exploring historical and contemporary visual culture. Located inside the city's former Ottoman Bank, the space is laced with magnificent neoclassical and oriental architecture. The centre includes an open library, a space for archival exhibitions, the Ottoman Bank Museum, an auditorium and a bookstore, plus a decidedly hip restaurant looking out to sea.

KargART

Kadife Sokak 16, Kadıköy (0216 449 1725, www.kargart.org). Ferry from Karaköy or Eminönü to Kadıköy. **Open** 12.30-8pm Tue-Sat. **Map** p251 W8.

Located above a popular bar in Kadıköy, KargART is easily the most experimental gallery on Istanbul's Asian shores. The exhibitions often feature works by young artists from the area, which attract a loyal local following. Free art-house films (original language with subtitles) are frequently shown.

Milk Gallery & Design Store

Balkon Çıkmazı 8/A, Galata, Beyoğlu (0212 251 5797, www.whatismilk.com). **Open** 1-7pm Tue-Sat. **Map** p246 M6.

Milk is a small gallery that shows work influenced by graffiti, street art, illustration and comics, by both local and international artists. There is also a display room for cult design objects, such as Lomo cameras, Ndeur shoes and limited edition prints.

INSIDE TRACK A-PEELING ART

Part art-incubation unit, part online-retrospective for young Turkish artists, **Banané** (www.bananemag.com) offers the first view of Istanbul's current crop of emerging talent. Run by Turko-Levantine crew Stephanie Gallia and Giulia Campaner, it's the first point of call for newcomers to the scene.

NON

Mısır Apt 163/4, Istiklal Caddesi, Beyoğlu (0212 249 8774, www.galerinon.com). **Open** 11am-7pm Tue-Sat. **Map** p248 N3.

Gallery NON is a relatively new space, located on the fourth floor of Istiklal Caddesi's Mısır Apartments, adjacent to the imposing St Anthony of Padua church. It hosts interdisciplinary group and solo exhibitions, showcasing both local and international artists. NON recently initiated Non-Stage, a project featuring internationally known performance artists.

Pist

Dolapdere Sokak 8/A/B/C, Pangaltı (no phone, www.pist.org.tr, www.pist-org.blogspot.com). Metro Osmanbey. **Open** check website for details.

An independent gallery located in the unlikely, off-centre district of Pangaltı. In a large, street-level space, Pist offers a lively interdisciplinary programme that includes solo installations displayed in the window, performances and collaborations with international artists' collectives. There are also pop-up exhibitions. Check the blog for details.

Pilot

Siraselviler Caddesi 83/2, Beyoğlu (0212 245 5505, www.pilotgaleri.com). **Open** 10.30am-6.30pm Tue-Sat. **Map** p249 O3.

In Istanbul's cosiest neighbourhood of Cihangir, Pilot (formerly known as Outlet) is a former 1970s nightclub turned 700sq m (2,300sq ft) exhibition space. The gallery represents contemporary artists – usually with a strong political stance – such as Sener Özmen, Burak Delier and Hamra Abbas.

Proje4L Elgiz Museum of Contemporary Art

Meydan Sokak, Beybi Giz, Plaza B Block, Maslak (0212 290 2525, www.proje4l.org). Metro ITU Ayazaga. **Open** 10am-5pm Wed-Fri; 10am-4pm Sat; by appointment Tue.

Originally created as a museum for temporary exhibitions, Proje4L – with a decade of experience under its belt – is now devoted to the private collection of art aficionados Sevda and Can Elgiz, which combines contemporary Turkish art with international pieces. The Project Rooms host exhibitions by Turkish artists that change every month.

★ Rampa

Şair Nedim Caddesi 21A, Akaretler, Beşiktaş (0212 327 0800, www.rampaistanbul.com). **Open** 11am-7pm Tue-Sat; by appointment Mon.

Located in one of the recently renovated Akaretler townhouses opposite Dolmabahçe Palace, Rampa stages cutting-edge contemporary exhibitions. In 2011, the popular spot hosted top Turkish artists Vahap Avşar and Ergin Çavuşoğlu.

Gay & Lesbian

Forget your preconceptions.

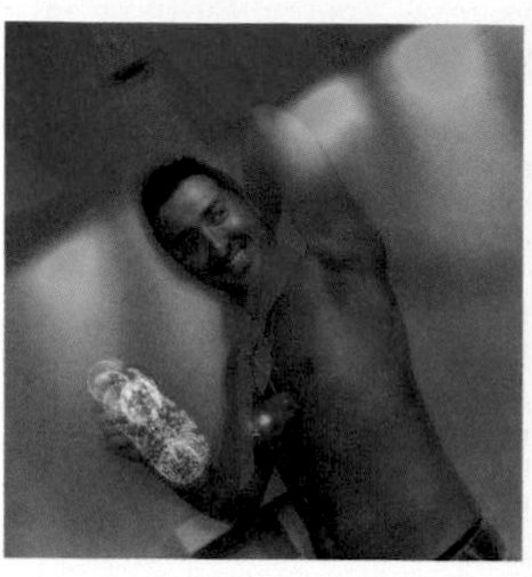

While Turkey's strictly secular nature means the gay community is not subjected to the ranting of religious figures, traditional family structure and values are still firmly in place and Istanbul is the only city in Turkey where a gay culture thrives. And it's a little different, with its own idiosyncracies: markers of sexual identity can be different to those in the West, and confusing to the foreign eye. No, those moustachioed men in tight jeans and bomber jackets, sauntering down the street hand in hand, are not the local Greenwich Village clones. They're just a couple of traditional guys in a country where public displays of male affection have been assumed to mean just that – and only that. And no, that doesn't mean you and your boyfriend can walk down the street hand in hand. Urban Turks are savvy enough to know when same-sex affection means more, and you'd draw the same reactions in the streets of Istanbul as in a small town in the American South, or in 1950s London. On the other hand, Istanbul has the most vibrant gay nightlife scene to be found between Prague and Cape Town.

THE GAY SCENE

The family structure means that a high premium is placed on knuckle-dragging masculinity and there's a lot of pressure to marry, which is one reason why so many bisexual and gay men present themselves in public as straight. Even for those few gay men with the financial means and firmness of character to strike out on their own, the downside of strong neighbourly ties is that liberated anonymity, even in large cities, is very difficult to achieve.

The whole concept of a gay rights movement complete with full social acceptance is a foreign import. The same is not true of gay sex. Oscar Wilde's 'love that dare not speak its name' had been expressed in loving detail in Ottoman court literature centuries earlier. It didn't need a name. It was just love, and nothing at all to be afraid of.

Ironically, it is in comparison to European norms that Turkey is now found wanting. And the legal codification of gay rights is among the criteria Turkey must fulfil should it eventually become part of the EU. As is the case in terms of geography and culture, Turkey lies somewhere between Europe and the Middle East,

Bars and clubs abound, Turkish baths are as steamy as ever, cyber hook-ups are an increasingly favoured sexual and social outlet for the closeted majority, and secluded public parks are wildly cruisy. While home-grown transsexual diva Bülent Ersoy has been revered for nearly three decades, and fellow singer Zeki Müren's gold lamé boots and thigh-baring tunics did his career no harm, until very recently even the campest celebrities have not been subjected to the 'outing' campaigns of the West, or pressured to 'admit' to their sexual orientations.

When it comes to gay culture, Turkey is neither permissive nor repressive, and the long, slow march to full acceptance will be won the same way it will (eventually) be won in the West: a family member, a friend,

INSIDE TRACK LEGALLY FOND

Homosexuality is not illegal in Turkey. It was decriminalised by the Ottomans in 1858, after a short-lived ban that had come about mainly as a result of European influences.

a colleague, a neighbour at a time. In the meantime, momentum marches on at Istanbul's annual **Gay Pride Parade** (June, www.prideistanbul.org), now extended to a week of workshops and activities, as well as the new **Trans Pride Walk** (also June), which began in 2010. Positive publicity continues at the yearly **!f Istanbul Independent Film Fest** (*see p184*), which showcases a selection of 'Rainbow Films'. And that's not to mention the unstoppable determination of a small but swelling group of queers, dykes and trannies determined to meet, party, have sex and settle down, whether society likes it or not.

VENUES

If you come to Istanbul expecting to find a gay nightlife scene comparable to that of major cities in the US and Europe, you will be disappointed – although incredible strides have been made, from just one bar in the 1980s to over a dozen by the early 21st century. In the last few years, however, the scene has grown decidedly less diverse.

While there have never been 'niche bars' catering exclusively to a mature crowd, leather queens or other subsets, there used to be a wider selection of more upmarket 'Western-style' venues. Of the three Western-style clubs that remain open, **Privé** has gone downmarket, and **Bar Bahçe** and **Love Point** have become the victims of their own success, unless well-heeled suburban PR ladies and their banker boyfriends are elements you'd like in your social mix.

That said, if you're in search of a truly Turkish experience, you're still in luck. There are at least half a dozen clubs and bars within walking distance of each other in Beyoğlu, tucked into side streets on both sides of Istiklal Caddesi. Expect a mix of scratchy techno dance tunes and Turkish pop, an average age barely over 20, minimal decor at best, a ventilation system unable to cope with the summer heat and drinks costing TL15. What you won't see much of are lesbians, although venues catering for them have risen – from none to one.

On the other hand, even if all of that's not your thing, on the right night, in the right mood, after the right number of overpriced cocktails, you just might find yourself somewhere, appreciating the sheer energy and lack of pretension, and a realisation will strike you that you have indeed strayed far from home.

Most places fill up only on Wednesday nights and weekends, if then. Don't bother turning up before midnight unless you're particularly enamoured with your own company, and be prepared to pay a nominal admission, usually in exchange for a drink ticket.

INSIDE TRACK ON THE WEB

Smooth and slick, www.absolutesultans.com peddles Istanbul as a sophisticated and super-sexy gay travel destination. As well as selling holidays, the company provides ungrudging free information via the website or phone. Turkey's oldest gay website, www.eshcinsel.net, has been in business since 1998. Reviews in Turkish of Madonna's latest album are unlikely to appeal to an international crowd, but visit the chat room to strike up pre-travel friendships. IstanbulGay (www.istanbulgay.com) is also an excellent resource.

Western

Not places in which chaps with chaps and cowboy hats hang out; by Western we mean the sort of bar where moneyed, liberated and largely moustache-free Turks tend to congregate. While still distinctly local in flavour, they're the kind of places where straights and women – lesbian or otherwise – will feel comfortable.

★ Bigudi Club

Mis Sokak 5, off Istiklal Caddesi, Beyoğlu (0535 509 0922, www.bigudiproject.net). **Open** 10pm-5am Wed-Fri. **Admission** free. **Map** p249 O2.

Lipstick chic is the order of the evening at Bigudi ('curlers'), Istanbul's first lesbian bar. The terrace club is all girls; the café-pub, one floor below, is open to everyone LGBT, and friends.

► *Lesbians will also enjoy the Rocinante Café Bar (Öğüt Sokak 6, off Sakızağacı Caddesi, Beyoğlu, 0212 244 8219), where arabesque and Turkish pop is played on Friday and Saturday nights.*

Cheeky Club

Küçük Bayram Sokak 1/A, Beyoğlu (0535 259 6060). **Open** midnight-6am daily. **Admission** TL25. **No credit cards**.

The local last-chance saloon, Cheeky Club starts to buzz around 3am, as thrill-seekers drift in to check out who's still available for the night. The edgy club boasts a darkroom out back.

★ Love Dance Point

Cumhuriyet Caddesi 349/1, Harbiye (0212 296 3358, www.lovedp.net). **Open** 11.30pm-4am Tue-Thur; 11.30pm-5am Fri, Sat. **Admission** free Tue-Thur; TL20 Fri, Sat. **Credit** MC, V. **Map** p247 P1.

Istanbul's only gay venue worthy of the title 'club', Love Dance Point has a full-size dancefloor, a no riff-raff door policy, professional sound system and groovy DJs. It draws a mixed crowd, most of whom are too focused on dancing and preening to notice anyone else but themselves.

Otherside the Club

Zambak Sokak 2/5, off Istiklal Caddesi, Beyoğlu (0212 293 8852, www.othersideistanbul.com). **Open** 8pm-3am daily. **Admission** free. **Map** p247 O1.

What used to be Istanbul's first gay restaurant is now a club, complete with house music, go-go boys and a tiny dancefloor. It's on the fourth floor of an apartment building, and decor is mismatched and glitzy. The main bar is in the former living room and the back room is the place to discreetly make bedroom eyes at your new friend.

Privé

Tarlabaşı Bulvarı 28/A, Taksim, Beyoğlu (0212 235 7999). **Open** 11pm-5am daily. **Admission** free Mon-Thur, Sun; TL25 Fri, Sat. **Map** p247 O2.

An after-hours club that used to mix the slightly sordid with the upmarket, Privé was the place where minor celebrities and socialites could slum in safety. In the last few years, though, the more unsavoury elements seem more in evidence. Be thankful for the hulking bodyguards at the door. The DJs shift a surprisingly progressive set.

XLarge

Kallavi Sokak 12, off Meşrutiyet Caddesi, Beyoğlu (0212 243 4943, www.xlargeclubistanbul.com). **Open** 11pm-5am Fri, Sat. **Admission** varies. **Credit** MC, V. **Map** p248 M3.

True to its name, this is a mega club, located in a former cinema. It features a ballroom-sized chandelier, the biggest bar of the venues in this chapter and two giant beds flanking the mezzanine bar. It's pretty busy, largely thanks to the recent DJ Mus-T programmes for avid dance music-lovers. The Las Vegas-style drag revue brings Lady Gaga and Madonna to the stage. A straight and pansexual crowd often roars in appreciation of the spectacle.

► *Not quite your thing? Nip around the corner to the brand-new Xsmall Club (Balyoz Sokak 10, off Meşrutiyet Caddesi) instead.*

Ala Turca

Be warned: some of these venues are minefields for anyone not sufficiently attuned to the local social dynamics. That tall, dark number cruising you from his dim corner could well be more of a homophobe than the most rednecked straight. Our list includes only the safer venues, but even so, brace yourself for the unexpected.

EKOO Club

Tarlabaşı Bulvarı 32, Taksim, Beyoğlu. **Open** 11.30pm-5am daily. **Admission** free. **No credit cards. Map** p247 O2.

A club that's particularly popular with bears, although all orientations – including straight – are welcome. It moved to brand-new premises near Taksim Square in 2011.

INSIDE TRACK KARAOKE CHIC

Pop stars in the making can start exercising those vocal chords: **Pinokyo Café Bar** (Büyükparmakkapı Sokak 26, Beyoğlu, 0212 292 6209) is Istanbul's first gay karaoke bar.

Chianti Café-Pub

Balo Sokak 31/2, Istiklal Caddesi, Beyoğlu. **Open** 10pm-12.30am Wed-Sun. **Admission** free. **Credit** MC, V. **Map** p248 N3.

A relatively recent addition to the ever-changing nocturnal landscape of Balohood (otherwise known as Balo Sokak), Chianti caters mainly to locals who fancy themselves as singers and enjoy the communal singing of Turkish pop. There's dancing between tables late into the evening. As much local flavour as you can find anywhere.

Durak Bar

Muratpaşa Sokak 9, Yusufpaşa, Aksaray. Tram Aksaray. **Open** 8pm-2am daily. **No credit cards.**

Turkish bears and other earthy types who won't do with the bright lights and thumping electronica of Beyoğlu gather here in the comparatively more exotic neighbourhood of Aksaray. The beer is cheap and folk music raunchily doled out by live performers. It gets busy around midnight at weekends.

★ Tek Yön

Sıraselviler Caddesi 63/1, Taksim, Beyoğlu (0212 245 1653, www.tekyonclub.com). **Open** 10pm-4am daily. **Admission** free. **No credit cards. Map** p248 M3.

Still one of the most happening places in town, able to retain a few bears even as its new sound system, video screen and club tunes have begun packing in the clubbers, middle classes and foreigners. For a Turkish night on the tiles in an unthreatening environment, this spot is your best bet.

Transgender

There are an estimated 3,000 transsexuals in Istanbul, many of whom survive through prostitution. Tranny admirers are drawn primarily from the ranks of the straight, and the bars and clubs they frequent are pick-up scenes dominated by moustachioed men in badly cut suits. You're bound to catch a glimpse of scantily clad 'girls' flocking towards **Club 1001 Gece** (Sıraselviler Caddesi 61/18, Taksim, Beyoğlu) – dancing takes place downstairs, with a cosy club for getting closer upstairs.

RESTAURANTS & CAFÉS

Frappe Istanbul

Zambak Sokak 10/A, off Istiklal Caddesi, Beyoğlu (0212 292 3834, www.frappeistanbul.com). **Open** 9am-2am daily. **No credit cards. Map** p247 O2.

This friendly gay café is a relatively recent addition to Istanbul's scene. A laid-back venue by day, Frappe transforms into a club come eve, complete with new basement level. Food is served from noon to 11pm, including midday breakfasts for post-partiers.

★ Sugar Café

Saka Salim Çıkmazı 3/A, off Istiklal Caddesi, Beyoğlu (0212 245 0096, www.sugar-cafe.com). **Open** 11am-1am daily. **No credit cards. Map** p248 N3.

Istanbul's first gay café – now a decade old – offers smart decor, strong espressos and home-made Turkish sweets. The cafe's handy location, informative staff and evening crowds make it a good starting point for a night of carousing.

HAMAMS & SAUNAS

None of Istanbul's hamams and saunas is officially gay, but the ones listed below cater almost exclusively to men unabashedly seeking a bit more than a good exfoliation. Their sheer numbers, and the decline in the popularity of public bathing among the population at large, have resulted in the small local hamams listed below becoming gay by default, simply because they've been swamped by an almost exclusively queer clientele. No matter how zealous the management's efforts to stamp out any monkey business, boys will be boys: clingy cloths are hitched up or allowed to slip down, groins are repeatedly lathered and rinsed. One notoriously busy hamam in the Sultanahmet district responded by adopting a women-only policy; others have helplessly thrown in the towel and sexual activity is tolerated, as long as it is not seen. Pointing out that a couple in the next room were moments ago having sex won't necessarily save you from a rapid ejection if you're spotted doing the same.

Çeşme Hamam

Yeni Çeşme Sokak 9, off Perşembe Pazarı Caddesi, Karaköy (0212 252 3441). **Open** 8am-7pm daily. **Admission** TL20. **No credit cards. Map** p246 L6.

A makeover several years ago did little to improve the forbidding appearance of this hard-to-find hamam, hidden among the backstreet hardware stores. The staff are apathetic enough to take a relaxed approach to the sight of great tubby things flirting (and more) in the underground bathing area.

Yeşildirek Hamam

Tersane Caddesi 74, Azapkapı (0212 297 7223). **Open** 6am-9.30pm daily. **Admission** TL20; TL27 with massage. **No credit cards. Map** p246 L5.

A neighbourhood hamam across from the Azapkapı Mosque at the base of the Atatürk Bridge. As good an introduction to the bathing scene as you'll get anywhere, with the added bonus of being relatively clean. The large, jam-packed sauna reeks of sweat and testosterone, if that's your thing.

Sugar Café.

Hamams

Scrub up on history.

British novelist Maggie O'Farrell wrote: 'If heaven exists, I hope it's a hamam.' After an afternoon at one of Istanbul's historic steam baths, any visitor would be hard pressed not to agree. For first-timers, it can be intimidating to strip off, stretch out and allow a stranger to knead your muscles into soft submission. But there's no need to fret – and no need to speak Turkish. You'll be guided through the process courtesy of expansive gestures: quickly cultivating your hamam taster into a blissed-out addiction.

Many hotels offer a sanitised, spa-inspired version of the city's ancient steam baths. Delightful as they are, it's worth taking the plunge and trying out a traditional hamam. In particular, Sultanahmet's 16th-century Roxelana Baths, freshly renovated and opened mid 2011, makes for an exquisite experience.

HAMAM HISTORY

Hamams were always intended to purify. Part of Islamic tradition is that followers should adhere to a strict set of rules for ablutions, washing hands, arms, face and feet with running water before praying. These rituals were not necessarily carried out in a hamam, but the link between the mosque and the hamam was always close, and the precincts of all major mosques incorporated a public bathhouse.

In the earliest times, the hamam was for men only, but the privilege was later extended to women. No mixing, of course: either the hamam would have two sections, one for each sex, or it would admit men and women at separate times of day. This schedule is still the case. In male-dominated Ottoman times, women particularly valued their visits as a rare freedom: far more than just somewhere to get clean, the hamam was a rare opportunity to be away from the home unchaperoned. Hamams were the favoured places for arranging marriages – somewhere a mother could get a good eyeful of any prospective daughter-in-law. When the wedding came along, the equivalent of an Ottoman stag or hen night was spent getting steamed, lathered, hennaed and depilated. For a husband to deny his wife access to the hamam was grounds for divorce.

Newborn babies would be taken out of the family home for the first time 40 days after birth for a visit to a hamam, an event that also marked the end of housebound confinement for the mother. And after a lifetime of hamam-going came to its inevitable end, a person's body would be carried in one last time to be washed, before being laid out at the mosque. Thankfully, this tradition has passed away; these days, there's no chance that you might have to share your steam room with a corpse.

Hamam-going itself has been on the verge of extinction since the advent of affordable internal plumbing. Whereas 80 years ago there were more than 2,500 bathhouses in Istanbul, now there are only about a hundred. Many of these spots struggle to survive. The few that flourish do so largely by courting the tourist dollar – hence some exorbitant admission prices.

BARE ESSENTIALS

For the uninitiated, entering a hamam for the first time can be a daunting experience. Lengthy menus offer such treats as massage, depilation and pedicures (also soap and shampoo, although you may prefer to bring your own – and don't forget a hairbrush or comb). Outside tourist-frequented hamams such as Çemberlitaş, Cağaloğlu and Galatasaray, these lists will be in Turkish. It all boils down to whether you just want to look after yourself, or whether you want to pay extra for the services of a masseur (who'll also give you a good soaping and scrub).

Once you've paid, you enter the *camekan*, a kind of reception area. Some of these entrances

Baths of Roxelana/Ayasofya Hürrem Sultan Hamamı.

are splendid affairs with several storeys of wooden cubicles, like boxes at an opera house, and a gurgling central fountain. You'll either get here, or will be directed to more modern dressing rooms. You will be given a colourful checked cloth, known as a *peştemal*, to be tied around the waist for modesty. Keep this wrap on at all times – it's bad form to flash. Women are less concerned and almost always ditch the *peştemal* in the steam room, though many keep on their knickers. Both sexes also get *takunya*, wooden clogs that can be lethal on wet marble floors. Plastic slippers are often substituted nowadays.

A door from the *camekan* leads through to the *soğukluk*, which is for cooling off and has showers and toilets; another gives on to the *hararet*, or steam room. These rooms can be plain or ornate, but are nearly always cloaked in marble and feature a great dome inset with star-shaped coloured glass admitting a soft, diffuse light. Billowing clouds of steam fog the air.

There are no pools, as still water was traditionally considered to be unclean. Instead, the *hararet* is dominated by a great marble slab known as the *göbek taşı* or 'navel stone'. Here, customers lie and sizzle like eggs on a skillet.

THE HAMAMS

Be warned that some of Istanbul's hamams can be run-down to the point of being downright filthy. We recommend sticking to the places reviewed below. For gay-friendly hamams, *see p191*. For hamam-style spas in hotels, *see p121*. Note that in tourist-targeted hamams, prices are often posted only in euros, although you're welcome to pay the equivalent in Turkish lira.

★ Baths of Roxelana/Ayasofya Hürrem Sultan Hamamı

Bab-ı Hümayun Caddesi, Sultanahmet (0212 517 3535, www.ayasofyahamami.com). **Open** 7am-11pm daily. **Admission** €70; €90-€165 with massage. **Map** p243 N10.

Directly opposite the Haghia Sophia, this stunning hamam was built in 1556 by the renowned architect Sinan for Sultan Süleyman's wife Roxelana. The baths were used as a carpet showroom for many years, but after a multi-million-euro renovation, they were restored to their original use and reopened to the public. Utterly opulent, the marble-swathed hamam is divided in two, providing mirror-image bathhouses for men and women. Packages are the priciest around, but the hamam is perfect for visitors seeking an indulgent experience – complete with traditional treats such as sherbet drinks and Turkish Delight.

Büyük Hamam

Potinciler Sokak 22, Kasımpaşa, Beyoğlu (0212 253 4229, www.buyukhamam.net). **Open** *Men* 5.30am-10.30pm daily. *Women* 8am-8pm daily. **Admission** *Men* TL14; TL18.50 with massage. *Women* TL12.50; TL16.50 with massage. **No credit cards. Map** p246 L3.

This no-frills hamam is favoured by locals. The name means 'the big bathhouse' – and it is Istanbul's largest. The *hararet* has 60 wash stations, compared to the usual dozen or so. The beautiful details are courtesy of the Ottoman architect Sinan. An open-air pool has been added to the men's section. The Büyük is a ten-minute walk from central Beyoğlu. Cross six-lane Tarlabaşı Bulvarı beside the Pera Palas Hotel and head west along Tepebaşı Caddesi, looking out for the minaret of Kasımpaşa Mosque.

INSIDE TRACK FAMILY WASH

Families and couples who don't mind a touristy experience should head to the **Süleymaniye Hamam** near its namesake mosque. Attendants speak some English. Children are welcome.

Cağaloğlu Hamamı

Prof Kazım Ismail Gürkan Caddesi 34, Cağaloğlu, Sultanahmet (0212 522 2424, www.cagaloglu hamami.com.tr). Tram Gülhane or Sultanahmet. **Open** *Men* 8am-10pm daily. *Women* 8am-8pm daily. **Admission** €35 with scrub; €50 with massage. **No credit cards**. **Map** p243 M9.

More or less unchanged since it was built in 1741, Cağaloğlu – pronounced 'jaah-lo-loo' – is Istanbul's most famous hamam. It is often used as a backdrop for soap ads and pop videos. The two-storey *camekan* has a baroque fountain, while the grand *hararet* seems inspired by the domed chamber of an imperial mosque. Illustrious bathers include Florence Nightingale, Omar Sharif and Kate Moss.

★ Çemberlitaş Hamamı

Vezirhan Caddesi 8, Çemberlitaş (0212 522 7974, www.cemberlitashamami.com.tr). Tram Çemberlitaş. **Open** 6am-midnight daily. **Admission** TL45; TL69 with scrub; TL117 with massage. **Map** p243 M10.

Possibly the cleanest and most atmospheric hamam in town. Built in 1584 by Sinan, it was commissioned by Nurbanu, wife of Sultan Selim the Sot, as a charitable foundation for the poor. The hamam has been in continual use ever since. There are sections for both sexes, but part of the ladies' wing was torn down in the 19th century. Women now change in a corridor rather than a proper *camekan*, although the main *hararet* is lovely. Close to the Grand Bazaar, the hamam is frequented by foreigners; as a result, the masseurs are perfunctory and more interested in hassling for tips. But there's usually someone at reception who speaks English, and if you're a hamam virgin, this pretty venue is a good place to begin.

Gedikpaşa Hamamı.

Galatasaray Hamamı

Turnacıbaşı Sokak 24, Galatasaray, Beyoğlu (men 0212 252 4242, women 0212 249 4342, www.galatasarayhamami.com). **Open** *Men* 7am-10pm daily. *Women* 8am-7pm daily. **Admission** TL50; TL60 with scrub; TL95 with massage. **Credit** MC, V. **Map** p248 N3.

Built in 1481, for almost 500 years this hamam was for men only. A small women's section was finally added in 1963. Little else has been altered. The *camekan* is particularly fine, and there's some beautiful tilework at the entrance to the men's steam room. Because it's used largely by locals, the steam room is hot, hot, hot – towels have to be laid on the *göbek taşı* before most foreigners can take the heat. Staff are shameless about hustling for tips, but they do give a good massage.

Gedikpaşa Hamamı

Hamam Caddesi 65-67, off Gedikpaşa Caddesi, Beyazıt (0212 517 8956). Tram Beyazıt. **Open** 6am-midnight daily. **Admission** TL35; T55 with massage. **No credit cards**. **Map** p242 L10.

One of Istanbul's oldest hamams, Gedikpaşa was built in 1475 by one of Mehmet the Conqueror's viziers, next door to the mosque that also bears his name. Although not in the same architectural league as the Çemberlitaş or Cağaloğlu, the interior remains largely intact. Both men's and women's sections are a little run-down but clean. The men's area includes a small pool and sauna.

★ Sülemaniye Hamam

Mimar Sinan Caddesi 20, Süleymaniye, Eminönü (0212 519 5569, www.suleymaniyehamami.com). Tram Eminönü. **Open** 10am-midnight daily. **Admission** €35 with scrub and soap massage. **No credit cards**. **Map** p242 K8.

This hamam, built by the venerable Mimar Sinan in 1557, was once part of a structure that included a mosque, hospital, school and an asylum. It's tourist friendly – in fact few locals visit – and so it's a comfortable option for an introduction. Note that the hamam is open to couples and families only – single visitors, male or female, will not be admitted. All the soapers are male. It's advised to make reservations.

★ Üsküdar Çinili Hamam

Çavuşdere Caddesi 204, Üsküdar (men 0216 553 1593, women 0216 334 9710, www.cinilihamam.com). **Open** 8am-10pm daily. **Admission** TL15; massage TL5, scrub TL5. **No credit cards**. **Map** p250 W2.

The best option on the Asian shore for a first-timer, this hamam was built in 1640 by Valide Sultan Kösem, wife of Sultan Ahmet I, with a section for each gender. Compared to European Istanbul's tourist-heavy hamams, the experience is wonderfully authentic – and one of the cheapest in town.

Music

An urban medley.

In Istanbul, music – from pop and hip hop to folk and arabesque – is ubiquitous. It can be heard pumping from cars, rooftops and every corner café. And pretty much everyone (yes, everyone) will make the time to stop and sing along.

Hit the local scene in Beyoğlu, where scores of small venues, including **Babylon** and **Ghetto**, host intimate live gigs. Tucked into an alleyway behind the Galata Tower, **Nardis** is a legendary spot to soak up Turkish and international jazz. For traditional *fasıl* music, simply head to the restaurants on **Nevizade Sokak** to hear wandering minstrels – it's completely normal for diners to put the meze on hold and break into song.

ARTS & ENTERTAINMENT

TICKETS AND INFORMATION

To find current information on live music events, visit the venues or pick up flyers in cafés and bookshops around Istiklal Caddesi. The monthly *Time Out Istanbul* (in English) has listings and previews, as does the Guide (www.theguideistanbul.com, bilingual). Both *ZeroIstanbul* and the fortnightly *Zip* are distributed free in bars and cafés around Beyoğlu (only in Turkish). For online listings, as well as advance tickets, try Biletix (www.biletix.com), My Bilet (www.mybilet.com) and Ticket Turk (www.ticketturk.com).

ROCK & WORLD MUSIC

Most of Istanbul's music venues are located on the side streets off Istiklal Caddesi – and they tend to be cramped and smoky. At many venues, the bouncers are in charge of the door policy, which means that men may have trouble entering if not accompanied by women, although foreigners usually get the nod. Many places include a drink in the price of admission. In addition to venues listed below, **Park Orman** in Maslak (www.parkorman.net) hosts big names.

Beyoğlu

★ Babylon

Şehbender Sokak 3, Asmalımescit, Tünel (0212 292 7368, www.babylon.com.tr). **Open** 9.30pm-2am Tue-Thur; 10pm-3am Fri, Sat. Closed mid July-mid Sept. **Admission** varies. **Map** p248 M4.

One of Istanbul's finest live music venues, this modestly sized brick vault with a mezzanine is located in the backstreets near Tünel. There's a lot of jazz, but Babylon is also the place for world music, electronica and anything avant-garde. The management consistently attracts the best local and international names: past performances have included Macy Gray, the Maccabees and Jane Birkin. Pick up the well-distributed monthly brochure for details. *Photo p196.*

► *Also on the premises is the Babylon Lounge: cocktails and other drinks are 50% off before 9.30pm.*

★ Ghetto

Kamer Hatun Caddesi 10 (0212 251 7501, www.ghettoist.com). **Open** 8pm-4am Thur-Sat. **Admission** varies. **Map** p248 N3.

Set in a former bakery, this stellar venue is a top spot to see international and Turkish performers, showcasing plenty of electronica, soul, jazz and funk. Past shows have included Tricky, De La Soul, the Levellers and Transglobal Underground. The club also houses a restaurant, Metto; during summertime, the action moves upstairs to the rooftop Ghetto Teras.

★ Indigo

Akarsu Sokak 1-5, off Istiklal Caddesi (0212 244 8567, www.livingindigo.com). **Open** 11pm-4am Mon-Thur, Sun; 11pm-5am Fri, Sat. **Admission** varies. **Map** p248 N3.

Better known as a nightclub, Indigo is also at the cutting edge for electronic live acts – although recent years have seen shows expand to encompass alternative Turkish bands too. It has built up a loyal audience of local rockers, so it's best to arrive early or buy tickets in advance.

Jolly Joker Balans

Balo Sokak 22, off Istiklal Caddesi (0212 249 0749, www.jjistanbul.com). **Open** 11am-2am Mon-Sat. **Admission** TL10-TL30. **Map** p248 N3.

The home of 'pop-rock' in Istanbul, Jolly Joker Balans started out with huge ambitions and attracted huge international bands to its well-appointed stage. It's still a smart venue that occasionally pulls in global guests, but today you're more likely to find local stars.

Mojo

Büyükparmakkapı Sokak 26, off Istiklal Caddesi (0212 243 2927, www.mojomusic.org). **Open** 10pm-4am daily. **Admission** varies. **Map** p249 O3.

A basement decorated with enormous posters of rock 'n' roll legends, Mojo is the type of bar where long hair and leather jackets never go out of fashion. Istanbul has dozens of similar joints, including many more on this very street. Cover bands have struck chords here every night of the week for almost a decade. Gigs usually begin at around midnight.

Peyote

Kameriye Sokak 4, off Nevizade Sokak (0212 251 4398, www.peyote.com.tr). **Open** midnight-4am daily. **Admission** varies. **Map** p248 N3.

Spread over several floors, this joint is a favourite of the city's alternative crowd. There's a small performance space on the second floor, where various local bands play original material. With capacity limited to 100, it's the place to discover some of Istanbul's finest new talent. The beer is cheap too.

► *Peyote is in the heart of the Nevizade area – perfect for drinks and dinner beforehand (see p138-140).*

★ Riddim

Sıraselviler Caddesi 35/1, Taksim (0212 251 2723, www.riddim.com.tr). **Open** 9.30pm-4am daily. **Admission** free Tue-Fri, Sun; TL30 Sat, includes 1 free drink. **Map** p248 N3.

The city's most popular spot for hip hop and R&B. The funky decor – a mix of checkerboard flooring and neon lights – helps to get the crowd going; big names such as Ja Rule, Busta Rhymes, Lil Jon and PitBull have all played here.

Roxy

Aslanyatağı Sokak 3, off Sıraselviler Caddesi, Taksim (0212 249 1283, www.roxy.com.tr). **Open** 8pm-2am Wed, Thur; 8pm-5am Fri, Sat. Closed July-Sept. **Admission** varies, but often comprises free drinks. **Map** p249 O3.

Roxy used to be a major live venue, but its weekend club nights became so successful that live music has been relegated to the odd midweeker or an addendum to city-wide festivals. These live events are eclectic, with artists ranging from the likes of Luke Haines to Chumbawumba via Japanese 'acid mothers' Afrirampo.

Studio Live

Hamalbaşı Caddesi 6, Galatasaray (0212 252 8797, www.studiolive.com.tr). **Open** 10pm-4am Fri, Sat. **Admission** varies. **Map** p248 N2.

Along with Balans, Studio Live caters for both international acts and local cover bands, with the occasional DJ party thrown into the mix.

Babylon. *See p195.*

> **INSIDE TRACK**
> **CROSSING THE BRIDGE**
>
> For a great introduction to the music scene in Istanbul, pick up a copy of *Crossing the Bridge*. The highly regarded 2005 film is directed by Fatih Akın and presented by Alexander Hacke, a bass player for German experimental band Einstürzende Neubauten. The two explore the many musical styles, crossing ethnic, social and age groups that converge on the Bosphorus.

The Asian Shore

Buddha

Kadife Sokak 14, Kadıköy (0216 345 8798, www.kadikoybuddha.com). Ferry from Karaköy or Eminönü to Kadıköy. **Open** 8pm-2am Mon-Thur, Sun; 8pm-4am Fri, Sat. **Admission** free Tue-Thur, Sun; TL10 Fri, Sat. **Map** p251 W8.
This student hangout on two floors is supplemented with a pleasant garden in summer. It gets busy early, with crowds turning up for passable Britpop and rock cover bands: concerts start around 10pm. The beer is cheap, the atmosphere convivial and relaxed.

Shaft

Osmancık Sokak 13, off Serasker Caddesi, Kadıköy (0216 349 9956, www.shaftclub.com.tr). Ferry from Karaköy or Eminönü to Kadiköy. **Open** 2pm-4am daily. **Admission** free-TL20, often includes 1 free drink. **Map** p251 W7.
The most established live venue on the Asian side, Shaft has a varied programme ranging from rock and blues to heavy metal and thrash.

JAZZ

In Istanbul, jazz has a revered status, with a hardcore of devotees and musicians who keep the scene vibrant. Jazz is the focus of the **International Jazz Festival** (*see p177*), the **Akbank Jazz Festival** (*see p178*) and the wonderful jazz bar **Nardis**. Both festivals draw an array of global stars (partly because of a very broad definition of jazz); thanks to Nardis, the line ups feature strong local players too.

In the past, many of Istanbul's great jazz musicians found recognition abroad before they made it big back home: Maffy Falay (discovered by Dizzy Gillespie), percussionist Okay Temiz and guitarist Önder Focan all emigrated to Scandinavia; percussionist Burhan Öçal moved to Switzerland; drummer Selahattin Can Kozlu went to Africa; and saxophonist Ilhan Erşahin moved to New York, where he has a bar, a record label and high-profile friends like Norah Jones.

Today, many Turkish musical talents are returning to their roots, encouraged by the fresh group of musicians making a name for themselves in Istanbul. Names to watch are pianists Kerem Görsev and Aydın Esen, who has worked with Pat Metheny, and trumpeter Imer Demirer. Of the old school, Öçal now records for the Doublemoon label, Erşahin makes regular visits, while percussionist Temiz now runs a 'rhythm school' in Galata (www.okaytemiz.com).

★ Jazz Café

Hasnün Galip Sokak 20, off Büyükparmakkapi Sokak, Beyoğlu (0212 245 0516, www.jazzcafe istanbul.com). **Open** *Mid Sept-June* 6pm-4am Mon-Sat. Closed July-mid Sept. **Map** p251 O3.
A dimly lit and cosy little venue allied to the 24-hour Jazz Café FM. Downstairs is a standard bar; upstairs is where the musicians perform to respectful silence. Veteran guitarist Bülent Ortaçgil plays frequently, while jazz maestros Erkut Kan and Kıbilay Kan perform Wednesdays and Fridays respectively.

KV

Tünel Geçidi 10, off Tünel Square, Beyoğlu (0212 251 4338, www.kv.com.tr). **Open** 8am-2am daily. **Admission** free. **Map** p248 M4.
This laid-back café (pronounced 'Kahve'), situated in a gorgeous, old-fashioned arcade off Tünel Square, hosts low-key jazz every evening in winter. Pianist Elvan Aracı performs most nights at 9pm.

★ Nardis Jazz Club

Kuledibi Sokak 14, Galata (0212 244 6327, www.nardisjazz.com). **Open** 8.30pm-midnight Mon-Thur; 8.30pm-1.30am Fri, Sat. **Admission** TL30. **Map** p246 M5.
A dedicated jazz venue, just a few steps downhill from the Galata Tower, for patrons who know their jazz. Small and sparsely decorated – bare floorboards and brick walls – Nardis benefits from an intimate atmosphere. The place is run by guitarist and regular performer Önder Focan and his wife, who also edit *Jazz* magazine. Food is served, if you want it. Reservations are essential for tables near the stage. The music usually kicks off at around 9.30pm or 10pm.

TURKISH MUSIC

Turkish music – blasting from taxis, echoing out of kebab joints, wafting through markets – is one of the more startling sensory surprises for the visitor to Istanbul. The market may be inundated with mainstream pop and rock, but locals haven't lost their taste for indigenous sounds. Turkey has a local music scene as diverse as world music centres such as Brazil, Cuba or West Africa.

Some of the music you'll hear is what's known as 'arabesque'. Much maligned by serious musical commentators – often with

INSIDE TRACK RAISING THE BAR

Some of the best live music can be heard in the bars of Beyoğlu. Try **Araf** (Balo Sokak 32, Beyoğlu, 0212 244 8301, www.araf.com.tr), perched at the top of a crumbling townhouse near Nevizade Sokak. Legendary gypsy jazz clarinet player Selim Sesler plays here on Tuesdays.

good reason – arabesque is a melancholic fusion of Turkish folk with borrowed 'oriental' frills.

In the days before electrified arabesque conquered Istanbul with its incessant dum-shikka-shikka, traditional Turkish music was one of the most influential in the world. The Ottomans understood a thing or two about melting pots. Instruments and musical styles from Central Asia and Persia were mixed with elements of Byzantine music, which encouraged many new sounds to flourish. Echoes of Ottoman music are still audible today in genres ranging from Jewish *klezmer* to Greek *bouzouki* to Romanian *lautar*. Today, Turkey's musical roots are still spreading in different directions.

SONGS OF OLD STAMBOUL

To get a sense of how this music flows through the city, spend an evening in a *meyhane*, one of the boozy backstreet restaurants. As you nibble on meze, a quartet of musicians (usually Roma) warms up the crowd with nostalgic songs from 'old Stamboul'. By the time the main courses arrive – several hours and shots of *rakı* later – the rhythm has stepped up and the diners are dancing around, or on the tables.

One striking feature of this music is the wide variety of rhythms. If you can't keep time clapping, that could be because it's in 9/8, 10/16, or some other bizarre signature. Also, Turkish scales often employ notes between the notes, sometimes referred to as quarter-tones.

Traditional Turkish music can be divided into four basic styles: folk, which generally has a regional or rural flavour; *fasıl*, the boisterous music found most often in *meyhanes*; Turkish classical (or Ottoman) music, the soundtrack of the court; and Sufi music, the ethereal sounds that inspire the dervishes to whirl.

Folk music

Halk müziği (folk music) is an important part of the local music scene. Usually what gets labelled as folk are the slightly modernised, *bağlama*-heavy songs played in bars. The *bağlama*, a long-necked lute also called a *saz*, was adopted by Atatürk's reformers as a national folk symbol because of its rural Anatolian connotations.

It's also the instrument favoured by the Alevi and Bektaşi, sects of Islam that stress inter-sectarian tolerance and equality between men and women, and are frowned upon by the orthodox majority. Their folk poets, known as *aşıks*, have been wandering the Anatolian plains since the tenth century or earlier.

Istanbul is also home to many immigrants from the Black Sea coast, whose characteristic instrument is the *kemençe*. The wonderfully chaotic music that comes out of this pear-shaped fiddle accompanies improvised musical 'duels' between the singers and players.

Bağlama bars, identified by signs announcing *halk müziği*, are especially prevalent in **Hasnün Galip Sokak** off Istiklal Caddesi and in **Kadıköy** on the Asian shore. With low seating, folk art and cosy kilims, these snug venues exude Anatolian nostalgia. It's not unusual to see family groups late at night, and men and women mingling more freely than is the norm in Turkey. Most venues offer two live sets a day, providing non-stop music from mid-afternoon until after midnight. Booze is served, tables are shared, and in addition to singing along, there's bound to be dancing. There is usually no admission charge, but patrons are, of course, expected to drink.

For a more sober experience, and probably more polished performances, head for the **Atatürk Cultural Centre (AKM)** (*see p205*), which hosts recitals by state ensembles such as the Modern Folk Music and Turkish Music Groups. Closed at the time of writing, it is scheduled to reopen in 2012.

★ Munzur

Hasnün Galip Sokak 21A, Beyoğlu (0212 245 4669). **Open** 6pm-4am daily. **Map** p249 O3.

From the outside, Munzur doesn't look that special. The inside is pretty nondescript, too, but when the live music starts this little bar suddenly becomes extraordinary. The outstanding quality of the musicians, who have a wicked way with a *bağlama*, is inspirational. Highly recommended.

Fasıl

Defining *fasıl* is one for the musicologists. At times it sounds like gypsy music, but it's also quite classical; or maybe it's just folk. In fact, it's all three – and more.

The word *fasıl* comes from Ottoman classical music. It refers to a suite involving different types of vocal and instrumental works strung together on the basis of their *makam* (mode and melodic shape). Today, *fasıl* bears very little resemblance to this style, except for the tendency of musicians to organise their compositions in a *makam*.

Unlike folk, which is basically bar music, *fasıl* is most commonly encountered in *meyhanes*. The musicians tend to appear later in the evening, by which time most of the diners are already warmed up by a few drinks. The vast majority of *fasıl* musicians touring the restaurants are Roma, skilled at working their audience into a state of *keyif* – or ecstasy. Not that anyone needs much encouragement to lose their inhibitions: most Turks don't have any. Every song is belted out by everyone in the room and tables are often pushed aside to create an impromptu dancefloor. Nostalgia is an essential element of *fasıl*, and most *meyhanes* are decorated with photos and prints that evoke the good old days of Beyoğlu.

Most *fasıl* venues offer set menus with drinks and music included, although it is customary to tip the musicians a few lira per person at the end of each set. Bring an appetite and try to go with a group of Turkish friends, and don't forget that a *fasıl* night is a participatory event.

A word of warning: if it's a slow night and the *meyhane* isn't filling up, the musicians may not play or the management may send them home early. This is more likely to occur early in the week and during the summer.

Shout Out to Istanbul

Turkey's hybrid hip hop scene.

Turkish hip hop has only recently hit the streets of Istanbul, but its roots can be traced back to late 1980s inner-city Berlin. The style, then as today, mixes the arabesque sounds of Turkish pop with the young, urban voice of the Turkish diaspora and those living in the *gecekondu*, or unplanned shanty areas, of Istanbul.

Islamic Force, originally from Berlin and with a name chosen to both reflect and combat negative stereotypes of Muslims, are credited with being the first to blend Turkish music with hip hop rhythms. But the first Turkish hip hop to make it to vinyl was 'Bir Yabanicin Hayat' ('The Life of the Stranger') by King Size Terror, a Nuremberg band. It told of the disenchantment and difficulties of life in Germany for the first- and second-generation immigrants who form the largest non-EU minority group in the country, numbering 1.7 million.

But it was the group Cartel that really brought Turkish hip hop to the fore. Based in Berlin, three groups of rappers came together for one eponymously named album, which has sold around half a million copies. They rapped mainly in Turkish, with just the odd smattering of German, and included traditional Anatolian instruments with the beats and bass of US hip hop. The album's artwork featured a red background with the letter C (representing the crescent on the Turkish flag), and on the sleeve was written, in English, 'What are they sayin?!'. Despite *Cartel* being banned in Turkey when it was released, it found its way into the underground scene, paving the way for the group Karakan – part of the Cartel line-up – to win Best European Act at the 1995 MTV awards. Around this time, Turkish hip hop became known as oriental hip hop.

At the beginning of the 21st century, artists such as Kool Savas (who released his most recent album, *Die John Bello Story 3*, in March 2010), Bass Sultan Hengzt and Eko Fresh found success in Germany, a resurgence that was documented by Neco Celik, a Turkish-German director in his film *Alltag*, filmed around Berlin's heavily Turkish Kreuzberg area.

In 2001, Turkish hip hop found its most successful proponent: Ceza, meaning 'the punishment'. Ceza (Bilgin Özçalkan) was born in Üsküdar on the Asian shore of Istanbul in 1976. Working with Turkish rappers Dr Fuchs, Sagopa Kaimer, Sahtiyan and Fuat, Ceza has done more than others to promote the mix of arabesque and hip hop. He is based in Turkey, but with connections with Germany, one of his biggest markets.

An international breakthrough came when he was featured freestyling in the documentary *Crossing the Bridge* and his song 'Holocaust' was featured on the movie's soundtrack. The film's producers described his staccato style as sounding 'as if he swallowed an AK-47, like a preacher on speed'. His latest album, *Onuncu Köy* (*Tenth Village*), was released in 2010.

The most successful female oriental hip hop artist is Aziza A, a Turkish German. One of the early stars of the genre, she is now also an actor and presenter. Born in Kreuzberg, she is known for her support of Turkish women in Germany. As her style has matured, elements of funk, soul, jazz and R&B have crept into her work.

To catch a show by these performers or any of Turkey's top hip hop stars, head to Istanbul's best live hip hop venue, Riddim (*see p196*).

Andon

Sıraselviler Caddesi 89, Taksim (0212 251 0222). **Open** 7pm-4am daily. **Map** p249 O3.

A four-storey venue close to Taksim. As well as being a *meyhane*, it's equipped with a wine bar, terrace restaurant and disco bar, not to mention Bosphorus views, accomplished musicians and smart service. The dimly lit interior creates a flattering backdrop for the dressed-up diners. A good place to start exploring *fasıl* if you're not ready to jump in at the deep end.

Doing the Oryantal

Swivel those hips.

The pelvis plays a prominent role in Turkish life. Belly-dancing shows are a staple of the package-holiday circuit, gyrations are a required movement for Turkish pop stars, while hip-swaying *dansöz* are celebrities.

Funny, then, that belly-dancing isn't a Turkish tradition. Sure, there were dancing girls in the harems, but the belly-dancing familiar to most – long-haired female *dansöz* in gauzy, sequined garments, undulating rhythmically – is actually an Egyptian import, which only caught on here during the 20th century. Turks acknowledge the dance's Arab heritage in their name for it: *oryantal*.

The Turks have embraced hip-swivelling with gusto. The average Turk can perform similar moves to the professionals, but they don't call it *oryantal*: when civilians gyrate it's referred to as *gobek atmak*, which literally means 'to fling one's belly'.

Belly-flinging wasn't always so acceptable. Once upon a time, the *dansöz* was considered a fallen woman, whose spangles and lamé were confined to entertaining men in seedy nightclubs.

That changed in the late 1970s, when a *dansöz* appeared on Turkish television for the first time. Nesrin Topkapı's five-minute spot transfixed the country, and she became an overnight celebrity. In the 1990s, it was the turn of Sibel Can to make the leap from seedy belly-dancing clubs to the charts. And in the 2003 Eurovision Song Contest, winner Sertap Erener brought belly-dancing into millions of living rooms across the world.

But traces of the demi-monde vibe remain. These famous names aside, the world of professional dancing is still pretty much wedded to its image of greasy banknotes stuffed into skimpy costumes.

Despina

Açıkyol Sokak 9, Kurtuluş (0212 232 6720). **Open** noon-midnight daily.

Located in the far-from-glamorous district of Kurtuluş, an area that was once home to a sizeable Greek community, Despina doesn't look promising at first. Its fluorescent lights and plastic flowers are a far cry from the snug *meyhanes* of Beyoğlu. However, some of the finest Turkish musicians frequent this historical place, drawing an appreciative and demonstrative audience, who submit requests for their favourite *oyun havaları* (dance songs). On the right night, this can be the best party in town. The easiest way to get here is by taxi.

Ehl-i Keyif

Kallavi Sokak 8A, off Istiklal Caddesi, Beyoğlu (0212 251 1010). **Open** noon-2am Mon-Sat. **Map** p248 M3.

Tucked away on its own little street off Istiklal, this classic little *meyhane* has decent food and, most weekend nights, an exhilarating atmosphere. It has one of the best reputations for *fasıl*, which makes reservations essential. Dancing in the street is not uncommon. Highly recommended.

Süheyla

Kalyoncukulluk Caddesi 19, Balık Pazarı, Galatasaray (0212 251 8347). **Open** 7pm-2am daily. **Map** p248 N3.

Another prime *fasıl* venue, in the Nevizade Sokak area, with two large rooms and good musicians. The set menu includes unlimited *rakı*: little surprise the place gets packed at weekends.

Turkish classical

Real Turkish classical music is rarely performed in public these days. In the new Turkish Republic of the 1920s, Ottoman music was considered elitist and backward, so the state did its best to bury it. There has been a slow revival over the last few decades; percussionist **Burhan Öçal** pays his respects with his classically inspired *Yeni Rüya* album. To hear other faithful renditions, look in music shops for Turkish classical music on the Doublemoon and Kalan labels.

Also known as Ottoman, Osmanlı or Court-Enderun music, Turkish classical music is based on the principle of *makam*. Like Indian *ragas*, the *makams* are modal. The melodies are subtle, the rhythms gentle and sometimes quite slow, although towards the end of a programme you'll often hear lively numbers as the pace picks up.

No single venue in Istanbul devotes itself exclusively to performances of Turkish classical music, although it does feature in the annual **International Istanbul Music Festival** (*see p177*).

Andon.

Atatürk Cultural Centre (AKM)
Atatürk Kültür Merkezi

Inönü Caddesi, Taksim Square (0212 251 5600). Closed for refurbishment. **No credit cards.** **Map** p247 P2.

The most likely place to find Turkish classical music. When the centre is open, the Türk Müziği chorus performs in the lower auditorium most Sundays from autumn to late spring. Closed for refurbishment until 2012.

Cemal Reşit Rey Concert Hall
Cemal Reşit Rey Konser Salonu

Darülbedayi Caddesi 1, Harbiye (0212 232 9830, www.crrks.org). **Box office** 10am-8pm daily. **Admission** TL10-25.

This large, comfortable auditorium with excellent acoustics is not far north of Taksim Square. Run by the Istanbul Municipality, the venue hosts occasional concerts of Turkish classical music.

Sufi music

They may be promoted as one of the enduring symbols of Turkey abroad, but the Whirling Dervishes, better known locally as the Mevlevi order of Sufis, are quite rare in Istanbul – not least because the sect is still technically outlawed in Turkey. You can catch a *sema* (religious whirling ceremony) in designated tourist spots, but it will likely be promoted as a colourful historical oddity, rather than an ecstatic connection with God through music, dance and *zikr* (a form of rhythmic breathing).

The **Galata Mevlevihanesi** in Tünel (*see p69*), a centre for Whirling Dervishes sanitised as a Museum for Classical Literature (Divan Edebiyat Müzesi), stages various performances each month exclusively for tourists. At the time of writing, it was closed for renovations, but is due to reopen at the end of 2012. Alternatively, you can visit the **Hocapaşa Culture Center** (Hocapaşa Hamam Sokak 3B, off Ankara Caddesi, Eminönü, 0212 511 4626, www.hodjapasha.com) five nights a week.

Genuine dervish ceremonies are not always accessible to the outsider. One place to catch one is in Fatih on Thursday evenings, at **EMAV** (Silivrikapı Mevlâna Cultural Center, Yeni Tavanlı Çeşme Sokak 6, Silivrikapı, 0542 422 1544, www.emav.org). More an act of worship than a performance, it's an unforgettable experience.

Another opportunity to hear Sufi music in Istanbul is during the **Mystic Music Festival** held at Cemal Reşit Rey Concert Hall every November. Check www.biletix.com for details.

FESTIVALS

The number of music festivals is multiplying every year. Events range from one night of performances in a touring show to a month of citywide activities. The Istanbul Culture and Art Foundation (www.iksv.org) organises a two-week **Jazz Festival** every July. Another key player on the scene is Pozitif (www.pozitif-ist.com), the organisation behind October's **Akbank Jazz Festival** (*see p178*), the **Efes Pilsen Blues Festival** (*see p178*), the **One Love Festival** (*see p177*), two days of eclectic open-air performances at Santralistanbul (*see p66*), and the **Rock 'n' Coke Festival** (*see p178*), a two-day event that hosts international and local acts out of town, complete with a Glastonbury-style campsite.

Local stars of pop and arabesque perform series of concerts each summer at the open-air theatres in Rumeli Hisarı and Harbiye. Look out for details on www.biletix.com.

The summer festivals held at beach clubs on the Black Sea coast usually include some kind of shuttle service from Taksim Square, but standards of organisation vary widely.

Nightlife

Boogie rights.

Turks love a good party – and Istanbul's nightlife reflects this attitude tenfold. Nightclubs are dotted throughout the city, but action tends to centre around two main areas. Year round, Istiklal Caddesi and Asmalımescit in Beyoğlu buzz with underground clubs and alternative venues. Here, it's all about the tunes – from cutting-edge electronica at Indigo to choice reggae at Dogzstar.

North of the city centre, superclubs are splashed along the Bosphorus, particularly between Ortaköy and Kuruçeşme. As warm weather washes over the city each spring, these open-air extravaganzas – often boasting multiple themed areas and international DJs – come into their own. Reina and Sortie are timeless, if blingingly ostentatious, picks. The floating island of Suada offers the chance to sip sundowners between two continents.

THE LOCAL SCENE

Given that Turks are obsessive followers of fads, club promoters tend to stick to tried and tested formulas. So although smaller clubs cater to most musical tastes, from rock and jazz to Latin or electronica, the majority of big clubs play house and techno. But what could be a lack of variety is offset by the frequency and variety of guest DJs who come to the city – the likes of Tiesto, Kruder & Dorfmeister, John Digweed and Paul Oakenfold. Istanbul also has plenty of talented DJs of its own: look out for Yunus Güvenen, Barış Türker and Murat Uncuoğlu.

New venues crop up every month – and big names such as **Crystal** (electronic, after hours), **Roxy** (rock, pop, theme parties), **NuPera** (electronic, dance, disco) or **Babylon** (excellent live acts and DJ nights) keep going strong.

Istanbul's lively party scene has its idiosyncrasies. Turks like to dress up, so make an effort not to look too casual. You won't find any rowdy, alcohol-induced behaviour at clubs or on the streets. But although disturbances are rare, belligerent bouncers can be a hassle. Drinks are generally expensive, due to heavy taxes on alcohol. Be warned that police sometimes raid clubs and crack down hard on anyone caught in possession of drugs.

The party doesn't start until after midnight. Fridays and Saturdays are the busiest nights, although there are sometimes special events on Wednesdays. Bars are busy on Thursdays, but it's usually dead in the clubs. From July to September, the party shifts to the shores of the Bosphorus (*see right* **Bosphorus Bling**).

For up-to-date nightlife listings, check out the monthly magazine *Time Out Istanbul* and the Guide (www.theguideistanbul.com).

INSIDE TRACK A SHOO-IN

If you want to be sure to make it past the notoriously tough bouncers stationed on the door of most Bosphorus nightclubs, make a dinner reservation at one of the venue's restaurants. It will guarantee you access all areas – and although dinner will be pricey, you won't have to pay the venue's entrance fee.

FESTIVALS & EVENTS

Despite drawbacks such as heavy-handed security and expensive taxi rides home, one-off raves and annual festivals in far-flung locales are a growth industry. Many events are held at the **Venue** (better known as Refresh The Venue, www.re-fresh.com.tr), with its huge indoor and outdoor arenas, on the outskirts of Maslak business district. Just beyond Maslak is **Parkorman** (www.parkorman.net), a huge bar/restaurant complex with a pool. During summer, the action moves to **Solar Beach** or **Burç Beach** in Kilyos on the Black Sea coast (*see p218*).

Big events are advertised around town, and clubs distribute flyers at bars, cafés and bookshops in Beyoğlu. Buy tickets online at Biletix (www.biletix.com), My Bilet (www.mybilet.com) or Ticket Turk (www.ticketturk.com).

CLUBS

★ 11:11

Meşrutiyet Caddesi 69, Beyoğlu (0212 244 8834, www.1111.com.tr). **Open** 10pm-4am Thur-Sun. **Admission** varies. **Map** p248 M4.

Looking something like a James Bond baddie's lair, also possibly resembling the inside of an ice cube, 11:11 (named after its opening date of 11.11.2009) is a busy venue that's popular with a more mature crowd. There are several different areas, each playing a different genre of music. A lounge bar also serves Asian and fusion food alongside good cocktails.

Anjelique

Salhane Sokak 5, Muallim Naci Caddesi, Ortaköy (0212 327 2844, www.istanbuldoors.com). Bus 25E, 40. **Open** 6pm-4am daily. **Admission** varies.

The most tasteful of the Bosphorus bunch of clubs. Anjelique's assets include stunning views over the water, above-average food and delicious apple martinis. There are resident and excellent guest DJs, but Western and Turkish sing-along pap predominates. *See below* **Bosphorus Bling**.

Arka Oda

Kadife Sokak 18, Kadıköy (0216 418 0277, www.arkaoda.com). Ferry from Karaköy or Eminönü to Kadıköy. **Open** noon-2am daily. **Admission** free.

Pick of the clubs that pack Kadıköy's Kadife Sokak, Arka Oda is an old Ottoman townhouse-turned-cushy vintage-styled venue. It's a good place to check out local up-and-coming bands; DJs are also top notch.

★ Babylon

Şehbender Sokak 3, Asmalımescit, Tünel (0212 292 7368, www.babylon.com.tr). **Open** 9.30pm-2am Tue-Thur; 10pm-3am Fri, Sat. Closed mid July-mid Sept. **Admission** varies. **Map** p248 M4.

More of a live music venue (*see p195*) than a club, the intimate Babylon hosts some of the best parties in town. Run by the prolific Pozitif group, it's one of the few places in Istanbul that offers more than techno. Nights range from funk to Oldies But Goldies parties, where cheesy ballads and dirty dancing are de rigueur.

Bosphorus Bling

When Istanbul gets hot, the hot people move outside.

If you like your nightlife flashy, you'll love the clubs along the Bosphorus between Ortaköy and Kuruçeşme. So-called superclubs like **Reina** and **Sortie** (for both, *see p204*) are a gaudy swirl of playboys, C-list celebs and gold-diggers sipping pricey cocktails as they sway to trashy Turkish and European pop. Patrons roll up in sports cars, or even speedboats. They might be soap stars eager to flash their cash; or upstarts trying to scramble onto the social ladder.

These clubs – particularly Reina – are notoriously elitist. A beer can cost TL17, a cocktail TL35, and a meal around TL150 per person. Entrance fees to the clubs, hovering around TL50, are equally exclusive. Other popular clubs include chic **Anjelique** (*see above*), **Çubuklu Hayal Kahvesi** (*see p204*) and **Suada** (*see p204*) on the Asian shore.

All these venues are at the peak of their popularity in summer, when the fine moonlit views offer cool respite for those stuck in the city. Some close in winter, others keep their indoor dancefloors open and close the outdoor spaces.

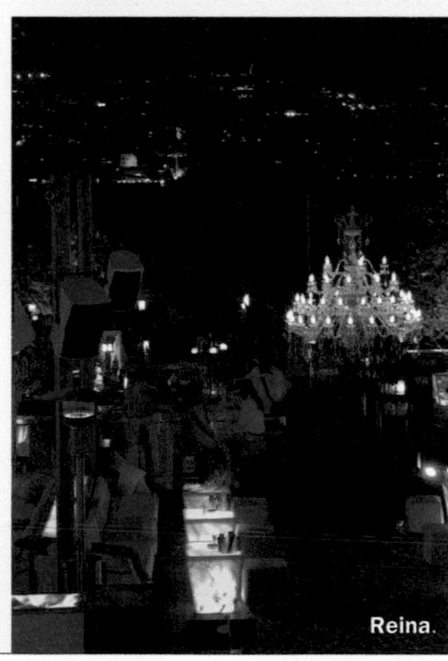

Reina.

ARTS & ENTERTAINMENT

Çubuklu Hayal Kahvesi

Burunbahçe Mevki Ağaçlık Mesire Yeri Çubuklu Caddesi 18, Çubuklu, Beykoz (0216 413 6880, www.hayalkahvesi.com.tr). Free ferries across the Bosphorus from Istinye. **Open** 7pm-4am daily. **Admission** varies.

Three restaurants (one specialising in artisan hamburgers), a club, concert venue and art gallery, all right on the waterfront in a leafy Asian suburb. Free boats whisk you across the Bosphorus to the club's private jetty (departing from Istinye Motor Iskelesi every 30 minutes from 7pm until closing time).

★ Dogzstar

Kartal Sokak 3, Galatasaray, Beyoğlu (0212 244 19147, www.dogzstar.com). **Open** 10pm-4am Wed-Sat. **Admission** free. **Map** p248 N3.

It may be small, but Dogzstar proves that size doesn't matter: this diminutive club in Beyoğlu has garnered quite a reputation: the laid-back, let-loose, reggae vibe here packs a punch. It can get a little cramped, but it's a good place to boogie.

★ Indigo

Akarsu Sokak 1-5, off Istiklal Caddesi, Beyoğlu (0212 244 8567, www.livingindigo.com). **Open** 11pm-4am Mon-Thur, Sun; 11pm-5am Fri, Sat. **Admission** varies. **Map** p248 N3.

Attracting a mix of local and foreign bands and DJs, Indigo is the definitive venue for fans of electronic music. Smack in the centre of Beyoğlu, it is also jammed every weekend. So be warned: if you don't like a bit of a mosh, or other dancers rubbing up against you, it might be best to steer clear.

Nu Club

Meşrutiyet Caddesi 67, Beyoğlu (0212 245 6070). **Open** 11pm-4am Fri, Sat. Closed June-Sept. **Admission** free. **Map** p248 M3.

The Nu Pera complex is known for its multiple fusion restaurants and amazing views from Nuteras (summer only). Come winter, the action moves downstairs to this intimate basement club. Top-notch local DJs such as Yunus Güvenen and Barış Türker are complemented with a guest DJ from Paris once a month. Unpretentious and great fun.

★ Off Pera

Canova Apartmanı, Gönül Sokak 14A, Asmalımescit, Beyoğlu (0212 249 2697). **Open** 10pm-4am Tue-Sat. **Admission** TL30. **No credit cards**. **Map** p248 N3.

The antithesis to the superclubs on the Bosphorus shores, tucked in the backstreets off Istiklal Caddesi. Head to Off Pera for quirky music, from '70s and '80s tunes to Turkish favourites (no house here), a tiny, packed dancefloor and killer cocktails.

Peyote

Kameriye Sokak 4, off Nevizade Sokak, Beyoğlu (0212 251 4398, www.peyote.com.tr). **Open** midnight-4am daily. **Admission** varies. **Map** p248 N3.

Spread over several floors, this joint is a favourite with the city's alternative crowd. Each floor has a different vibe. It's well known for live music, and the open roof terrace is also a popular place for drinks, to be enjoyed before descending to the ground floor for the trance and electronica music from the resident DJ. Peyote also has a small performance space on the second floor, where various local bands play original material.

Reina

Muallim Naci Caddesi 44, Ortaköy (0212 259 5919, www.reina.com.tr). Bus 25E, 40. **Open** 7pm-4am daily. **Admission** varies.

The city's most famous nightclub, Reina is paparazzi heaven. It's a stunning waterfront venue with the expected amazing views, and resembles a swanky food court with a big dancefloor in the middle. It attracts rich brats, playboys, celebs and wannabes. The music is pure Euro Med trash, and loud.

Roxy

Aslanyatağı Sokak 3, off Sıraselviler Caddesi, Taksim (0212 249 1283, www.roxy.com.tr). **Open** 8pm-2am Wed, Thur; 8pm-5am Fri, Sat. Closed July-Sept. **Admission** varies, but often comprises free drinks. **Map** p249 O3.

This established venue is a showcase for mainstream rock and pop bands. The place is usually packed with sociable, easygoing regulars, swigging bottled Sex On The Beach (usually free with your admission fee). Look out for Roxy's regular theme parties.

Sortie

Muallim Naci Sokak 141, Kuruçeşme (0212 327 8585, www.sortie.com.tr). Bus 25E, 40. **Open** *Summer only* 6pm-4am daily. **Admission** varies.

Sortie has successfully replicated the Bosphorus bling formula. Like many of the area's neighbouring clubs, it's a nightspot that is well known for the collection of pricey (seven!) restaurants that surround the central bar area. Big and brash in the summer, Sortie is closed in winter.

Suada

Just offshore Kuruçeşme (0212 263 7300, www.suadaclub.com.tr). Free ferries from Kuruçeşme harbour. **Open** 10am-1am daily. **Admission** varies.

Floating in the Bosphorus just off the Kuruçeşme waterfront, the man-made island of Suada ('water island') is home to multiple restaurants (Italian, Cretan, a kebab joint, steakhouse and two seafood spots), a massive open-air swimming pool and – as of 2011 – a brand-new outpost of Beyoğlu's hip restaurant and club, 360 (*see p134*). At its best between May and September, some of the island's venues shut down over winter.

Performing Arts

Bright lights on the Bosphorus.

Turkey doesn't have a long tradition of Western-style performing arts. The Ottomans cultivated their own courtly music (*see p200*), while the general population has long had a dedicated passion for home-grown folk and traditional art. Until recent years, Western performing arts have generally appealed to only a minority of Turks, almost entirely from the well-travelled upper classes. However, the scene is expanding fast.

Kadıköy's historical **Süreyya Opera House** was completely renovated and reopened in 2007. It's now home to the **Istanbul State Opera & Ballet**. The city also hosts a handful of international events, including the **Istanbul Theatre Festival** and the **International Puppet Festival** (for both, *see p176*). New venues, visits from foreign theatre companies and touring dance troupes all contribute to the growing scene.

CLASSICAL MUSIC, OPERA & BALLET

Western-style classical music has an unusual history in Turkey. In the early decades of the 20th century, Atatürk banned traditional Ottoman classical music, categorising it as regressive and elitist. He promoted Western-style music instead, which, in the early years of the Republic, was put to the service of Turkish nationalism.

Today, Istanbul is home to a respectable – if small – classical music, opera and ballet scene, and also hosts the major annual **International Istanbul Music Festival** (*see p177*). And there is one area in which Istanbul can compete with any major city in the world, and that's the unique venues where concerts and events are held, including ancient underground cisterns, Byzantine churches and Ottoman palaces. The standard venues are also very good; the **Atatürk Cultural Centre** is chief among them.

Tickets for concerts, opera and theatre can be bought online from Biletex (www.biletix.com).

★ Akbank Culture and Arts Centre

Istiklal Caddesi 8, Beyoğlu (0212 252 3500, www.akbanksanat.com). **Performances** usually 8pm Mon-Sat. **Map** p249 O2.

This arts centre has a 135-seat, multi-purpose concert hall, and hosts all sorts of cultural activities.

Atatürk Cultural Centre (AKM)

Inönü Caddesi, Taksim Square (0212 251 5600). Closed for refurbishment until 2012. **No credit cards**. **Map** p247 P2.

Istanbul's premier performing arts venue. Behind the brutalist 1960s design, the interior is surprisingly grand and vibrant. It has two main concert halls, with a capacity of 1,300 and 520.

Bosphorus University Albert Long Hall Cultural Centre

Nispetiye Caddesi, Boğaziçi Üniversitesi, Bebek (0212 359 6609, www.klasikmuzik.boun.edu.tr). Bus 25E, 40. **Performances** normally 7.30pm. **No credit cards**.

The Albert Long Hall is an iconic symbol of Bosphorus University, and an important venue for concerts by leading local and foreign musicians, orchestras and companies. The university's South

INSIDE TRACK THEATRE SEASONS

Istanbul's performance season runs from November to May; summer is usually dead. Check the classical music and theatre sections in the monthly *Time Out Istanbul* magazine or *The Guide* (www.theguideistanbul.com) to keep track of what's on.

INSIDE TRACK CHILDREN'S THEATRE

Got a budding star in the family? The Learning Center (*see p180*) runs Saturday drama courses for kids.

Campus, where the Hall is located, is in Rumeli Hisarı, near the Fatih Sultan Mehmet Bridge.

Cemal Reşit Rey Concert Hall

Darülbedayi Caddesi 1, Harbiye (0212 232 9830, www.crrks.org). **Open** *Box office* 10am-8pm daily. **Performances** 8pm daily. Closed June-Sept.

This venue, the 860-seat home of the municipal CRR Symphony Orchestra, has a diverse programme, including Turkish religious and traditional music. It's a key venue for several festivals, including October's International Mystic Music Festival, December's International CRR Piano Festival, January's International Istanbul Baroque Days, April's International Dance Festival and the International Youth Festival in May. Tickets are available from www.biletix.com.

Enka Ibrahim Betil Auditorium

Sadi Gülçelik Spor Sitesi, Istinye (0212 276 2214, www.enkasanat.org). Bus 40B. **Performances** 8pm Mon-Sat; 11.15am Sun.

A 600-seat modern auditorium with perfect acoustics. It hosts a variety of events, including drama, concerts, folk dancing and ballet, and regularly plays host to the local metropolitan and state music and dance companies.

► *There is also an open-air venue, Enka Eşref Denizhan Açık Hava Tiyatrosu, which is used for events during June and July.*

★ Garajistanbul

Kaymakam Reşat Bey Sokak 11, off Yeni Çarşi Caddesi, Galatasaray (0212 244 4499, www.garajistanbul.org). **Performances** varies.

A forward-thinking performing arts centre, not afraid to lend its stage to any discipline, from cutting-edge theatre to the International Puppet Festival. The programme covers theatre, dance, music, literature and arts shows, both home-grown and from abroad.

► *There is an art-house cinema, bar and café on the premises.*

Iş Art and Culture Centre

Iş Towers (Iş Kuleleri), Levent (0212 316 1083, www.issanat.com.tr). Metro Levent. **Box office** 9am-6pm daily. **Performances** 8pm Mon-Sat; 3pm Sun. Closed June-Oct.

An 800-seat concert hall with a prestigious programme and an unconventional location: the basement of one of the highest skyscrapers in Levent. Classical music concerts are performed by Turkish and foreign symphony and chamber orchestras. Other draws include jazz and world music.

Lütfi Kırdar Convention & Exhibition Centre

Gümüş Caddesi 4, Harbiye (0212 373 1100, www.icec.org). Metro Osmanbey.

The convention centre houses one of the city's biggest auditoriums, seating up to 3,500 people. Although it's not a dedicated music venue, it's actually one of Istanbul's top venues for classical music, along with the AKM.

★ Süreyya Opera House

Bahariye Caddesi 29, Caferaşa, Kadıköy (0216 346 1531, www.sureyyaoperasi.org). Ferry from Karaköy or Eminönü to Kadıköy. **Box office** 10am-6pm daily. **Map** p251 X8.

First opened in 1927, this frescoed opera house – which was used as a cinema for 50 years – was thoroughly restored and reopened to the public in 2007. It now showcases classical Turkish performances. It's also home to the renowned Istanbul State Opera and Ballet.

THEATRE

Theatre in Istanbul is vital and varied, with more than 30 stages across the city – the best-known are listed below. The best chance for seeing good theatre in English is during the **International Istanbul Theatre Festival** (*see p177*), when dozens of foreign companies perform plays in their original languages. In most cases, though, performances will be in Turkish. Also be aware that many theatres are closed from June to September.

Kenter Theatre

Halaskargazi Caddesi 9, Harbiye (0212 246 3589, www.kentertiyatrosu.org). Metro Osmanbey.

Maya Sahnesi

Halep Pasajı, Istiklal Caddesi, Beyoğlu (0212 252 7452, www.mayasanat.com). **Map** p248 N3.

Muhsin Ertuğrul Stage

Gümüş Caddesi 3, Harbiye (0212 455 3919). Metro Osmanbey.

Pera Theatre

Sıraselviler Caddesi 26, Taksim (0212 245 4460, www.tiyatropera.com).

Foreigners are in luck here: the company performs works in both English and Turkish.

Ses-1885 Ortaoyuncular Theatre

Halep Pasajı 62/90, off Istiklal Caddesi, Beyoğlu (0212 251 1865, www.ortaoyuncular.com). **No credit cards. Map** p248 N3.

Sport & Fitness

Breaking a sweat.

Istanbul is a city obsessed with football. From taxi drivers to hairdressers to university professors, everyone has their favourite local team – be it Galatasaray, Beşiktaş or Fenerbahçe – and often times the multicoloured scarf and branded credit card to go with it.

Get beyond football (or occasionally basketball), and you'll soon notice that Istanbullus are not prone to participate in sports 'for the fun of it'. But attitudes are slowly changing. Adventure sports organisations have begun to spring up around town. New vehicle-free lanes, used for jogging and cycling, are in place. And over recent years, the local municipality has installed dozens of exercise grounds, complete with low-impact machines for stretching, along the shores of the Bosphorus and the Sea of Marmara.

SPECTATOR SPORTS

All sporting events and fixtures are listed in the local press and at the online ticketing agency **Biletix** (www.biletix.com) or **Ticket Turk** (www.ticketturk.com).

Football

Istanbul is home to Turkey's three biggest clubs: **Galatasaray**, **Beşiktaş** and **Fenerbahçe**. The Black Sea side **Trabzonspor** plus **Bursaspor**, known as the 'Green Crocodiles', complete the 'big five'. The domestic league (Süper Lig) runs from August to May. For an intense atmosphere, try to catch one of the Istanbul derbies.

To satisfy the TV companies, matches are staggered over the whole weekend, from Friday evening to Sunday evening. Tickets usually go on sale two or three days before a match, although for all but the biggest games it is surprisingly easy to pick them up at the stadium on the day. For matches involving the big three, tickets can also be bought in advance via booking agency Biletix (www.biletix.com).

★ Beşiktaş

Inönü Stadium, Dolmabahçe Caddesi, Beşiktaş (0212 236 7201, www.bjk.com.tr). **Tickets** League games TL25-TL200. **Tickets** from Biletix. **Map** p247 R1/2.

National league champions and Turkish Cup winners in 2009, the Beşiktaş 'Black Eagles' are resurgent. The club's Inönü Stadium is the city's most conveniently located, opposite Dolmabahçe Palace. Some stands offer great views over the Bosphorus. *Photo p209.*

★ Fenerbahçe

Şükrü Saracoğlu Stadium, Kadıköy (0216 261 1907, www.fenerbahce.org). Ferry from Eminönü or Karaköy to Kadıköy, then 10B bus. **Tickets** League games TL30-TL225. **No credit cards. Map** p251 Y8.

Despite winning a record number of Turkish league championships, including the 2010-11 season, Fener has been plagued with controversy surrounding charges of match-fixing. Atatürk's favourite team, Fenerbahçe has historic links with the Turkish army, despite its decidedly unmilitary nickname – 'the Canaries'. The home stadium is in the wealthy suburb of Fenerbahçe, on the Asian side.

INSIDE TRACK
CROSSING CONTINENTS

Every year in October, thousands of runners cross the Bosphorus Bridge from Asia into Europe during the city's annual marathon (www.istanbulmarathon.org). If you can't make the date, but are still keen to stretch your legs, join Istanbul running club Adım Adım (www.adimadim.org), which organises regular weekend walks and group jogs in the leafy Belgrad Forest.

Galatasaray
Türk Telekom Arena, Şişli (0212 305 1929, www.galatasaray.org, www.turktelekomarena.com.tr). **Tickets** League games TL13-TL160. **No credit cards**.
Easily Turkey's most famous club, Galatasaray boasts a string of European successes, crowned by victory over Arsenal in the UEFA Cup final in 2000. Known to fans as 'Cim Bom' for reasons no one can explain, Galatasaray see themselves as the aristocracy of Turkish football – an ideology supported by their fans' ultra-fierce reputation. As of 2011, the club now play in Şişli's new Türk Telekom Arena.
► *For the Galatasary football club museum, see p71.*

Basketball

While international soccer success has tended to eclipse Turkey's long-running love affair with basketball, the game still has a large fan base, and a handful of Turkish-born players have moved on to the NBA. The national squad have ranked sixth worldwide over the past two years' World Championships, with hopes running high for London's 2012 Olympic games.

The basketball season lasts roughly from October to June. Tickets for all but the biggest games are readily available on the day, or can be bought in advance. Information on games and fixtures is available on the Turkish Basketball Federation website (www.tbf.org.tr).

Anadolu Efes Spor Kulübü
Sinan Erdem Spor Salonu, Ataköy Olimpik Yüzme Havuzu ve Spor Kompleksi, Zuhuratbaba, Bakırköy (0212 559 0914, http://en.efesbasket.org). Tram Bakırköy. **Tickets** TL9.50-TL23, from Biletix.
Founded in 1976, Efes Pilsen have won the Turkish title 13 times. In 1996, they scored their biggest success when they bagged the European Korac Cup.

Grease is the Word

Take a jar of olive oil, pour it all over yourself, then wrestle.

Two heavy-set men with moustaches are covered in oil and rolling around the floor. One hand slips down the other's leather trousers – it's the only place to get a good grip – and a man is thrown on his back. Yes, this grappling is indeed a sport: it's *yağlı güreş*, Turkey's national sport of oil wrestling. The Kırkpınar oil-wrestling tournament, held every year in Edirne, near the Bulgarian and Greek border, is the world's longest-established sporting event. With the first tournament taking place in 1346, it preceded football's FA Cup by more than half a millennium.

Grappling while covered in oil has been an essential part of the Central Asian Turkic culture for more than 3,000 years. The word *pehlivan*, meaning wrestler, was first used around the turn of the first millennium. As the Turks spread across Western Asia and into Anatolia, they brought the sport of *yağlı güreş* with them. The original function of the oil is disputed. Some believe it was used to repel mosquitoes, while others maintain that it was just used to make it more difficult to wrestle – which it undoubtedly does.

The sport really rose to prominence during the Ottoman conquest of Rumeli, the area that would become the southern Balkan regions of the Ottoman Empire, during the reign of Orhan I (1326-61). Wrestling became popular in military camps during the campaigns, to fend off boredom. Legend has it that one bout lasted for two days, leading to the death of both fighters from exhaustion. The prize, as decreed by Orhan's brother, Süleyman Pasha, was a pair of trousers made from buffalo hide – known as *kispet*, and still worn today. The two soldiers were buried under a fig tree and several years later, upon returning to the site, springs had developed; the area became known as Kırkpınar (Forty Springs), and a tournament has been held here most years since 1357 (only an estimated 70 years have been missed).

During the Ottoman era, wrestlers studied the art in schools called *tekke*. Much like Japanese sumo wrestling, spiritual development was considered at least as important as the physical aspect of the sport. Today, the rituals remain. The leather *kispet* is worn by all the *pehlivans* and, of course, gallons of olive oil are used to grease themselves up beforehand. Unlike Olympic wrestling (a sport in which Turkey excels, with 28 golds to date), a fight is won when someone manages to carry his opponent – or, to put it another way, 'when an umbilicus is exposed to heaven'.

The Kırkpınar tournament is usually held at the end of June in Edirne. See www.kirkpinar.org for details.

Beşiktaş Milangaz
BJK Milangaz Arena, Gelincik Sokak 2, off Yıldırım Oşuz Göker Caddesi, Akatlar, Etiler (0212 283 6600, www.bjkbasket.org). Metro 4. Levent. **Tickets** TL10-TL25, from Biletix.
Although Beşiktaş haven't won the championship since the 1970s – lagging behind their footballing colleagues – the squad are still locally adored.

Fenerbahçe-Ülker
Ülker Sports Arena, Ataşehir (0216 347 8438, www.fenerbahce.org). Ferry from Eminönü or Karaköy to Kadıköy, then 10B bus. **Tickets** TL710-TL20, from Biletix.
In 2006, Fenerbahçe merged with Ülkerspor and pilfered the stronger squad's roster in a bid to unseat perennial champions Efes Pilsen: it worked, as they won the national championship in 2007, 2008, 2010 and 2011. As of December 2011, they play in their new home stadium in Ataşehir.

Galatasaray Medical Park
Galatasaray Spor Kulübü
Abdi Ipekçi Arena, 10 Yıl Caddesi, Zeytinburnu (0212 679 7420, www.galatasaray.org). Tram Zeytinburnu. **Tickets** TL7-TL15, from Biletix.
While Galatasaray were once top of the various local leagues, the team have struggeld to beat their competitors in recent years. However, in 2011 they secured second place in the Turkish Basketball League and qualified for Euroleague.

Beşiktaş. *See p207.*

INSIDE TRACK WEIGHING GOLD

The failure of Turkey's bids to host the Olympic Games (thus far) hurts, but as a competing nation they continue to excel in two Olympic sports: wrestling and weightlifting. Halil Mutlu is Turkey's most famous Olympian, winning three consecutive golds (1996, 2000, 2004) in the 56kg category. He also won five World Championships and broke more than 20 world records. Mutlu's hero and countryman, Naim Süleimanov, also won three Olympic Golds. Most of Turkey's Olympic golds (28) have been won for wrestling.

ACTIVE SPORTS

With sparse facilities and little leisure time, few Turks actively participate in any sports other than the odd football match played on one of the city's many five-a-side pitches. In Kadıköy and Bakırköy, cycle paths line the coastal roads, although they're equally popular with joggers. Along the shores of the Bosphorus and the Sea of Marmara, as well as in most parks, the Istanbul municipality has established small exercise areas with equipment for stretching. In general, exercise in Istanbul is otherwise a habit confined to the well-heeled.

Adventure sports

Ministry of Tourism efforts to pitch Turkey as an ideal destination for adventure enthusiasts have attracted the attention of locals too.

Adrenalin
Necatibey Caddesi, Gayret Han 53/A, Karaköy (0212 293 1530, www.adrenalin.com.tr). Tram Karaköy. **Open** 10am-8pm Mon-Sat.
Adrenalin offers training in outdoor adventure sports, prefaced by classroom sessions on surviving the experience. Activities run the gamut from weekends camping in the Istanbul suburbs to mountain-climbing courses. Trainers all speak English.

DSM No Limits
Öz Plaza, Kayışdağı Caddesi 23, 2nd Floor, Içerenköy (0216 469 4858, www.nolimits.com.tr). Ferry from Eminönü or Karaköy to Kadıköy, then bus 10B. **Open** 9am-6pm Mon-Sat.
An adventure sports centre that organises group activities including rafting, mountain climbing, caving, camping, trekking and paragliding, all under the leadership and guidance of expert trainers. English is spoken.

Gezici YAK

Recep Paşa Caddesi 14/10, off Cumhuriyet Caddesi, Taksim (0212 238 5107, www.geziciyak.com). **Open** 9am-7.30pm Mon-Sat; 11am-4pm Sun. **Map** p247 P1.
Organises day treks in the local area and river and rafting trips further afield. The company also organises scuba diving trips and training, for which a doctor's certificate is required. English is spoken.

Swimming

The city's few Olympic-size pools are located in university campuses or members-only sports complexes, but you can get a day pass or membership at several hotels.

★ Çırağan Palace Hotel Kempinski

Çırağan Caddesi 32, Beşiktaş (0212 326 4646, www.kempinski.com). Bus 25E, 40. **Open** 7am-11pm daily. **Rates** Day pass €100 Mon-Fri; €160 Sat, Sun. 40% discount under-12s; free under-6s.
Right on the banks of the Bosphorus, this 33m (108ft) outdoor pool has the most spectacular setting in Istanbul. The indoor pool is a third of the size.

Hilton Istanbul

Cumhuriyet Caddesi, Harbiye (0212 315 6000, www.hilton.com). **Open** *Outdoor pool* 7am-6pm daily. *Indoor pool* 7am-10pm daily. **Rates** TL60 Mon-Fri; TL95 Sat, Sun. Half-price under-12s; free under-6s. **Map** p247 P1.
The outdoor pool is approximately half Olympic size, while the indoor pool is 18m (60ft) long. The price includes use of all the health club facilities. After 3pm, the price of a day pass drops to TL30 on weekdays and TL60 on weekends.

Beaches

Although Istanbul is surrounded by water and the municipality has sponsored numerous high- profile clean-up campaigns, swimming within city limits is still a dodgy proposition. The upper Bosphorus, near Sarıyer, is cleaner but subject to treacherous currents.

Solar Beach & Party

Turhan Yolu 4, Kilyos (0212 201 2612, www.kilyossolarbeach.com). **Admission** TL25 Mon-Fri; TL40 Sat, Sun.
In addition to jet skiing, bungee jumping and trampolining, Solar Beach hosts rave parties most summer weekends come nightfall. During high season, the club runs shuttle buses to Taksim Square.

FITNESS

Weightlifting and bodybuilding are beloved of Turkish men of all ages and income brackets. Cheaper gyms tend to be dominated by men, but women will find this new addition hassle-free – not least it's expensive enough to keep out the oglers. Most big hotels also have fitness centres.

★ Mars Athletic Club

Kanyon Mall, Büyükdere Caddesi, Levent (0212 353 0999, www.marsathletic.com). Metro Levent. **Open** 6.30am-11pm Mon-Fri; 9am-9pm Sat, Sun. **Rates** Day pass TL100.
One of five Mac Clubs around town, this super sleek gym offers high-tech equipment, as well as three types of yoga, hardcore Pilates and kickboxing lessons. There are English-speaking trainers and a gorgeous rooftop terrace.

Çırağan Palace Hotel Kempinski.

Escapes & Excursions

Burgazada. *See p216.*

Escapes & Excursions

Get out of town.

On sunny days many locals choose to leave the chaos of the city behind. And there's no better escape than getting out on to the Bosphorus, the narrow straits that cleave Europe and Asia in two. A daytime cruise up this breezy waterway takes in banks dotted with former embassies, summertime retreats and more than a few gorgeous Ottoman *yalı* (waterfront mansions). At the Bosphorus's northern tip, cruisers can dine on fresh fish in **Sarıyer** or **Anadolu Kavaşı**.

South of the city, the Princes' Islands – each one entirely car-free – make an idyllic getaway. Hire a bike, hop aboard a fayton (horse-drawn carriage) or simply stroll along these clement shores. Or, heading north, make your way to one of the lively Black Sea beaches at **Kilyos** or hike through the Belgrad Forest's acres of lush greenery.

THE BOSPHORUS CRUISE

The standard Bosphorus cruise takes six hours and costs all of TL25. Ferries depart daily year round from Eminönü's Boğaz Iskelesi dock, 100 metres east of the Galata Bridge. Daily cruises depart at 10.35am. Between April and early November, an additional cruise departs at 1.35pm; from June to September there's often a third service at noon. On Sundays between April and early November, a two-hour, non-stop cruise (TL10) departs from the same spot at 2.30pm. In summer and at weekends, be sure to board the boat at least 30 minutes before departure to get a seat.

From Eminönü, the first stop is Beşiktaş near Dolmabahçe Palace. The ferry then tacks back and forth between the European and Asian shores, stopping at several Bosphorous villages along the way: notably Kanlıca, Yeniköy, Sarıyer, Rumeli Kavağı and Anadolu Kavağı. You can get off wherever you like, but you will have to make your own way onwards or back into town. Most first-timers stay on board until Anadolu Kavağı, where three hours are allotted for lunch at one of the fish restaurants, before reboarding the ferry, which then traces the same route back to Eminönü.

On Saturdays from June to mid September, a Moonlight Trip (TL20) leaves Eminönü at 7.15pm or Ortaköy at 7.40pm. The ferry arrives at Anadolu Kavaği at 8.50pm, and departs at 10pm, returning to Beşiktaş at 11.05pm and Eminönü at 11.30pm. For further information, updated fares and timetables, check the bilingual Istanbul Şehir Hatları website (www.sehirhatlari.com.tr).

Numerous private operators run shorter boat trips too. These typically only loop as far north as Rumeli Hisarı, after which the boat returns to Eminönü. There are no stops en route. Boats depart from Eminönü roughly every half hour between 10.30am and 6pm (4pm October to April). Touts who roam the wharfs sell tickets for TL10-TL15, but it's worth bargaining. Alternatively, head to Eminönü's TurYol (www.turyol.com) ticket kiosk just west of the Galata Bridge: hour-and-a-half cruises (TL12) depart from here hourly, from around noon to 6pm.

KANLICA

The first major sights – and, indeed, the last if you opt for the shorter cruise – are the twin fortresses of **Rumeli Hisarı** (*see p85*) and **Anadolu Hisarı**, looming on opposite shores of the Bosphorus.

Just before the second great suspension bridge, the 1,096-metre (3,595-foot) **Fatih Mehmet Bridge**, a battered, barn-like structure hangs over the water on the Asian side. This is the historic **Amcazade Hüseyin Paşa Yalısı**, Istanbul's oldest waterfront mansion, built in 1699. When French writer and long time local resident Pierre Loti visited in 1910, he pleaded, 'Of all the *yalıs* on the Bosphorus, you must save the Amcazade Yalı': after more than a century, his wish has been granted, as the attractive *yalı* has finally undergone renovations over recent years.

First stop on the standard Bosphorus cruise is **Kanlıca** on the Asian shore, a lovely village dotted with picturesque mansions and backed by the lush Mihribad Forest Preserve. But Kanlıca's main claim to fame is bacterial: since the 17th century, it has been celebrated for its rich yoghurt, the milk coming from sheep grazing on the hills around nearby Beykoz. A pleasant diversion is a walk up a leafy path to **Khedive's Villa** (Hıdiv Kasrı), a former summer residence of the 19th-century rulers of Egypt. The villa itself is a stately structure built in 1907. It has manicured lawns, a children's play area and an outdoor café, making it ideal for a tranquil morning. The restaurant serves Ottoman and Turkish cuisine – without alcohol. Weekend brunch buffet (9am-1pm) will set you back TL26. During weekdays it's open from 9am to 11pm for breakfast, lunch or dinner. Meze are between TL7 and TL9, with kebabs, grilled fish and other mains around TL20. Kanlıca is linked by a couple of daily ferries to Arnavutköy and Bebek on the European shore.

On departing Kanlıca, the Bosphorus cruise noses back towards Europe. Shortly after Istinye Bay is the stunning **Ahmet Atıf Paşa Yalısı**, a white neo-baroque fantasy of turrets and Ottoman roofs, created by Italian architect Alexandre Villaury for the original proprietor of the Pera Palace hotel (*see p103*).

Further north is Beykoz, a larger and livelier town. This working settlement offers a sense of real Turkish life among the wealth of other coastal towns. There are more amenities and shopping options than Kanlıca. Of interest is the house of Ahmet Mithat Efendi (1844-1912), the respected journalist, author and publisher of *Tercüman-i Hakikat*, the longest running Ottoman newspaper. The polymath published more than 250 works that covered subjects such as philosophy, the Turkish identity and papers decrying the Ottoman rule.

YENIKÖY

The Bophorus ferry then pulls in at **Yeniköy**. As the Ottoman Empire deteriorated in the early 19th century, increasingly desperate rulers used lavish gifts of land as a way of securing the support of foreign embassies in Istanbul. Yeniköy was considered choice real estate, and the waterfront is lined with the greatest concentration of restored Bosphorus mansions, several of which remain the summer residences of the city's consulates.

Just south of the landing is the boxy, white shuttered **Sait Halim Paşa**, also known as the Pink Lion Mansion because of the two stone lions on the quay. Sait Halim was grand vizier under Sultan Abdül Hamit in the dying days of the empire. The hapless Halim ended up taking much of the rap for the empire's disastrous decision to fight on Germany's side in World War I. Adding fatal injury to insult, he was shot dead by an Armenian extremist soon after the war. North of the landing is another Bosphorus landmark, the **Twin Yalı**, a symmetrical semi-detached, whose art nouveau scrollings mark it out as a work by Raimondo D'Aronco.

As the ferry departs Yeniköy it passes a string of rambling European summer embassies, including a vast pink edifice, partially screened by trees, belonging to Austria. About a mile north, spires and gables mark out the fantastic **Huber Mansion**, another D'Aronco design. The Hubers made a massive fortune flogging Mauser rifles to the Ottoman government in the dying days of the empire; they were also renowned for their lavish parties, earning them regular appearances in the late-19th-century versions of *Hello!* magazine. The Huber Mansion is now the official Istanbul residence of the Turkish president. The forested slopes surrounding both these mansions give an idea of how most of the Bosphorus shoreline looked not so long ago.

Several more summer embassies follow in quick succession. With its distinctive bell tower, Germany's looks rather like a Black Forest town hall. Though dilapidated, the summer residence of the Italian Embassy remains supremely elegant. And the British ambassador's summertime retreat is a small cottage set in luxuriant gardens.

SARIYER

The shoreline recedes to accommodate Büyükdere Bay, where the Bosphorus is at its widest (3.5 kilometres, or just under two miles). As the ferry approaches land, you will see a curious, flat-fronted building distinguished by bold yellow and white cross-hatching. This *yalı* houses the **Sadberk Hanım Museum**, stuffed with Ottoman costumes, archaeological and ethnographic artefacts, as well as beautifully hand-painted tiles.

The Bosphorus cruise's next port of call is **Sarıyer**, beside the turreted **Naval Officers'**

Club. Built in 1911, the latter bears the seal of Sultan Mehmet V Reşat. It is now a restaurant and social club for naval officers and their families.

Sarıyer, the largest village on the Upper Bosphorus, is one of Greater Istanbul's more conservative suburbs. As recently as 1995, a local woman was stoned to death here on suspicion of being a prostitute. For the morally unblemished, it is a lovely place to wander (if you disembark here, you can catch bus 25E back to Kabataş). There's a fine old fish market just north of the ferry landing, plus several good seafood restaurants.

On Sular Caddesi, various *dolmuş* depart for the next waterside village, Rumeli Kavağı. En route they pass the **burial place of Telli Baba**, a mystic Muslim saint. Would-be brides come to pray at his tomb and take away a charmed piece of golden wire, apparently guaranteed to secure them a husband. Newlyweds traditionally return on their wedding day to reattach the wire to the saint's tomb and pay homage to Telli Baba's matchmaking skills. On Saturday and Sunday afternoons, there are usually major traffic jams as convoys of husband-seekers pile up along the narrow road beside the Bosphorus.

RUMELI & ANADOLU KAVAĞI

Rumeli Kavağı is a sleepy little place – no more than a string of houses and restaurants clustered around the ferry landing and the coastal road. From here, the road runs north up the Bosphorus, passing dozens of restaurants set into the cliffs and a few small, sandy private beaches, which usually charge entrance fees of around TL20.

Just before the coastal road ends abruptly at the gates of an army base is **Altınkum**, the best of the area's beaches, accessible via a narrow footpath between the trees. There is a restaurant serving meze and cold beer. The water is marked off by a line of buoys – stick within this line if you're swimming, as the Bosphorus is swept by strong currents further from the shore.

From Sarıyer, a couple of metres left of IDO harbour, boats depart for nearby Büyük Liman and Menekşe beaches in the morning, returning to Sarıyer late afternoon.

The last stop for the ferry cruise is **Anadolu Kavağı** on the Asian shore, which is almost opposite Rumeli Kavağı. Passengers have plenty of time to explore the village and eat in one of the many fish restaurants, which cater almost exclusively to passing tourist trade.

Alternatively, clamber up to **Yoros Castle**, which looms on the headland north of the village, offering commanding views of the Black Sea. Originally, the site of a temple to Zeus, where ancient Greek sailors would make a sacrifice to ensure safe passage through the straits, the present fortress was built by the Byzantines, occupied by the Genoese in the mid 14th century, until it was seized by the Turks, who fortified the battlements. The castle lay abandoned until it was opened to the public in the 1980s. Descending from the castle, take the steep path across the heath, which leads to a teahouse with half a dozen rickety tables and amazing views.

Khedive's Villa
Hıdiv Kasrı

Çubuklu Yolu 32, Kanlıca (0216 413 9253, www.beltur.com.tr). **Open** 9am-10pm daily. **Admission** free.

Sadberk Hanım Museum
Sadberk Hanım Müzesi

Piyasa Caddesi 27-29, Büyükdere (0212 242 3813, www.sadberkhanimmuzesi.org.tr). **Open** 10am-5pm Mon, Tue, Thur-Sun. **Admission** TL7. **No credit cards**.

BELGRAD FOREST

Stretching over the hills and valleys north-east of the city, Belgrad Forest is popular with summer picnickers, cyclists and joggers. All leafy glades and oak, pine, plane and beech trees, the place has a distinctly Balkan feel. It is actually named after the Serbian residents entrusted by Süleyman the Magnificent with guarding the forest reservoirs that served as the city's water supply under the Byzantines and Ottomans. Even today, you'll come across the remains of the reservoirs and aqueducts. The Serbs were booted out in the 1890s by the paranoid sultan Abdül Hamit II, who suspected they were poisoning the water.

In centuries past, the wealthy European residents of Istanbul would retreat to Belgrad village in summer to escape the heat and bouts of pestilence. In 1771, Lady Mary Wortley Montagu described the village as an Arcadian idyll, whose inhabitants would meet every night 'to sing and dance, the beauty and dress of the women exactly resembling the ancient nymphs'. All that's left of Belgrad village are a few bumps in the forest floor, hidden near one of the main picnic areas

Upper Bosphorus.

Exploring the Princes' Islands

Dissidents, minorities and horse-drawn carriages – island life, Istanbul-style.

Set in the Marmara Sea off Istanbul's Asian shore, the Princes' Islands have come a long way since they were used as a place of exile and imprisonment. In the 19th century, they were 'discovered' as a luxury location for the summer houses and pleasure palaces of Istanbul's mainly non-Muslim elite: particularly Greeks, Armenians and Jews. Today, the islands continue to offer a glimpse of the old ethnic mix of Istanbul.

Almost all the houses are built of wood, fretted and carved into lacy designs and set in well-tended gardens. The islands are entirely car-free, and the streets echo with the clip-clop of *fayton*, horse-drawn carriages. The overall effect is of a 19th-century time capsule.

There are nine islands in total, of which four can be visited. Furthest from European Istanbul (20 kilometres, or 12 miles) is **Büyükada**, the largest and most popular island. It has traditionally been home to a large Jewish population. **Kınalıada** is predominantly Armenian, **Burgazada** is Greek and **Heybeliada** is mostly Turkish.

KINALIADA

Kınalıada, the smallest of the islands and the closest to Istanbul, is the least green. Its name (from *kınalı*, Turkish for 'dyed with henna') comes from the reddish tinge of the shoreline cliffs, although the absence of greenery today is down to historical copper mining and plentiful modern housing.

Sights in the town include a fine modernist mosque, the **Kınalıada Camii**, erected in 1964, and the 19th-century Armenian church, the **Surp Krikor Lusavoriç**, on Narciciyi Sokak, a ten-minute walk inland from the ferry landing. En route, pass by the grilled sheep's head vendors on Akasya Caddesi, which is also the place to hire bikes.

Where to stay & eat

There is no accommodation on Kinalıada. The Greek taverna, **Çınaraltı** (Çınaraltı Köşk Sokak 16, 0216 381 5407) in Çınaraltı Meydanı, or square, has been going for 125 years. In summer, live Greek and Armenian music livens up the evenings.

BURGAZADA

Burgazada is best known for its connections with Turkish short-story writer Sait Faik (1906-54), who lived on the island from 1939 until his death. He was a specialist in brief vignettes of the lives of his neighbours. Gay or bisexual, Faik probably enjoyed the freedom from the censorious mores of the city that island life could offer. His former home is now the modest and free **Sait Faik Abasıyanık Museum** (Çayırı Sokak 15, 0216 381 2132, closed for restoration at the time of writing), which includes a musty collection of his works and his death mask. The local landmark is the Greek Orthodox **Church of St John the Baptist** (Aya Yani).

Where to stay & eat

The **Mehtap 45 Butik Otel** (Mehtap Sokak 45, 0216 381 2660, doubles TL170) is set on top of a peaceful hill, but still close to town. The area around the ferry landing is laden with fish restaurants, of which the Greek-owned **Barba Yani** (Yalı Caddesi 6, 0216 381 2404, meal with drinks TL35-TL45) has live Greek music on Fridays and Saturdays.

HEYBELIADA

The name means 'saddlebag island' – a good description of how Heybeliada looks, with a low landmass between twin summits. It's a summer favourite with picnickers, and is ringed by lovely seaside paths. The island is also home to a naval academy, visible immediately to the left of the ferry landing.

The best way of getting around is in a horse-drawn carriage, picked up on Ayyıldız Caddesi, parallel to the seafront. An island tour takes 45 minutes and costs TL35. Views from the hilltop Greek Orthodox monastery (around a 20-minute hike from the ferry landing; monastery closed to the public) are sublime.

Where to stay & eat

The **Merit Halki Palace** (Refah Şehitleri Caddesi 94, 0216 351 0025, www.halkipalacehotel.com, doubles TL150) is set in a 19th-century Ottoman mansion. In summer its swimming pool is open to non-residents (TL30 weekdays, TL45

Kinaliada.

weekends). Opposite, Karamanyan (Refah Şehitleri Caddesi, www.istanbulislands.com, apartments TL490-TL990/week) rents four stylish self-catering apartments by the week. Heybeliada's waterfront is brimming with restaurants. For value for money, hit **Ambrosia** (Ay Yıldız Caddesi, 0216 351 1388), for fish and meze.

BÜYÜKADA

The largest Princes' Island is appropriately named: *büyük* means 'big', while ada is Turkish for 'island'. From 1929 to 1933, Büyükada was the home of Leon Trotsky, who bashed out his *History of the Russian Revolution* in exile at the Izzet Paşa Köskü, a restored wooden mansion at Çankaya Caddesi 55. The island was probably the safest place for him, given that at the time Istanbul was also home to some 34,000 White Russians, living in exile after a crushing defeat by Trotsky's Red Army.

The island is now a hugely popular but exclusive summer resort – a kind of Turkish take on the Hamptons. For the casual visitor, it's a gorgeous place for a long walk along leafy lanes scented heavily with blossom. The main settlement and ferry landing are on the northern tip of the island. East is a corral of horse-drawn carriages. Drivers offer big (TL50) or small (TL40) tours of the island, both of which end up at the foot of the hill, where you can climb up a cobbled path to St George's Monastery (Aya Yorgi) – or hire a donkey for TL4. As you climb the steep slope up to the monastery, note the hundreds of pieces of cloth tied to the branches of the trees near the top: each represents a prayer, tied by the faithful of all religions, mostly women hoping for a child.

At the top are fine views and an excellent garden restaurant. The monastery's chapel is usually open to visitors, with icons depicting the old dragon-slayer, plus an assortment of saintly relics.

Where to stay & eat

Just west of the clock tower is the Splendid **Palas** (Nisan Caddesi 23, 0216 382 6950, www.splendidhotel.net, doubles from $130, closed Nov-Apr). The boutique **Ascot** (Çınar Caddesi 6, 0216 382 2888, www.ascot.com.tr, doubles from TL75) boasts a swimming pool, Finnish sauna and traditional Turkish breakfasts al fresco. To sample authentic island life, try the **Kıyı Restaurant** (Çiçek Yalı Sokak 2, 0216 382 5606), a low-key *meyhane* that plays Greek music and is famous for its meze. A meal costs around TL50 per person including drinks.

GETTING THERE

Regular ferries to the islands depart from Kabataş. They stop at each of the islands in turn, taking an hour and a half to reach Büyükada (50 minutes to Kınalıada). The fare is TL3. Departure times change with the season, but in summer there are around six to ten sailings a day from 9.20am onwards. Be sure to arrive at least 30 minutes before departure, particularly in summer and on weekends, in order to secure a seat. For schedules and information, call 0212 444 4436 or visit www.ido.com.tr. TurYol (www.turyol.com) also runs regular crossings to Büyükada: its ferries tend to be faster (and pricier), but the slow, open-air sail remains a pleasure in itself.

by Büyük Bend reservoir, one of the oldest parts of the Byzantine water system.

Following Mahmut II's purge of the Janissary corps in 1826, those who escaped the massacre fled into the forest, where they took up traditional woodland pursuits such as shooting the sultan's deer and ambushing local traders. The sultan's radical response was to set the whole forest on fire.

Also worth visiting is the **Long Aqueduct**, on the road to Kısırmandıra, another work by Mimar Sinan, built for Süleyman the Magnificent in 1563. The stream it crosses is the Kağıthane Suyu, which eventually flows into the Golden Horn.

Getting there

From Kabataş take the 25E bus (or the 40 from Taksim) to Büyükdere. Take a *dolmuş* for Bahçeköy, on the east side of the forest, a 1.5-kilometre (one mile) walk to Büyük Bend.

THE BLACK SEA COAST

North of the twin landmarks of Rumeli Kavağı and Anadolu Kavağı, the mouth of the Bosphorus widens to meet the **Black Sea** (Karadeniz). Much of the coast is an off-limits military zone, but there are small enclaves of civilian life. On the European side, there's the fishing port of **Rumeli Feneri** and **Kilyos**, one of Istanbul's most popular beach resorts, mirrored on the Asian side by the resort of **Şile.**

RUMELI FENERI

Rumeli Feneri means 'European Lighthouse'. Perched atop sheer cliffs overlooking the entrance to the Bosphorus, the lighthouse was built by the British during the Crimean War. But the namesake village is most famous for the ancient Symplegades or 'clashing rocks' – two large humps at the end of the L-shaped harbour. In ancient mythology, these rocks were regarded as living creatures that would dash out to crash into passing boats. One such vessel was Jason's *Argo*, which managed to make it through the straits to the Black Sea, thanks to a neat trick with a pigeon and a helping hand from the goddess Athena.

These days, Rumeli Feneri is a working fishing village – a laid-back Sunday lunch venue for the few Istanbullus who have discovered it. On the Black Sea side of town is an Ottoman fort, once the area's main customs clearing house. Also of archaeological interest is the stone altar on top of the Symplegade closest to shore, which was used to make sacrifices to the sea god, Poseidon, and to light fires to warn passing ships. You can scale the rocks as long as you've got walking shoes and a head for heights.

One of the most exclusive spots on Istanbul's Black Sea coast, the **Golden Beach Club** at Rumeli Feneri boasts an attractive beach and endless facilities including a restaurant, beach bar, beach volleyball, cycling tracks, climbing wall, mini-golf, paintball and sea-trampoline. If you make a reservation one day in advance, you can be picked up from Sarıyer.

Golden Beach Club

Marmaracık Koyu, Rumeli Feneri (0212 228 1007, www.goldenbeachclub.net). **Admission** TL15 Mon-Fri; TL25 Sat, Sun, incl lounger & umbrella.

KILYOS AND DEMIRCIKÖY

Many of Kilyos's long sandy beaches are seriously overdeveloped – unfortunately, a formula that's being repeated all along much of the Black Sea coast near Istanbul. **Solar Beach Club** (0212 201 2612, admission TL25, TL40 weekends, including lounger & umbrella), the most upmarket of Kilyos's private beaches, becomes a party venue during the summer nights, when raves, concerts and other special events draw crowds. It also has lifeguards, a childcare centre, small shops and a food court. Sun-worshippers on a budget should head to Kilyos's free (and very popular) public beach. **Dalia Beach** (0212 204 0368, www.clubdalia.com, admission TL20, TL25 weekends, including lounger & umbrella) at Demirciköy, two kilometres (1.25 miles) from Kilyos, is much quieter and has a small fish restaurant. Access is by taxi (around TL5); or you can take the 151 bus from Sarıyer.

Note that all beaches on the Black Sea coast tend to be windy (perfect for keen kite-surfers) and that seas here are subject to very strong currents. Swim with care.

Getting there

Kilyos is 15 kilometres (10 miles) north of Sarıyer, where regular *dolmuş* depart from Sular Caddesi (the *dolmuş* rank is just before you arrive at Sarıyer bus terminal, opposite the old municipality building). The journey takes half an hour and costs TL3. The last *dolmuş* back to Sarıyer from Kilyos leaves at about 8pm. Rumeli Feneri can be reached by bus or taxi (around TL15) from Sarıyer.

Buses 150 (Haciosman Metro–Rumeli Feneri), 151 (Kilyos–Demirciköy) and 152 (Haciosman Metro–Sarıyer) depart from Sarıyer every 15 minutes during summer weekends and every half hour on weekdays. In winter, buses depart every 45 minutes, with the last bus returning at around 10pm.

Directory

Getting Around

ARRIVING & LEAVING

By air

Istanbul's international **Atatürk Airport** is around 25km (15 miles) west of the city centre in Yeşilköy. The compact international terminal (Dış Hatlar) has several shops, restaurants, bars, a massage parlour, post office, 24-hour banking, exchange bureaux, car hire, a tourist office and hotel reservation desk. From landing to clearing customs usually takes 20 minutes. Security checks can delay check-in, so arrive at least 90 minutes before your flight.

A second international airport, **Sabiha Gökçen**, in Kurtköy on the Asian side was intended to be used by three million travellers a year: it now handles close to 12 million passengers annually. Easyjet and many charter flights arrive here. It is 35km (22 miles) from the city centre, but direct buses transport means it's not the hassle it once was.

Atatürk International Airport
Atatürk Hava Limanı Yolu
Yeşilköy (24-hr English flight information 0212 463 3000, www.ataturkairport.com).

Sabiha Gökçen Airport
Kurtköy (0212 585 5000, English flight info at www.sgairport.com).

There are three options for getting from either airport to the city centre: bus, light rail/underground (Atatürk only) or taxi. The choice depends on where you're staying and how much time you've got.

The easiest option is with Hava (0212 445 4700, www.havas.net). Hava operates a reliable **express airport bus service** from both airports, which leaves for four different destinations from a signposted stop outside the arrivals hall. The only one of use to most visitors is the Taksim service – fine if you're staying in Beyoğlu or Taksim – which starts at 4am then half-hourly until 1am (5am-midnight from Sabiha Gökçen), stopping en route at the Bakırköy Sea Bus Terminal, Aksaray and Tepebaşı (just short of Taksim). The fare is TL10 (TL12 from Sabiha Gökçen), collected by a conductor on board the bus.

The **underground**, or 'light metro', takes you to Aksaray in half an hour and costs just TL2; change in Zeytinburnu for the tram to Kabataş (for Taksim), which stops at Sultanahmet en route (both TL4). Services run from 6am-midnight daily.

Taxis can be taken from the rank outside the arrivals hall. Fares are metered. Journeys to the centre of Sultanahmet should be around TL35 (half as much again at night). The ride takes about 20 minutes but can stretch to 45 minutes if the traffic's bad. To Taksim, it costs around TL40 and takes anywhere between 20-50 minutes. Taxis from Sabiha Gökçen will be around half as much again.

By rail

The days of the Orient Express are long gone. Rail travel from Europe to Istanbul is now the preserve of backpackers, adventurers and the lower-income end of Turkey's Balkan diaspora.

Up until February 2011, it was possible to travel to Istanbul from Thessaloniki in Greece. Unfortunately, at the time of writing this route has been cancelled. Direct services from Europe to Istanbul remain the daily train from Belgrade (departing at 7.50am), which stops at Sofia en route (7.15pm), and arrives in Istanbul at 7.50am the following day; and the daily Bosphorus Express, which departs Bucharest at 1pm and pulls into Istanbul at 7.50am the following morning.

Trains from Europe arrive at Sirkeci Station (*gar*), beside the Golden Horn in Eminönü. From here, it's a short walk or tram ride up the hill to **Sultanahmet**. A taxi to Taksim costs around TL8.

Trains from destinations to the south and east terminate at **Haydarpaşa Station** on the Asian shore. International arrivals include the Trans-Asya, which departs from Tehran every Wednesday at 9.25pm and limps into Istanbul – as of late 2011, via one change in Ankara – some 68 hours later.

Sirkeci (from Eminönü) and Haydarpaşa stations are connected by ferries, though the Marmaray Tunnel (due to open in 2013) will soon supply speedy under-Bosphorus crossings. Information lines serve Sirkeci (0212 527 0051) and Haydarpaşa (0216 348 8020 ext 336) between 7am-midnight daily, but are in Turkish only. Timetables for international and national services are posted on the state railway (TCDD) website (www.tcdd.gov.tr); the English-language version of the site is refreshingly good.

Sirkeci Station
*Istasyon Caddesi, Eminönü (*0212 527 0051*, for international reservations only 7am-midnight daily).*

Haydarpaşa Station
Haydarpaşa Istasyon Caddesi, Kadıköy (0216 336 4470, for reservations 6am-6pm daily).

By road

Turkish coach companies (such as Ulusoy and Varan) run regular services from many European cities. Be prepared for lengthy waits at border crossings – particularly with Bulgaria, where it can take up to three hours to clear customs.

Travellers arriving by coach disembark at the international and inter-city bus terminal (*otogar*) in Bayrampaşa, about ten kilometres (six miles) from the city centre. There are courtesy minibuses to Taksim and Sultanahmet. The underground 'light metro' connects the terminal to Aksaray, where you can trudge to the Taksim bus stop across the road, or take a tram to Sultanahmet.

Istanbul Main Bus Terminal
Büyük Istanbul Otogarı, Bayrampaşa (0212 658 0505, www.otogaristanbul.com).
Open 24hrs daily.

Ulusoy
Inönü Caddesi 47, Gümüşsuyu, Taksim (0212 244 6373/Call centre 0212 444 1888, www.ulusoy.com.tr). **Open** 24hrs daily. Twice-weekly buses to and from Greece (Thessaloniki, 12hrs, TL88; Athens, 21hrs), Germany (Münich, 48hrs; Frankfurt, 55hrs) and Italy (Ancona via Munich). The English website is difficult to use – booking are best made in person at Ulusoy's office.

Varan
Inönü Caddesi 19, Gümüşsuyu, Taksim (0212 251 7474/Call centre 0212 444 8999, www.varan.com.tr).
Open 24hrs daily.
Weekly buses to and from Austria (Vienna, 33hrs, Salzburg, 37hrs, Linz, 39hrs, TL240-255); Germany (Berlin, TL295).

PUBLIC TRANSPORT

Public transport is cheap and improving all the time, thanks to a municipal campaign to defeat the city's chronic traffic problem. The result is reinforcement to the entire transport infrastructure: extensions to metro and tram lines, new bypasses and underpasses, new sea bus routes and funiculars are all under way or completed, and a trans-Bosphorus tunnel (Marmaray) is due to open in 2013. But for the time being, Istanbul endures gridlock along major arteries.

Happily, the two areas where visitors are likely to spend most time – Beyoğlu and Sultanahmet – are easily explored on foot. However, buses are useful for heading up the Bosphorus coast to Ortaköy, Arnavutköy, Bebek and beyond, while trips to the districts of Üsküdar and Kadıköy on the Asian shore are best undertaken by ferry or sea bus. The easiest way to get to shopping and business districts in Nişantaşı, Teşvikye, Etiler and Levent is via the new metro line that runs north from Taksim.

The informative website of the IETT (www.iett.gov.tr*)*, the local transport authority, has an excellent English version that includes maps and timetables.

Fares & tickets

Istanbulkart, which replaced the much-loved Akbil travel pass in 2011, is an electronic travel pass that can be used on all public transport except *dolmu* and minibuses. You get a ten per cent discount on fares. Istanbulkarts are available for a small refundable deposit (TL10) from booths at all main bus, sea bus and metro stations. Similar in appearance to an Oyster card, the Istanbulkart functions by waving the card in front of the orange machine located next to the driver on buses, or alongside the turnstiles at all metro, light rail, tram and ferry stations. Recharge at Jetonmatik machines located at bus, metro and tram stations, ferry terminals, or at kiosks marked with 'Istanbulkart' or 'Akbil'.

Metro, trams & Tünel

The metro and tram systems provide a comfortable and efficient alternative to clogged roads and crowded buses. However, coverage currently remains scant. At present, the metro runs from Şişhane north to Maslak, stopping at Taksim, Osmanbey, Şişli, Gayrettepe, Levent and 4. Levent. Extensions will take the line south of Şişhane to the sea bus jetty at Yenikapı.

Another option is the 'light metro', which connects Aksaray (west of the Grand Bazaar) to the Esenler bus terminal and on to the airport.

The city's only modern tram runs from Zeytinburnu via Aksaray, Sultanahmet, Eminönü by the Galata Bridge and six more stops including Karaköy and Kabataş; the ferry and sea bus terminal.

This is a useful service for visitors, linking the Grand Bazaar, Haghia Sophia, Sultanahmet, Topkapı, the Egyptian Bazaar and the Golden Horn. You can also use the tram to visit the city walls. Buy tokens in advance from kiosks at tram stops or from nearby shops – the attendant will point you in the right direction) and feed them into the automatic barriers outside the platform. A single trip on the tram costs TL1.50 irrespective of your destination. The service runs from around 6am-midnight.

A funicular connects Kabataş to Taksim Square, (connecting at the metro).

A 125-year-old funicular, known as *Tünel*, ascends from Karaköy to Tünel Square at the southern end of Istiklal Caddesi. It's a very short run, but saves a tiring climb up (or down) the sheer slope. The service runs 7am-10pm Mon-Sat and 7.30am-10pm Sun and costs TL2. At Tünel, it connects with a century-old tram that shuttles up mile-and-a-half-long Istiklal Caddesi to Taksim Square and back. Istanbulkart can be used for either. Otherwise, you need to buy a token for the funicular at the entrance, and a ticket for the tram onboard. Tickets for either the tram or funicular cost TL2.

Buses

Most city buses (*belediye otobüsü*) are operated by the municipality, but there are also private versions (*halk otobüsü*). Municipal buses are red and white or green; all have IETT written on the front. Private ones are pale blue and green, and usually more modern.

Buy tickets (*bilet*) for municipal buses onboard. On private buses, pay a conductor seated in the doorway (they will begrudgingly accept coins, but no large bills). Both IETT and private buses accept Istanbulkarts (*see above*) and charge the same fare (TL2).

Newer buses have electronic signboards with route information. Bus stops also have route maps. Still, the sheer number of routes and the interminable traffic and roadworks can make bus travel tricky – consider buses with the same number but different following letter as different routes. Bus services run from around 6am to 11pm. Kabataş, Beşiktaş and Taksim are the main bus terminals north of the Golden Horn. The following are useful bus routes:

Taksim – **Topkapı** 83
Taksim – **Bahçeşehir** 76D
Taksim – **Ortaköy** DT1, DT2
Taksim – **Edirnekapı** 87
Taksim – **Kadıköy** 110
Taksim – **Sarıyer** 40
Taksim – **Otogar** 83O
Otogar – **Eminönü** 91O
Otogar – **Beşiktaş** 28O
Kabataş – **Reşitpaşa** 22RE
Kabataş – **Sarıyer** 25E
Topkapı – **Beşiktaş** 28T
Sarıyer – **Kilyos** 151
Sarıyer – **Beşiktaş** 40B
Aksaray – **Airport** light metro
Edirnekapı – **Beşiktaş** 28

Dolmuş & minibuses

A *dolmuş* (which means 'full') is basically a shared taxi that sets off once every seat is taken. *Dolmuş* run fixed routes (starting points and final destinations are displayed in the front window) but with no set stops – although within city limits, *dolmuş* stops are often designated with a large 'D'. Passengers flag the driver down to get on (if there's room) and holler out to be let off (Inecek var!). For local journeys, there's one fixed fare (usually TL3). Ask a fellow passenger how much it is or just watch what everyone else is paying. *Dolmuş* run later than buses, often as late as 2am.

Minibuses are more crowded than dolmuş, and less frequent. Minibus fares are lower, but chances are you'll make your journey standing while being blasted by tinny Turkish pop. Pay and get on/off as you would a *dolmuş*. The main routes are from Beşiktaş to the upper Bosphorus districts.

Water transport

Boats and ships of all sizes shuttle between the European and Asian shores, operating to summer (mid June-mid Sept) and winter timetables. Timetables are available from ferry terminals; times are also posted online. The main services run between Eminönü, Karaköy, Kabataş and Beşiktaş on the European side, and Üsküdar and Kadıköy on the Asian shore. Departures are every 15 minutes or so.

There are also regular services running up the Golden Horn to Eyüp from Eminönü Haliç Iskelesi (just west of Eminönü). Less frequent commuter services criss-cross the Bosphorus, starting from Eminönü and calling at Ortaköy, Arnavutköy, Bebek, Kandilli and beyond.

Ferries also depart from Kabataş and *Yenikapı* to the Princes' Islands. The popular Bosphorus tour departs from Eminönü three times daily – *see p212.*

The modern catamarans (called *deniz otobüsleri* or 'sea buses') are faster but more expensive. You can pick up timetables from the ferry terminals or check online (*see below*).

City Line Ferries
Şehir Hatları
Evliya Çelebi Caddesi 1-4, Kasımpaşa (0212 444 1851, www.sehirhatlari.com.tr).

Istanbul Fast Ferry
Istanbul Deniz Otobüsleri
Kennedy Caddesi, Sahil Yolu, Hızlı Feribot Iskelesi, Yenikapı (0212 444 4436, www.ido.com.tr).

TAXIS

You won't have a problem finding a taxi, day or night. Licensed taxis are bright yellow, with a roof-mounted *taksi* sign. They're all metered, and relatively cheap by European standards. If the meter isn't running, get out.

During the day, the meter displays the word *gündüz* (day rate); the clock should start with TL2.50. From midnight to 6am the *gece* (night) rate kicks in, adding 50 per cent to the fare. The day rate is TL1.40 per kilometre. A trip between Sultanahmet and Taksim Square costs TL8-TL10. There's no room for haggling and no need to tip. Cabbies are not necessarily streetwise. It's not unusual for your driver to ask you, other drivers or passers-by the way. If you cross the Bosphorus bridges, the toll (TL4) will be added to the fare.

DRIVING

Driving is not recommended. Heavy congestion doesn't stop speeding, although the limit is 50kmh (30mph), rising to 120kmh (75mph) on motorways. Seat belts are the law, but observance of regulations is laughable.

If you take your own car to Turkey, prepare to be entangled in red tape. Drivers must provide registration documents and a valid international driving licence at point of entry. Cars, minibuses, caravans, and motorbikes can be taken into Turkey for up to six months without a *carnet de passage* or *triptyque*. Your vehicle is registered in your passport and you're issued a certificate that should be carried at all times along with your driving licence and passport. If you stay in Turkey for more than six months, you must leave and re-enter the country, or apply to the Turkish Touring & Automobile Association for a *triptyque*. You won't be allowed to visit another country without taking your vehicle, unless you cancel the registration at the local customs office. Drivers from Europe also need a Green Card, which is available from your insurance company.

A rarely enforced law requires all cars to be equipped with a fire extinguisher, first-aid kit and two triangles.

Turkish Touring & Automobile Association
Türkiye Turing ve Otomobil Kurumu
1 Oto Sanayi Sitesi Yanı, Seyrantepe, 4.Levent (0212 282 8140, www.turing.org.tr).
Turkey's equivalent of the AA.

Breakdown services

Gökşenler
Atatürk Oto Sarayı Sitesi 2, Kısım Sokak, Gökşenler Plaza 213, Maslak (0212 286 6141, www.goksenler.com). **Open** 8.30am-6.30pm Mon-Fri; 8.30am-3.30pm Sun. 24-hour emergency service.

Istanbul Traffic Foundation
0212 289 9800.
24-hour towing services.

Car hire

Rental rates generally include VAT, insurance with third-party liability, and unlimited mileage, but are still relatively high. The rates below include VAT and insurance.

Avis
Mete Caddesi, Ayyıldız Apt 12/A, Taksim (0212 244 9350, www.avis.com.tr). **Open** 9am-7pm daily. **Rates** TL115-TL195 per day. **Other locations** Atatürk Airport (0212 465 3455).

Budget
Abdülhak Hamit Caddesi, Inal Apt 72/A, Taksim (0212 297 4393, www.budget.com.tr). **Open** 8.30am-7pm daily. **Rates** TL88-TL250/day. **Other locations** Atatürk Airport (0212 465 6909).

Europcar
Topçu Caddesi 1/A, off Cumhuriyet Caddesi, Taksim (0212 254 7710, www.europcar.com.tr). **Open** 8.30am-7pm daily. **Rates** TL100-TL260/day. **Other locations** Atatürk Airport (0212 465 3695).

Parking

Street parking is difficult and not always legal, in which case you're liable to get towed. Use the plentiful car parks; you may have to leave the keys so that cars can be shuffled.

CYCLING

Terrible traffic, steep hills, slippery cobbles, and countless potholes make Istanbul very challenging for cyclists. However, the wide road alongside the Bosphorus north of Ortaköy is great for biking, with lovely views and a sea breeze. A hired bike is ideal for getting around the Princes' Islands where cars are banned. Bikes (from around TL10 per day) are available from rental shops clustered around each island's ferry terminal.

WALKING

The tourist hubs of Sultanahmet, the Bazaar Quarter and Beyoğlu are all perfect for exploring on foot (and Beyo lu's main drag, Istiklal Caddesi, is pedestrianised). There are very few main roads, while the narrow, sloping backstreets are better suited to pedestrians than cars. Pay attention when crossing roads, as drivers often jump lights.

GUIDED TOURS

All hotels will be able to organise guided tours. Istanbul Walks (www.istanbulwalks.net) is a highly regarded, independent tour organiser.

Resources A-Z

TRAVEL ADVICE

For up-to-date information on travel to a specific country – including the latest on safety and security, health issues, local laws and customs – contact your home country government's department of foreign affairs. Most have websites with useful advice for would-be travellers.

AUSTRALIA
www.smartraveller.gov.au

CANADA
www.voyage.gc.ca

NEW ZEALAND
www.safetravel.govt.nz

REPUBLIC OF IRELAND
foreignaffairs.gov.ie

UK
www.fco.gov.uk/travel

USA
www.state.gov/travel

ADDRESSES

When writing an address, the house number comes after the street name, with a slash separating the flat number. If it's on a side street (*sokak*), the custom is to include the nearest main street or avenue (*caddesi*). This main street is usually written first. So the address of Mehmet Aksoy, who lives in Flat 7 at 14 Matrar Sokak, off Sıraselviler Street, in the district of Cihangir, will be written like this:

Mehmet Aksoy
Sıraseviler Caddesi
Matar Sokak 14/7
Cirhangir
Istanbul

ATTITUDE & ETIQUETTE

Istanbullus are generally polite, open and interested in foreigners. It's a laid-back city, so don't be surprised if a meeting starts late or food takes a while to turn up. The relaxed vibe extends even to high-end restaurants. Diners will generally look smart, but jackets and ties aren't necessary.

BUSINESS SERVICES

Although Istanbul is alive with opportunity, the city is also fraught with difficulties for business. Of the many foreign companies that have successfully entered the Turkish market, few have done so alone. Foreign concerns have either bought controlling interests in local businesses, or work with Turkish partners. Corruption and interminable bureaucracy make it essential to have an efficient local representative, preferably with plenty of *torpil* ('influence').

Turkish employees work long hours and take few holidays, but seem to have inherited their administrative methods from the Byzantines. Things are slowly changing, but official paperwork still takes forever to complete, while the vocabulary of the average civil servant more often than not seems to consist entirely of negatives. Most foreign companies farm out tasks such as getting work permits and residence permits to local lawyers or accountants. Dealings with private-sector business are less fraught, and the AKP government has been trying to ease red tape to encourage more foreign investment.

Conventions & conferences

Istanbul Convention & Visitors Bureau (ICVB)
Istanbul Ticaret Odası Ek Hizmet Binası
Reşadiye Caddesi 7, Eminönü (0212 522 5555, www.icvb.org). Help with arranging a conference.

Istanbul Convention & Exhibition Centre (ICEC)
Lutfi Kirdar Uluslararasi Kongre ve Sergi Sarayi
Gümüş Caddesi 4, Harbiye (0212 373 1100, www.icec.org). Large convention centre near Taksim.

Courier & shippers

DHL
Cumhuriyet Caddesi 26/D, Taksim, Beyoğlu (0212 245 5851, www.dhl.com.tr). **Open** 9am-6pm Mon-Sat.
International service only. Customer services 24 hours daily.

UPS
Aksakal Sokak 14, off Küçük Ayasofya Caddesi, Sultanahmet (0212 517 4102, www.ups.com.tr). **Open** 8.30am-7.45pm Mon-Fri; 8.30am-5pm Sat.
International and national deliveries.

Federal Express
Taş Ocağı Yolu 19, off Fabrikalar Caddesi, Mahmutbey, Bağcılar (0212 445 0808, www.fedex.com/tr). **Open** 8am-11pm Mon-Fri; 8am-8pm Sat.
International service only.

Office services

Deloitte
Sun Plaza, Bilim Sokak 5, Maslak, Şişli (0212 366 6000, www.deloitte.com).

PricewaterhouseCoopers
Ninth floor, B Blok, BJK Plaza, Süleyman Seba Caddesi 48, Akaretler, Beşiktaş (0212 326 6060, www.pwc.com/tr).

IBS
Agahamami Caddesi, Aga Han 1/6, Cihangir (0212 252 2460, www.ibsresearch.com). **Open** 9am-6pm Mon-Fri.
English-owned and run. It produces the comprehensive, indispensable guide *Doing Business in Turkey*.

Wordsmith
Refik Saydam Caddesi, Akarca Sokak 39, 5th Floor, Beyoğlu (0212 237 1979, www.wordsmith.com.tr). **Open** 9am-6pm Mon-Fri.
Advertising, promotional films and translation.

Useful organisations

Foreign Economic Relations Board
Dış Ekonomik Şlişkiler Kurulu
TOBB Plaza, Talatpaşa Caddesi 3, 5th Floor (0212 339 5000, www.deik.org.tr). **Open** 9am-6pm Mon-Fri. **Map** p248 N3.
Organises joint business councils between Turkey and dozens of

countries worldwide. Also has a small library and resource centre.

Istanbul Convention & Visitors Bureau (ICVB)
Istanbul Ticaret Odası Ek Hizmet Binası
Reşadiye Caddesi 7, Eminönü (0212 522 5555, www.icvb.org). **Open** 9am-5.30pm Mon-Fri.
Provides information and services related to conventions and meetings in Istanbul.

CUSTOMS

Foreign visitors can import up to one 100cc (or two 75cc) bottle(s) of alcohol (including wine), 200 cigarettes, 50 cigarillos and ten cigars. You may be asked to register electronic equipment to ensure it leaves Turkey with you. You may need proof of purchase for antiques and a carpet. If an item is more than 100 years old there is some red tape, which the dealer should help with. For more details, visit www.gumruk.gov.tr or call 0312 306 8000.

DISABLED ACCESS

Hilly Istanbul is tough on anyone with restricted mobility. Roads and pavements are narrow, bumpy, and often cobbled, kerbs are high, and stairs ubiquitous. However, public transport is more accessible than before: the metro has elevators, the light railway and trams are accessible; and some 450 'low-riding' Mercedes buses have been provided to facilitate disabled access. Apart from a handful of top hotels, few buildings make any provisions for the disabled, although Mayor Kadir Topba – in power since 2004 – claims this issue high on his agenda.

DRUGS

Turkey is a major transit point for heroin smugglers. The use of marijuana, cocaine and ecstasy is also on the rise. Enforcement is uneven, but heavy-handed; police conduct random sweeps of bars and nightclubs. You may be body-searched and checked for needle tracks. Sentencing for drug offences can be extremely severe. Carry ID at all times, especially if you're out on the town.

ELECTRICITY

Electricity in Turkey runs on 220 volts. Plugs have two round pins. Adaptors for UK appliances can be found in hardware shops and on street stalls, but it's still best to bring one from home. Transformers are required for US 110-volt appliances. There are frequent, brief power cuts, so it's not a bad idea to bring a torch.

EMBASSIES & CONSULATES

All foreign embassies are located in Ankara, but many countries also have a consulate in Istanbul.

Australian Consulate
Ritz Carlton Residences, Asker Ocagi Caddesi 15, Elmadag, Şişli (0212 393 8542, www.turkey.embassy.gov.au). **Open** 8.30am-12.30pm, 1.30-5pm Mon-Fri.

Canadian Consulate
Tekfen Tower, 16th Floor, 209 Buyukdere Caddesi, 4.Levent (0212 385 9700, www.canadainternational.gc.ca). **Open** 9am-noon, 2-5pm Mon-Thur, 9am-noon Fri.

Republic of Ireland Honorary Consulate
Meridyen Iş Merkezi, 4th Floor, Ali Rıza Gürcan Caddesi 417, Merter (0212 482 1862, www.irlconsulist.com). **Open** 9am-5pm Mon-Fri.

New Zealand Honorary Consulate
Inönü Caddesi 48/3, Gümüşsuyu, Taksim (0212 244 0272, www.nzembassy.com). **Open** 8.30am-5pm Mon-Fri. **Map** p247 P2.

UK Consulate
Meşrutiyet Caddesi 34, Tepebaşı, Beyoğlu (0212 334 6400, http://ukinturkey.fco.gov.uk). **Open** 8.30am-1pm, 1.45-4.45pm Mon-Fri. **Map** p248 M3.

US Consulate
Üç Şehitler Sokak 2, Istinye (0212 335 9000, http://istanbul.usconsulate.gov). **Open** 7.45am-4.30pm Mon-Fri.

EMERGENCIES

For police, *see p227*. For hospitals and health, *see below*.

Police 155
Fire 110
Emergency/Ambulance 112

GAY & LESBIAN

For more information on the gay and lesbian scene, *see p188-191*.

LAMBDA Istanbul (0212 245 7068, www.lambdaistanbul.org).
This umbrella group has links to international organisations, including the International Gay and Lesbian Association. LAMBDA is involved in a range of legal, social, cultural, health and political issues of concern to the gay community.

HEALTH

Turkey's health services suffer from an overstretched, underfunded public sector. There is no GP system, state hospitals are jammed, and underpaid doctors often have to take on private patients. In contrast, private hospitals have state-of-the-art equipment, look like five-star hotels, and milk their patients royally. If you need medical aid, the simplest solution (especially if you have insurance) is to go straight to a private hospital, where you'll get immediate attention and are pretty sure to find English speakers. Many private hospitals also run dental clinics.

No vaccinations are required for Istanbul, although cases of rabies have been reported in recent years. Stray dogs with a yellow tag in their ear have been vaccinated. It's best to avoid tap water; cheap bottled water is readily available.

Accident & emergency

American Hospital
Amerikan Hastanesi
Güzelbahçe Sokak 20, Nişantaşı (0212 444 3777, www.americanhospitalistanbul.org).
Well equipped and well staffed, the American Hospital also has a dental clinic.

European Florence Nightingale Hospital
Abide-i Hürriyet Caddesi 164, Şişli (0212 212 8811 or 444 0436, www.groupflorence.com).
Modern and well equipped, specialises in treating children.

German Hospital
Sıraselviler Caddesi 119, Cihangir, Taksim (0212 293 2150, www.uhg.com.tr). **Map** p249 O3.
Part of the Universal Hospitals Group, it incorporates an eye hospital and dental clinic.

International Hospital
Istanbul Caddesi 82, Yeşilköy (0212 468 4444, www.internationalhospital.com.tr).
Five minutes from the airport, it has cutting-edge technology, eye and dental clinics.

Taksim State Emergency Hospital
Taksim Ilkyardım Hastanesi
Sıraselviler Caddesi 112, Cihangir, Taksim (0212 252 4300, www.taksimhastanesi.gov.tr). **No credit cards. Map** p249 O3.

A state-run hospital that recently got a much-needed overhaul. It only deals with emergencies.

Contraception & abortion

Contraception can be found at any pharmacy (*see below*). Abortion (*kürtaj*) is legal in Turkey up until the tenth week of pregnancy.

Dr Hakan Topalismailoğlu
Halaskargazi Caddesi Doğançay, Apt 216 (0212 233 4647, www.kurtajrehberi.net).

Dentists

Dental treatment is also available at the **American Hospital** and the **International Hospital** (for both, *see left*). Dental tourism has become increasingly popular in Istanbul.

Dentistanbul Dental Hospital
Yildiz Caddesi 71, Beşiktaş (0212 310 5600, www.dentistanbul.co.uk).

Opticians

See p171 **Shops & services**

PHARMACIES

Pharmacies (*eczane*) are plentiful. Pharmacists are licensed to measure blood pressure, give injections, clean and bandage minor injuries, and suggest medication for minor ailments – many prescription medicines are available over the counter in Turkey. However, few pharmacists speak English. Opening hours are typically from 9am-7pm Mon-Sat. Every neighbourhood also has a duty pharmacy (*nöbetçi*) that is open all night and on Sundays. *see p172.*

STDs, HIV, AIDS

Yeniden
Halaskargazi Caddesi, Kücükbaçe Sokak, Yuvam Apart 351/1 (0212 219 0303, www.yeniden.org.tr).
Yeniden works mainly with young people regarding AIDS, STDs, HIV and on addiction issues.

ID

It is illegal not to carry photo ID at all times. It's unlikely that tourists are asked by authorities to show ID, and almost never to buy alcohol.

INSURANCE

Turkey is not covered by EU mutual health insurance schemes, so visitors are advised to get private insurance policy. Anyone with a full residence permit is entitled to national health care.

INTERNET

Almost all hotels offer internet access and many travel agents have a couple of online computers. Wireless access is widespread, and available in most upscale cafés and restaurants, including Gloria Jeans and Starbucks.

The majority of phone sockets take the US-style RJ11 plug, although a few older hotels use a Turkish model for which there don't seem to be any adaptors.

The following is a reputable internet provider with English-speaking technical staff and back-up services.

Turknet
0212 355 1718, http://kurumsal.turk.net

There are many internet cafés in Sultanahmet, especially on and around Divan Yolu, as well as in Beyoğlu. The whole of Istiklal Caddesi is covered by free blanket WiFi. Initial access is by text from any cell phone.

Bohem Internet Cafe
Büyükparmakkapı Sokak 9, 3rd Floor, off Istiklal Caddesi, Beyoğlu (0212 243 8684).
This third-floor café has various computers as well as WiFi.

LANGUAGE

For more on language, *see p230,* **Vocabulary**. For **language classes**, *see p227.*

LEFT LUGGAGE

There are left luggage facilities at both **Sabiha Gökçen Airport** and **Atatürk Airport**. It costs between TL10-TL20 depending on the size. They are open 24 hours. There's also left luggage storage at Istanbul's Büyük Otogarı Bus Terminal as well as at both Haydarpaşa and Sirkeci train stations.

LEGAL HELP

For criminal legal help, contact the consulates, *see p224.*

Martinez-Echevarria, Perez y Ferrero
Büyükdere Caddesi, Maya Akar Center 100-102 C Swiss Offices (0212 318 9060, www.martinez echevarria.com).
A consultancy and law firm that specialises in real estate, financial, investment, mergers, labour and urban law.

LIBRARIES

While there are excellent Spanish and French libraries in Beyoğlu, there isn't a single English-language library open to the public since the closure of the British Council library after the 2003 bombing.

Istanbul Library/ Çelik Gülersoy Foundation
Ayasofya Pansiyonları, Soğukçeşme Sokak, Sultanahmet (0212 513 3660, www.turing.org.tr). **Open** 9am-noon, 1-4.30pm Mon-Fri. **Map** p243 N10.
Antique and modern books on Istanbul in several languages, stored in an Ottoman house beside Topkapı Palace. The specialised tomes are used primarily by academics and specialists. Free WiFi.

LOST PROPERTY

To report a crime or lost property, go to the Tourist Police station (0212 527 4503) opposite Yerebatan Sarnıcı in Sultanahmet. Most officers speak English or German. If your passport is lost or stolen, you generally have to fill out a police report before the consulate will deal with you.

MEDIA

Magazines

Most magazines are ephemeral unless backed by one of the big media groups. Established leaders are *Tempo* and *Aktüel*, which mix news, fashion and gossip. *Cornucopia* is a beautiful quarterly magazine covering Turkish history, archaeology, architecture and food. There are a slew of licensed international titles, including the monthly *Time Out Istanbul* with both English and Turkish editions.

Our competitor *Istanbul: The Guide* also includes hotel, restaurant and club reviews, but only appears every other month.

Newspapers

National newspapers fall into two broad categories, secular and pro-Islamist. The secular press is monopolised by two empires – the Do an and Sabah groups; between them, they account for around 60 per cent of the market.

DIRECTORY

The most highbrow papers are *Cumhuriyet* (*Republic*), a foundering left-of-centre paper, and *Radikal*, a Do an title. Competition comes from three big hitters: *Hürriyet*, *Sabah* and *Milliyet*, indistinguishable popular dailies that occupy the centre. Journalistic standards are undermined by low pay. The real news comes from the columnists – usually at least one per page.

The main pro-Islamist daily is *Zaman*, distinguished by good coverage of international literature and film, and the first Turkish newspaper to go online. By far the worst Islamist paper is the hate-mongering Yeni *Akit*, with its habit of insinuating that successful business leaders are closet Jews or Christians.

Weekly satirical comics sell well. Popular titles include *Gır Gır*, *Penguen* and *LeMan*. No subject is taboo, and the humour, while crude, is usually on the mark.

Istanbul has two competing daily English newspapers: *Hürriyet Daily News (www.hurriyetdailynews.com)* and *Today's Zaman* (www.todayszaman.com). Both are great reads for cultural, historical and political background.

Foreign newspapers and magazines are easy to find, but rarely arrive before late afternoon. The best places to look are the news stands in Sultanahmet and around Tünel and Taksim Squares, or the bookshops on Istiklal Caddesi.

Radio

The airwaves over Istanbul are so crammed with broadcasts that it's practically impossible to pick up any station without overlapping interference. Stations generally offer either Turkish or foreign music, but rarely both. One exception is Açık Radyo (94.9), which intercuts topical talk shows (often in English) with world music. Stations offering dance and pop music include Metro FM (97.2), Capital Radio (99.5), Kiss FM (99.8), Power FM (100.0) and Number One FM (102.4). Virgin (99.4) specialises in pop and contemporary music; Radyo Eksen (96.2) is the best channel for alternative music. For Turkish music, try Kral FM (92.0), Best FM (98.4) and Nostalji (107.4). For Western classical music tune into ITU Radyosu (103.8). You can pick up the BBC news in English on NTV Radyo (102.8) at 6pm daily, and at 7am and 10.30pm Monday to Friday.

Television

Turkey has 30 national channels, and countless more regional stations. Perhaps unsurprisingly, production values are low. The exceptions are CNN Turk and NTV, which feature excellent news, documentary and sports programmes. Cable TV is available, offering improved reception of terrestrial channels, plus BBC Entertainment, CNN, Discovery, Eurosport and MTV. Digital TV is represented by Digitürk, which carries programmes from Europe and the US, plus all the biggest Turkish TV and radio stations.

MONEY

Local currency is the Turkish lira, or TL. After taming inflation with IMF help, Turkey lopped six zeros off its currency in 2005 and the New Turkish Lira (YTL) was born – although as of 2010, it's simply Turkish Lira, or TL, again. TL banknotes come in denominations of 5, 10, 20, 50, and 100.

Travellers' cheques can be cashed at banks or post offices, but are usually not accepted at exchange bureaux. You always need to have your passport with you to cash cheques. Banks charge different commissions, and some charge none at all; but the post office usually offers the best deal.

Banks & ATMs

Cashpoints are common. Most machines will accept cards linked into the Cirrus or Plus networks, and supply Turkish lira or cash advances on major credit cards, provided you know your PIN.

Most banks provide telephone and internet banking, which can be less frustrating than shabby counter service. Non-residents can open a savings account at a Turkish bank in any currency: although you'll need to provide both your passport and a Turkish tax ID number. You'll be asked to sign a routine account agreement. Be sure to choose a branch that is near your place of residence or work, because you'll only be able to draw cash from this branch without incurring charges. Cash can be deposited at any branch. With a current account, you can also apply for an ATM card. Getting a credit card isn't so easy: you need a residence permit, employment, proof of income, and a Turkish guarantor, as well as patience.

Most banks will accept transfers even if you don't have an account. The drawback is that the money doesn't always arrive instantly, and the bank will block the money for up to 20 days. There is a way around this: you can withdraw the money in Turkish lira at the bank's discretionary rates, or by paying a hefty commission. The quicker and more reliable alternative is to use Western Union Money Transfer. This service is now offered by all branches of Denizbank, Finansbank and Ziraat Bankası. If you're expecting to receive money, turn up at any branch of these banks with your passport and transfer details (amount of transfer, plus 'money transfer control number'). You should be able to draw the money instantly in dollars, euros or TL.

Akbank
www.akbank.com.

Citibank
www.citibank.com.tr.

Garanti Bank
www.garantibank.com.tr.

HSBC
www.hsbc.com.tr.

Yapı Kredi Bank
www.yapikredi.com.tr.

Bureaux de change

Some shops and restaurants will accept payment in US dollars, sterling or euros, but there are dozens of exchange bureaux (*döviz bürosu*) in the main tourist districts. These speedy counters are easier to deal with than banks, where transactions can take forever and exchange rates are generally lower. Bureaux de change have long opening hours, generally from from 9am to 7.30pm Monday to Saturday. Some exchange offices also open on Sundays, although lack of competition means exchange rates can be poor.

Çetin Döviz
Istiklal Caddesi 31, Taksim, Beyoğlu (0212 252 6428). **Open** 9am-8pm daily. **Map** p249 O2.

Çözüm Döviz
Istiklal Caddesi 41/B, Beyoğlu (0212 244 6271). **Open** 9am-7.30pm Mon-Sat; 11am-6pm Sun. **Map** p249 O2.

Klas Döviz
Sıraselviler Caddesi 6/F, Taksim (0212 249 3550). **Open** 8.30am-10pm daily. **Map** p249 O2.

Lost/stolen credit cards

American Express
0212 310 2315, +44 1273 696 933, www.americanexpress.com.tr.

Represented in Turkey by Garanti, AmEx is far less widely accepted than Mastercard or Visa because of high commission charges.

Mastercard
00 800 13 887 0903.

Visa
00 800 13 535 0900.

OPENING HOURS

Opening hours are extremely variable in Istanbul, but here are some general guidelines:

Banks 9am-12.30pm, 1.30-5pm Mon-Fri.
Bars 11am or noon-2am daily.
Businesses 9am-6pm Mon-Fri.
Municipal offices 8am-12.30pm, 1.30-5.30pm Mon-Fri.
Museums 8.30am-5.30pm Tue-Sun.
Petrol stations 24 hrs daily.
Post offices *see below*.
Shops 10am-8pm Mon-Sat. In main shopping areas shops stay open until 10pm and also open on Sunday. Grocery stores (bakkal) and supermarkets are open 9am-10pm daily. Most neighbourhoods will have a 24hr grocery store.

POLICE

See p224 **Emergencies**.
Crime is low in Istanbul. The main thing to beware of is bag-snatching and pickpocketing, especially in tourist areas like Sultanahmet, or crowded places such as Eminönü and Beyoğlu.

Single women can get hassled, but this is generally confined to verbal comments. That said, women should not wander around the quieter streets of Beyoğlu, Taksim or Tarlabaşı late at night unaccompanied.

The police have a reputation for incompetence, excessive use of force, and an appetite for back-handers – which they have generally deserved.

Tourist police
Yerebatan Caddesi 6, Sultanahmet (0212 527 4503, www.iem.gov.tr*). Tram Sultanahmet.* **Open** 24 hrs daily. **Map** p243 N10.
The place to report thefts, losses or scams. Most officers speak English.

POST

Post offices are recognisable by their yellow and black PTT signs.

Stamps can only be bought at post offices. Postcards cost TL0.70 to Europe, TL0.80 to the US and Australia. Airmail letters up to 50g cost TL1.50 to Europe, TL1.75 to the US and Australia.

For parcels, airmail rates start at TL39 to the UK, TL38 to the US, and TL45 to Australia for the first kg, with an extra TL8 , TL17 and TL24 respectively for every additional kg. Rates for surface mail are TL34 to the UK, TL24 to the US and TL29 to Australia.

The contents of all parcels will be inspected at the post office, so it's best not to seal them and bring tape with you.

Beyoğlu
Tom Tom Kaptan Sokak 22, off Yeni Çarşı Caddesi, Galatasaray (0212 252 0140, www.ptt.gov.tr). **Open** 8.30am-5pm Mon-Fri. **Map** p248 N3.

Sirkeci
Büyük Postane, Büyük Postane Caddesi 1/25 (0212 511 3818, www.ptt.gov.tr). **Open** 8.30am-5pm Mon-Fri. **Map** p243 N9.

Taksim
Cumhuriyet Caddesi 2 (0212 243 0284, www.ptt.gov.tr). **Open** 8.30am-5pm Mon-Fri. **Map** p249 P2.

Post restante

Poste restante mail should be sent to the central post office at Sirkeci, addressed as follows:

Recipient's name
Poste Restante
Büyük Postane
Büyük Postane Caddesi 1/25
Sirkeci
Istanbul

To collect mail, you need to bring your passport, and to pay a small fee for each letter that you receive.

RELIGION

Istanbul has a strong Jewish tradition and is still the home of the Greek and Armenian Orthodox Patriarchates.

Christian

Christ Church (Anglican)
Serdari Ekrem Sokak 52, Tünel, Beyoğlu (0212 251 5616, www.anglicansistanbul.blogspot.com). **Services** 9am, 6pm Mon-Sat; 9am,10am Sun. **Map** p248 N5.

Union Church of Istanbul (Protestant)
Postacılar Sokak, Beyoğlu (0212 244 5212, http://ucistanbul.org). **Services** 9.30am, 11am, 1.30pm, 3pm Sun. **Map** p248 N4.

St Anthony's (Catholic)
Istiklal Caddesi 325, Beyoğlu (0212 244 0935). **Open** 8am-7.30pm Mon-Sat, 9am-12.30pm and 3-7.30pm Sun. **Services** English 8am Mon-Sat, 10am Sun. **Map** p248 N3.

Haghia Triada (Greek Orthodox)
Meşelik Sokak 11/1, Taksim, Beyoğlu (0212 244 1358). **Services** Short 8.30am, 5pm daily (4pm in winter). Full-length 9am Sun. **Map** p249 O2.

Üç Horon (Gregorian Armenian)
Balık Pazarı, Sahne Sokak 24/A, Beyoğlu (0212 244 1382). **Open** 9am-5pm daily. **Services** 9.30am-1pm Tue; 9am-1pm Sun. **Map** p248 N3.

Jewish

Security at Istanbul's synagogues has been tight ever since two suicide bombings on synagogues in November 2003. To visit a synagogue, you must first obtain permission by telephoning 0212 292 0385. If you're attending prayers, it's sufficient to simply turn up with your passport. Prayers are usually held daily at 7.30am, with Shabbat services at 8am. Friday evening services take place at sunset.

Neve Shalom Synagogue
Büyük Hendek Caddesi 61, Galata, Beyoğlu (0212 293 7566, www.nevesalom.org). **Open** 9am-5pm Mon-Thur; 9am-1pm Fri.

SMOKING

A ban prohibits smoking in all indoor public spaces in Turkey. All public transport, public offices, banks, shops, restaurants, bars and cafés in Istanbul have been smoke-free since 2009.

STUDY

The most significant public universities are **Istanbul University**, Beyazıt (0212 440 0000, www.istanbul.edu.tr/english), **Boğaziçi University** (Bebek, 0212 359 540, www.boun.edu.tr) and **Galatasaray University** (Çırağan Caddesi 36, Ortaköy, 0212 227 4480, www.gsu.edu.tr).

Language courses

Turkish is taught at various private schools and colleges; many also offer individual tuition. All of the following schools offer daytime, evening and weekend classes. You can also find private tutors and notices for students seeking language exchanges posted on central bulletin boards within each of these centres.

Efinst Turkish Centre
F Blok, Aydın Sokak 12, off Korukent Yolu, Levent (0212 282 9064, www.turkishlesson.com).
Dilmer Language Teaching Centre
Tarık Zafer Tunaya Sokak 16, off Inönü Caddesi, Taksim (0212 292 9696, www.dilmer.com). **Map** p247 Q2.
Tömer Language School
Tel Sokak 47, off Istiklal Caddesi, Taksim (0212 249 1648, www.tomer.ankara.edu.tr). **Map** p249 O3.

TELEPHONES

Dialling & codes

Istanbul's districts have different area codes: 0212 for Europe; 0216 for Asia. You must use the code whenever you call the opposite shore, but when dialling from abroad omit the zero. The country code for Turkey is 90.

Mobile phones

There are three GSM networks: Turkcell, Vodaphone and Avea. If you bring your UK mobile, you'll have no problem using your phone as long as you've set up a roaming facility. However, because the Turkish system operates on 900 MHz, US mobile phones won't work.

A cheaper option is to invest in a local SIM card, or *hazır kart,* available through all the GSM operators. Find an authorised dealer, present your passport, and pay the subscription fee (around TL40-50), which includes roughly 25 minutes of talk-time within Turkey. Top-up cards are sold all over the place (look for the *hazir kart* sign) in units of TL5-TL300 (although exact available top-up amounts vary according to network).

It's essential to note that any Turkish SIM card will only work in your foreign mobile phone for approximately 15 days. After this period, your mobile will be blocked. The reasoning behind this annoying situation seems to be to encourage the purchase of Turkish mobile phones, which start around TL60. If you're travelling within Turkey for longer than two weeks, there is a way around buying a pricey brand-new mobile: you can register your foreign handset with the Turkish government at any Turkcell, Vodaphone or Avea store for free. In practice, however, almost all attempts to do so are bogged down in bureaucracy and are generally unsuccessful.

Operator services

Call 115 for the international operator. Directory assistance is 11811, but only in Turkish.

Public phones

Public phones now operate with pre-paid cards (*telefon kartı*). Some newer phones also take credit cards. Phone cards can be bought at post offices or, at a small premium, from street vendors and kiosks. They come in units of 50 (TL3.75), 100 (TL7.50), 200 (TL15) and 350 (TL19). Metered calls (*kontörlü*) can be placed at post offices or private phone and fax offices (*telefonşofisi*), but they charge over the odds.

Public phone rates are about TL1.20 a minute to the UK and US, TL1.80 to Australia. Reduced rates for international calls operate from 10pm to 9am Monday to Saturday, and all day Sunday and holidays. For local and national calls, cheap time is 8pm to 8am midweek and all weekend.

TIME

Turkey is two hours ahead of Greenwich Mean Time (GMT) and seven hours ahead of New York. There is no Turkish equivalent of am and pm, so the 24-hour clock is used. Daylight-saving runs from the last Sunday in March to the last Sunday in October.

TIPPING

Although not obligatory, the rule of thumb is to leave about ten per cent of the bill at cafés and restaurants. Service is occasionally included, in which case it'll say *servis dahil* at the bottom of the bill. If in doubt ask: '*Servis dahil mi?*' Tipping hotel staff, porters and hairdressers is discretionary, but TL1-TL2 is the norm. Hamam attendants expect more like 25 per cent. It's not necessary to tip taxi drivers.

TOILETS

Public toilets are plentiful. They'll be signposted 'WC' (when asking, use the term *tuvalet*); the gents' is *Bay*; the ladies' is *Bayan*. Public facilities often consist of a hole in the floor. Toilet paper in these places is a rarity, so carry a pack of tissues (*selpak*). City plumbing cannot cope with toilet paper, so use the bin provided. Hotels, bars and restaurants all have Western-style (*alafranga*) toilets.

TOURIST INFORMATION

The Ministry of Culture and Tourism has tourist information kiosks, where staff speak English, all over town. See www.gototurkey.co.uk for further information.

Atatürk Airport
International Arrivals (0212 663 0798). **Open** 24 hrs daily.
Beyazıt
Beyazıt Square (0212 522 4902). **Open** 9am-6pm daily. **Map** p242 K10.
Hilton Hotel
Cumhuriyet Caddesi, Şişli (0212 233 0592). **Open** 9am-5pm daily. **Map** p247 P1.
Karaköy Seaport
Karaköy Limanı Yolcu Salonu içi, Karaköy (0212 249 5776). **Open** 9am-5pm Mon-Sat. **Map** p246 N6.
Sirkeci Station
Istasyon Caddesi, Sirkeci (0212 511 5888). **Open** 9am-5pm daily. **Map** p243 N8.
Sultanahmet Square
Divan Yolu 3 (0212 518 1802). **Open** 9am-5pm daily. **Map** p243 N10.

International Turkish tourist offices

For additional international Turkish tourist offices, see www.goturkey.com

UK
4th Floor, 29-30 St James Street SW1A 1HB (+44 20 7839 7778, www.gototurkey.co.uk).
USA
821 United Nations Plaza, New York, NY 10017 (+1 212 687 2194, www.tourismturkey.org).

VISAS & IMMIGRATION

Visas are required by most nationalities; they can be bought at the airport upon arrival. At press time, rates were as follows: UK Ĺ10; USA $20; Canada $60; Australia $20; Ireland $20. New Zealanders don't need a visa. Fees must be paid in sterling, euros or dollars. Credit cards or travellers' cheques are not accepted. Visas are valid for three months. Overstaying your visa, even by a single day, will earn you a fine of around TL150 ($100) when you finally leave the country. *See right* for information on work visas.

If you have a work permit, you're automatically entitled to residence as long as your permit is valid. Otherwise, residence applications should be filed with the Turkish Consulate General in your country of residence. The laborious application procedure for British passport holders is detailed online at www.invest.gov.tr.

Upon arrival in Istanbul, you must register with the Foreigners' Branch (Yabancılar Şube Müdürlüğü, http://yabancilar.iem.gov.tr) at any local police station within one month of the visa/work permit being issued. Residence permits are valid for one or two years; you can also apply for a five-year permit. Expect to pay upwards of TL225.

WEIGHTS & MEASURES

The metric system is used.

WHEN TO GO

Between December and March Istanbul is cold, grey and blustery. Temperatures average 5C (42F), but humidity and windchill make it feel much colder. The city is usually buried under several feet of snow at least once every winter.

Summers can be oppressive; temperatures average 25-30C (78-88F) from June to August, occasionally rising beyond 35C (104F). The humidity can be draining during the day, but when it cool down at sunset people go to the Bosphorus to enjoy languid evenings at waterfront cafés.

The best weather is in spring and autumn, when days are temperate and evenings mild. Occasionally, poyraz, a chill Balkan wind, and *lodos*, hot, humid gusts from the south, can result in a 'four seasons in a single day' effect.

AVERAGE TEMPERATURES

MONTH	MINIMUM °C	MAXIMUM °C
January	3	8
February	2	9
March	3	11
April	7	16
May	12	21
June	16	25
July	18	28
August	19	28
September	16	24
October	13	20
November	9	15
December	5	11

Public & religious holidays

Turkey's five secular public holidays last one day each. Banks, offices and post offices are closed, but many shops stay open and public transport runs as usual.

Religious holidays are different. They last three or four days; if these happen to be midweek, the government often extends the holiday to cover the whole working week. The city shuts down as Istanbullus flock to the country. Coaches and flights are jammed.

Observance of Ramazan, the Islamic month of fasting, is widespread. Many Turks abstain from food, drink and cigarettes between sunrise and sunset. This has little impact on visitors, as most bars and restaurants remain open, but it's bad form to flaunt your non-participation by smoking or eating in the street, especially in religious districts, such as Fatih and Üsküdar. Here, Ramazan nights are the busiest of the year. At sundown, eateries are packed with large groups breaking their fast together. Sultanahmet Square turns into an extravaganza of food and music at twilight. The end of Ramazan is marked by the three-day Şeker Bayramı, or 'Sugar Holiday', when sweets are traditionally given to friends and family.

The main event in the Islamic calendar is Kurban Bayramı (the Feast of the Sacrifice), which marks Abraham's near-sacrifice of Isaac. Traditionally, families buy a *kurban*, which could be a sheep, bull, goat or camel, which they sacrifice on the first or second day of the feast. The meat is shared with relatives, neighbours and the poor. There are now stricter regulations on slaughtering sites and methods, which has reduced the bloodbath effect, but the faint-hearted are advised to keep away from mosques.

Islamic religious holidays are based on a lunar calendar, roughly 11 days shorter than the Gregorian (Western) calendar. Consequently, Islamic holidays shift forward by ten or 12 days each year.

New Year's Day (*Yılbaşı Günü*) 1 Jan.
National Sovereignty & Children's Day (*Ulusal Egemenlik ve Çocuk Bayramı*) 23 Apr.
Youth & Sports Day (*Gençlik ve Spor Bayramı*) 19 May.
Ramazan Holiday (*Ramazan Bayramı*) 20 July-18 Aug 2012; 9 July-7 Aug 2013.
Şeker Bayramı 19-21 Aug 2012; 8-10 Aug 2012.
Victory Day (*Zafer Bayramı*) 30 Aug.
The Feast of the Sacrifice (*Kurban Bayramı*) 24-28 Oct 2012; 14-18 Oct 2013.
Republic Day (*Cumhuriyet Bayramı*) 29 Oct.

WOMEN

Few special rules apply for women in Istanbul. With some provisos, you needn't dress any differently than at home, certainly not in the more European areas such as Beyoğlu. Probably best to leave the micro minis and short shorts at home, though. To avoid being stared at, wear trousers or skirts that come to the knee. And in more conservative areas, and particularly in mosques and churches, keep your shoulders covered.

In touristy areas you may get hit on. It's usually harmless, but all the same it can be annoying. It's also generally easy to shrug off. Avoid eye contact; don't beam wide smiles. Don't respond to invitations, come-ons or obnoxious comments. If a man is persistent and in your face, try saying 'Ayıp', literally 'shame on you'. Chances are someone will intervene on your behalf. It seldom extends beyond that, but should you need help, the word is '*Imdat*'.

WORK

Work permits can only be obtained through a sponsoring employer. In principle, your job should only be doable by a foreigner. Getting the permit is a long, bureaucratic process. First, the employer submits an application for authorisation to the Treasury in Ankara. This stage can take a couple of months. You then submit your own application to the Turkish Consulate General in your country of residence (which shouldn't be Turkey) and wait about six weeks for it to be processed. When it's ready, you must collect it from the consulate in person with your passport. Back in Turkey, you still need a residence permit (*see left* **Visas & immigration**).

DIRECTORY

Vocabulary

Making the effort to use a few phrases will be greatly appreciated. For information on language courses *see p227*.

PRONUNCIATION

All words are written phonetically and except ğ there are no silent letters; so post office, *postane*, is pronounced 'post-a-neh'. Syllables are articulated with equal stress. The key is to master the pronunciation of the few letters and vowels that differ from English:

c – like the 'j' in jam; so cami (mosque) is 'jami'
ç – like the 'ch' in chip, so çiçek (flower) is 'chi-check'
ğ – silent, but lengthens preceding vowel
ı – an 'uh', like the 'a' in cinema
ö – like the 'ir' in girdle
ş – like the 'sh' in shop, so şiş (as in kebab) is pronounced 'shish'
ü – as in the French 'tu'

ACCOMMODATION

air-conditioning klima
bathroom banyo
bed yatak
bed & breakfast pansiyon
breakfast kahvaltı
double bed çift kişilik yatak
hotel otel
no vacancies yer yok
room oda
shower duş
soap sabun
towel havlu
vacancy yer var

DAYS OF THE WEEK

Monday pazartesi
Tuesday salı
Wednesday çarşamba
Thursday perşembe
Friday cuma
Saturday cumartesi
Sunday pazar

EMERGENCIES

accident kaza
ambulance ambülans
doctor doktor
fire yangın
help! imdat!
hospital hastane
medication ilaç
pharmacy eczane
police polis
sick hasta

ESSENTIALS

a lot/very/too çok
and ve
bad/badly kötü
big büyük
but ama/fakat
good/well iyi
I don't speak Turkish Türkçe bilmiyorum
I don't understand anlayamadım
leave me alone (quite forceful) beni rahat bırak
Mr/Mrs bey/hanım (with first name)
no hayır
OK tamam
or veya
please lütfen
small küçük
sorry pardon
thank you teşekkürler/mersi/sağol
yes evet
this/that bu/şu

GETTING AROUND

airport havalimanı
bus otobüs
bus/coach station otogar
car park otopark
entrance giriş
exit çıkış
left sol
map harita
no parking park yapılmaz
petrol benzin
platform peron
right sağ
road yol
station gar
street sokak
train tren

GREETINGS

good morning günaydın
good afternoon/goodbye iyi günler
good evening/goodbye iyi akşamlar
good night/goodbye iyi geceler
goodbye güle güle (to the person leaving)
hello merhaba

QUESTIONS

do you have change? bozuk paranız var mı?
do you speak English? ingilizce biliyor musunuz?
how? nasıl?
what? ne?
when? ne zaman?
where? nerede?
where to? nereye?
which (one)? hangi(si)?
who? kim?
why? niye/niçin/neden?

SHOPPING

bank banka
cheap ucuz
credit card kredi kartı
expensive pahalı
how many? kaç tane?
how much (price)? kaç para?
I would like....istiyorum...
is there/are there any? var mı?
post office postane/PTT
price fiyat
stamp pul
till receipt fiş

SIGHTSEEING

castle kale
church kilise
closed kapalı
free bedava/ücretsiz
open açık
mosque cami
museum müze
palace saray
reduced price indirimli
ticket bilet

TIME

at what time? saat kaçta gün
hour saat
minute dakika
today bugün
tomorrow yarın
week hafta
what time is it? saat kaç?
when? ne zaman?
yesterday dün

NUMBERS

0 sıfır; 1 bir; 2 iki; 3 üç; 4 dört; 5 beş; 6 altı; 7 yedi; 8 sekiz; 9 dokuz; 10 on; 11 onbir; 12 oniki; 20 yirmi; 21 yirmibir; 22 yirmiiki; 30 otuz; 40 kırk; 50 elli; 60 altmış; 70 yetmiş; 80 seksen; 90 doksan; 100 yüz; 1,000 bin; 1,000,000 milyon; 1,000,000,000 milyar.

Further Reference

BOOKS

Istanbul has a lively literary scene. Authors whose work has been translated include Turkey's national poet, **Nazım Hikmet**, and award-winning fiction writers **Orhan Pamuk** (*see p71* **The City's Narrator**) and **Yaşar Kemal**. Most of the titles listed here are available in Istanbul.

Fiction

Ali, Tariq *The Stone Woman* (2000)
Historical novel by former Trotskyist activist in which an Ottoman noble family observes the decay of the empire.

Christie, Agatha *Murder on the Orient Express* (1934)
One of the passengers of the fabled train is bumped off.

de Souza, Daniel *Under A Crescent Moon* (1989)
True-life tale of a guy banged up in Istanbul for drug smuggling.

Greene, Graham *Stamboul Train* (1932)
Lesser yarn about a bunch of characters crossing central Europe on the Orient Express. Greene's advance wouldn't stretch beyond Cologne, so all the eastern detail was cribbed from Baedeker.

Kemal, Yashar *Memed, My Hawk* (1961)
The book that established Kemal as one of Turkey's greatest contemporary writers is a gritty insight into Turkish rural life.

Nadel, Barbara *Death by Design* (2010)
The latest in a series of Inspector Ikmen thrillers, this Istanbul crime novel takes on local counterfeiting and terrorist conspiracy.

Pamuk, Orhan *Museum of Innocence* (2006)
A sensation in his native Istanbul, Pamuk scooped the Nobel Prize for Literature in 2006. This tale of romantic longing is set in Istanbul during the late 1970s.

Unsworth, Barry *The Rage of the Vulture* (1982)
Booker Prize-winner Unsworth once taught English in Istanbul. His detailed imagery enriches this tale of political intrigue, as the 'vultures of Europe' circle the dying Ottoman Empire.

Non-fiction

Ashman, Anastasia M & Eaton Gökmen, Jennifer *Tales from the Expat Harem (2006)*
Reflections on local culture by female expats

Beck, Christa & Fausting, Christiane *Istanbul: An Architectural Guide (*1997)

Brownworth, Lars *Lost to the West: The Forgotten Byzantine Empire That Rescued Western Civilization (2008)*
Gazetteer of nearly 100 of the city's most significant buildings.

Hellier, Chris & Venturi, Franscesco *Splendors of Istanbul: Houses and Palaces Along the Bosphorus* (1993)
Glossy photos of the interiors of lavish waterside mansions.

Hull, Alastair & Luczyc-Wyhowska, Jose *Kilims: The Complete Guide* (2000)
A lavish but practical large-format paperback.

Hutchings, Roger & Rugman, Jonathan *Atatürk's Children: Turkey and the Kurds* (2001)
One of the best books on an explosive national issue – the conflict in the country's south-east.

Kinzer, Stephen *Crescent and Star* (2002)
Opinionated and engaging account of contemporary Turkey by the former *New York Times* correspondent for Istanbul.

Mango, Andrew *Atatürk* (2002)
Latest in a long line of Atatürk bios.

Mansel, Philip *Constantinople: City of the World's Desire* (1996)
Grand discourse on the rise and fall of the imperial capital.

Norwich, John Julius *A Short History of Byzantium* (1998)
A tour of the Byzantine Empire's history, which captures every tawdry and riveting detail.

Orga, Irfan *Portrait of a Turkish Family* (1989)
A haunting autobiography that follows a wealthy Istanbul family's demise following World War I, offering insight into Turkey's transition from empire to republic.

Pope, Hugh & Nicole *Turkey Unveiled* (2000)
Balanced assessment of the contemporary political and cultural landscape by two long-term Istanbul journalists.

Procopius *The Secret History* (1982)
The first-century Byzantine historian wrote the official biography of Justinian; in these salacious diaries, he gives his own, account of the tyrannical emperor.

Travel

Freely, John & Sumner-Boyd, Hilary *Strolling Through Istanbul* (2003)
A companion for city wandering, with an emphasis on history and architecture from the Byzantine to the Ottoman age

Kelly, Laurence (ed) *Istanbul: A Traveller's Companion* (1987)
Historical writings and travellers' tales covering places, people, courtly life, and social diversions.

Montagu, Mary Wortley *Turkish Embassy Letters* (1763)
London socialite Lady Montagu was a diplomatic wife in Istanbul from 1716-18 and an amusing correspondent, equally at home with court politics and harem gossip.

FILM

Journey Into Fear
(Norman Foster, 1942)
World War II spy thriller co-written, produced by and starring Orson Welles.

Istanbul (Joseph Pevney, 1957)
Suspected diamond smuggler (Errol Flynn) returns to Istanbul to find his old flame, whom he thought was dead, is still alive.

From Russia with Love
(Terence Young, 1962)
'He seems fit enough. Have him report to me in Istanbul in 24 hours.' 007 casually dispatches Eastern Bloc assailants in various tourist spots and gets to shag two wrestling gypsies.

America, America
(Elia Kazan, 1963)
Autobiographical film (Kazan was born in Istanbul) picturing the working-class neighbourhoods of Istanbul through the eyes of the director's uncle.

Topkapı (Jules Dassin, 1964)
Caper movie in which a small-time con-man (Peter Ustinov) gets mixed up in a big-time jewellery heist. Good fun, and Istanbul looks stunning.

Murder on the Orient Express (Sidney Lumet, 1974)
Albert Finney, Lauren Bacall, Ingrid Bergman, Sean Connery and John Gielgud ham it up something rotten.
Midnight Express (Alan Parker, 1978)
Still misshaping views of Turkey and the Turks thirty years on. A great movie? Perhaps, but an inexcusably racist one.
Pascali's Island (James Dearden, 1988)
Based on a novel by Barry Unsworth. Pascali (Ben Kingsley) is a spy for the Ottoman sultanate.
Hamam (Ferzan Ozpetek, 1996)
Italian man visits Istanbul, repairs bathhouse, falls for local boy. A gorgeously photographed, lushly scored ethno-homo romp.
In This World (Michael Winterbottom, 2002)
Account of two Afghans smuggled across countless borders between Pakistan and Britain, featuring dingy sweat-shop scenes in Istanbul.
Tinker Tailor Soldier Spy (Tomas Alfredson, 2011)
Gary Oldman and Colin Firth reinterpret Le Carré's classic.
Skyfall (Sam Mendes, 2012)
Daniel Craig and Javier Bardem on the ancient Istanbul streets.

MUSIC

Rock and pop releases on local labels are not widely available outside Turkey, but traditional Turkish music can be tracked down in specialist stores. Two fine labels are Kalan Music (www.kalan.com) and Traditional Crossroads (www.rootsworld.com). Golden Horn (www.goldenhorn.com), based in California, has a decent catalogue of traditional Turkish music and jazz.

Fasıl

There are few *fasıl* recordings on the market. Generally, the older the recording, the better. Look out for albums by Müzeyyen Senar, Zeki Müren and newcomer Muazzez Erso, and reissues by Hamiyet Yüceses and Safiye Ayla.

Zeki Müren *1955-63 Recordings* (Kalan)
Gorgeous melodies complemented by Müren's alto voice.

Folk music

Bosphorus *Balkan Dusleri* (Ada Müzik)
Turkish classical musicians revive the Istanbul Greek repertoire.
Ali Ekber Çiçek *Klasikleri* (Mega Müzik)
One of the most respected exponents of the saz.
Mehmet Erenler *Mehmet Erenler ve Bozlakları* (Folk Müzik Center)
Anything by saz maestro Erenler is worth picking up.
Neşet Ertaş (Kalan)
A collection of work by Ertaş, a cult figure on the Turkish folk scene.
Muhabbet *Volumes 1-7* (Kalan)
Fantastic *aşık* – Alevi mystical songs – performed by top names.

Ottoman, classical & court music

Erol Deran *Solo Kanun* (Mega)
This is what Turkish classical music should be: subtle and virtuosic.
Emirgan Assemble *Klasik Osmanlı Müziği* (Kalan)
A sampler of Ottoman instrumental works, featuring *kemençe, ud, kanun, ney* and percussion.
Kani Karaca *Kani Karaca* (Kalan)
Something of a national treasure, Karaca is a hafız, someone who can recite the Koran from memory, with voice bound to raise goosebumps.
Various *Gazeller 1&2* (Kalan)
Amazing archival recordings of traditional vocal improvisations, rescued from ancient 78rpm vinyl.
Various *Lalezar* (Istanbul Büyük Belediye)
Four-CD set of Ottoman music, including compositions by sultans and imperial dance music.

Rock & pop

Sezen Aksu *Serçe* (EMI)
The glitzy queen of pop churns out an album every two years, but this, her 1978 debut, is still her best.
Ceza *Med Cezir* (Hammer Müzik)
Ceza's intense lyrical flurries kick-started the Turkish hip-hop scene.
Cem Karaca *Best of* (Yavuz ve Burç Plakçilik)
A prominent – and still beloved – rocker from the 1960s until his death in 2004.
Erkin Koray *Şaşkın* (Kalite Ticaret)
Great intro to Turkish psychedelia by one of its leading lights.
Barış Mançolo *Mançoloği* (Stereo)
Anatolian rocker turned TV celeb whose early death immortalised him as a legend of Turkish rock.
Erkan Oğur *Fuad* (Kalan)
Erkan brings jazz and blues to Turkish instruments and melodies – or vice versa.
Tarkan *Dudu* (Istanbul Plak)
The sound of Istanbul for a huge percentage of its population.
Various *East2West* (Doublemoon)
An eclectic, jazz-soaked sampler from the Doublemoon label.

Roma (Gypsy)

Ciguli *Ciguli* (Dost)
Accordion-led recording that made Ahmet Ciguli a star.
Roman Oyun Havaları *Volumes 1 & 2* (EMI-Kent)
Istanbul's top Roma session musicians thump out dance tunes.
Mustafa Kandıralı *Caz Roman* (World Network)
The 'Benny Goodman of Turkey', with cameos from other famous *fasıl* musicians.
Selim Sesler & Grup Trakya *The Road to Keşan* (Traditional Crossroads)
Songs and dances from Keşan, a Roma town on the Turkish-Greek border. Excellent sleeve notes.

Sufi religious

Asitane *Simurg* (Istanbul Ajans)
A young ensemble featuring *tanbur, kemençe, ney* and *bendir*.
Mercan Dede *Secret Tribe Nar* (Doublemoon)
Mercan Dede (aka DJ Arkın Allen) splices traditional mystic instruments with electronica.
Doğan Ergin *Sufi Music of Turkey Vol 2* (Mega)
Meditative improvisations.
Music of the Whirling Dervishes *Sufi Music of Turkey* (Mega)
Music to twirl by.
Various Mevlana *Dede Efendi* (Kalan)
1963 recording featuring some of the finest performers of the genre.

WEBSITES

Great Buildings Online
www.greatbuildings.com
Take a virtual tour of Haghia Sophia or explore Sinan's masterpieces.
Istanbul Food
www.istanbulfood.com
Culinary insiders guide
Istanbul City Guide
www.istanbulcityguide.com
English-language listings updated daily, plus features and news.
Turkey Travel Planner
www.turkeytravelplanner.com
A comprehensive aid for organising your travels through Turkey.
The World Factbook – Turkey
www.cia.gov
The CIA's factual take on Turkey.
Foreign & Commonwealth Office – Turkey www.fco.gov.uk
The UK government's advice.

Content Index

Venue Index

★ **indicates a critic's choice**

INDEX

INDEX

N

O

P

R

S

T

U

V

W

X

Y

Z

Advertisers' Index

Please refer to the relevant pages for contact details.

Maps

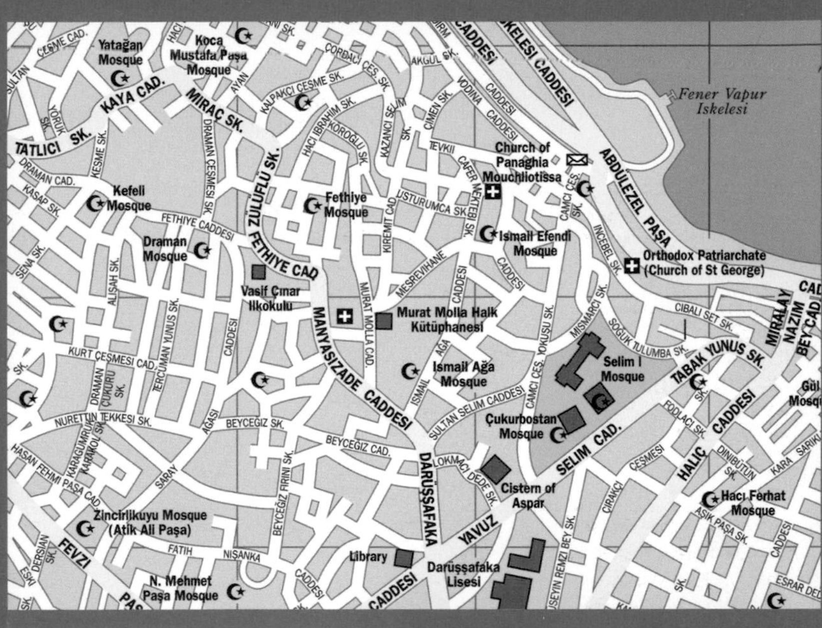

Major sight or landmark	
Hospital or college	
Railway station	
Parks	
River	
Motorway	
Main road	
Main road tunnel	
Pedestrian road	
Steps	
City Wall	
Tram	
Airport	
Church	
Mosque	
Metro station	M
Area name	FATIH

Istanbul Overview

ŞIŞLI
NIŞANTAŞI
MECIDIYE
Atatürk Museum
HALASKARGAZI CADDESI
VALIKONAĞI CADDESI
TEŞVIKIYE CADDESI
ABDI IPEKÇI CADDESI
BARBAROS CADDESI
Malta Köşkü
Yıldız Palace
Yıldız Park
TEŞVIKIYE
British Council
Imperial Porcelain Factory
To Ortaköy
Bentley Hotel
Cemal Reşit Rey Concert Hall
Military Museum
Lütfi Kırdar Concert Hall
Harbiye Open-air Theatre
KURTULUŞ CADDESI
HARBIYE
KADIRGALAR GEÇIDI
MÜVEZZI CAD.
ÇIRAĞAN CADDESI
Çırağan Palace Hotel Kempinski
BEŞIKTAŞ CADDESI
Naval Museum
Mimar Sinan Museum of Fine Arts
Dolmabahçe Palace
BEŞIKTAŞ
YENIŞEHIR DERE CADDESI
TARLABAŞI BULVARI
TAKSIM SQUARE
ISTIKLAL CADDESI
KABATAŞ
BEYOĞLU
NECATIBEY CADDESI
Bosphorus (Borazici)
TOPHANE
PAŞA LIMANI CADDESI
See p250
KARAKÖY
SAHIL YOLU
DOĞANCILAR CADDESI
Leander's Tower
ÜSKÜDAR
TOPTAŞI CADDESI
GÜNDOĞUMU CADDESI
ÜSKÜDAR - HAREM SAHIL YOLU
Sirkeci
Sirkeci Station
Topkapı Place
Gülhane
KENNEDY CADDESI (SAHIL YOLU)
Haghia Sophia
YOLU
SULTANAHMET
Cankurtaran Station
HAREM
DOKTOR EYÜP AKSOY CADDESI
Harem Bus Terminal
Florence Nightingale Museum
Selimye Barracks
TIBBIYE CADDESI
SELIMYE
Sea of Marmara
(Marmara Denizi)
See p251
Haydarpaşa Station

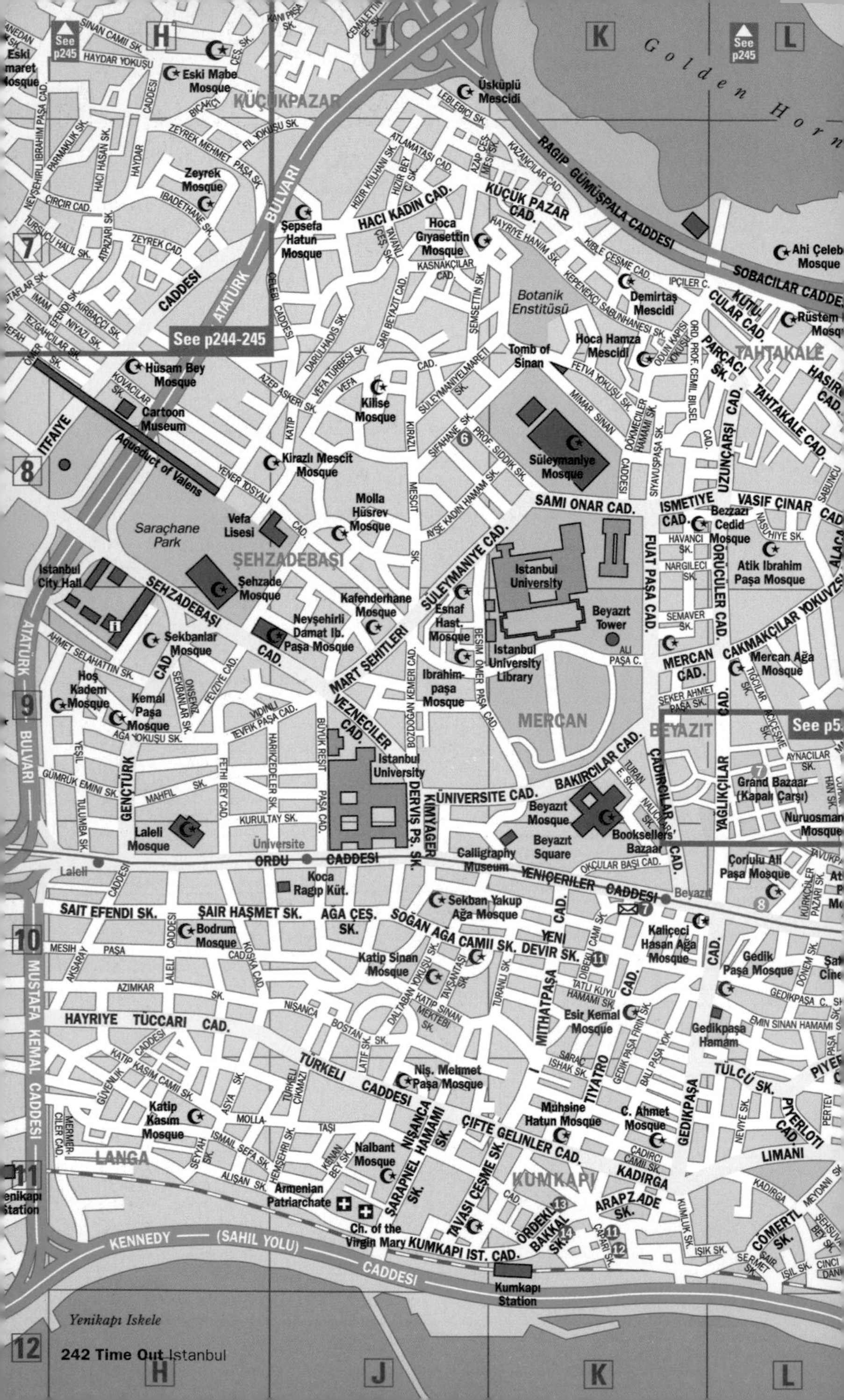
Golden Horn
Küçükpazar
Şehzadebaşı
Mercan
Beyazıt
Tahtakale
Langa
Kumkapı
Süleymaniye Mosque
Istanbul University
Grand Bazaar (Kapalı Çarşı)
Aqueduct of Valens
Saraçhane Park
Istanbul City Hall
Botanik Enstitüsü
Tomb of Sinan
Beyazıt Tower
Beyazıt Mosque
Beyazıt Square
Booksellers' Bazaar
Calligraphy Museum
Laleli Mosque
Cartoon Museum
Armenian Patriarchate
Ch. of the Virgin Mary
Kumkapı Station
Yenikapı Iskele
Atatürk Bulvarı
Mustafa Kemal Caddesi
Kennedy (Sahil Yolu) Caddesi
Ordu Caddesi
Yeniçeriler Caddesi
See p244-245
See p245

South of the Golden Horn

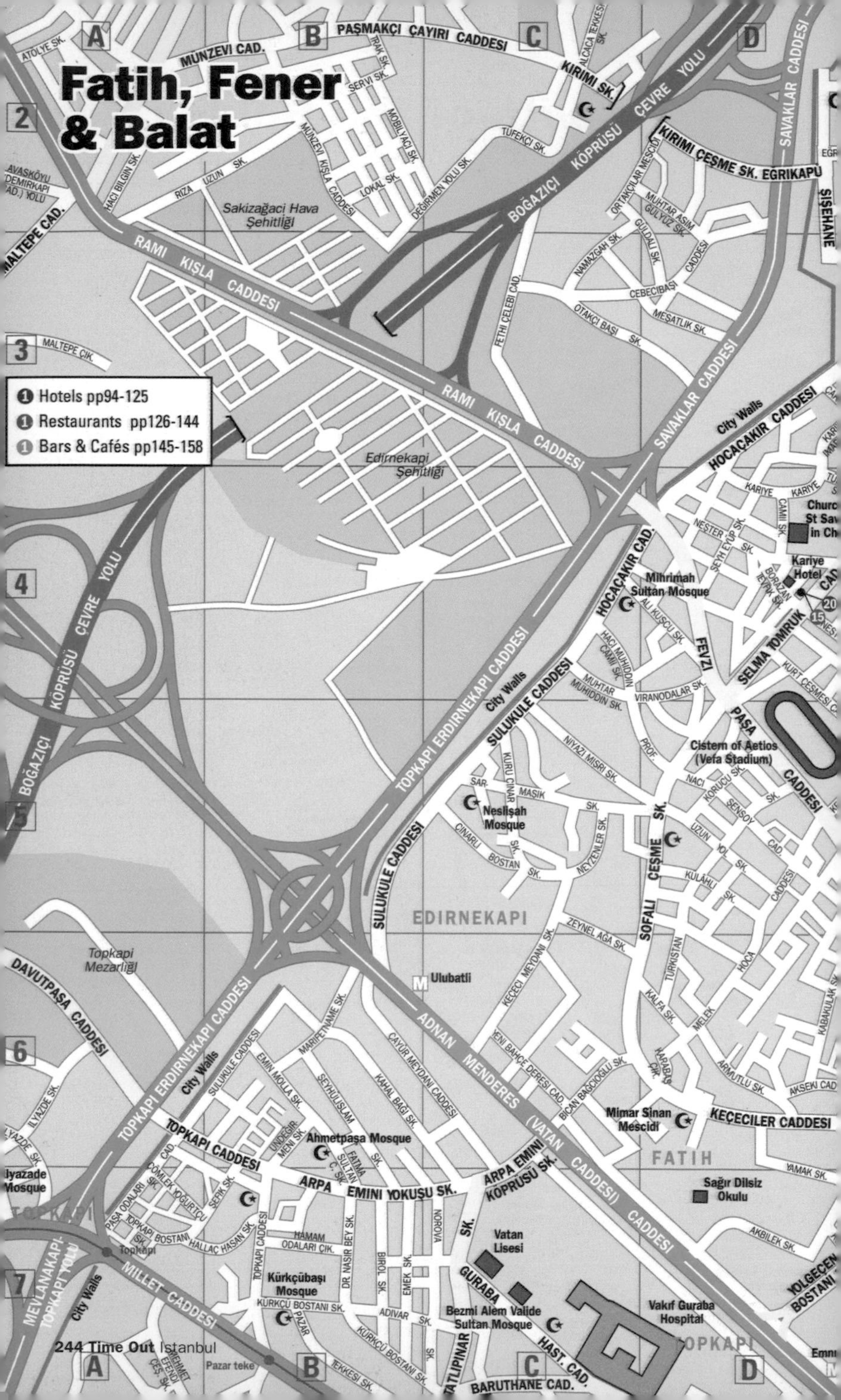

Fatih, Fener & Balat
Hotels pp94-125
Restaurants pp126-144
Bars & Cafés pp145-158
A
B
C
D
2
3
4
5
6
7
ATOLYE SK.
MUNZEVI CAD.
PAŞMAKÇI ÇAYIRI CADDESI
ALCACA TEKKESI SK.
KIRIMI SK.
SERVI SK.
TRAK SK.
MOBILYACI SK.
MUNZEVI KIŞLA CADDESI
LOKAL SK.
DEĞIRMEN YOLU SK.
TÜFEKÇI SK.
KIRIMI ÇEŞME SK.
EGRIKAPU
SAVAKLAR CADDESI
ŞIŞEHANE
HACI BILGIN SK.
RIZA UZUN SK.
Sakizağaci Hava Şehitliği
MALTEPE CAD.
RAMI KIŞLA CADDESI
BOĞAZIÇI KÖPRÜSÜ ÇEVRE YOLU
ORTAKÇILAR MESCIDI
MUHTAR ASIM GÜLYÜZ SK.
NAMAZGAH SK.
GÜLDALI SK.
CEBECIBAŞI CADDESI
FETHI ÇELEBI CAD.
OTAKÇI BAŞI SK.
MEŞATLIK SK.
MALTEPE ÇIK.
Edirnekapi Şehitliği
City Walls
HOCAÇAKIR CADDESI
KARIYE
CAMII SK.
Church St Saviour in Chora
NEŞTER SK.
ŞEYH EYÜP SK.
BORAZAN TEVFIK SK.
Kariye Hotel
HOCAÇAKIR CAD.
Mihrimah Sultan Mosque
ALI KUŞÇU SK.
HACI MUHIDDIN CAMII SK.
FEVZI PAŞA CADDESI
SELMA TOMRUK
KURT ÇEŞMESI
MUHTAR MUHIDDIN SK.
VIRANODALAR SK.
SULUKULE CADDESI
TOPKAPI ERDIRNEKAPI CADDESI
NIYAZI MISRI SK.
PROF.
Cistern of Aetios (Vefa Stadium)
NACI
KORUCU SK.
SENSOY
KURU ÇINAR SK.
MAŞIK
Neslişah Mosque
ÇINARLI BOSTAN SK.
NEYZENLER SK.
SOFALI ÇEŞME SK.
UZUN YOL SK.
KULAHLI SK.
EDIRNEKAPI
ZEYNEL AĞA SK.
KEÇECI MEYDANI SK.
TURKISTAN
HOCA
KALFA SK.
MELEK
Topkapi Mezarliği
DAVUTPAŞA CADDESI
Ulubatli
ADNAN MENDERES (VATAN CADDESI) CADDESI
MARIFETNAME SK.
ÇAYÜR MEYDANI CADDESI
KAHAL BAĞI SK.
EMIN MOLLA SK.
ŞEYHÜLISLAM
YENI BAHÇE DERESI CAD.
BICAN BAĞCIOĞLU SK.
HARABI ÇIK.
ARMUTLU SK.
AKSEKI CAD.
KABAKULAK SK.
Mimar Sinan Mescidi
KEÇECILER CADDESI
FATIH
YAMAK SK.
Sağır Dilsiz Okulu
ILYAZDE SK.
Ilyazade Mosque
TOPKAPI CADDESI
UNDEĞIRMENI SK.
Ahmetpaşa Mosque
FATMA SULTAN C. SK.
ARPA EMINI YOKUŞU SK.
ARPA EMINI KÖPRÜSÜ SK.
ÇÖMLEK YOĞURTÇU
SEFIK SK.
PAŞA ODALARI SK.
TOPKAPI BOSTANI SK.
HALLAÇ HASAN SK.
TOPKAPI
Topkapi
HAMAM ODALARI ÇIK.
TOPKAPI CADDESI
DR. NASIR BEY SK.
BIROL SK.
EMEK SK.
NOROVA
Vatan Lisesi
AKBILEK SK.
YOLGEÇEN BOSTANI SK.
MILLET CADDESI
MEVLANAKAPI-TOPKAPI YOLU
Kürkçübaşı Mosque
KURKÇU BOSTANI SK.
ADIVAR SK.
PAZAR
GURABA HAST. CAD.
Bezmi Alem Valide Sultan Mosque
Vakıf Guraba Hospital
TATLIPINAR
BARUTHANE CAD.
Pazar teke
TEKKESI SK.
MEHMET EFENDI ÇEŞ. SK.

Golden Horn
(Haliç)
Balat Vapur Iskelesi
Fener Vapur Iskelesi
Camialtı Shipyard
Aynalı Kavak Kasrı
Musevi Hastanesi
Church of Hiresdagabet
Ahrida Synagogue
FENER
St Stephen of the Bulgars
Church of Panaghia Mouchliotissa
Orthodox Patriarchate (Church of St George)
Yatağan Mosque
Koca Mustafa Paşa Mosque
Kefeli Mosque
Fethiye Mosque
Ismail Efendi Mosque
Draman Mosque
Vasif Çınar Ilkokulu
Ilkokulu
Murat Molla Halk Kütüphanesi
Ismail Ağa Mosque
Selim I Mosque
Çukurbostan Mosque
Gül Mosque
Cistern of Aspar
Hacı Ferhat Mosque
Zincirlikuyu Mosque (Atik Ali Paşa)
Library
Darüşşafaka Lisesi
N. Mehmet Paşa Mosque
Kumrulu Mosque
Altay Mosque
Fatih Sarıçlar
Mesih Ali Paşa Mosque
Yeni Doğan Mosque
Eski Imaret Mosque
Eski Mabed Mosque
Zeyrek Mosque
Fatih Mosque
Bali Paşa Mosque
OLD GALATA BRIDGE
DEMIRHISAR CADDESI
AYVANSARAY CAD.
BALAT VAPUR ISKELESI CADDESI
MÜRSEL PAŞA CADDESI
ABDÜLEZEL PAŞA CADDESI
FEVZI PAŞA CAD.
YAVUZ SELIM CADDESI
DARÜŞŞAFAKA CADDESI
ISLAMBOL CADDESI
HALIÇ CADDESI
MANYASIZADE CADDESI
FETHIYE CAD.
SELIM CAD.
KEÇECILER CAD.
HIRKAI ŞERIF CAD.
AKŞEMSETTIN CADDESI
AKDENIZ CADDESI
TABAK YUNUS SK.
MIRALAY NAZIM BEY CAD.
OKMEYDANI CAD.
AYNALI KAVAK CAD.
KASIMPAŞA HASKÖY
ITFAIYE CADDESI
ATATÜRK BULVARI
0 400 m
0 400 yds
See p242
E F G H
2 3 4 5 6 7

Beyoğlu
KURTULUŞ
TEPEBAŞI
ASMALIMESCIT
TÜNEL
ŞIŞHANE
GALATA
TOPHANE
DOLAPDERE CADDESI
ATATÜRK BRIDGE
Hasan Paşa Park
Kasımpaşa Stadı
UK Consulate
Istanbul Arts Centre (Theatre)
Bedreddin Mosque
Kasım Paşa Mosque
Büyük Kasımpaşa Mosque
Galatasaray Square
Galatasaray Lycée
St Anthony of Padua
Büyük Londra Hotel
Armenian Church of the Holy Trinity
Pera Palas Hotel
Pera Museum
Palais de France
Russian Consulate
Tomtom Kaptan Mosque
St Mary Draperis
Swedish Consulate
Christ Church
Galata Mevlevihanesi
Okçu Musa Mosque
Galata Tower
Hoca Ali Mosque
Azapkapı Çeşmesi
Azapkapı Sokullu M. Paşa Mosque
Arap Mosque
SS Peter & Paul
Beyoğlu Hospital
Church of St Benoit
Church of St Panagia
Jewish Museum
Kemankeş Must. Paşa Mosque
Yeraltı Mosque
Fish Market
Karaköy Square
See p242

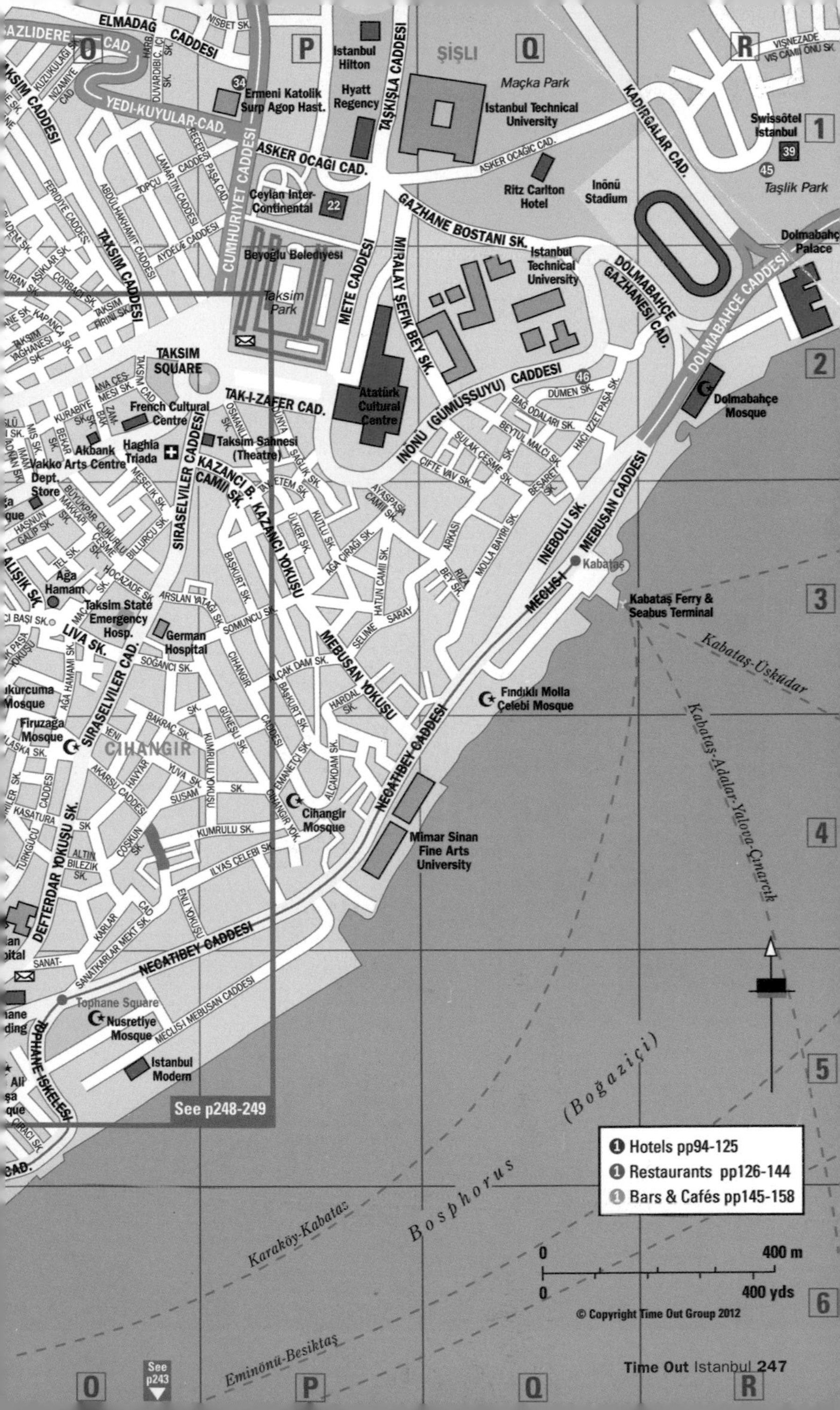

O
P
Q
R
1
2
3
4
5
6
ELMADAĞ CADDESI
NISBET SK.
BAZLIDERE CAD.
KUZUKULAĞI SK.
NIZAMIYE CAD.
TAKSIM CADDESI
HARBIYE
DUVARDIBIÇ İÇİ SK.
YEDI-KUYULAR-CAD.
Istanbul Hilton
Hyatt Regency
Ermeni Katolik Surp Agop Hast.
TAŞKIŞLA CADDESI
ŞIŞLI
Maçka Park
Istanbul Technical University
KADIRGALAR CAD.
VIŞNEZADE
VIŞ CAMII ÖNÜ SK.
Swissôtel Istanbul
Taşlik Park
ASKER OCAĞI CAD.
ASKER OCAĞIC CAD.
Ritz Carlton Hotel
Inönü Stadium
Ceylan Inter-Continental
CUMHURIYET CADDESI
RECEP PAŞA CAD.
TOPÇU CADDESI
LAMARTIN CADDESI
FERIDIYE CADDESI
ABDÜLHAKHAMIT CADDESI
AYDEDE CADDESI
GAZHANE BOSTANI SK.
Beyoğlu Belediyesi
MIRALAY ŞEFIK BEY SK.
METE CADDESI
Dolmabahçe Palace
DOLMABAHÇE GAZHANESI CAD.
DOLMABAHÇE CADDESI
Taksim Park
TAKSIM CADDESI
TAKSIM FIRINI SK.
TAKSIM SQUARE
TAK-I-ZAFER CAD.
Atatürk Cultural Centre
INÖNÜ (GÜMÜŞSUYU) CADDESI
DÜMEN SK.
BAĞ ODALARI SK.
BEYTÜL MALCI SK.
HACI İZZET PAŞA SK.
Dolmabahçe Mosque
French Cultural Centre
Akbank Arts Centre
Haghia Triada
Taksim Sahnesi (Theatre)
Vakko Dept. Store
SIRASELVILER CADDESI
KAZANCI B. CAMII SK.
KAZANCI YOKUŞU
SULAK ÇEŞME SK.
ÇIFTE VAV SK.
BESARET SK.
INEBOLU SK.
MEBUSAN CADDESI
AYASPAŞA CAMII SK.
AĞA ÇIRAĞI SK.
ARKASI
MOLLA BAYIRI SK.
RIZA BEY SK.
Kabataş
MECLIS-I
Kabataş Ferry & Seabus Terminal
Kabataş-Üsküdar
Ağa Hamam
Taksim State Emergency Hosp.
German Hospital
LIVA SK.
ARSLAN YATAĞI SK.
SOMUNCU SK.
SOĞANCI SK.
MEBUSAN YOKUŞU
SELIME
SARAY
HATUN CAMII SK.
ALÇAK DAM SK.
Fındıklı Molla Çelebi Mosque
Kabataş-Adalar-Yalova-Çınarcık
Firuzağa Mosque
SIRASELVILER CAD.
CIHANGIR
BAKRAÇ SK.
AKARSU CADDESI
HAVYAR
YUVA SK.
SUSAM
KUMRULU YOKUŞU
Cihangir Mosque
ALÇAKDAM SK.
EMANETÇI SK.
NECATIBEY CADDESI
Mimar Sinan Fine Arts University
DEFTERDAR YOKUŞU SK.
KASATURA
TÜRKGÜCÜ
ALTIN BILEZIK SK.
ÇOŞKUN SK.
KUMRULU SK.
ILYAS ÇELEBI SK.
ENLI YOKUŞU
KARLAR
SANATKARLAR MEKT SK.
NECATIBEY CADDESI
Tophane Square
Nusretiye Mosque
MECLIS-I MEBUSAN CADDESI
Istanbul Modern
TOPHANE ISKELESI
See p248-249
(Boğaziçi)
Bosphorus
Karaköy-Kabataş
Eminönü-Besiktaş
See p243
❶ Hotels pp94-125
❶ Restaurants pp126-144
❶ Bars & Cafés pp145-158
0
400 m
0
400 yds

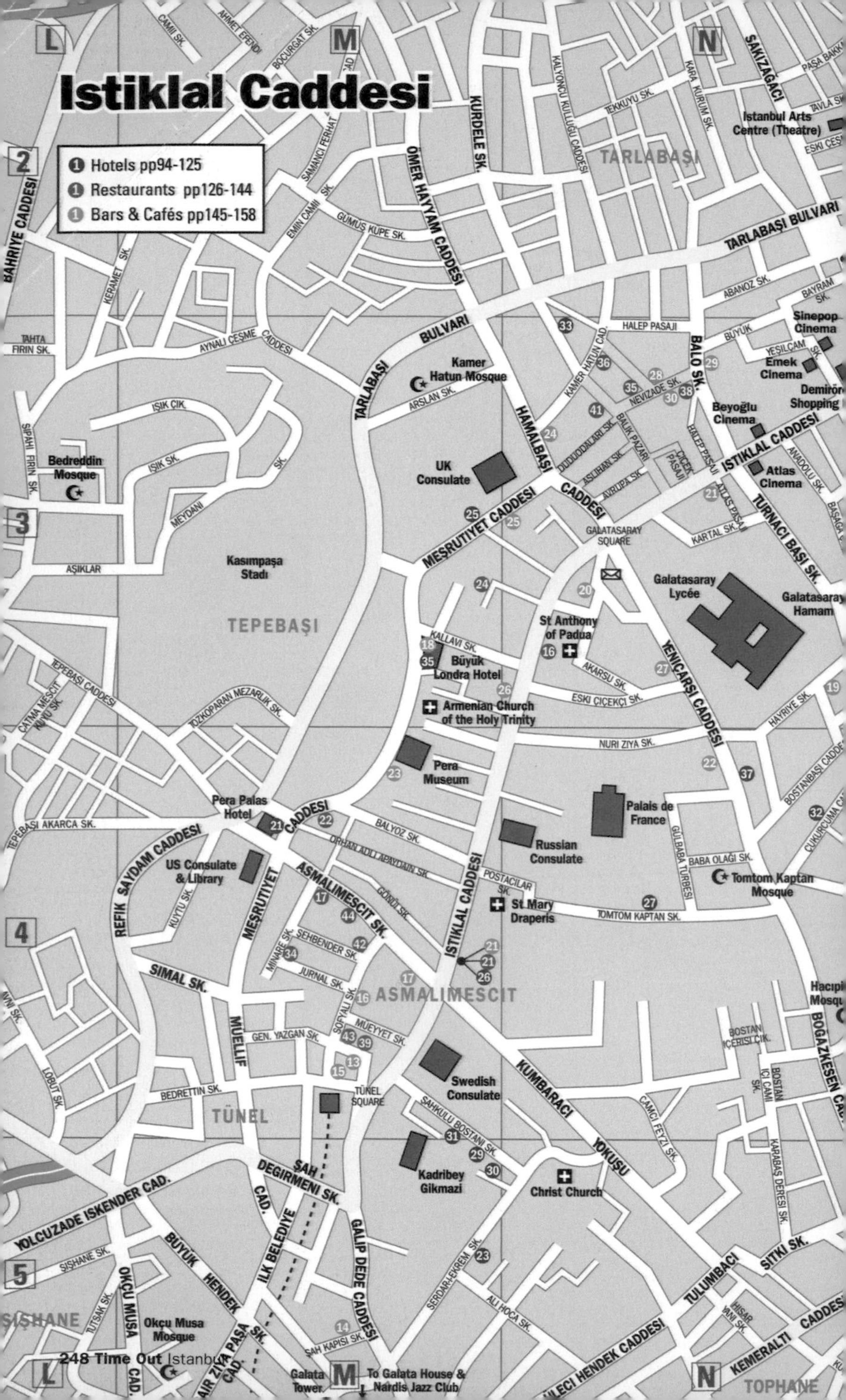

Istiklal Caddesi
Hotels pp94-125
Restaurants pp126-144
Bars & Cafés pp145-158
TARLABAŞI
TEPEBAŞI
ASMALIMESCIT
TÜNEL
ŞIŞHANE
TOPHANE
Istanbul Arts Centre (Theatre)
Sinepop Cinema
Emek Cinema
Beyoğlu Cinema
Atlas Cinema
Kamer Hatun Mosque
UK Consulate
Bedreddin Mosque
Kasımpaşa Stadı
Galatasaray Lycée
Galatasaray Hamam
St Anthony of Padua
Büyük Londra Hotel
Armenian Church of the Holy Trinity
Pera Museum
Pera Palas Hotel
Palais de France
Russian Consulate
US Consulate & Library
Tomtom Kaptan Mosque
St Mary Draperis
Swedish Consulate
Kadribey Gikmazi
Christ Church
Okçu Musa Mosque
Galata Tower
To Galata House & Nardis Jazz Club
GALATASARAY SQUARE
TÜNEL SQUARE
ISTIKLAL CADDESI
TARLABAŞI BULVARI
MEŞRUTIYET CADDESI
YENIÇARŞI CADDESI
KUMBARACI YOKUŞU
ÖMER HAYYAM CADDESI
HAMALBAŞI CADDESI
GALIP DEDE CADDESI
BOĞAZKESEN CAD.
REFIK SAYDAM CADDESI
YOLCUZADE ISKENDER CAD.

O
P
Q
2
3
4
5
Taksim Park
TAKSIM SQUARE
Marmara Hotel
TAK-I-ZAFER CAD
METE CADDESI
MIRALAY ŞEFIK BEY SK.
Gümüşsuyu Askeri Hast.
Atatürk Cultural Centre
INÖNÜ (GÜMÜŞSUYU) CADDESI
French Cultural Centre
Akbank Arts Centre
Haghia Triada
Taksim Sahnesi (Theatre)
KAZANCI BAŞI CAMII SK.
ISTIKLAL CADDESI
Vakko Dept. Store
SIRASELVILER CADDESI
SADRI ALIŞIK SK.
Taksim State Emergency Hospital
German Hospital
Ağa Hamam
LIVA SK.
MEBUSAN YOKUŞU
Fındıklı Molla Çelebi Camii
Çukurcuma Mosque
CIHANGIR
Firuzağa Mosque
Cihangir Mosque
Mimar Sinan University
NECATIBEY CADDESI
DEFTERDAR YOKUŞU SK.
Italian Hospital
Tophane Building
Tophane Square
Nusretiye Mosque
Tophane Nargile Cafes
Istanbul Modern
TOPHANE ISKELESI
Kılıç Ali Paşa Mosque
0
200 m
0
200 yds
© Copyright Time Out Group 2012

Üsküdar
Hotels pp94-125
Restaurants pp126-144
Bars & Cafés pp145-158
U
V
W
X
Y
Z
1
2
3
4
To Beşiktaş
To Kabataş
To Eminönü
Şemsi Paşa Mosque
Hakimiyet - i Milliye Meydanı
Mihrimah Sultan Mosque
Ağa Mosque
Şeyh Mosque
Yeni Valide Mosque
Mimar Sinan Çarşısı
Rumi Mehmet Paşa Mosque
Kara Davut Paşa Mosque
Karakadı Alaatin Mosque
Kaptan Paşa Mosque
Ayazma Mosque
İmrahor Mosque
Müsahipzade Celal Theatre
Şehit Süleyman Paşa Mosque
Ahmediye Mosque
Doğancılar Mosque
Nasuhi Mosque
Atik Valide Mosque
Çinili Mosque
Bülbül Deresi Mezarlık
Leander's Tower
ÜSKÜDAR
PAŞA LIMANI CADDESİ
HAREM ÜSKÜDAR YOLU
BAĞLARBAŞI CADDESİ
BULBULDERE
SELMANIPAK CAD.
SELAMI ALI EFENDI CAD.
UNCULAR CAD.
HAKIMIYET - I MILLIYE CAD.
DOĞANCILAR CAD.
KATIBIM AZIZ BEY SK.
EFENDI CAD.
HATMI SK.
ÇAVUŞDERE CAD.
TOPTAŞI CAD.
GÜNDOĞUMU CADDESİ
TAVUKÇU BAKKAL SK.
HALK DERHANESI SK.
TUNUS
SELIM PAŞA CAD.
DOLAP SK.
400 m
400 yds
0
© Copyright Time Out Group 2012

Kadıköy

Kadıköy
Haydarpaşa Station
Dolmuş for Üsküdar
Bus Station
Ferry Terminal
To Karaköy & Eminönü
Mustafa Iskele Mosque
Osmanağa Mosque
Söğütlüçeşme Mosque
Söğütlüçeşme Station
Bull Statue
Sureyya Cinema
Rexx Cinema
Rüştü Saraçoğlu Stadium
Kızıltoprak
HASANPAŞA
OSMAN AĞA
ZÜHTÜPAŞA
MODA
HAYDARPAŞA RIHTIM CAD.
SÖĞÜTLÜÇEŞME CADDESI
SÖĞÜTLÜÇEŞME CAD.
HALIT AĞA CADDESI
INKIŞAF CAD.
SARAY ARDI CADDESI
FAHRETTIN KERIM GÖKAY (KAYIŞDAĞI) CADDESI
BAĞDAT CADDESI
KUŞDILI CADDESI
YOĞURTÇU ÇAYIRI CAD.
BAHARIYE CADDESI
MODA CADDESI
DR. ESAT IŞIK CADDESI
T. EMIN BEY CAD.
RECEP PEKER CADDESI
SERASKER CADDESI
400 m
400 yds
© Copyright Time Out Group 2012

Street Index

Istanbul transport

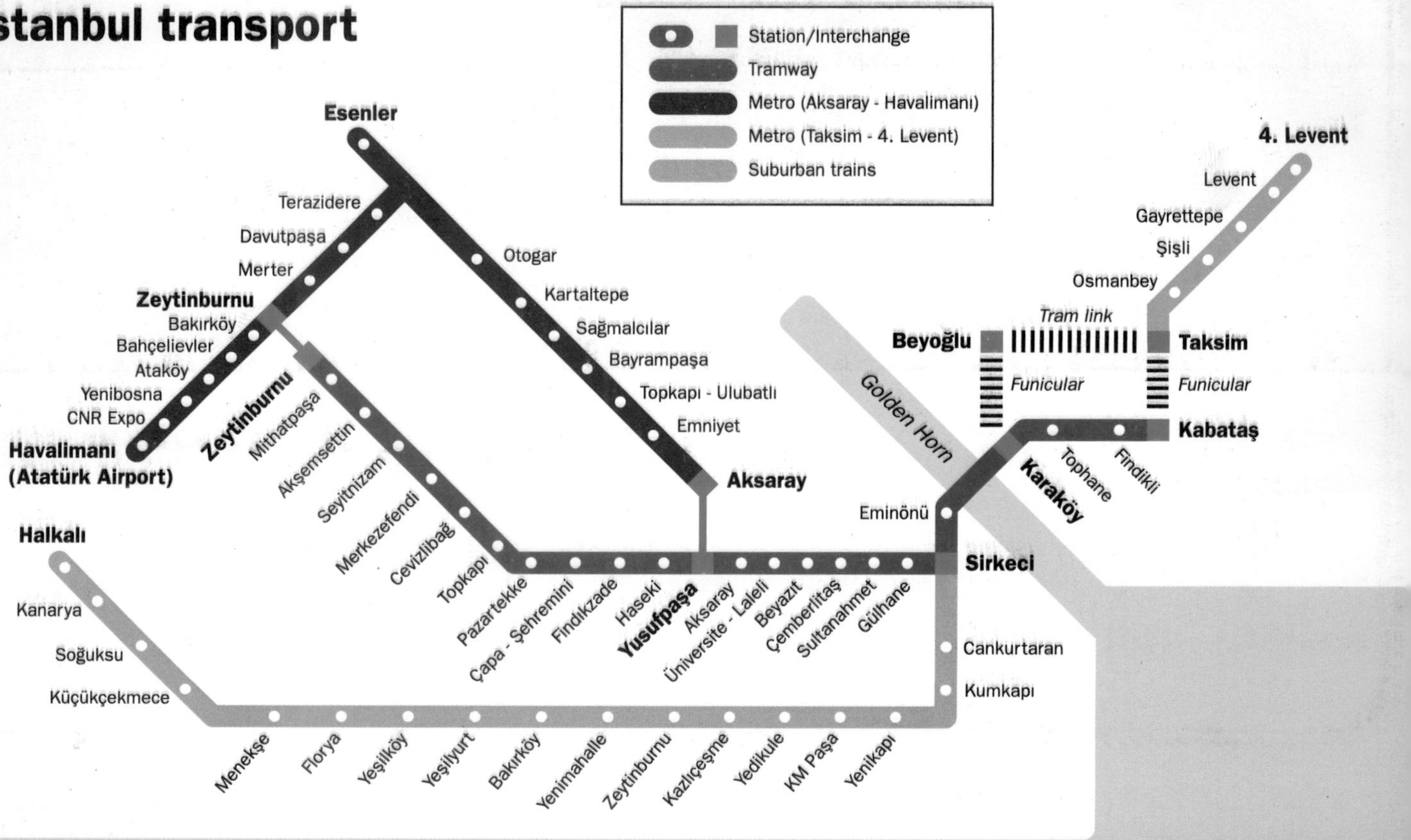

Station/Interchange
Tramway
Metro (Aksaray - Havalimanı)
Metro (Taksim - 4. Levent)
Suburban trains

Esenler
Terazidere
Davutpaşa
Merter
Zeytinburnu
Bakırköy
Bahçelievler
Ataköy
Yenibosna
CNR Expo
Havalimanı
(Atatürk Airport)

Otogar
Kartaltepe
Sağmalcılar
Bayrampaşa
Topkapı - Ulubatlı
Emniyet
Aksaray

Zeytinburnu
Mithatpaşa
Akşemsettin
Seyitnizam
Merkezefendi
Cevizlibağ
Topkapı
Pazartekke
Çapa - Şehremini
Fındıkzade
Haseki
Yusufpaşa
Aksaray
Üniversite - Laleli
Beyazıt
Çemberlitaş
Sultanahmet
Gülhane
Sirkeci
Eminönü
Karaköy
Tophane
Findikli
Kabataş

Golden Horn

Beyoğlu
Tram link
Taksim
Funicular
Funicular

4. Levent
Levent
Gayrettepe
Şişli
Osmanbey

Halkalı
Kanarya
Soğuksu
Küçükçekmece
Menekşe
Florya
Yeşilköy
Yeşilyurt
Bakırköy
Yenimahalle
Zeytinburnu
Kazlıçeşme
Yedikule
KM Paşa
Yenikapı
Kumkapı
Cankurtaran